Sexuality

A Biopsychosocial Approach

Chess Denman

First published 2004 by
PALGRAVE MACMILLAN
Houndmills, Basingstoke, Hampshire RG21 6XS and
175 Fifth Avenue, New York, N.Y. 10010
Companies and representatives throughout the world

PALGRAVE MACMILLAN is the global academic imprint of the Palgrave Macmillan division of St. Martin's Press, LLC and of Palgrave Macmillan Ltd. Macmillan® is a registered trademark in the United States, United Kingdom and other countries. Palgrave is a registered trademark in the European Union and other countries.

ISBN 0–333–78648–3

This book is printed on paper suitable for recycling and made from fully managed and sustained forest sources.

A catalogue record for this book is available from the British Library.

Library of Congress Cataloging-in-Publication Data
Denman, Chess, 1959– .
    Sexuality : a biopsychosocial approach / Chess Denman.
        p. cm.
    Includes bibliographical references and index.
    ISBN 0–333–78648–3 (pbk.)
    1. Sex therapy. 2. Psychosexual disorders—Social aspects. 3. Sexual disorders—Social aspects. I. Title.

RC556.D465 2003
616.85'830651—dc21   2003053573

10 9 8 7 6 5 4 3 2 1
13 12 11 10 09 08 07 06 05 04

Printed in China

Contents

Acknowledgements   x

Introduction   1
    The aims of this book   1
    The biopsychosocial approach   2
    'Clients', 'patients' and case examples   6

1 Approaches I: biology and sociobiology   10
    Biological processes in sexuality   10
    Medical aspects of sex and sexuality – not just a
      medical matter   19
    Sociobiology and evolutionary psychology   29
    Conclusion   36

2 Approaches II: anthropology and sociology   37
    Anthropology   38
    Sociology   49

**3 Approaches III: psychological approaches to
sexuality**   64
    Psychoanalysis   64
    Freudian perspectives   66
    Jung and Jungians   76
    French analysts   80
    English developments   83
    American analysts   88
    Psychoanalysis and biology: recent developments   93
    Conclusion: psychoanalysis, lovemaps and the erotic
      imagination   95

4 Politics   98
    Introduction: why politics?   98
    Freudiomarxists   100
    Feminism   102
    Feminism, psychotherapy and psychoanalysis   107
    Feminism, psychoanalysis and biology   114

Structuralism and poststructuralism		116
Psychoanalysis and postructuralism		117
Queer theory		123
Sexual politics and therapeutic practice		128

5	**Male and female heterosexuality**	**131**
	The female sexual life cycle	131
	The male sexual life cycle	149

6	**Lesbians and gay men**	**169**
	Sexuality and identity	169
	Why are some people homosexual?	170
	General principles of therapy with gay men and lesbians	176
	Gay men	178
	Lesbians	188

7	**Transgressive and coercive sex**	**198**
	Transgressive sex and perversion	199
	Causes of transgressive sex: psychoanalytic views	200
	Causes of transgressive sex: non-analytic perspectives	202
	Transgressive sexual acts and psychiatric disorders	204
	Women and transgressive sex	205
	Specific forms of transgressive sex	207
	Coercive sex	217
	Treating sexual aggression	220
	Child sexual abuse	221
	Perversion, transgression and normality	224

8	**Transgendered people: the plasticity of gender**	**227**
	Introduction	227
	Definitions	227
	Causes of gender dysphoria: biological and sociocultural issues	233
	Causes of male to female transsexualism	235
	Causes of female to male transsexualism	237
	Treatment options	241
	Political considerations	247
	Psychotherapy of transgendered, transvestite and intersex conditions	249

9 Sexology and sex therapy   **251**
Introduction   251
Sexology: a historical review   251
Sex therapy   256
Techniques to treat specific sexual disorders   263
Critique   275
Improving sexology and sex therapy   279

10 Sex in the consulting room   **281**
Sexual feelings towards the therapist   281
Sexual feelings of therapists towards patients   284
Gender and erotic transference/countertransference   287
The renunciation of sex in the consulting room and
   in the Oedipus complex   293
Transference, countertransference and the erotic
   imagination   294
Sexual relationships between therapists and patients   295
Who has sex with patients and why do they do it?   295
Who is abused?   297
The outcome of sexual relationships in therapy   300
Treating patients who have been sexually exploited   301
Primary prevention of abuse   303
Discussing the taboo   305

11 Conclusion   **308**
Taking stock   308
The erotic imagination   315
Pathology and the erotic imagination   324
Erotic imagination and culture   329

References   331
Index of Names   358
Index of Case Examples   364
Index of Terms   365

Acknowledgements

If writing about sex were as much fun as having it then those who have helped me would have had a much less onerous task. Jules Mackenzie provided many hours of research, referencing, copy-editing, criticism and support to a not always appropriately grateful partner. Peter Denman and Steffi corrected some of the many errors of style and punctuation which littered the text – those which remain are entirely my responsibility. Many more of my friends have patiently endured hearing a great deal more about sex than they might always have liked and have offered me advice and moral support. I am gateful to them. My editors Ann Scott, Alison Caunt and Andrew McAleer always responded encouragingly and calmly to a range of panics, phobias and anxieties.

CHESS DENMAN

Introduction

The aims of this book

Sexual feelings and sexual expression form a regular part of the experience of most human beings and, while therapists and theorists have disagreed about the centrality of sexual experience in human psychology, none have suggested it to be an unimportant part of human life. Sexual feelings can bring pleasure or suffering, can occasion murder or marriage, yet, in our culture, in therapy or out of it, sex remains a difficult subject to discuss with any sense of balance. Discourses based on suppression and silence have given way, first, to ones based on hygiene and good sense and more recently to discourses characterised by conflicts between hedonism and repression. None of these attitudes to sex leave much room for the personal exploration and expression of sexuality. Instead, powerful external and internal social injunctions dominate sexual expression. For these reasons, although patients may not volunteer it, sex is often a problematic issue in their lives combining with and compounding other difficulties. This means that, whatever overt problem a therapist may be treating, sexual matters can suddenly appear and require attention.

Therapists are just as much subject to cultural pressures and social injunctions in relation to sexuality as their patients. They may find it difficult to disentangle their own value judgements from clinical issues relating to pathology. Stepping out of a strongly held sexual value and belief system, however difficult, is important. If therapists do not maintain perspective on their own value system they run the risk of labelling as psychopathological experiences or acts which merely represent infractions of their personal moral system. As a result, ideological assumptions may lead therapists to make unbalanced judgements of the causes and consequences of the symptoms and behaviours their patients describe and often, as a result, to use a reduced or incorrect range of therapeutic interventions.

This book suggests that part of the antidote to these problems lies in acquiring a wide knowledge base about sex. It tries to provide therapists with some of the basic information and theory which they will need when treating patients with sexual problems. It also has three further aims. One is to demonstrate the importance of a biopsychosocial approach to therapy and to show how, when some therapies fail to adopt such an approach, this is detrimental to patients. Another aim has been to demonstrate the advantages and complexities of adopting a permissive non-judgemental and non-pathologising attitude to variation in sexual practice. Lastly, where possible, the book uses the idea of erotic imagination to try to discuss the positive potential of sex for personal and social transformation.

The ideas of taking both a sex-positive, and a non-judgemental stance are, to an extent, self explanatory although their detailed application is complicated and controversial. Both ideas will be covered as they arise in the text. The notion of the erotic imagination is specifically introduced at the end of Chapter 3. The biopsychosocial approach needs more immediate explanation and elaboration.

The biopsychosocial approach

The biopsychosocial approach outlined by Engel (1980) and taken up specifically in relation to sexuality by Rossi (1994) offers an overarching paradigm connecting biological, cultural and psychological domains. In relation to the practice of medicine Engel outlined a model of interacting and intertwining influences from these three domains. He believed that none of these realms could be neglected in any analysis of a patient's problems. In the context of the study of human sexuality the biopsychosocial approach starts by assuming that all three domains will contribute to the origins and quality of a sexual behaviour or experience.

Adopting a consistently biopsychosocial approach amounts to saying that it is always an error to neglect any one of the biological or the social or the psychological domains. The biopsychosocial approach can be viewed as a progressive narrowing of focus from statements of the most general nature about human affairs to statements of a highly individual and specific kind. Although we vary in our biology and in the evolutionarily driven behavioural strategies which we employ, these variations are for the most part coarse, tightly driven by biology, and applicable to large groups of people. At the social and cultural level variation is much more marked. Anthropology, sociology and cultural theory form a not entirely separable set of disciplines which cover this territory. They concentrate on describing rules for human behaviour and experience based on the needs of groups of individuals and often emphasising the roles of tools or artefacts. Biological and evolutionary factors are still important. For example, there is evidence that the cultural variations in the way mate selection is controlled represent a range of intra- species competition strategies, which cope with variations in the relative ratio of men to women in a society (Buss 1994). Last, at the psychological level, individual experience shapes behaviour and experience even as it selects from a biologically and culturally constrained menu of activities. Even though the individual level seems at first the 'weakest' level it can exert reverse influence on culture and even on biology. Social activism, genocide, embryo selection and assisted reproduction, and transgendered individuals seeking surgery are all examples, good and bad, of such reverse influences.

The first three chapters follow this narrowing focus, dealing successively with biology and sociobiology, psychology and psychoanalysis, and anthropology and sociology. A fourth chapter considers political activism in relation to sex – largely feminism and queer theory – and its theoretical foundations in psychology and cultural studies. The rest of the book considers specific topics in relation to sexuality, always maintaining the biopsychosocial perspective. These later chapters often flesh out aspects of the biology, cultural theory and psychology relevant to their topic area which receive short shrift in the initial chapters.

How might a biopsychosocial approach inform therapeutic practice?

Joan presented to the child psychiatry clinic with her son Peter. The school had referred them because Peter's behaviour was said to be sexually disinhibited. From the demeanor of mother and son it was clear that the mother was highly anxious about her child's behaviour and that he had been subjected to considerable cross-questioning about it. It was therefore difficult to get a clear account of the behaviour itself. The suggestion from the school was that Peter had repeatedly attempted to persuade female classmates and girls in younger classes to lift up their skirts and show him their genitals. The class teacher reported that his behaviour was often unruly and that he used sexual swear words frequently. Confronted, he had denied the behaviour and become sullen.

The case raises many issues. Only one will be followed up. Our attitude to the clinical situation will be substantially altered by Peter's age. If Peter is 14 years old then our view of the nature of his sexual activity, experience and wishes alters dramatically over our attitude to a Peter who is 6 years old. Partly this is because, from a biological perspective, sexual development in childhood is crucially influenced by puberty, when interest in sexual and sexual behavior becomes both stronger and more focused. 6-year-old Peter will be pre-pubertal while his 14-year-old namesake will be in the midst of puberty or nearing its end. This biological information informs both our view of Peter's psychology and also cultural expectations and norms about sexual behaviour.

Psychological processes are also age-related and operate differently in relation to a 6-year-old or a 14-year-old child. Children acquire knowledge of sexuality from a range of sources and their analyses of sexual situations generally grow more complex as time passes. Partly this is as a result of developing cognitive abilities, but also it is as a result of a socially sanctioned, culturally specific, graded exposure to sexual material. One aspect of this analysis is a child's developing awareness of social expectations of their behaviour. In each culture we can develop a rough timetable for the development of this awareness. Generally, in our culture we would regard Peter at 14 as displaying a strikingly age inappropriate lack of awareness of the likely social consequences of his acts and this would be one of many reasons for worrying about his development.

Six-year-old Peter is in a different position. Broadly, a 6-year-old who is trying to look under girl's skirts is not nearly so age-inappropriate, although some children would have been socialised to suppress this behaviour somewhat earlier. So, because in our culture we allow children latitude to break social rules until a certain age, we are inclined to view 6-year-old Peter's behaviour as less serious. Culturally, we are also inclined to see pre-pubertal children as less sexually motivated (an attitude which probably understates young children's sexuality). Instead, to explain the behaviour, we attribute motivations to the child which our culture values, such as curiosity or experimentation. But it doesn't take much further evidence to tip the balance away from such kindly perspectives. Peter's sexual swearing and unruly behaviour, while regrettable, are not seen as pathological in a 14-year-old whom we expect to be rebellious and at times unruly. In a 6-year-old, sexual swearing and unruly behaviour seem more worrying. They might simply indicate sexualised aspects of his upbringing, but this seems unlikely given his mother's overtly controlling attitude. Instead, things could be quite serious. One cause of sexual disinhibition in young children, as defined by Western norms, is exposure to age-inappropriate sexual experiences.

Alongside this largely social and cultural analysis would need to be set psychological considerations. Peter's sullen silence signals that he has some understanding that his behaviour is putting him in difficulties and that his mother is exposing him to a rapid lesson in its consequences. Peter is ashamed; having already internalised social standards about sexuality his shame now makes it hard for him to seek help. So, our speculations and worries about Peter vary depending on his age and on the domain of explanation used to consider his case.

Naturally, Peter and his mother also have theories and anxieties about what is going on. Their attitude, worries and manner of seeking help will depend on their own culture-bound, psychologically processed and biologically based analysis of the situation they face as they reflexively assess their own motivations, and the motivations and responses of others.

Here are two ways the therapist in the case could have acted:

Vignette 1
The therapist knew that he must find a way to get Peter to open up and talk. He greeted Peter and his mother in the waiting room and showed them into a comfortable therapy room. He then immediately invited Peter to use any of the toys and drawing materials in the room to play with.

Vignette 2
The therapist knew that he must find a way to get Peter to open up and talk so he greeted Peter and his mother in the waiting room. He explained to both of them that he would like to talk

to Peter on his own first but added that there would be plenty of time for them all to talk together during the consultation.

It is at once clear in which vignette Peter is 6 and in which he is 14. The therapist's actions reveal standard therapeutic manoeuvres worked out in relation to children's biologically based developmental stage, cultural expectations based on who has charge of the care of children, and psychological strategies designed to get Peter to relax and open up. The strategies employed involve a tacit biopsychosocially based analysis of the expectations of all those involved. If this analysis is not done correctly then problems can result.

Had the therapist of 6-year-old Peter tried to separate him from his mother and see him alone, then in all likelihood Peter would have protested and little would be observed in the consulting room other than phenomena associated with fear in new situations. Peter's mother would very likely have interpreted the separation from Peter as a sign that some serious, possibly sexual, infraction was being investigated, even that social services might become involved. She could have become obsequious or belligerent, but either way her main aim would have been to keep Peter with her, rather than let him fall into the hands of fantasised accusers. Thus the therapist's hypothetical failure to deal with Peter's age appropriately involves a failure to analyse correctly the psychological and cultural factors influencing Peter and his mother.

Peter's therapist's biopsychosocial analysis was tacit. In this book the emphasis will often be on an explicit use of the biopsychosocial model in relation to sexuality.

'Patients', 'clients' and case examples

As the rest of this book works through the biopsychosocial model frequent case examples are given. A few remarks follow which address some of the issues that arise from the use of clinical material in the book.

The term 'patient' is used throughout this book and is preferred to the term 'client'. There are two reasons. First, patients when surveyed have expressed a preference for being called patient rather than client. Second, the connotations of the term client are not as benign as they might at first seem. Clients, after all, consult solicitors and prostitutes. The term 'user', referring to someone who uses mental health services, is also prevalent but seems more appropriate to that subset of individuals in contact with formal mental health. Arguably, it has no less objectionable connotations than 'client'.

All the case examples used are fictions created by drawing on the author's actual clinical experience. This controversial decision needs defending. In 1999, the International Committee of Medical Editors issued common guidance for all medical journals in relation to publication of clinical materials. The twin standards they adopted were consent and accurate presentation. The psychotherapeutic community, and particularly the psychoanalytic community, have not traditionally adopted either of these standards in an uncomplicated way. The guidelines produced a thoughtful response from the editor of the *International Journal of Psychoanalysis* (Tuckett 2000) who discusses the competing needs of consent and accurate presentation, in the special circumstances of the psychodynamic tradition, which result from its need to report intimate details. He argues against the International Committee that the obtaining of consent may not always be appropriate for each piece of published data. He also suggests that some elements of disguise may be helpful in protecting the patient, and innocuous in relation to presenting the facts of the case.

Gabbard (2000) agrees and suggests that only in certain circumstances – when the patient might read about him or herself inadvertently – is consent necessary. He also points out that informed consent may distort the accuracy of the clinical text since, if the patient is to see the text, then the therapist may censor aspects of the account (for example, difficult countertransference issues).

To my mind, Gabbard is correct on the impossibility of obtaining consent. I have treated relevant cases over a period much longer than the conception and writing of this book, and it is impossible to know in advance whose material may be an important example. To ask retrospective consent from all the patients whose cases I might wish to cite, would be a breach of my duty of care since it would at least in some, not always predictable, cases be detrimental to them. Asking every prospective patient to consent to potential future publication is useless since such a vague consent could not be regarded as informed. This leaves disguise as the only recourse for presenting clinical material. Gabbard is a proponent of disguise (the only course he can take since he rejects consent) and rejects the worry that disguise always risks a serious distortion of the clinical material.

To be successful disguise must satisfy two criteria. It must be adequate to protect the patient and it must preserve all relevant aspects of the clinical material undistorted. The adequacy of disguise in protecting the patient depends on sufficient conceal-ment, and needs to be strong if the patient is to fail to recognise themselves. Gabbard (2000) suggests that the account can be disguised only in relation to people other than the patient if patients' capacity to recognise themselves in the account is viti-ated by its appearance in a publication to which the patient is unlikely to have access. This is clearly wrong. There have been situations where a case report, published in an obscure journal, was taken up by a second author whose critique was published in a less obscure journal where it was read by the patient who recog-nised themselves, then traced back the original account. To add to the confusion, Gabbard also points out that patients sometimes recognise themselves in accounts which are not about them.

Thus the strongest form of disguise is needed. The task of ensuring that this disguise does not distort the clinical material is particularly difficult. Different authors judge it differently. We know for example that both Freud and Klein felt it acceptable to write about their own children (Freud's paper 'A child is being Beaten' is thought to describe Anna (Young-Bruehl 1989), his daughter, and Klein is thought to have discussed the treatment of her daughter Melita, in a paper (Grosskurth 1987) without revealing this fact. No modern therapist would regard this as a fact which could be withheld without extreme violence to the account.

However, disguise is only problematic if it is suggested that case reporting has evidential weight as opposed to illustrative value. This question, which is related to the problem of the status of psychotherapy and psychoanalysis as scientific disciplines, turns out to be very complicated. For those who take the view that, in relation to establishing facts about the outcome and mecha-nism of therapy, the traditional scientific method of empirical testing as elaborated in most biomedical and psychiatric research, is the 'gold standard', then the genre of the single case, accurately reported or not, never, or rarely, establishes matters of fact. For those whose grounding is in textual analysis, literary criticism and postmodern thought, the notion of constructing a clear case history, which could act as an undistorting window through to some true account of a case, is not credible. Thus, whether one takes a radical anti-realist view of descriptive acts and views reality as a negotiable construction, or whether one adheres to the more realist view that while accounts describe a particular perspective on a real (for example, independently agreeable) situation all accounts are, to quite a large extent, matters of perspective, single case reports are a groundless basis for establishing causal links. So it turns out that the project of an undistorting disguise is both futile (case histories have no evidential weight) and impossible.

What solutions can be adopted? To an extent the cases in this book are what Gabbard (2000) would call composites, in that they represent the condensation of many different cases into illustrative types. Gabbard recommends this process for particularly sensitive material and says he used it when discussing the treatment of cases of therapists who have made sexual boundary violations. Similar processes have been used by a number of other writers, for example O' Connor and Ryan (1993). None of the authors who use this method seem willing to acknowledge that, to the extent that this boiled-down account is then personalised into a 'case' story rather than presented as a general principle, this process amounts to fiction.

This is not so terrible since, arguably, fiction turns out to be what psychotherapists who presented their cases in any guise were writing all along (Hillman 1983). Once the function of fictional case accounts is acknowledged to be at once illustrative, educative, entertaining and polemical then their value obtains a new footing. So, in this text fictional accounts are designed to illustrate and elaborate the argument of the text but not to establish it. They are derived from my practice, but no patient I have treated or supervised is directly represented in these pages.

1 Approaches I: biology and sociobiology

Biological processes in sexuality

An acknowledgement of bodily and biological processes in conditioning experience is central to the biopsychosocial model. Our biological nature was developed as a result of evolutionary processes and expresses itself in physiology and anatomy. Thus the two disciplines which deal with these aspects of human sexual experience are sexual anatomy and physiology, and evolutionary theory. Scientific sexologists have defined a range of descriptive terms to serve as labels for different aspects of sexual anatomy and behaviour. A review of these terms provides a useful introduction to the complexities and contradictions of biological sex.

Definitions

Generally sexologists reserve the terms sex or gender to describe the quality of being biologically male or female, but to describe an individual this way first requires assigning them to a category. This is not a simple task. Categorising an individual's sex using biological characteristics can be done in a range of ways which can give conflicting results. Biological sex has several subcategories which include chromosomal sex, hormonal status, internal sexual organs, external sexual organs, and 'brain sex'.

Chromosomal sex

Almost all individuals are born with either two X chromosomes or with an X and a Y chromosome in the nuclear material of their cells and this genetic patterning determines chromosomal sex.

Chromosomes determine sex by changing a biological default position which is largely female. Maleness develops only if a Y chromosome is present. We know this because some individuals are born with different chromosomal arrangements including XO, XXX, XYY and XXY. In these people the presence of a Y chromosome in any arrangement produces a male individual. That said, some of these genetic variations produce a range of difficulties in sexual development and other areas.

The effects of chromosomal make-up are apparent only after a long developmental pathway which, in interaction with the environment, turns genetic instructions (the genotype) into individual characteristics (the phenotype). Twists and turns along this pathway can divorce chromosomal sex from phenotypic characteristics. Even so our ideas about genes – that they are basic or fundamental – have given chromosomal sex a social function. Athletes and other sports people who wish to compete as male or female have their gender determined by tests of chromosomal make-up, making chromosomal sex, rather than gender identity or any features of gendered biology, the determinant of the gender category in which an athlete may compete.

Hormonal elements

Although the first part of sexual differentiation is genetically determined, hormonal influences soon take over and determine how the gonads and other sexual characteristics will develop. For this reason, if hormonal influences are disturbed, a bewildering range of conditions in which genotypic and phenotypic sex are at variance, can develop. Androgen insensitivity syndrome is an example. In this condition genotypic males develop into externally phenotypic females because of a constitutional insensitivity of the tissues to the influence of testosterone. Often the condition is only noticed at puberty when the 'girl' fails to menstruate. Internally these individuals have rudimentary testes rather than ovaries and there is no uterus or upper vagina. Individuals with this condition face two difficult psychological challenges of which therapists need to be aware. First, they must cope with the news that they are not securely the sex they thought they were. Although most have a secure identity as female the idea that they are genetically male is disturbing. Second, they face coping with infertility. Sadly, many patients must also come to terms with the fact that it was thought prudent by doctors and parents alike to lie to them and conceal the true nature of their condition.

Internal sexual organs

Male internal sexual organs include the testis and its associated tubing while female internal sexual organs include the uterus and fallopian tubes. Innumerable pre- and post-natal developmental difficulties may beset these organs and produce infertility or sub-fertility. Internal organs, particularly female ones, have probably always had powerful but with varying significance for women and men. At the beginning of this century, the idea that girls knew innately about their internal spaces and phantasised about them anxiously was an important part of a female inspired readjustment of Freudian theory (Klein 1932, Sayers 1986). Certainly, more recently, as medical knowledge and imagery about the interior of bodies has become more widespread, conscious ideas about how the insides of our bodies are arranged are often relevant to sexual anxieties in women. For example:

Sarah was referred for treatment of post-traumatic stress disorder. She had been sent to hospital as an emergency with abdominal pain which developed over the space of a single evening. A medical and surgical nightmare then developed involving repeated surgery, including hysterectomy, and a long period spent in intensive care in a kind of twilight state. During consultation Sarah had many worries and problems, which would need psychological help, but enquiry about her sex life produced the specific fear that because her hysterectomy had included the removal of her cervix her vaginal vault would have been left open at the top. During intercourse she imagined that semen would be injected into her abdomen and she worried about it accumulating there. For this problem, diagrams of her internal anatomy, pre- and post operation, and an explanation of the procedure for hysterectomy were helpful but there were also many issues, including those related to her new, traumatically created, self-image as 'fragile and in danger', to deal with.

External genitalia and secondary sexual characteristics

The term external genitalia refers to the vulva in females, comprising the vagina and vaginal opening, the urethra surrounded by the clitoris and the labia minora and labia majora. In men, the external genitalia comprise the scrotum and penis. External genitalia are evident at birth and it is on the basis of these that gender is usually assigned. Their significance to us as individuals and culturally is incalculable and the vast and complex web of phantasy, fantasy, art, supposition, science and pseudo-knowledge which surrounds them has at times almost obscured their biological base.

Brain sex

The existence and influence of biological correlates of sex in the central nervous system causes heated debate. One problem is that the outcome of these debates is thought to be relevant to the oppressed status of women and also to the status of certain sexual preferences in our society and its chance of being altered. Other worries concern the implied loss of autonomy thought to result from discoveries of biological substrates for behaviour. Those who view biological discoveries as eroding human dignity, react against them. Those whose position of power is reinforced, may exploit them (Moir and Moir 1999).

Even so, after a period of some uncertainty, the dust does seem to be settling. There is some reason to suppose that brains are in some senses male or female. This is not however a single quality of brains but rather a group of qualities, which includes aspects of experienced gender, gendered behaviour and sexual preference. What is far from clear is the extent to which these aspects are set or can be altered by cultural or psychological forces.

In our culture, beliefs about the biological basis of sexual preferences or of gender identity, based on presumptive cerebral hardwiring, have become important to some individuals. Transgendered people identify themselves as being a different sex from their biological one. They claim that this discordance is a consequence of being biologically a certain sex in their brains but not their bodies. They argue that this means their condition is an illness and not simply a preference. The argument is important to transgendered individuals because authorities have accepted it as a reason to offer and to fund gender reassignment surgery.

The gender assigned at birth

Strictly, the gender assigned at birth is not a biological category at all. It may be at variance with any of the other categories defined so far. Its importance derives from the fact that the gender assigned at birth is usually the one recorded on a birth certificate and used to a greater or lesser extent by authorities in determining issues such as the kinds of marriage an individual may validly contract. Often, at least for a while, the child is reared in accordance with this gender.

The following terms, along with gender assigned at birth, have less well established roots in biology. Such biological factors as have been identified are the source of enduring controversy at once scientific, ideological and frankly political.

Gender identity

This term refers to the way an individual will answer the question, printed on so many forms, 'What sex are you?' although more strictly it should perhaps refer to the answer to 'what sex do you feel?' In many individuals an unequivocal answer is possible, but for others aspects of gender identity may not be so firmly set.

Sex role

Sex role refers to culturally normative behavioural differences between the sexes. Fierce and unresolved debate continues over the extent to which each aspect of sex role behaviour found in our culture and in other cultures can be attributed to biological, psychological or cultural factors. The urgency of these arguments results from the presumption that certain types of origin lend legitimacy or inevitability to cultural practices which advantage some (generally, until recently, men) and disadvantage others (normally women but increasingly men). Crudely, two camps emerge. The first is biological and essentialist and favours inbuilt separations of male and female roles, arguing that these roles are biologically based and hence immutable. The other, often feminist, is associated with blurring or mobility of roles, and supposes that the origins of sex roles are cultural or psychological and hence plastic. This squaring off into camps is catastrophic because none of the internal linkages within each camp is logically justified (there is, for example, nothing inherently immutable about biology or inherently plastic about psychology). Furthermore, the powerful political consequences of each view often result in arguments based on hope rather than evidence.

Patients who consult with sexual difficulties do not escape these debates. They often have self-expectations based on their own view of appropriate sex role behaviour for them. It is therefore no surprise that some of the most frequent causes of difficulties with sex and sexuality arise from a mismatch between self-imposed sex role standards and actual performance. Often there are conflicting sex role standards between individuals involved as well.

Sexual preference/sexual orientation

The term 'sexual preference' refers to the kinds of sex which a person wants to have, while the term sexual orientation is generally reserved to describe sexual preferences for same-sex or cross-sex pairings. Sexual orientation is almost always fairly central to an individual's identity. Being heterosexual, homosexual or bisexual opens and closes doors to a range of cultural experiences, family organisations, fears and anxieties. Sexual preferences by contrast may refer to a fairly trivial issue in a person's life, for example a preference for dark haired women or a particular fetish. However, some sexual preferences in some cultures – for example SM (sado-masochism) in parts of our culture – may also become 'identities' for the people involved.

Sexual response cycle

Scientific sexologists have also made a study of the physiology of sexual activity. To some this dispassionate regard may seem to miss the point of sex. However, a working knowledge of the physiology of sex can help therapists confronted with sexual problems and can help patients to understand what is going on in their bodies. The following account draws heavily on Bancroft (1989), whose text is authoritative. Various classifications of the sexual response cycle have been attempted. The most commonly known is Masters and Johnson's excitement, plateau, orgasm, and resolution system (Masters and Johnson 1966). However, there are, as Bancroft (1983) points out, difficulties with this system particularly with the 'plateau' phase, because orgasm can occur out of sequence. Bancroft also criticises Kaplan's (1979) triphasic division into desire, excitement and orgasm, arguing that her distinctions between arousal and desire are somewhat arbitrary. Nevertheless, it remains convenient to give an account of sexual response in terms of this kind of categorisation.

Sexual desire

The neurobiology of sexual desire in men and women remains largely obscure. There are clearly times when, for biological reasons, people are more or less likely to experience sexual desire. Fatigue, stage of the menstrual cycle, physical illness and drugs are all capable of influencing sexual desire. Because none of these factors have an overriding effect they are best thought of as setting the level of arousability in each individual at any time.

Arousal and excitement

Smell, visual signals, and touch are all important in sexual arousal, though all these are subject to very powerful mediation from higher centres in the brain. Thus, stimulation of different parts of the body can at different times be experienced as revolting or arousing. Individuals who have suffered a break in the spinal cord may develop erotic sensitivity in the area of skin just above the first level which has lost sensation. Such phenomena testify to the neurobiological complexity of erotic sensation.

Arousal produces variable and non-specific changes in things like blood pressure, heart rate, and pupil size. Specific signs of arousal occur in the genitals (erection in men and engorgement of the labia in women). Genital responses can occur in the absence of subjective arousal (especially erection in men) but when they do occur, awareness of them may then produce subjective arousal. Genital arousal during sleep is well known in men but also occurs in women. Medically it can be an important phenomenon because the presence of nocturnal erections in a man who otherwise has severe erectile difficulty can signal that the difficulty does not have a peripheral organic origin.

As women become aroused there is also a generalised increase in blood flow in the genital area. The clitoris (which is anatomically analogous to the penis) erects to a variable degree but as arousal increases may retract as the structures around it engorge. Engorgement also results in release of fluid from the walls of the vagina. It serves to lubricate the vagina and make entry of the penis easy and pleasurable. The fluid also changes the vaginal environment to make it more likely that sperm will survive.

Orgasm

Orgasm in men is a complicated series of muscular and neurological events which remain in part obscure. In men, it is generally preceded by a short period in which there is awareness that ejaculation is inevitable, followed, first, by the building up of spermatic fluid in the urethra near the prostate gland and then its rhythmic expulsion. In women, orgasm is characterised by rhythmic contractions of the outer third of the vagina but there may also be uterine contractions and contractions of the anal sphincter. Female orgasmic response is less consistent than male orgasmic response and may vary in duration, and in the number of contractions experienced. During orgasm the top third of the vagina balloons. The reason is not clear but some biologists have suggested that it allows for the formation of a pool of sperm close to the cervix, which may then draw up the sperm, thus aiding conception.

Freud distinguished between mature vaginal orgasms and immature clitoral ones. The early scientific studies of Kinsey *et al.* (1953) and of Masters and Johnson (1966) provided women with strong reasons for thinking that there was no such difference in orgasmic response. Since then, other researchers have found differences possibly related to differences in peripheral cutaneous stimulation as opposed to stimulation of deeper stretch receptors (Singer 1973, cited in Bancroft 1989). Some workers who have found a difference have associated proneness to anxiety with reliance on vaginal intercourse (Fisher 1973 cited in Bancroft 1983). It is clear that, in this area, emotional and wish-fulfilling ideas on the part of the researchers, the mental set of the women involved in the research, and the extreme difficulty of doing mechanical studies in intimate settings, combine to make unbiased research in this area difficult.

However, the most important feature of the largely futile female orgasm debate is the lingering sense of anxiety and doubt with which some women are left and of which the following case history is an example:

> Sheila presented to the clinic complaining of being sexually unresponsive. Since her marriage she had not enjoyed sex although she enjoyed the physical closeness and became readily aroused. She was quite able to masturbate to orgasm but felt that these orgasms didn't count and friends had assured her that orgasm during intercourse was a very different affair. Suggestions for alternative methods of lovemaking and experimentation with her husband were met with blank rejection, in particular those which involved any kind of manual stimulation of her genitals during intercourse which were seen by her as 'not counting'. A psychodynamic approach, centring on the possibility of underlying anxieties which might be making sexual response during intercourse less intense, was begun on the basis that it might be more in tune with her own health beliefs. Even here it was hard for the therapist to find any room for manoeuvre. Eventually Sheila left treatment with no resolution of her difficulties.

The psychological experience of orgasm is, as one might expect, variable. Reports of altered experience of consciousness are common. Some research has been directed towards determining whether there is a neurological basis for this but again, as one might expect, the results of these researches vary. After orgasm the physiological manifestations of arousal resolve and they do so more rapidly if orgasm occurs than if it does not. Men and women differ in that, for men, a period of unresponsiveness to sexual stimulation ranging from a few minutes to a number of hours follows orgasm. In women, there is a variable capacity for further orgasmic response.

Summary

A clear understanding of the biological basis of human sexuality and the human sexual response is clearly essential to offering basic sexual advice. Even though this kind of information has become much more widely disseminated, most sex therapists have experience of cases where couples were not sure how sex was done and of men and women whose understanding of the nature of each other's sexual responsiveness was sketchy or deficient:

> Paula and John presented for therapy because John was angry that Paula seemed sexually unresponsive to him. Paula on the other hand was bewildered. She said that she enjoyed sex with John. He angrily retorted that she never had an orgasm so she definitely was not enjoying sex. Paula again said she did enjoy sex and did sometimes have an orgasm. John would have none of this and accused her of faking arousal. The therapist was unclear just where to start in this case, whether on the mistrust, or the misinformation, or the pent-up feeling. In the end he opted initially for a psycho-educational approach and talked about signs of male and female arousal. Learning about this calmed John down to an extent – he felt he had something concrete to look for. This prepared the way for a more inter-personal perspective.

Medical aspects of sex and sexuality – not just a medical matter

In the case of Paula and John, an understanding of the biological nature of sexuality helped begin a therapeutic dialogue. Sexual physiology and anatomy does not always work well. Therapists also need to understand the potential medical conditions which patients may experience. Sometimes they may be able to identify situations in which a medical referral is appropriate. Much more often they will be dealing with the emotional and cognitive consequences of established conditions, an area often neglected by medical professionals. Issues of considerable complexity can be involved.

Jane was a respected but closeted senior professional in a public position. As a result of an increasingly open personal life and a campaign by a vindictive ex-lover she had recently been outed as a lesbian. In therapy she was filled with self-loathing and self-recrimination. The therapist found himself in something of a quandary. He wanted to interpret Jane's self-recrimination as an example of internalised homophobia (discriminatory views against the self held by gays and lesbians). Exploration of Jane's self-loathing and rejection of her lesbian sexual orientation led suddenly to the revelation that Jane was experiencing pain during sex. Any deep penetration felt excruciating. Jane worried that she might be lesbian because she couldn't 'take' a man's penis and linked this idea to experiences of sexual abuse involving penetration in childhood. Jane's lesbian lover often wanted to use sex toys, including a dildo, and, when refused by Jane, would, on occasion, suggest that Jane was not truly lesbian. In the midst of all this the therapist noted that Jane's menstrual periods were irregular and also painful.

Jane's pain on penetration was linked in her mind with common notions about lesbians as inadequate women and also with cultural stories about sexual abuse and its consequence. Jane's lover may also share some of these mainstream cultural ideas but may also have expectations and frustrations centred in a particular lesbian subculture, which values sex toys and may be dismissive of non-penetrative 'vanilla' sex. However, pain on deep penetration and irregular painful menstruation are symptoms of a number of medical conditions. It turned out that Jane had endometriosis, a fairly common and distressing condition that can often cause pain on penetration. This discovery produced some relief and a range of new difficulties because endometriosis is hard to treat. The therapist's knowledge of both factual material and current debates surrounding lesbian sexuality allowed him to tread surely through a difficult treatment. Lack of knowledge in any of a range of areas could, all too easily, have led to a lack of balance and clinical error. The size and complexity of the topic means that the following brief account of common medical issues is included only as a goad to further reading.

Medical and organic causes of low sexual desire

Almost all 'disorders' of desire are not primarily biological in origin. Occasionally, low sexual desire is associated with hormonal problems so that, for example, falling androgen levels may be the cause of declining sexual desire in men as they get older. Any disturbance of good health may be associated with a lowering of desire. Freud (1914) thought that the reason for this was narcissistic cathexis – a redistribution of libido (perhaps better rendered as concern) from objects to the self. This sounds plausible but biological mechanisms must also play a large part in many cases.

Sexual symptoms in men

Erectile failure is mostly a psychological problem without organic basis. However, it can also be caused or contributed to by a wide range of physical conditions. Furthermore, once it has occurred, anxiety over future performance may contribute to its perpetuation even when the physical cause has resolved. Organic causes do exist and are medically important. Probably erectile failure which is persistent rather than occasional, and particularly beginning without an obvious provoking psychological cause, should be medically investigated. Painful intercourse in men may be caused by a number of local conditions of the penis including many sexually transmitted diseases.

Sexual symptoms in women

Painful intercourse in women can be divided into pain on penetration or pain on deep thrusting. These two symptoms have different causes. One of the most common causes of pain on penetration is attempting penetration before the woman is sufficiently aroused and the vagina is well lubricated and has elongated. Pain on deep penetration can be caused by vigorous thrusting against pelvic ligaments or the ovaries, which can hurt.

More serious conditions which cause pain on penetration include sexually transmitted diseases, which often impair vaginal lubrication (although it is important to note that in women sexually transmitted diseases may be asymptomatic and present for the first time with infertility). Oestrogen deficiency can develop after the menopause and leads to a poorly lubricated vaginal wall resulting in soreness on penetration. Deep pain on intercourse is more likely to be medical in origin than superficial pain. Common causes include pelvic inflammatory disease, and endometriosis. Anorgasmia in women is largely a psychological issue. However, in a few women there is evidence linking a lack of certain reflexes in the genital region associated with poor response to psychological treatment (Brindley and Gillan 1982, cited in Bancroft 1989). They suggest this might indicate an underlying physical problem in these women, but since some women give accounts of a capacity for orgasmic response from non genital stimulation a lack of reflexes may not be a total handicap. Some women have pain on orgasm which is bad enough to make them frightened to have sex. Probably muscle spasm is involved in the genesis of this pain but this is not certainly established.

Specific medical conditions associated with sexual difficulty

Another way in which medical problems associated with sexual functioning present to therapists is with patients who have an established medical diagnosis or treatment and need to cope with the sexual consequences, real or imagined, of their diagnosis or its treatment.

Diabetes

Diabetes is a major cause of sexual dysfunction in men. Diabetes damages small arteries and nerves causing erectile problems. Psychological factors interact with biological damage in determining the degree of difficulty with sexual functioning for any given amount of damage from the disease. (Bancroft *et al.* 1985) There are a number of treatments, both psychological and medical, available to diabetic men with erectile failure.

Sexual functioning in diabetic women has not been well studied. In such studies as have been done there does not seem to be a significant degree of impairment. However, some diabetic women have vaginal dryness. Where being diabetic had an impact on sexual functioning this was mediated by psychological factors such as responses to the threat of the illness.

All diabetics need careful monitoring. They need to take an unusual degree of responsibility for themselves and for the functioning of their body. Their lives are subject to restrictions and they may face the threat of future ill health, which many resent. So for any diabetic in therapy, the self-management of their illness is likely to become a topic within the therapy and it is in this context that sexual functioning may come to the fore:

> Peter was a 17-year-old diabetic man who presented with extreme shyness increasing to social phobia. Over the past year he had been isolating himself in his room and refusing to go out with his friends. He was brought to assessment by his parents, who were also insistent on accompanying him into the consulting room. The pattern of interactions in the interview took a characteristic course. The assessor would address some question or comment to Peter, a long pause would follow, and then Peter's father would interject with 'What Peter would like to say is . . . '. Peter had been diagnosed as diabetic at the age of 2 and had needed regular insulin ever since. Generally his diabetes had been well controlled and he had been taking over some responsibility for his injections. Then some years ago he seemed to tolerate a change in his diabetic medication (from animal to human insulin) poorly and had a few episodes of fainting caused by low blood sugar. His mother seems to have taken on the task of regaining diabetic control and negotiating with doctors. She still took primary responsibility for his injections.
>
> When eventually Peter could be seen alone he talked of his anxieties about going out with peers because of his fear that he would have to inject himself while he was with them. He was also deeply ashamed of being a virgin and felt his friends would jeer at him if he revealed this fact. He avoided having any relationships with women because he worried that he would be rejected as ugly and unsightly because he had scarred areas on both thighs and his stomach from the repeated injections. He felt that if he were to start a sexual relationship his mother would find out and this would be unbearable. It was clear that he was complicit in being dominated by his mother and also resentful of it.

Peter's mother reacted to her son's illness with concerned control. As he reached adulthood her involvement with his body limited his privacy and stalled his capacity to develop a different intimate relationship.

Cardiovascular diseases

Heart disease is bad for sexual functioning. A large part of its effect is because patients fear dying during sex. Moderate sexual activity is equivalent to climbing about two flights of stairs or a short walk (Bancroft 1989), so much of this fear is unjustified. Even so, heart attacks have entered popular culture as events likely to occur during active sex and it can be hard to reassure patients.

High blood pressure is another important source of sexual dysfunction in men. The furring up of small arteries, which may underlie high blood pressure, can affect the blood supply to the penis and produce erectile failure. Also, many of the drugs used to treat hypertension and heart disease produce sexual side effects which can be severe and which range from loss of desire to erectile difficulty.

Prostatectomy

The prostate gland sits just below the neck of the bladder and behind the pubic bone. Prostatectomy is a common surgical operation in older men either treating a benign enlargement in the prostate or treating a cancer in the gland. The operation can cause a reversal in the flow of spermatic fluid at ejaculation up into the bladder rather than down and out of the tip of the penis. A small proportion of men also suffer erectile difficulty as a result of the operation. Men who have not been warned about retrograde ejaculation before surgery can become very upset as a result when they discover the effect. Gay men who have anal sex report pleasurable stimulation from the penis as it rubs or strikes the prostate which lies just behind the wall of the rectum. As with so many issues related to gay sexuality, the idea of the prostate as a sexual organ has been neglected and as yet no studies have investigated this aspect of sexual functioning in gay men who have had prostatectomies.

Gynaecological problems in women

Hysterectomy tends not to be associated with much sexual dysfunction. Patients whose surgery was done to correct severe bleeding are often relieved by the results of surgery and report improved sexual function. Hysterectomies which are combined with removal of the ovaries are not so benign. They are generally performed in more serious conditions and, in pre-menopausal women, result in an abrupt menopause unless hormone relacement therapy is given, combined with irrevocable loss of fertility.

Childbirth will be considered later as a biopsychosocial event. However, from a medical standpoint, it may be associated with a number of complications which can have effects on sexual responsiveness. A fair proportion of women suffer some damage to the nervous structure of the pelvis during childbirth. This can cause conditions such as vaginal prolapse and stress incontinence which alter body image and have a negative effect on sexual functioning. Even the surgery for prolapse of the vagina can itself directly result in a loss in sexual functioning in one in five cases (Bancroft 1989) and many more have poor sexual functioning, from before the surgery, which is not regained.

Sexual aspects of medical involvement in fertility

Contraceptive methods and attitudes to pregnancy have a range of psychologically mediated effects on sexual functioning. More direct effects are largely limited to complaints of altered sensation and pleasure as a result of barrier methods and possible depression of female desire resulting from taking the contraceptive pill.

Individuals or couples for whom fertility is an issue describe complex and often highly detrimental effects of threatened fertility on sexuality. These are mostly psychological in origin rather than biological, although women who take drugs to enhance ovulation and to prepare for cycles of in vitro fertilisation report a range of effects from these.

Sexually transmitted diseases – safe sex

Sexually transmitted diseases represent an area of intense psychological difficulty. No sexual encounter can any longer fail to take account of the risks of infection with HIV or with other sexually transmitted agents. Although the health risks of agents other than HIV may in some areas be greater than that posed by HIV it has become the paradigm sexual infection.

HIV-infected individuals secrete the virus in all their body fluids and there is a risk of transmission if body fluids from an infected individual find their way past the barrier of the skin into the blood stream of a non infected person. Heterosexual coitus, anal sex, and to a very small extent oral sex and kissing may all be associated with cause via tiny breaches in the skin through which the virus may pass. Blood transfusions and intravenous drug use, which involves sharing needles, offer further routes of transmission. Because different activities vary in the risk they pose infection is not evenly distributed in the population. In the West, but not in Africa, gay men and intravenous drug users were and still are badly hit. Notwithstanding, anyone can become infected with HIV.

Current advice on sexual activity counsels that it is wise for both individuals in a sexual encounter to act as though either person may be HIV-positive unless they have very good reason not to do so. If sex which involves one or more penises is contemplated, then condoms should be used if it results in ejaculation into one or other of the people involved. Debate over the necessary precautions for other kinds of sex raged for a while but a consensus is emerging. Sex toys, such as dildoes, which are inserted into an orifice, should be covered with a condom, which should be changed if the same toy is used on another person or when moving from anal sex to another orifice. Some people feel that oral genital sex with a woman may be risky and suggest the use of a latex dental dam. This is particularly advisable when sex is happening during the woman's menstrual period. Kissing has very rarely been associated with infection and when it occurs active oral infection is the culprit. Most people do not take special precautions when kissing. An important advantage of these safe sex precautions is that they offer protection from a range of other sexual diseases.

Many gay men and intravenous drug users suffered and continue to suffer terribly as their friends and former lovers die from AIDS-related illnesses. Early on, some of the discrimination to which they were subjected amounted to a vicious unreasoning hatred. Many who have been infected are advised to take an unpleasant cocktail of drugs that reminds them regularly of their infected status. For all these reasons gay men present with a range of sexual complaints linked to their HIV-status. They may, for example, find it difficult to reconcile themselves to the idea that their sexual activity has infected others or that a former lover infected them. Some become asexual, while others react with anger and hatred or with denial and refuse to countenance the practise of safe sex. Yet another group have rebelled against the medicalisation and control of their bodies that the therapeutic regime of drugs imposes and have refused further treatment. For the most part, though, the gay community's response to HIV and AIDS has been rational, supportive and exemplary. It should provide a model for other communities faced with a sustained catastrophe. Gay communities have done much to re-eroticise an experience of sex which had become fraught with risk and the rituals to avoid it (see, for example, Preston and Swann 1987).

HIV is not the only serious sexually transmitted disease. Hepatitis B and C may be life-threatening. Other less life-threatening conditions can still cause significant morbidity, particularly in women, because they may take root without declaring themselves openly or sharply. The risk is of chronic pelvic inflammatory disease which can lead to pain and infertility and may be caused by agents like chlamydia and gonorrhoea. Viruses, particularly genital warts and herpes simplex virus, are also now associated with cervical cancer.

Psychiatric illness

Loss of libido is a key symptom of depressive illness while, not surprisingly, increased libido may be associated with mania. The other psychiatric illnesses, such as schizophrenia and neurotic disorders, are less well studied. Almost all psychoactive agents can cause erectile and orgasmic failure, including the major tranquillisers and most classes of antidepressant. The newer class of antidepressants called specific serotonin reuptake inhibitors, of which Prozac is one of the best known agents, are particularly likely to cause erectile failure in men and anorgasmia in women. Specialists can try to improve the situation by adding other drugs to counteract this side effect. Despite the dismal reputation of these drugs, some patients taking them report paradoxical effects of increased sexual responsiveness. This might be due partly to the lifting of the depression.

Alcohol and drugs

Quite a few drugs can have effects on sexual functioning and they are amongst the commonest causes of sexual dysfunction. It is traditional to divide them into prescription drugs and non-prescription drugs. Amongst prescription drugs there are a few particularly well known offenders, like antidepressants, but there is also a long list of other agents which may be implicated. It is wisest to advise a medical opinion in such cases.

Alcohol
Alcohol has complex dose-related effects on sex. In lower doses it may at least appear beneficial by reducing anxiety and social constraints. In higher doses alcohol reduces the capacity for sexual performance, most evidently in men because it reduces their capacity to get and maintain an erection. In the longer term, chronic abuse of alcohol results in toxic effects in a large number of different systems in the body and these effects decrease sexual functioning

Non-prescription drugs
Systematic research into the sexual effects of non-prescription drugs is understandably sparse! Cannabis, like alcohol, increases sensitivity to touch and general sensuality resulting in increased sexual pleasure. It can also increase the latency to orgasm but this delay tends to be experienced pleasurably rather than negatively. Research on the harmful effects rarely seems very balanced but there is some suggestion that cannabis may be associated with longer-term depressant effects on testicular and ovarian function. Heroin inhibits sexual responsiveness. Many commentators, particularly from psychoanalytic backgrounds, have been impressed by the idea of a parallel between mainlining heroin, which produces a 'rush' and then a letdown, and the arousal – orgasm – recovery cycle of sex. Such a parallel can be strength-ened by appeal to the symbolism of needles. Cocaine is popularly thought to enhance sex, but there is little evidence for this and

chronic use is associated with low desire. The effects of amphetamines remain unclear as do those of ecstasy although, anecdotally, ecstasy is an inhibitor of sexual response and so in some rave parties a trade in Viagra (Sildenafil) which enhances sexual performance has developed.

In conclusion

This review of biological and medical aspects of sexuality has offered immediate causal explanations for sexual phenomena either in terms of physiological functioning or of disease and dysfunction. Therapists need this information to assist them in helping patients with sexual problems and medical issues. However, another, more theoretical, biological discipline – sociobiology and evolutionary psychology – approaches biological and psychological aspects of sexuality from a causal perspective that looks to their formation through evolutionary time in response to ecological pressures. Evolution works by a process of natural selection which operates on variation thrown up by repeated sexual reproduction. This means that sociobiologists, because they are interested in evolution, are very interested in sex.

Sociobiology and evolutionary psychology

Sociobiologists and evolutionary psychologists attempt to explain human behaviour on the basis of evolutionary processes. The term sociobiology was coined by Wilson (1975) and referred initially to an extension of evolutionary theory into ethology. Wilson and others soon became interested in the social behaviour of humans and extended the applications of sociobiology. Later, theorists taking a less behaviourist stance began to consider human psychology from an evolutionary perspective. They called themselves evolutionary psychologists. Some proponents of this approach attribute social behaviour largely to biological factors shaped by evolution.

Darwin (1859) described how natural selection was the engine which drove evolution. He showed that variations within a species (which Mendel later showed were carried by genes coded, we now know, in DNA) affect an individual's capacity to produce healthy offspring. Parents who display a beneficial, genetically coded trait pass it on to their offspring who reproduce more successfully than those without the trait and, as a result, over time the trait spreads through the population. Since Darwin's day, evolutionary theory has become progressively more complex as the strange paradoxes of a blind process of random mutation and natural selection, which appears purposively to produce organisms of staggering complexity, have been charted out.

For an evolutionary psychologist, human sexual behaviour has developed as the result of a long evolutionary process. Genetically coded alterations in behaviour which tend to increase the inclusive fitness of an individual spread through the population. Genetically coded behaviour that reduces inclusive fitness tends to disappear. Inclusive fitness is a term designed to cope with the paradoxes generated by the understanding that natural selection works on organisms but variation, producing new traits, is generated by mutations in genes. Altruism is a good example of such a paradox. How could self-sacrifice be selected by evolution? Any overly self-sacrificing individual would not reproduce well so selfishness should spread through the population. It turns out that altruism is maintained as a trait because the relatives of an individual carry at least some of the same genetic material. Self-sacrifice by that individual may then benefit copies of his or her genetic material residing in relations, if enough of them are saved to reproduce. Altruism is found in animal species and it can be shown that the fine print of a cost benefit analysis for the genes circumscribes the degree of altruism displayed.

Human sexual behaviour is a problem for sociobiologists. We seem to indulge in a range of activities that appear to reduce our inclusive fitness. These range from priestly celibacy and homosexuality through to infanticide. Faced with these behaviours, evolutionary psychologists may argue that the behaviour in question, like altruism, has subtle advantages. They may also argue that evolution, being a mechanism which takes generations to work, is slow to catch up with the changed situation presented by the modern age. In the past things were different. For example, humans differ from many animal species by being in a continuous state of readiness for sexual intercourse. Some evolutionary biologists have wondered whether such a state of affairs was once adaptive. They suggest that in prehistoric times, when hunter gatherer tribal structures were the main social organisation, women only ovulated at those times of the year when there was sufficient food to push their body weight above a critical level required to maintain ovulatory cycles. If this were the case, a continual readiness for reproduction seems less like profligacy on the part of nature and more like an insurance system for making certain that babies were conceived as soon as times were good. Only modern high standards of nutrition have resulted in the appearance of continuous reproductive capacity (Taylor 1997).

Darwin described more than one competition-based mechanism by which evolution occurs. He pointed out that, while there is obvious competition between species for resources, there is also competition within species for reproductive resources. He called this second mechanism sexual selection. Sexual selection can be carried out in two ways. First, animals can compete with each other for access to a mate. For example, stags lock horns in a dominance contest. Another way competition occurs is by female preference for a trait such as the peacock's extravagant tail.

Sexual selection turns out to be important in developing evolutionary accounts for sexual and apparently non sexual behaviour. It has been argued (Miller 2000) that capacities for artistic production developed because of sexual selection. This is because one possible feature of a characteristic being used for sexual selection is apparent uselessness, high cost, and manifest beauty (like the peacock's tail). Features with these qualities signal the strength of the individual by showing that they can devote spare capacity to a seemingly useless activity. Human artistic production, it is argued, is a 'fitness indicator' rather in the same way that a glossy pelt or evident body fat may also indicate reproductive fitness.

Miller also uses the idea of 'runaway selection', and suggests that females may have had a preference for males who are good conversationalists. If so, they would selectively chose such males thus favouring the trait. However, by favouring it in men the females would also tend to acquire it themselves since, genetically they are very similar. Thus enhanced, the females become more discerning and demanding, and so push the trait on in males, and then in females, ever further. Miller also manages to argue that such a mechanism would favour advanced listening skills in females and talking skills in males!

One of the problems of explanations using sexual selection now becomes apparent. There are clearly a whole range of plausible mechanisms and explanatory routes. Since all explanations are retrospective, theorists are open to the criticism of finding only what they were looking for. Feminists have pointed out that the theories often seem to support sexist views of human behaviour roughly appropriate to the 1950s. Indeed, the early man on whom evolution is supposedly working can seem all too closely akin to Fred Flintstone. The case of a male skeleton found with a long thin object in a grave is an example of sexist assumptions (Taylor 1997). For a long time this skeleton was thought to be male and the long thin object was called a sword. More recent sophisticated techniques have shown that the skeleton is female and so the long thin object is now called a stick. Sometimes even the data on which theory is built has been tampered with. The Spanish, in the sixteenth century, were outraged by the extent of homosexual practice and transvestism that they found amongst the indigenous peoples of South America and systematically destroyed all sculptures, jewellery and monuments which celebrated such practices (Taylor 1997).

Apart from practical difficulties, sociobiology also has many ideological critics who object to its premises. Lerner (1992), for example, has reacted vehemently to sociobiology, criticising it for being reductionist and oppressive. He finds it abhorrent that human beings are reduced to temporary carriers of the genes whose will they serve. Lerner cites objectionable sociobiological texts in which it is argued that men go to war largely to gain the right of impregnating a new population of women. He also shows how sociobiological theories have been recruited in support of right-wing views. He is joined by feminist critics, who have also responded with horror to the sexist world of systematic female inferiority which it seems to portray (Reed 1978.)

Certainly both early and more recent proponents have managed to subscribe to views which are, to many, thoroughly objectionable as the following quote demonstrates:

> It may seem unfair that a woman assistant solicitor earns £3000 less than a man, but is she as profitable? It appears that she is much more likely to be doing unprofitable legal aid work because it makes her feel useful to society and good about

herself while he is chasing the high-profit cases. We are told that women engineers earn less than their male counterparts .... Engineering, for obvious biological reasons, is an almost exclusively male preserve but once the social scientists tacked on 'food engineering' to the engineer category, it suddenly appeared to have a considerable number of less well paid but highly qualified women. (Moir and Moir, 1999:187).

Notwithstanding the outrageous sexism implicit in many sociobiological texts, a repeated difficulty with some feminist and humanist argument is a tendency to reject theories with unpleasant consequences without any inspection of the merit of their arguments. Buss (1994), a key proponent of sexual selection theory in relation to human mate selection, takes up this point by arguing that the view involves the naturalistic fallacy. He points out that many opponents of evolutionary theory oppose it on the basis that they do not like the facts it reveals – for example that women marry for power and status but men marry for youth and beauty. They object, he argues, because they confuse descriptions of fact with prescriptions for social order. Throughout his book Buss argues that the 'natural' state of affairs need not be desirable but that acknowledging it and its causal origins is a first step on the road to change. Buss's argument is worth considering but he tends to assume a much easier separation of fact from value than can, in practice, be achieved.

Having been cautioned by the difficulties of the sociobiological project, it is still useful to consider the ways in which sociobiological explanations deal with issues of sexuality in practice. Adult male humans have the longest and most flexible penises of any living primate. Even more unusual is the thickness of the erect male penis, which relies on an unusual (for primates) system of vasocongestion. Why should this be, in evolutionary terms? Evolutionary theorists are not sure but their speculations about the reasons for this show the kind of reasoning typically employed.

Any heritable differences in sperm quality and sperm delivery equipment will be under intense sexual selection. One common explanation sees 'sperm competition' as the reason behind the penis's vital statistics. Sperm competition has been documented in many primates where females have numerous sexual liaisons so sperm from many males must compete to reach the ovum. Within one ejaculate some sperm is geared to fertilisation, some is geared to blocking the sperm of other males and some is geared to attacking other male's sperm. The argument runs that the longer the penis the closer it can get to the woman's cervix giving the sperm it delivers an advantage. This argument has a number of problems, among which are the counter claims that it is the force of penile ejaculate and its volume that determines where sperm ends up. The great apes, who have multiple partners, have evolved large testicles to produce copious quantities of sperm. They ejaculate forcefully but their penises are small.

Perhaps, therefore, what is important about the human penis is instead its flaccid visibility. With the adoption of erect posture and relative hairlessness the penis certainly became more visible – but why should females select for penile size? Another possibility is that the large penis evolved through female choice as a tactile stimulator. Copulatory thrusting is not necessary for sperm delivery and Miller (2000) suggests that females take the vigour of thrusting as an index of general fitness. Others suggest that penises go on developing to better stimulate the clitoris, a suggestion which seems difficult to support in view of the relative inefficiency of penile thrusting as a method for clitoral stimulation.

If the size of the human penis troubles evolutionary biologists, the very existence of the clitoris is troublesome. Gould and Lewontin (1979) see the clitoris as an accidental spin-off from the male body plan, adding that since conception can occur in its absence it is unimportant from an evolutionary perspective. This explains, for Gould, why female orgasm seems less reliable than male orgasm. However, despite its externally small size, internally the clitoris is a major organ. Furthermore, Baker and Bellis (1993, cited in Taylor 1997) suggest that the clitoris has a functional dimension. They suggest that female masturbation plays an important part in the process, generating uterine contractions that help a woman to keep a particular man's sperm in play for several days after intercourse. The clitoris would therefore allow females to select which male's sperm will finally impregnate her. They point out that the location of the clitoris toward the top of the pubic area and a little away from the vaginal opening allows comfortable masturbation without the risk of infection. Yet another explanatory line suggests that the clitoris serves interpersonal functions. Eibesfelt (1989, cited in Miller 2000) has viewed female orgasm as a reinforcement mechanism for promoting long-term pair bonding that keeps a female faithful to her mate though, in suggesting this, he is left wondering why clitorises have such trouble in provoking orgasm. Perhaps the difficult-to-please clitoris is exploited by choosy females, who use the difficulty of stimulating the clitoris correctly as a selection mechanism for males who provide pleasurable foreplay. Such males, it is argued, are brighter, more sensitive, and interpersonally attuned and as such are more likely to make a generous parental investment for their children.

No consistent story on the clitoris emerges. Instead, the persistent difficulty sociobiologists have with non reproductive aspects of sex is highlighted. Consistent with this difficulty, evolutionary theorists have a hard time with homosexuality. Some, like Stevens and Price (1996), are able to produce some theoretical suggestions; others like Buss (1994) regard homosexuality as an enigma.

Evolutionary theory mainly defines areas which resist change in normal life spans. Stevens and Price (1996), however, suggest a number of strategies. Among them is the recommendation that the problem should be framed to the patient in evolutionary terms and they should be helped to select between a range of evolutionarily sanctioned strategies. On other occasions, it is suggested that explaining the difficulty to the patient in terms of its evolutionary adaptiveness helps the patient to understand their predicament and is remoralising. These are somewhat weak suggestions, and in general evolutionary psychology is strong on theory and weak on action. It provides very little purchase for the therapist or the political activist seeking to improve a state of affairs in a patient or in a current culture. At worst it threatens to strand the patient in a bleak and immoral world. At other times it can give permission to individuals whose wishes do not fit well with current sexual mores. In the following, not entirely comfortable vignette, the therapist uses evolutionary theory strategically to gain a patient's confidence:

Colin was a 40-year-old labourer who presented complaining of compulsive sexual adventuring which hurt his wife and repeatedly got him into trouble. He had presented at assessment reluctantly and with a hangdog expression and he made it perfectly clear that he would rather be elsewhere. After hearing his story the therapist said that the assessment was for him, not for anyone else, and that he would quite understand if he did not feel he needed help. Colin looked surprised. The therapist went on to explain that some theorists thought that men were evolutionarily programmed to try to have sex with a wide range of women. Colin agreed that he thought it was 'in my nature'. The therapist leaned forwards and said conspiratorially 'yes, but only the stupid get caught'. In subsequent sessions Colin and his therapist worked chiefly on the risky aspects of Colin's sexual adventuring, risk management of which improved considerably.

From a sociobiological perspective Colin, literally, and his therapist, vicariously could be thought of as both having got their clubs out and started to wander through the forest in search of a spare piece of the nubile gene pool! Such a vision sums up both the best and the worst in sociobiology. It can offer striking, if sometimes unpalatable, explanations for our social arrangements and it can also serve as window dressing for unacceptable behaviours or provide justifications for entrenched privilege.

Conclusion

This chapter has sought to establish that whatever else it is, sex is a biological business. Large parts of what we do, how we wish to do it and how we have difficulty in doing it are strongly conditioned by biological factors. Sexual responses are partly, therefore, adaptations to environmental pressures. But in what environment were they formed? How can we guess at the selection pressures that formed them? Sociobiological theories are now sufficiently long in the tooth for us to have several examples of their recruitment for ideological purposes. But sociobiology's critics seem ideologically driven also. Therapists confronting sexual problems need to be as clear about the biology and sociobiology of sex as they can, given the current state of knowledge. Often this will mean acknowledging that not much is known for sure.

2 Approaches II: anthropology and sociology

Human sexual experience is shot through with the influence of language and culture and it is various beyond belief. For this reason, neither biology nor psychology can provide the whole of any explanation of the social affair which is human sexuality. For a number of decades work carried out in a range of disciplines (cultural anthropology, sociology, history, social psychology, and feminism) challenged approaches to sexuality which emphasised its universal features (perceived as most prevalent within biological and psychological perspectives). They focused their attention on the social, cultural, economic and political forces shaping sexual variation. It is a field studded with conflicting positions on almost every aspect of theory and practice. One thing remains constant. Ironically, it is the fact of social diversity across time, and across and within cultures, which undercuts any easy claims of sexual universality and any easy standard of sexual normality. The topic is too large for a single chapter to cover all aspects. Instead, topic areas in anthropology and sociology are presented.

The aim in this chapter is to present the kind of information and the sort of approach which should be in the mind of the therapist when approaching sexual problems from a cultural and social perspective. Conspicuous, by its absence, in this chapter is any attention to those large traditions in anthropology and sociology which have taken up a radically reflexive and self-critical stance, not only in relation to the apparent institutions and assumptions of the West but also to the covert power structures which maintain influence by shaping the very structure of thought itself. These theorists, often structuralists or poststructuralists, because of their consistent focus on power are covered in the chapter on politics and sexuality.

Anthropology

Anthropology is the study of different cultures. Initially, as a discipline, it was applied to structurally simple, 'primitive' societies. More recently, cultures or sub-cultures closer to home have been studied. The key methodology of anthropology is participant observation (Ashkenazi and Markowitz 1999), a methodology which has evident difficulties when sexuality is the subject of study. Initially ethnographers, acting as participant observers, were enjoined to take the status of as neutral an observer as possible. Particularly important was the maintenance of moral neutrality, which was supposed to be achieved by a stance of benevolent universalism that saw all cultures as equally valuable (Goldenweisser 1937). The object of participant observation was the creation of an ethnographic record, which contained descriptions of a culture's behaviour, customs, social practices, myths and stories. On the basis of this record, anthropologists theorised about the causes, functions and meanings of the behaviours they had observed and things they had been told. The objective was always to provide a description of the way in which the culture under observation functioned as a culture.

In the 1960s this seemingly value-neutral stance was challenged as being in practice both heterosexist and male-dominated (Ashkenazi and Markowitz 1999). The neutral observer turned out to be anything but neutral. Instead, by silence, by topic selection, and through the terms of their analysis, anthropologists introduced major cultural biases. Interestingly, this passage from avowed innocent neutrality towards a more anguished or problematic understanding of the sources of bias in observation exactly parallels the increasing problematisation of the concept of the neutral analyst which was to occur in psychoanalytic circles.

Anthropologists have had a great deal to say about marriage and kinship, which they have always viewed as an important cultural phenomenon. Until recently sex, as such, was a more difficult topic, although it did become more openly discussed as experience and phenomenon in the 1990's, when the sexuality of other cultures was reclaimed as something more than just 'exotic customs'. (Markowitz *et al.* 1999:11). However, anthropological reflections on family, sexuality and culture are all relevant to the study of sexuality and to therapeutic endeavours in relation to sexual difficulty.

Even though anthropologists have turned to the topic of sexuality late, their earlier reflections on questions of kinship remain relevant. Anthropologists distinguish between two kinds of kinship: affinity – based on a sexual connection, and consanguinity – based on genetic relation. Within cultures, however, kinship structures do not always conform to these biologically based definitions. An example in our own culture of kinship not based on affinity or consanguinity is the creation of godparents as additional kin by ritual. Questions of kinship are bound together with ritual structures such as marriage, and social arrangements, the organisation of households and the structuring of inheritance. There is a wide range of possible social organisations. One of the commonest is a patrilineal society. In such a society kinship structures are altered when a man marries a woman. She then has to sever her ties with her natal group and join her husband's group. In doing so she takes part in a property transaction in which money (in the form of a dowry) changes hands and in which she becomes, to an extent, property. In such societies divorce is rare and children are considered part of their father's tribal group.

Another, very different, form of social organisation is a cognatic society. In such a society group membership is not fixed at birth but chosen later, often at marriage. Women are allowed to inherit, retain continued rights in the woman's natal group and have access to easy frequent divorce (Ortner 1981, cited in Caplan 1987). Unlike patrilinial societies, where attitudes to sexuality centre around the control of female fertility and the protection of blood lines, in cognatic societies attitudes to sexuality centre around the use of sexuality as a resource for women.

These two structures have particular relevance in our own culture. Arguably our culture is slowly moving from a patrilineal to a cognatic one. As our society moves slowly away from one structure towards another the two can frequently be found in conflict. When this conflict represents either generational or gendered divisions as well it can be severe and difficult to resolve. One common conflict centres on the nature of the wedding ceremony which will be performed. The ritual structure, which gave to the bride's family the right to the structuring of this process, has given way to innumerable variations. The potential for causing offence can be considerable. The problems of cognatic structures are particularly highlighted when the partners come from different religious groupings and the nature of the ceremony to be performed can be seen to represent a very visible form of choice between groups. Patrilineal and cognatic structures also have different implications for the form of household organisation which the couple adopt:

> Helen and Paul found the terms of their marriage difficult to negotiate and presented because Paul was convinced Helen was having an affair. Paul thought Helen should keep house and that he should always know where she was. Helen resented the intrusion on her freedom. There were rows and, when they came to blows, Helen often escaped the marital home to spend time with her mother where Paul suspected, with some justice, that Helen and her mother tended to badmouth him. Paul resented this, feeling he should have first call on Helen's time. Additionally, Paul wanted children badly while Helen wanted to delay. This division of opinion was reflected in the senior generation also, where Helen's mother counselled delay and Paul's was desperate for grandchildren. Paul easily assumed that these children would take his surname and Helen resented this and wanted them to take her surname.

Aspects of Paul's expectations have a 'patrilinial' feel – he has a call on her time, he wants children and particularly ones with his name. Some aspects of Helen's way of relating have an 'exogamous cognatic' tinge – she returns to her home tribe, is less keen to see herself in a child-producing kinship structure, and not at all keen to affiliate herself or her offspring to Paul's surname tribe. The therapist was torn both ways, feeling in sympathy with Helen over Paul's wish to control her and his ill treatment of her, but feeling in sympathy with Paul over Helen's tie to her mother. The therapist found himself stepping in and trying repeatedly to make everything all right.

In supervision, stepping back to look at the situation from an anthropological perspective helped the therapist to disengage from a state of controlling concern but also helped the therapist to locate Helen and Paul's dilemma within a larger understanding of our culture. The therapist was able to transmit to the couple some notion that their dilemma was part of a wider social picture which let them gain some distance on the situation.

While liberal sympathies might see in our culture's move from patrilineal to cognatic structuring of kinship and descent an advance, certainly for women and perhaps more generally for human rights, there may be a more sinister undertow. Anthropologists have pointed out that tight kinship structures are less relevant in post-industrialised societies. This is because the privatisation of property erodes a sense of group membership and the state may have an interest in furthering such erosions. This is because states, and indeed other large organisations such as churches or the army, dislike strong descent groups which may challenge official authority.

Although different kinds of inheritance arrangement are found in human cultures, patrilineal structures are the most common. Behavioural anthropologists have suggested that the reason for this lies in the differing investments which men and women have in their offspring. In general, it is argued female children will maximise their reproductive capacity irrespective of parental investment and furthermore that male children are more likely to produce offspring than female ones. So, parents invest in sons in order to maximise the number of grandchildren they will have and patrilineal inheritance enshrines this. Running through this kind of argument is a belief in the power of biology, shaped by selection pressures, to affect the nature of human society so that, from a genetic/evolutionary perspective, behaviours which maximise the production of descendents are likely to be favoured over an evolutionary timescale. In support of their argument anthropologists of this persuasion point out that in societies where there are few opportunities for men to mate, strategies are altered in such a way as to maximise the production of kin. In these situations female children become a better bet and cultural rules often promote hypergamous mating by low-status women. That is to say, families lower down the social structure invest in females who are propelled into polygamous unions with high-status males where they have a good chance of reproducing. However, there could be more immediate reasons, particularly in pre-industrialised societies, why strategies which produce lots of grandchildren are selected – they may, for example, provide care for their grandparents and parents as they age – and, as cultures vary one would expect that strategic assessments of ways to obtain maximum benefit would change.

Very likely the distribution of causation between strategies will prove more genetic in origin than cultural theorists might wish, and less biologically programmed than evolutionary biologist's claim. From a therapeutic perspective the debate is less relevant than attempting to see how cultural imperatives of whatever origin may affect the representation of erotic and sexual possibilities. This can be seen in the case of exogamy – another area where biological mechanisms have been theorised as important in governing cultural practices. The exogamy rule obliges members to marry outside their immediate grouping and is in a way an extension of the incest taboo. Its effect is to force exchange between different cultural groups based on trade in women. Depending on custom, and doubtless the prevailing balance of advantage between the sexes and groups, the exchange of women is accompanied either by a dowry or a bride price. Anthropologists have seen in exogamy an engine which forces social intercourse between different groups and is responsible for driving forward the development of culture and society. Erotically it has led to a number of easily identifiable eroticised images and relationship scripts. The 'Man from Laramie – the frightening stranger with so many notches on his gun' – is arguably an eroticised vision of an out-group male whose status as a potential exogamous mate is deliciously ambiguous. In the same vein, the story of the vampire whose bite (itself a thinly disguised sexual advance) recruits the unsuspecting virgin to the vampire tribe, may reflect fantasies about the man from outside, but may also recapitulate scenarios in which groups which contain a surfeit of males resort to stealing women from other tribes.

The out-group female is also eroticised. The exchange of miniature paintings of marriageable women between high-status males in Europe, in a pre-photography era, is strikingly similar to the use which has been suggested for small figurines of women – the Venuses which represent very early prehistoric figurative sculptures (Taylor 1997). These images travel as proxies, or possibly even promissory notes, for women who will be exchanged between powerful dynastic groups. In the case of the Venuses, as in the cases of the miniature paintings, erotically determined conventions of female beauty probably had more influence over the nature of the representation than any concern for accuracy.

Social rules invite social transgressions and transgressive sexualities are also defined by the normative cultural structures. Eloping and its less active relative, hopeless romance between social classes, both take their specific excitement and danger from setting love against convention. Thus differing kinship structures, inheritance rules and the entailed household organisations will invite different kinds of erotic elaboration:

> Shiv presented for therapy in a state of turmoil having become impotent with his wife. He said that his mother had died and that he had been grieving for her. He took her ashes back to India for the family and gave up eating mangoes for a year in her memory. During this time he did not think much about sex. Then, a year later on the anniversary of his mother's death things were meant to get back to normal but he had felt unable to be with his wife. Shiv and his wife had lived with his mother and some younger sisters. Mother had been very much the matriarch of the house with Shiv's wife in a rather subservient role. Now Shiv's wife was the senior woman in the household. As therapy proceeded Shiv realised he felt angry with his wife whenever he saw her in the place where he remembered his mother.

There is an extra strong bond between mothers and sons in some Indian – Hindu cultural arrangements. Women marry into their husband's household and gain status as they produce male children and as senior women die off. Ultimately, a woman's sons procure her status as the matriarch of a household of her own. Shiv's response is one which might be an expected class of difficulty within his cultural setting.

Cultural relativism and its limitations

The difference between cultures has led some anthropologists and cultural theorists to a radical scepticism over the capacity for investigators ever to understand another culture. They frequently cite errors in cultural understanding as evidence for this difficulty. However, in order to have identified these errors as such, cultural theorists, however critical, must have succeeded in some degree of cultural conversion in which they have confidence. Complete scepticism is amply justified but complete nihilism about cross-cultural understanding could only be logically consistent with a complete cessation of all attempts to understand or relate to other cultures. While questions about the epistemological foundations of anthropology may seem abstruse from the point of view of a practising therapist, a similar set of considerations must apply to attempts to compare or evaluate moral standards between cultures. This is important because the close linkage between what cultures consider moral and their conception of human flourishing means that much psychological health and ill health is intimately linked to an individual's standing in relation to whatever is considered normative for a subculture or culture. Thus, comparing moral norms between cultures cannot be escaped if any cross-cultural view of sexual function is to be achieved. Evidently moral standards vary between cultures; the question is how to view activities or proscriptions which seem unacceptable by any moral standard. A completely relativist standpoint, which argued that cultures are free to set any norms they please, threatens to sanction activities (say, for example, the routine abuse of children) which many people from our culture would have difficulty ever seeing as acceptable. On the other hand, a completely absolutist perspective (which might resemble that taken by some Christian missionaries in the nineteenth century), would brand all cultures that departed from a very specific view of sexual behaviour and modesty as immoral. Obviously a middle position needs to be found by therapists practising mainly in our own culture, and thinking about where to draw the line can provide helpful perspectives on the therapeutic task of making similar distinctions within our own culture.

Marriage has often been treated by anthropologists as a cultural universal, but it is not the same thing amongst different cultures. Certainly marriage cannot simply refer to the acquisition of sexual rights, even if these are exclusive. Instead, we normally conceive of marriage as combined in some form of sexual access with a set of rights and obligations which are publicly sanctioned and socially binding. These frequently specify subsequent domestic arrangements and the status of inheritance rights of children. Some societies do not have anything which resembles marriage. The Nyar cast in India are a matrilineal group in which paternity is thought relatively unimportant. At puberty children are placed in male–female pairs and put through a ceremony which has been called by western observers 'marriage'. The pair go through a ceremony, cohabit for a few days and then part never to see each other again. Thereafter the woman lives with her mother's family and takes lovers who have neither rights nor obligations. Her children live with her in her mother's home. It is clear that the so-called marriage ceremony confers none of the social rights, obligations, or sequelae which may be expected as a result of marriage. Instead it functions much more like an initiation ceremony in which the children are fitted for sexual availability. Current emphasis on the need for children to have secure knowledge of their paternity in our culture, and an increasing emphasis on family stability as a guarantor of mental health, means that Nyar customs seem alien. Can we say that they are inevitably pathological? Certainly in our culture, households composed of successive generations of women and visited by roving unattached males are not regarded as a stable base for childrearing. But living arrangements which appear to result from the breakdown of previously accepted social structures within our own culture do not seem analogous to a social structure embedded within a long-standing ritualised arrangement. In this case perhaps what is right for the Nyar may not be right for us.

The Kikuyu and Hausa provide another example. They are African tribes who live only a few miles from each other. Despite this, Nelson (1987) shows that their views on female sexuality are radically different from each other. Kikuyu feel that only virgins can do without sex – once a woman has had sex she will be insatiable and cannot be faithful. The Kikuyu practise female circumcision to limit female pleasure and thereby keep girls under control by limiting their sex drive. Kikuyu men often forbid their wives contraception to prevent them having affairs. By contrast, Hausa men value women who have been prostitutes because it is felt that having sowed their wild oats they are less likely to stray when married.

The contrast between these two groups raises some deep questions. Both tribal groups are keen to control female activity once they enter a breeding pair, even if the methods and beliefs deployed to this end vary. The concern of these cultures to control post-marital female sexuality is a respect in which they resemble our own and many other cultures. Does this make female marital fidelity something of a moral universal? If so, the probable reasons which lie behind it are not morally inspiring since they are rooted in male needs to ensure that offspring in which they will invest time and support (when they could be occupied siring further kin) are, in truth, their own. Even sharper moral questions arise in relation to the practice of female circumcision, which has been widely condemned and has become one culturally sanctioned practice which it is acceptable to condemn despite the prevailing climate of cultural relativism. Matters grow even more fraught morally when the practice of circumcising boys is raised. Some people see this practice as unacceptable while others see, in attempts to ban it, nothing short of genocide. Yet both female and male circumcisions are procedures which have no Western medical justification and which may be accompanied by post-operative complications which include reduced adult sexual functioning. Probably our less conflicted condemnation of female circumcision is due to our perception of it is a much more mutilating procedure. Even so, strong advocates of female circumcision still exist and elide their arguments with an increasing Western trend for female genital surgery designed to enhance rather than reduce sexual pleasure.

Culture and ritual

The issue of circumcision raises a more general question about the status and function of ritualised sexual practices. In a general way these practices do not find favour in our culture, which has adopted a rather medicalised and individualised perspective on sexual activity. For Western commentators ritual satanic abuse and sadomasochistic enactments may be the only kinds of ritual sex they can call to mind. Georges Battaille, a French writer and novelist, produced a long, highly theoretical and at times plainly whimsical meditation on the links between ritual and eroticism in his book (Battaille 1987). Battaille argues that the only animals to be erotic, as opposed to sexual, are humans. For Battaille death, birth and eroticism are intimately linked and the aim of eroticism is to replace a deep sense of discontinuity (we must all die alone) with a feeling of continuity. Battaille reasons further that eroticism is linked intimately with extremes of violence and disruption.

He contrasts self-possession with nakedness and argues that obscenity is the name we give to the uneasiness that nakedness brings on as it threatens to disrupt our sense of self-possession. From this position it is not surprising that Battaille moves on to consider the nature of taboos. These he argues are necessary to combat violence and protect the world of work but are also the essence of eroticism, which lies in the transgression of taboos. Transgression is not the ending of the taboo but rather its legitimated suspension, and ritual figures in his scheme as the means by which transgressions are sanctioned. Battaille is therefore able to argue that both marriage and ritual orgy are alike in so far as they are structures which break the taboo on sexual expression and allow it, within certain limits.

Battaille's thoughts are easily subject to the criticism that a wealth of theorising is backed up by scant quantities of evidence. However, his vision of a world suffused with dark violent forces and shaped by primitive and magical thinking is enticing when the task is to analyse grotesque sexual phenomena. Current cultural concerns over paedophilia have lead to exaggerated responses, both legal and cultural. One characteristic of these is a turning against paedophiles in which violent opprobrium is sanctioned. Battaille might argue that the social ritual in which a paedophile is identified licences an explosion of violence and the breaking of taboos (this time against violence) which maintain civilised behaviour. He might suggest further that the ferocity of the attack is rooted in a violent identification with the paedophile urge to sexually violate the child. He might wonder whether society, in building up children as vulnerable innocents who know nothing of sex, also builds up the licentious urge to violate and join with children. Thus the hatred of paedophilia is linked to the violation of children and to their pure innocence in a mutually reinforcing cycle.

The task of psychotherapists is to reapply the insights of anthropology to therapeutic practice. Robert Stoller, an American analyst, moved increasingly towards an anthropologically informed investigation of sexual practices. In his later work Stoller (1993, 1996) used ethnographic methodologies extensively on aspects of our own culture. His successive works on the subject of sexuality move steadily away from analytic certainties grounded in a universalisation of a single culture (Stoller 1975) and an easy knowledge of 'sexual normality', towards the use of ethnographic methodology in an atmosphere of benevolent curious neutrality and an acknowledgement of sexual diversity (Stoller 1991). Later books are able to discuss the role of ritualised enactments in sexual expression (see, for example, *Pain and Passion*, 1991), but even in later works Stoller's basic thesis involves appeal to an earlier trauma which is being re-enacted in order to be resolved, and he remains unwilling to see such sexual activities as normal. Instead, he increasingly argues that all sexual activities, even the overtly normal, involve such re-enactments.

Stoller was able to use anthropological methodology as a basis for increasing his explanatory range and the scope of his sexual compassion and imagination. Less work has been done on drawing information from other cultures into the knowledge base of therapy. Jungian therapists, whose tradition sanctions a wide-ranging view across other cultures in order to gain an under-standing of the workings of a common imaginative structure theorised to be universally present in humanity (the collective unconscious), might have been well placed to do this work, and there are some examples (Cowan 1982), but a general distaste for sexual matters has limited investigation in this area:

> Pauline presented for therapy, her body covered in slashes and piercings. To the therapist's eye she seemed grotesque. It was difficult at times for the therapist even to look at her. Each week there were either fresh cuts or fresh piercings. Pauline distinguished quite sharply between these two activities in rela-tion to her body. The cutting was a solitary activity done when she was distressed and she saw the cuts as ugly and wanted plastic surgery to reduce the scarring. The piercings were done in company with her boyfriend as part of sexual activity and regarded by her as aesthetically pleasing.

For Stoller, both Pauline's piercing and her self-harming would be re-enactments aimed at mastering childhood trauma that involved significant pain and humiliation. For Battaille, Pauline's cutting would have been irrelevant but her piercings might have been viewed as ritual erotic acts enacted within a cultural setting in which body piercing had taken on specific meanings. A Jungian therapist might not choose to point to the erotic significance of the piercing but instead might discuss the religious values of self-harm, ranging from the Catholic mortification of the flesh, ritual self-harming in certain Shia Muslim rituals, to Hindu practices involving wearing large bamboo structures attached to the flesh by hooks.

Sociology

We imagine that we know our own culture but often we only know a small part of it. This leads to the illusion that we are representative of our own culture which, as a result, can lead us to generalise from our experience in ways which may turn out to be unjustified. In any case, our understandings of our actions often concentrate on their personal meanings and neglect the extent to which our ways of behaving are part of a social prescription with collective aims.

Sociological perspectives can help with this as long as it is kept in mind that no single knowledge base or theoretical perspective exists for therapists to acquire. As in the case of anthropology, so in sociology, there is no single tradition which sets out the 'sociology of sex'. Indeed, in the past, major sociologists often ignored the topic. There were some important exceptions, including the work of Michel Foucault (*History of Sexuality*, 1981). More recently sex has been directly considered by sociologists working from within a feminist or gay and lesbian perspective (Weeks 1985), but also, within the mainstream, by sociologists such as Anthony Giddens (1992).

Three topic areas will be examined. First, a historical perspective on the sociology of sex in the eighteenth and nineteenth centuries is presented, with the aim of demonstrating how social variables affect sexual attitudes. Next, the work of Anthony Giddens is discussed to show how the important work of this fairly mainstream sociological theorist bears on the topic of sexuality. Giddens is particularly important because he shows how personal concerns arise from sociological forces. Last, some specific therapeutic methodologies, which share an explicit focus on the social nature of man, are presented. While these methodologies have not as yet been directly applied to sexuality it is easy to see how they can be relevant.

Historical sociology

Hawkes' (1996) account of the sociology of sex devotes a chapter to tracing the development of sexual attitudes in the eighteenth and nineteenth centuries. She suggests that Enlightenment thought challenged the immediate linkage of sin and sex. In particular it challenged the notion that sex was degraded because it was an animal activity. Nature came to be positively valued and sex, because natural, was also valued. Open descriptions of sexual activity were permitted; standards of sexual behaviour, including the censure of prostitution and adultery, were relaxed. Even so, there remained plenty of evidence of unease and ambivalence over sexual discussion and a developing discourse on the dangers of sexual excess. In particular, sexual expression amongst the lower classes, on the part of women, and outside heterosexual coitus, was repressed. Thus sexual liberty was not discussed in front of the servants, women were expected to remain feminine (that is not to express active sexual striving) and homosexual acts became, for the first time, associated with a type of individual and with acts that were against nature.[1] For this reason Porter (1982, cited in Hawkes) argues that Enlightenment sexuality is really a refined sexuality. Hawkes suggests that, as the century proceeds, limited radicalism is overrun by increasing prudishness as part of a more general rejection of the hedonism of the Georgian era.

The nineteenth century began with an uneasy bourgeoisie whose attitude to sexuality was overtly repressive but covertly fascinated. Concerns over prostitution loomed large and it has been suggested that these both revealed urges to repress sexuality and indulged a vicarious fascination with sex and low life. Female sexuality became equated with the control of male sexual activity, either by inflaming or regulating desire. There are probably links between this view and the increasing male anxiety over women's increasing economic freedom from marriage. A new moral rhetoric of female responsibilities now had to take over from the economic necessities that had once regulated female behaviour.

Social commentators on sexuality in our own age might do well to consider the frightening possibility that current sexual liberal-

---

1 The idea that homosexual identity is a relatively recent construction is, of course, hotly contested (see, for example, Mohr 1992).

ity may give way under a range of pressures. These may include fears about the reproductive capacities and inclinations of the 'lower orders' (a preoccupation which occupied the Enlightenment and was also strong in the nineteenth century) whose sexual knowledge can, because of mass media, no longer be held in check as compared with the elite. Sexual repression could also result from a more general preoccupation with discipline and social responsibility which governments need to foster in times of economic difficulty or of war. As in the nineteenth century, our culture continues the sexual demonisation of the poor and the outcast based on the crude fear that they will out-reproduce the ruling classes. Our culture also, increasingly, relies on images of bestiality in the depiction of the lives of what it perceives as the under class. All in all aspects of modern, third-way, straight-talking, state-sponsored philanthropy, such as welfare for work, have a strongly nineteenth-century feel to them.

Anthony Giddens

There is one modern sociology of sex, however, which has a much more Enlightenment cast to it than a nineteenth-century one. Ironically, its exponent is also strongly associated with third-way politics. Giddens is one of the most important recent sociologists to consider sexuality and his approach is, by and large, strongly sex-positive. His importance lies in the way he reflects on the social origins and social implications of modern sexual arrangements, arguing that they have both been responsible for shaping the modern era while reflexively being shaped by it. His interest in these arrangements is therefore part of a larger task of describing the project of 'self-creation' that is part of 'reflexive modernity'. By this he means that modern ways of living involve individualised journeys of self-development and individualised assessments of relevant social and other knowledge bases, as opposed to a pre-modern traditionalist approach in which long-honoured ways of doing things (tradition) set norms of behaviour. For Giddens the rise of romantic love is intimately bound up with modernisation and the construction of narratives of the self. The canonical form for a tale of romantic love is a story about two lives and their relations with little reference to the surrounding setting. Giddens argues that, because of this, long-term romantic relationships kicked off the construction of self narratives which now become independently pursued.

Giddens also argues for the emergence of 'plastic sexuality'. Plastic sexuality is sexuality freed from its intrinsic relation to reproduction and used instead as a vehicle for personal identity development. Giddens suggests that plastic sexuality emerged as a result of social trends initiated in the eighteenth century, including the limiting of family size. It became further developed with the introduction and widespread use of contraception in the 1960s. Giddens argues that once sexual relationships were no longer centred exclusively on reproduction (or its possibility) they were also freed from being defined solely in terms of the rule of the phallus. Women could pioneer changes in the nature of the sexual relationship and have sought to introduce a new emotional egalitarianism at the centre of sexual relationships. Giddens argues that the transformation of intimacy which has developed could have radical possibilities if the female-led changes in the personal sphere extend to the public sphere. The aim of maximising economic growth may be replaced by the aim of maximising emotional fulfilment. Whereas Freud saw sex as an unruly force needing curbing and control before civilisation could emerge, Giddens sees, at least in plastic if not reproductive sexuality, utopian possibilities for the development of civilisation.

Giddens supports his argument by demonstrating the way in which sex is influenced by, and in turn influences, wider social practices. His idea of sexuality as a life style – more a matter of social conditioning and personal choice than biology – provides an important counterbalance to the views of sexuality as biologically or psychologically determined. He dethrones 'normal' sexuality from any pretensions of biological or cultural hegemony and legitimates a wider range of individual choice in the expression of sexual feelings. This aim has not achieved universal endorsement amongst psychotherapists. Young (2001), for example, reviewing Giddens' work from a psychoanalytic perspective, struggles with this liberalising view and ultimately concludes that a Kleinian analysis of sexuality cannot accommodate the levels of freedom which Giddens proposes. For Kleinians there are quite prescriptive universals and some kinds of sexual expression violate what amount, in their view, to natural laws of the psyche.

Giddens' work may be open to criticism from another direction. His book on sexuality (Giddens 1992) contains a vast swath of theorising, much of it highly psychologised. His discussion of sex addiction (Giddens 1992, Chapter 5) is a good example. It contains a wide range of highly generalised statements, both sociological and psychological, none of which are backed up by any evidence base other than the odd anecdote or appeal to general historical facts. His discussion of womanisers succeeds in pathologising these individuals both in terms of their individual psychology and in relation to the development of reflexive modernisation. It comes, therefore, to the not entirely revolutionary conclusion that womanisers are sad, compulsion-driven individuals who would be better off if they could be faithful. The difficulty with Giddens' work is that the weight of his theory undermines the main value of sociology – its capacity to marshal, present and then theorise from facts about our social world in a way which both generates new insights but which is also open to challenge from further facts. Ironically, such a sociology would have exactly the relation to fact which Giddens sees as a vital part of reflexive modernisation.

The value of more factually based sociological perspectives on clinical material can be appreciated by thinking about the following case:

Kiri is 30, and has three children by three partners. All her partners have been unemployed men and in each case she got pregnant early in the relationship with little suggestion or expectation that the men involved would stay around. She continues to be involved with a number of men in relationships in which payment or coercion may be involved. Now her 14-year-old daughter Eloise is pregnant.

Kiri came to treatment suffering with depression and anxiety. When Eloise announced that she was pregnant Kiri and her current partner had an angry break-up after an argument about whether Eloise should have a termination. Kiri then telephoned social services to say that they must come and take the children into care. Now she is terrified that they will refuse to return the children. She talks tearfully in the therapy session of her regret at her own pregnancy at 16. She had been the oldest in a family of six siblings and was used by her mother, who she experienced as harsh and hating, as an auxiliary caregiver to younger siblings. Kiri's pregnancy with Eloise resulted in her being thrown out of the family home as not fit to raise a child.

Kiri's psychological and social problems cannot be understood from within a personal framework. Her problem is part of a larger social problem which interacts with both biological and psychological factors. The decline in the age of puberty now makes it biologically possible for all younger teenagers to get pregnant, but teenage pregnancy is also unevenly spread across the population. Coming from a single-parent family of origin, having low school attainment and being friendly with sexually active peers are among the social factors which predispose to a younger age of first intercourse (Rossi 1997), which is a risk factor for young pregnancy. These findings also point to a class link to the phenomenon of teen pregnancy. The ghettoisation of poverty and the association of poverty with teen pregnancy have, in some areas, produced communities in which teen pregnancy is both endemic and multigenerational.

Appraisal of a case like Kiri's will be affected by the way in which the problem is perceived by therapist and patient and their perceptions are likely to be shaped by cultural attitudes. Politicians and the press have created an image of a tidal wave of teen parenthood, caused by young women's unregulated sexual behaviour and poor women sponging off the state, even though this is unwarranted. In America, for example, teen motherhood cannot be said to have grown as a consequence of welfare because the value of welfare has reduced (Schwartz and Rutter 1998). Interviews with teens who are pregnant do not indicate the kind of planning and forethought necessary for their pregnancy to be a thought-out monetary strategy. Indeed, being able to see a future for oneself is actually associated with abstaining from sex or using contraception (Pipher 1994, in Schwartz and Rutter 1998). In fact, teen pregnancy rates themselves have not increased at all. Instead they have declined along with a general decline in pregnancy rates but, because they have not declined as much as pregnancy rates in other age ranges, they form a rising proportion of the figures.

The therapist can draw a number of useful points from the sociology of Kiri's case. An understanding of the exigencies of poverty will help the therapist see that none of the players in the drama would seem quite so dysfunctional if they had enough money to live on. The therapist could also use the finding that a capacity to see a future for oneself is associated with lower levels of teen pregnancy and greater self-esteem and try to increase Kiri's sense of self-efficacy and, through Kiri, the self-efficacy of Eloise and the other children.

Therapeutic methodologies based in social sciences

Interpersonal therapy (Klerman and Weisman 1994) and cognitive analytic therapy (CAT) (Ryle 1990) both try to take account of human social functioning, and research on the effects of social difficulty on mood and wellbeing (for example, Brown and Harris 1978). Neither has as yet spent much time theorising sexuality explicitly but they are both capable of being applied to sexual difficulties (see, for example, Denman and De Vries 1998). Recently CAT therapy has also introduced an explicit acknowledgement of the importance of the biopsychosocial model (Ryle and Kerr 2002) in its theoretical framework. This means that should it turn its attention to sexuality it will have firm foundations.

Interpersonal therapy was used to treat Kiri. This therapy sees Kiri's depression as related to current interpersonal conflict and role transition and focuses exclusively on encouraging her to try to solve difficulties in her current social relationships. It seeks to mobilise the patient's own resources by helping them to maintain a consistent focus on two or three agreed difficulties in the therapy sessions. In the event Kiri agreed to use her difficult relationship with her own mother as one focus and her relationship with Eloise as another. These two difficult relationships provide examples of what IPT calls interpersonal disputes. In the therapy the focus was on helping Kiri to define her main disagreements with her mother and helping her to voice these reasonably to her mother in a way that avoided a tendency to escalate the arguments into an increasingly acrimonious recitation of ancient wrongs. In relation to her daughter, work focused on getting Kiri to define what were age-appropriate responses for her daughter and what were responses which were 'right out of order'. In this way Kiri was able to reflect on her own childhood as she worked on her relationship with her daughter. As therapy progressed the therapist was able to persuade Kiri to accept a third focus. This was her tendency to sexual adventuring. Kiri's initially hostile response to questions about this area gave way to an admission that her sexual relationships were not always satisfying to her and that she was afraid of some of the men with whom she was involved. The IPT therapist conceptualised this (somewhat awkwardly) in terms of IPT's theory of role transition, seeing Kiri as trying to negotiate moving from an adolescent version of sexuality to a more adult one. Kiri was able to make some decisions about her relationships and, importantly, extracted herself from two of them.

Cognitive analytic therapy (CAT) was devised by Ryle (1990). It is a brief focal intervention in which consistent stress is laid on the way in which people are formed and continually influenced by their social interactions. Using the work of Vygotsky as a basis, humans are represented as learning animals capable of self-consciously using 'higher functions' to influence malfunction in other areas of life. The term 'reciprocal role' is used to describe the socially imparted knowledge of paired social roles which together encode social knowledge about the relationships between people, between the self and others, and between the different parts of the self. Talcot Parsons' theory of social roles (1951) was the inspiration for this idea but in the hands of Ryle and his co-workers, it developed from a concept with similarities to that of the persona developed by Jung (a mask over the real self) into a much more flexible tool for describing inner experience and inner and outer relationships.

Reciprocal roles describe the parts agents play in enacting certain kinds of relationships and are learned by observation and enactment throughout life. Examples might include 'care-giver in relation to care-receiver' or, less benignly, 'contemptuous of others in relation to contemptible'. Adopting one pole of a reciprocal role in relation to another person often exerts a strong pressure on that person to reciprocate and enact the congruent role. Clinical CAT theory delineates the repertoire of reciprocal roles a patient may adopt and the inter- or intrapersonal complications which result. Objectives in therapy include developing an overview when roles are diverse and not very consciously deployed and thereby promoting integration, sidelining harsh or negative roles which have persistent negative effects, or devising strategies for altering maladaptive sequences of behaviour, thinking and acting which derive from a role but which serve detrimentally to reinforce it or another undesirable role.

The following case history therefore provides an example of the ways in which CAT techniques can be adapted for use in cases where sex is one of the problems:

Dave and Fiona were both professionals. Dave, a senior lawyer, worked in town much of the week. Fiona had had a professional career but had become unwell with a mixed anxiety and depressive state after the birth of their second child. For the past five years she had stayed at home, incarcerated by a phobia of driving. She had grown increasingly bitter at her confinement and her husband's career advances. Dave had expanded his life outside the home, slowly coming to ignore his wife's difficulties as they proved intractable to any intervention on his part. His absences and the complexities introduced into their arrangements by her inability to drive were the cause of frequent rows. Fiona had had extensive psychiatric and psychotherapeutic treatment over the years and had little good to say about any of it.

Referral resulted from a major crisis in their relationship because Fiona had galvanised herself to consult a divorce lawyer, saying that Dave had raped her. The lawyer had raised the possibility of pressing criminal charges with Fiona but she had backed off and then, initial papers having been served, also got cold feet about the divorce proceedings. However, since the divorce papers had mentioned the rape Dave was aware of her accusation and was horribly distressed by it.

Both parties entered therapy with radically different stories about their relationship. Until that point Dave said that the marriage was all right apart from Fiona's illness, which he attributed to postnatal depression. He felt their sex life had been preserved throughout, for which he was grateful, feeling that this had helped him stay in the marriage, despite sexual longings which had nearly resulted in an affair at one stage. Their current estranged state was horribly painful to him. Fiona said that the marriage had always been unfulfilling for her but found the prospect of a divorce unbearable.

Dave's childhood, as one of a large family run on bohemian

lines, had been mostly happy. He described himself as a child as being a 'Johnny head-in-air'. Only later in life had he recalled the many emotionally charged fights and reconciliations which he witnessed between members of the household and which mostly ended in sex. The therapist's suggestion, that his marriage to Fiona and establishment of a conventional household and career represented something of a backlash against his childhood, produced a wry laugh of recognition.

Fiona's early life had been as the only child of high-powered academics. As a child she could recall her parents asking another couple if they had 'got a good one yet'. By this they meant had one of the other couple's children showed academic promise? Fiona was a clever child but not one of those children who could achieve results without considerable hard work. Every advantage was offered to her by slightly preoccupied parents who expected in return the highest academic standards. When she went to a new school Fiona found herself disliked and began to fail academically. Consequently parental love was withdrawn. Socially she had little nourishment and she began to fantasise about a 'lovely mummy' to replace her demanding mother. Such fantasies were futile and she remembered, as an adolescent, resolving to put away all softness and longing. Asked about sex she said it was discussed in the home exactly once, when her parents produced a factual textbook for her to read.

In CAT therapy a diagram of the reciprocal role structure helps all parties to see what is going on (Figure 2.1).

Using the historical information given, and other facts, the therapist hypothesised that Dave's chief reciprocal role structure was largely ignoring and denying (but secretly vigilant and terrified) in relation to noisy, struggling and dangerous. Dave's response to emotional difficulty was to withdraw and become a 'Johnny head-in-air'. This gave him seeming invulnerability but was in truth based on an underlying vigilance for danger. The birth of a son may have exacerbated this characteristic in Dave who withdrew from the chaos and disorder of a young baby. Fiona, on the other hand seemed to find herself often stuck in one or other pole of a 'critical and conditional' – 'criticised and striving' reciprocal role which itself existed along side a rarely enacted

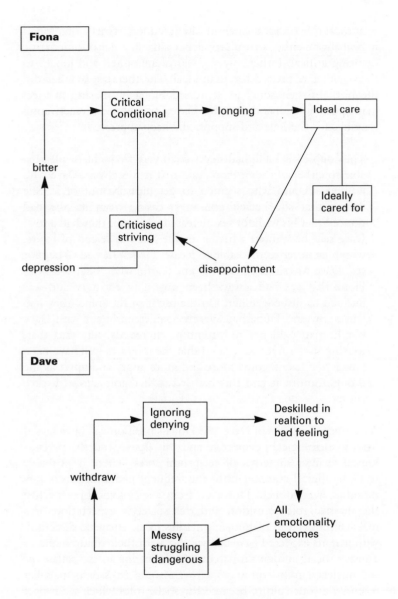

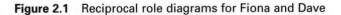

Figure 2.1 Reciprocal role diagrams for Fiona and Dave

reciprocal role of 'ideal carer–ideally cared for'. Thus Fiona found herself always either striving to silence a harsh inner or outer critic or being critical. Either way she was disappointed and lonely, as she or her care proved less than ideal. The therapist wondered if the birth of their son had depressed Fiona by making her feel inadequate and abandoned by Dave, and also by reactivating longings for the love and support she had suppressed:

> The couple's sex life had never been very frequent or pleasurable to either of them. Fiona said that it was always Dave who wanted sex and who seemed to get pleasure out of it. She denied that she herself got any pleasure from it. She had noticed that his wish for sex increased whenever they had a row. Dave said he wanted a better sex life but was scared of Fiona, whom he never seemed able to please. He felt he had to beg for sex. Dave was shocked and became tearful when he heard from Fiona that sex had always been only a wifely duty and was inclined to disbelieve her. On the night of the 'rape' they had had a row and Fiona had silently acquiesced in sex with Dave but he had paid her no attention afterwards. She said that, looking back on it she realised that she might as well have been raped. She had become more and more angry and upset as she thought about it and this had led to her going to a divorce lawyer.

A number of aspects of Dave and Fiona's position can be analysed from a sociological perspective and this fleshes out the psychological analysis in terms of reciprocal roles. There is probably some biological component to the frequent phenomenon of low mood after childbirth. However, from a sociological perspective the massive role transition and our society's expectation of a massive redirection of human energies in an altruistic direction, with parents expected to make 'sacrifices' for their children, places a heavy social burden on parents. Childbearing in the setting of the nuclear family represents a psychosocial stressor of peculiar intensity in our culture because the social roles which we expect parents to adopt are particularly idealised.

The introduction of the idea of rape also makes Dave and Fiona's situation exceedingly painful. The recognition of a crime of rape in marriage is recent and marks a shift from seeing women as sexual property (rape used to be a crime against a man's property not a woman's person) to seeing women as consenting agents. This shift is vital but it tends to assume that a parallel debate about consent has reached a sufficiently mature stage. Some debates in our culture about consent in rape are framed around a discourse which sees the woman as *agent provocateur* and the man as having been goaded to a point of sexual no-return beyond which he can no longer be expected to consider consent further. Others see female consent as capable of being withdrawn at all stages of a sexual encounter. Fiona's 'consent' or lack of it and Dave's 'crime' fall into neither of these juridical categories. Instead, Fiona and Dave are arguing about the emotional qualities of their relationship. Yet these qualities are themselves culturally embedded. CAT's use of the concept of reciprocal roles provides a tool for seeing how elements of cultural expectations in the form of social roles become internal expectations in the form of internal reciprocal roles. Where social roles are ambiguous or conflicted then the internal reciprocal roles which members of society imbibe will be at a minimum similarly conflicted.

From a larger perspective, Fiona's relationship style in relation to sex is fairly classical for some women in our culture. She views sex as a mechanical adjunct to a relationship and values the relationship-promoting aspects of sex – something that she feels Dave often does not give her. Dave's view of sex is also fairly stereotypically masculine for our culture. For him sex is a relaxation in itself and does not need to come overburdened with other relationship duties. From a micro-cultural perspective, Dave's family culture may have combined with larger expectations of sex to teach him the syllogism that sex is a tool to deploy in helping to achieve respite and distance from emotional tangles. Fiona on the other hand may have fused her micro- and macro-cultural experiences to generate the assumption that sex is a duty and a reward for good behaviour. CAT's concept of reciprocal roles can usefully be extended to encompass the notion of sexual reciprocal roles or to see sex serving a relationship function:

The therapist drew out these assumptions about sex and their likely effects on the relationship in the form of a second diagram.

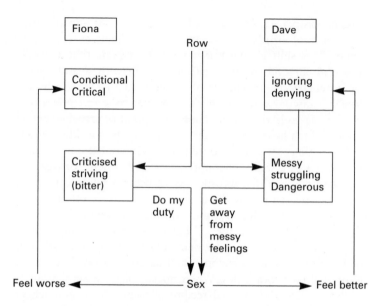

Figure 2.2 Reciprocal role diagram showing how Dave and Fiona's reciprocal role patterns interact when they have a row

This helped Fiona and Dave to understand their different contributions to the sexual difficulties they found themselves in. They took the diagram away and made several modifications based on their own observations during the week. Later sessions of therapy concentrated on using the diagrams as a way to understand, monitor and later intervene in the phenomena described. As therapy ended, Dave and Fiona were more optimistic, but anxious as well, particularly as all parties conceded that it was easy to fall back into old patterns.

Both IPT and CAT provide different ways of integrating social and cultural knowledge into a perspective which tries to weld together the interpersonal and the intrapersonal, while Jungian therapies have the potential to integrate ritual/cultural/aesthetic elements of sexuality into the mixture. However, all the therapies discussed so far lack the kind of sustained concentration on the variability of personal meanings involved in sexual fantasy and expression. This is provided by psychoanalytic accounts of sexuality, which are covered in the next chapter. They also lack any analysis of agency in the political sphere or, in the guises so far presented, much sense of the potential critiques of their claims which might be developed by social theorists who adopt a reflective or critical stance in relation to the categories of knowledge used in their analysis. These elements are covered in Chapter 4.

3

Approaches III: psychological approaches to sexuality

Introduction

Therapists feel on their strongest territory when they consider the psychological aspect of the biopsychosocial approach. Sexuality is, after all, an intensely personal experience. Yet, oddly, few psychological theories have had very much to say about the details of sex. Cognitive therapists and theorists have approached sexuality from the basis of learning theory and a theory of motivation and experience driven by cognitive appraisal. Their approach is mainly practical and is covered in the chapter which deals with sex therapy (Chapter 9). Sexual and marital therapists have also used a range of other theoretical bases for their work and this topic is also covered in Chapter 9.

Psychoanalysis

Introduction

One particular psychological approach – psychoanalysis – has had by far the greatest and most detailed amount to say on the topic of sex. Indeed, in some sense the entire subject matter of psychoanalysis is sex and sexuality, since Freud thought that libido (sexual drive) was the key dynamic force in the psyche. For Freud, and to a greater or lesser extent for each of his followers, sexuality is the conditioning force shaping other, not apparently sexual, phenomena. The primacy accorded to sex differentiates psychoanalytic theory from all other psychological theories. Even when overt sexual activity is not under consideration sexual wishes are hypothesised to lie behind other phenomena:

Phil, a frustrated painter, presented for therapy in a disgusted state. He felt 'a contemptible shit', he was impotent and felt blocked in his painting. The notion that painting was just masturbation, spurting paint helplessly onto the canvas, dominated his thinking as an obsessional accompaniment to each brushstroke. Perhaps he had never been a 'real' artist only a piss artist and a wanker. He was also anxious that therapy aimed at restoring his potency would disable him as an artist.

Phil's abuse of psychoanalytic ideas about sex to flagellate himself shows how widespread they have become. This is largely due to the complexity and detail which psychoanalytic theory brings to the phenomena under discussion and to the strong affective charge and narrative drive of its explanations. But fecundity is the source of both the potential of psychoanalysis and its greatest difficulties. The psychoanalytic canon contains theories of every kind, often contradictory, sometimes even self-contradictory. Although it is possible to mine the wealth of psychoanalytic theorising for a host of insights and to use them as the basis for even further theorising, the problem is that it is often impossible to know what the basic psychoanalytic theory of any particular area is. At times even compassing the range of theory can be a bewildering and even dispiriting exercise.

However, more difficult even than this, is the long and only partly corrected tendency of psychoanalytic theorists to confuse personal, moral and sexual preferences for sexual pathology:

Nora attended for supervision. Her patient was a 67-year-old man whose wife had recently died. He began a series of fairly casual affairs with women. Supervision initially focused on the potential meaning of these affairs in relation to the transference. Was Nora's patient displacing loving or erotic feelings for her onto these women and 'acting out'? Nora felt critical of the behaviour and rather inclined to fantasise that it was potentially coercive or perverse, even in the absence of any evidence of either of these elements. Later reflection tempered these feelings. Nora and her supervisor wondered if both of them were having difficulty allowing older people a license to engage in casual sex that they would more easily have extended to younger adults. Nora's supervisor speculated on the extent to which expectations of sexual decorum in older adults are based on an expectation that they maintain cultural standards which were the norm when they were young. Another reason for their disquiet might have been psychological difficulties in imagining the self as old or difficulties in dealing with the aesthetics of older bodies in sexual activity. From a more analytic standpoint Nora and her therapist wondered if Nora's snap judgement, and the force of fantasy behind it, was fueled by difficulties in conceiving of her parents in bed actively involved with each other.

This rather mild example of a tendency to regard behaviour which is not usual, or is aesthetically unappealing, as pathological can be replicated, sadly with less self-awareness, throughout much of the analytic literature. It makes much analytic theorising about sexuality difficult to read and it poses a difficult question. Just how far does psychoanalytically inspired prejudice in relation to some sexualities reveal a more deep-rooted infection or dysfunction in psychoanalytic theorising about other sexual activities more generally? To attempt an answer to this question requires a review of the psychoanalytic theory of sexuality.

Freudian perspectives

Freud's views on human sexuality and its role in the genesis of mental disorder were formulated alongside his developing theory of the structure of the psyche. His first theory, the seduction theory, argued that hysteria was a consequence of the traumatic effects of early seduction. In many ways this view was not all that original since it relied on traditional views of sex as an adult concern and of childhood innocence, but added the extra element of late-onset pernicious effects due to the premature exposure of children to sex. Freud abandoned the seduction theory for reasons which it has been suggested were more self-serving than scientific (Mason 1984; Crews 1995) and came to argue that a hysteric's pathogenic ideas of having been seduced are wishful fantasies, not true memories. As a consequence Freud came to feel that we must all have active sexual wishes in childhood. Hysteria was retheorised as the result of an, only partially successful, attempt to repress childhood sexual wishes that have been rendered obnoxious by the demands of civilisation, acting through parental pressure. Later theorists question the legitimacy of this argument, suggesting either that Freud was wrong to abandon the seduction theory and that neurosis is indeed caused by early traumatic abuse (Milner 1987, Masson 1984), or that Freud induced the 'memories' of sexual abuse in his patients (the memories he was later to dismiss as wishful fantasies) by coercion and suggestion (Crews 1995):

> Jill was 19. She presented with a history of cutting and burning herself. She had severe mood swings and a habit of behaving seductively with male health professionals. She drank excessively and got into fights with neighbours who disliked the loud music she played at unsocial hours to drown out the voices of an angel and a devil on either side of her. The devil called her slut or slag and urged her to harm herself. The good voice often told her she would be all right when she got to heaven. Jill had been sexually abused as a child first by her stepfather and then by a foster father. It was thought she might still be sexually involved with both.

Diagnostically, Jill is likely to fulfill the criteria for borderline personality disorder. In so far as convincing sequelae of childhood sexual abuse have been established, later 'personality disorder' does appear to be a potential outcome. There are also some histrionic features to her presentation (seductive behaviour, dramatic pseudo-psychotic symptoms). Bell (1992) has argued that this kind of patient who is now thought to suffer from a borderline personality disorder, may be far more like the 'hysterical' patients described by Freud than change in diagnostic fashion might suggest. Certainly these patients fit the description of a group of hysteric patients with poor prognosis described by Zetzel (1968). Ironically, therefore, it may well be the case that Freud's first formulation was the most accurate.

Analysis of his own dreams (Freud 1900) and those of his patients led Freud to conclude that the dreams contain coded evidence of childhood sexual wishes. This led in turn to a view of sexuality which expanded the timespan for the operation of the sexual instinct back into earliest infancy and expanded the range of activities called sexual to ones involving a wide range of bodily experiences. Freud's self-analysis was precipitated by the death of his father. During it he had a disturbing dream which, after a lengthy self-analysis, he felt contained death wishes towards his father and sexual wishes towards his mother. This led Freud, drawing on the Oedipus myth, in which Oedipus inadvertently has sex with his mother and kills his father, to suppose that his wishes were a universal phenomenon – which he called the Oedipus complex. He argued that young children's open expression of affection for opposite sex parents is evidence for the Oedipus complex. The theorised hostility towards the same-sex parent is experienced as risky and is not usually so openly expressed. Oedipal constellations were often highly ambivalent and emotionally charged with fear towards the same-sexed parent, who becomes a hated rival. Oedipal constellations are also not clear-cut. Freud, for example, allowed for a 'negative' oedipal complex, with love for the same-sex parent and hostility towards the opposite-sexed one:

> Tom and his cousin, both 6, played together in the bath. They discussed the fate of a shared toy frog. At times he was allowed to be with Tom at others with his cousin but always, in the end, the frog got thrown out of the bath. As the game grew more animated the frog went on undiscussed journeys as the boys touched him to their genitals. There was much giggling and now the frog was forcibly ejected from the bath. He had been a bad frog. Tom said to the frog, 'You are a bad frog. You cannot come into the bath. It is our bath. We are in it, not you.'

In this innocent but transparently oedipal scene Tom and his cousin arrange a scenario in which they take the role of oedipal parents to the frog. It is frog who is ejected from the bath (bedroom) because the 'parents' are together and because the frog has bad impulses which are not allowed. Play like this partly represents wish-fulfilment (I am not excluded from the parent's bedroom instead I can exclude) but also partly play directed at mastery (in this case repression) and self-control of sexual wishes.

Once the Oedipus complex is activated it retrospectively reorganises pre-existing elements of childhood sexuality, including perverse elements, and, importantly, includes memories of experiences which had not previously been read by the developing child, as sexual. Many impulses are repressed in order to resolve conflicts between wishes and parental prohibitions. They become consciously experienced as disgusting. Freud's view is that children are polymorphously perverse – that is, subject to a diversity of strong sexual impulses which in adult life seem perverted and are repressed more or less successfully. In maturity people fight and only partially win running battles against antisocial and disruptive sexual impulses. The outcomes of these battles are always compromises, some successful others less so.

The three essays on the theory of sexuality (1905) represent Freud's next large statement on the psychoanalytic theory of sexuality. He begins with an analysis of perversions. Freud first characterises each instinct as having a source, an impetus or pressure, an aim, and an object. Next Freud argues that the sexual instinct is not characterised by genital sex but rather by rhythmic stroking of any part of the body. This makes for an image of a childhood at once innocent and subject to the greatest diversity of sexual impulses – essentially an image of Eden. Notwithstanding this initially permissive framework – possibly even because of it – Freud works through the vicissitudes of subsequent sexual development until he arrives at a point where genital heterosexual coitus is the only finally satisfactory adult compromise between the range of sexual wishes and prohibitions.

What of individuals whose adult sexuality is not characterised by an exclusive focus on heterosexual coitus? Freud sees these individuals as expressing sexual deviations and he uses the distinction between aim and object to divide sexual deviations into those of object and those of aim. Deviations in relation to sexual object such as paedophilia are, Freud argues, learned consequences of developmental experiences. Anomalies of sexual aim extend the area used for sex or linger over intermediate relations to sexual object. They involve the use of oral or anal cavities for sex or expand the use of the component instincts of sexuality such as exhibitionism and masochism to replace genital sex. Although Freud's final sexual state is strongly normatively prescribed, he emphasises strongly that all sexual outcomes are a compromise between the sexual instinct, seen in some senses as innocently diverse, and the demands of civilisation, seen as the prohibiting parent writ large.

The three essays also cover the development of childhood sexuality. Freud discusses the linkage between aim and object in the powerful suggestion that repeated experiences of satisfaction and instinctual gratification form a permanent linkage between the aim of the instinct and the objects that satisfy it. This formulation is similar in some respects to an associationist or learning theory explanation for sexual development and particularly for specific sexual preferences. However, Freud's theory is preferable to cognitive or Piagetian formulations because it explicitly uses desire (as opposed to idea) as the mental element which is successively transformed by experiences of satisfaction. Later analysts seem to have failed to recognise the radical value of this formulation. It was abandoned by object-relation theorists, who tried to weld the instinct directly to the object without the intervention of experience. In America concentration on the 'normal' pattern also precluded consideration of the experiential contingency of development and obscured the complexity, diversity and elusiveness of desire.

Freud then describes a single normative line of sexual development in more detail. The first stage is concerned with feeding. Freud argues that the infant derives oral sexual satisfaction from sucking, and orally infused sexual awareness comes to pervade the infant's mind in the first year of life. Next the social obligation to control elimination leads to experiences of praise and punishment which fuse with the sexual pleasures of defecation, toilet training and anal masturbation. So, in the second year of life, anal sexual ideas replace oral ones. Beginning at about 3 or 4 years of age, social pressure against anal sexuality combines with discovery of pleasures of masturbation and inaugurates a new stage – the phallic – which peaks at 5–6 years of age. Each successive stage of sexual development does not so much replace its predecessor, but rather is layered on top of it so that traces of the earlier sexual stages can often be discerned in adult life.

In his later work Freud elaborates these psychosexual stages of development and outlines a range of character types. He argues that differences in childhood sexual experience have effects on adult formation of character. A major case history – the Rat Man – demonstrates the link between strict toilet training and fantasy material, or free associations, linked to anal references. The Rat Man presented to Freud with an obsession about a rat torture which involved rats eating their way into his anus. He had suffered a strict toilet training as a child and also demonstrated obsessional character traits. Freud came to feel that an anal character was definable by preoccupation with anal themes in free association and personality traits of orderliness, cleanliness, parsimony, and obstinacy. Freud's followers characterised the personality traits associated with the other psychosexual stages. Oral characters were thought to be either generous and unduly optimistic or, if deprived in childhood, envious and pessimistic. Curiosity and exhibitionism characterised the phallic stage. Freud's follower Abraham was an important developer of these theories, taking them forward in biologically based subdivisions. For example, looking at psychological changes occurring when teeth develop he argued that the capacity to bite and take pleasure in hurting could be distinguished as an oral sadistic stage.

At 5 or 6 sexual curiosity, sexual wishes towards the parents, an awareness of parental genitals and, Freud argues, the sight of mother without a penis, culminate in the catastrophic theory that mother was once a boy who challenged the father and was castrated in childhood as a punishment. This fate the boy child wishes to avoid at all costs. Emergency manoeuvres include expedient identification with the same-sexed parent (a form of identification with the aggressor), superego formation (or modification) and a wave of sexual repression. With these in place a period of apparently reduced interest in sex, called latency, begins.

Freud's model, set out in the three essays, is an attempt to square an impossible circle. His initial conditions for sexual development are ones of a polymorphously perverse, bisexual, infant. The final condition he accepts as normal is heterosexual genitality. For Freud this transition is achieved by a single universal developmental path. However it is dependent on contingent social experiences which Freud suggests successively confine the acceptable linkages between instinctual object and aim. Because of this contradiction later theorists were to argue at length about the potential for variations in psychosexual development between cultures.

The tension between the permissive opening of the three essays and their rigid endpoint is diminished by a series of footnotes to the essays which successively chip away at their initially radical stance, narrowing the acceptable scope and freedom of the sexual instinct. Notwithstanding, a key insight articulated by Freud within his theory of sexuality is the idea that sexuality is necessarily a conflicted ambivalent compromise, whatever its external manifestation:

> William, a senior professional, consulted with depression. He had outwardly a highly successful life. He was married with three children and held down a responsible job in the public eye. At first his depression seemed difficult to understand. Coming out of the blue it had first been treated unsuccessfully with antidepressants (a lack of success largely attributable to the fact he did not take the tablets). In therapy no evident precipitant could be discovered. Then, one session, William revealed that in the evenings after work he would on occasion visit prostitutes with whom he wanted anal sex. Particularly distressing to him was his wish to see and smell faeces during sex. He was worried he would be caught and this it turned out was the chief content of his depressive round of thought. In his childhood William had experienced a period of 'treatment' for 'constipation' involving enemas and having objects inserted into his anus by a mother who seems, at least, to have been driven by anxious motivations but also possibly erotically excited by her son's bowel functions. William had no memory at all of his feelings during this period and described it in a flat tone as something he called 'evidently relevant'. He described his wife as an anxious woman who had attracted him because of her orderliness and fastidiousness. He was clear that she would be revolted by his sexual wishes but found it difficult to follow the therapist's suggestion that the combination of ways in which she was both like and unlike his mother might have been a strong reason for his choosing her.

William's case demonstrates a link between early experience and later sexual behaviour. It also shows how adult relationship and erotic choices are compromise formations, in this case between painful alternatives. Later analysts looking at the case would detect further elements not contained in Freud's formulation, such as the compulsive repetition and sexualisation of trauma from a new position of mastery, as an attempt to deal with that trauma and/or aggressive and hostile elements in his behaviour.

William's case also illustrates how complex the function of sexual intercourse is in Freud's framework since it, like other non-sexual activity, serves as cover for functions derived from the sexual drama of childhood while also being directly sexual itself (Mitchell and Black 1995). Freud thought that for a woman, sexual intercourse provides the fantasy of the possession of the father's penis, as a compensation for the narcissistic wound of her sense of castration. For a man sexual intercourse offers the fantasy of possessing the mother sexually at last, and triumphing over father.

The differing fantasies in play during sexual intercourse reveal that it is at the stage of the Oedipus complex that the sexual development of girls and boys diverges. Before that the little girl is, according to Freud, in effect a little boy. By this Freud means that at this stage female psychosexual experience is active and centred on the clitoris which the girl sees as being a penis. At the point when the Oedipus complex kicks in the little girl sees her castration not as a threat but as an accomplished fact. For Freud this grim oedipal realisation has a number of baleful consequences for girls and women. Since castration is not a threat, women fail to form as solid a super-ego as boys and this, along with penis envy, tends to give them, Freud suggests, a less strong moral sense. Women then transfer their sexual interests to men and change from active to passive sexual aims. They accept, reluctantly, the second best option of femininity, finding some compensation for the lost penis in admiring that possessed by the boy baby they hope for. Girls, unlike boys, must therefore make three renunciations. They give up their first love object, the mother. They exchange their active sexual strivings for passive ones. They give up the clitoris as a source of pleasure for the vagina. Faced with these difficulties Freud thought that many girls never become completely heterosexual:

> Andrea and Paul consulted for couple therapy. Paul did almost all the talking and said there were difficulties in their sex life. Paul complained that Andrea showed no active interest in sex but simply lay back and let him do whatever he wanted. She never refused any activity but always participated, where required, in a limp distant way. Andrea felt sex was a dirty and disgusting duty. When childhood sexual experiences were

reviewed Andrea revealed two which seemed relevant to her. First, she said she had only once seen her mother naked and had been immediately disgusted by this sight for reasons she couldn't make out. Second, she remembered a profoundly humiliating incident in the kitchen when her mother held up a nightgown of Andrea's and said it smelled. She had said that Andrea must have been masturbating and that she was too grown up for such behaviours.

Ironically Andrea's psychosexual development may have proceeded too far along Freudian lines. Her active sexual strivings squashed by fear of castration (seeing mother's body naked) and sexual prohibition. However, while Freud might have suggested that Andrea read mother's stern prohibition as an oedipal exclusion from father, modern feminist analysts might be more able to see in this scene mother's role in transmitting the culturally sanctioned repression of female sexuality of all kinds.

Freud's followers' reactions to his theory of female sexuality

Women analysts took a role in reshaping Freud's ideas about female sexuality from an early stage and their influence is evident in 'Female sexuality' (Freud 1931). In this text Freud re-emphasises the role of mother in female development, and while a standard masochistic narcissistic femininity is the desired outcome Freud suggests that other non-feminine outcomes are common enough. In one there is a general inhibition or revulsion against sex. The other involves clinging to masculinity and potentially a homosexual outcome.

Freud's followers reacted variously to his revised theories of female sexuality. Some accepted or extended his views (Deutsch 1946), while others (for example, Horney 1967) questioned his approach. Two objections were commonly expressed. First, it was argued that pre-oedipal girls had knowledge of themselves as feminine and of their female genital and so did not assume that they were little boys before the Oedipus complex. Second, it was maintained that men suffered from an equivalent envy to penis envy – envy of the womb. These two developments were important because they argued that women had something as physical and as creative as the penis to offer up as proof of identity. Politically, though, the effect of this appeal to and celebration of female biology – one repeated in chronological waves during the feminist movement – can be something of a trap. This is because possession of a penis goes along with an entry into a world of social and political supremacy and casual or low investment procreation. Possession of a womb offers no wider entry into the social world. Instead it indicates the single (because socially constructed as comprehensively absorbing) role of motherhood. In therapy also, by concentrating exclusively on female biology and the patient's relation to it, the patient's entry into the wider political world can be denied:

> Leonora had been accepted for analytic training when she became pregnant. There was considerable disquiet at this development. Some trainers expressed the view that it would not be possible for her to do right both by her child and her training. Others wondered about the possible emotional impact of looking after a baby while considering catastrophes of early development in case material. Leonora felt that there was obvious justice to comments related to issues of timetabling and childcare but pointed out that male candidates for training whose wives had children during this time were never subject to similar scrutiny.

Psychoanalysis since Freud

After Freud, psychoanalysis fissioned into numerous schools with varying theoretical preoccupations. As a result the subsequent history of the psychoanalytic theory of sex is of a range of contributions from analysts whose underlying premises vary. Sometimes differences of opinion are related to sex; sometimes they are driven by other theoretical concerns. In many ways the most important development was the overall downgrading of sexual motives as the causal mechanism behind adult non-sexual and even sexual behaviour. Only a small part of the massive analytic diaspora which followed Freud is presented below. Feminist analytical approaches are dealt with separately in Chapter 4, on Politics.

Jung and Jungians

Jung was one of the earliest analysts to question the central role of the erotic in Freud's scheme. He put in place of libido, as erotic, a more general concept of libido as an energy which motivated curiosity and creativity. Having done this, he developed an extended and complex system which has a great deal to say about the difference between the sexes and about psychological growth but is not much interested in theorising sexuality. Notwithstanding, Jung introduced two ideas which have considerable appeal. He suggested that erotic activity and erotic imagery represented passionate creative union within the psyche and therefore served to promote psychological growth. This idea was consistent both with his spiritual preoccupations and with his tendency to investigate the purpose or function of an experience rather than its cause:

> Phillipa was stuck in an unresolved dilemma. She wanted to abandon her career in medicine, finding it oppressive and unrewarding, but her upper-class and rather stuffy parents had set their hearts on a daughter who would become a doctor. Phillipa herself was not sure what else she might do. Meanwhile she was off sick with depression and the medical school was pressing her to make a decision, at least about her immediate future. Phillipa's therapist had begun to despair that she would ever take a positive decision of any sort. Then, suddenly, Phillipa started a relationship (her first) with a much older Rastafarian man she had met one day on the tube. The expectable chorus of alarm went up in their social network. In therapy Phillipa talked only about having sex – a new thing for her. Neatly, the fact that this was unprotected sex contrived to push the therapist into the position of becoming another admonishing figure. One day in therapy the therapist said crossly, 'You've got us all lined up where you want us now, haven't you?' Phillipa was furious, she stormed about the room, broke a few ornaments, and left. There was enough bond between the therapist and Phillipa that a few months later Phillipa, now pregnant, telephoned to update the therapist. She was living with her partner and working in a shop. Before ending the call Phillipa said, 'I had to find a new way you know.'

It isn't clear how things will work out in this situation but what is clear is that the sexual relationship Phillipa started, in an unorthodox way with an unorthodox person, is serving a whole range of developmental functions. Jungian therapists would tend to concentrate on the developmental possibilities and risks opened up by it rather than only appreciating the defensive and avoidant functions it may also serve.

Some Jungian analysts have found this teleological approach needs balance. Samuels (1989) who belongs to a school of Jungians who try to reclaim Freudian insights and values into their thinking, has turned this functional Jungian approach on the Freudian concept of the primal scene, i.e. the worrying, horrible, exciting sight of the parents in bed together. In Freudian, and particularly post Freudian theory, this scene twists the knife of the Oedipus complex, forcibly ramming home the child's exclusion from the special relationship of its parents. Samuels shows how it appears in both differentiated and primitive forms in the imagery and dreams of patients. It serves the function of driving the process of analysis forward and its reappearance marks stages of the individuation process – a Jungian term for a process of psychological development towards wholeness. Sexuality is therefore an expression of the individuation process in symbols (Guggenbuhl-Craig 1980).

Just as sexual images may stand in for individuation processes so actual sexual expression and sexual longing may be part of the individuation process. Jung's second important sexual idea concerned the incest taboo. He argued that this was a more important psychocultural entity than the Oedipus complex. The taboo on incest sets up a cycle of sexual longing, fantasy and renunciation which then acts as the motor for individual development. Here Samuels' work on erotic playback is very valuable (Samuels 1989). He looks at the relationship between father and daughter and suggests that it offers the daughter a chance to be seen as someone other than a copy of mother. This is promoted by optimal (that is renounced but not repressed) erotic playback between the daughter and her father. Failures of this playback in either direction (too much or too little) may damage the daughter's development. Samuels' ideas are capable of elaboration in a number of important directions.

Anna was her famous father's youngest and most dutiful child. She emulated him and followed in his footsteps professionally. Her father speculated that fantasies she had revealed to him showed her envy of older siblings. Half-hearted attempts to find her suitable partners were made but she never showed any inclination to marry, nursing her father through his final illness and carrying on his work in creative and important ways. In later years she lived with a female friend and professional colleague. Pictures of her in old age wearing her father's coat carry an almost unbearable poignancy.

Speculation on Anna Freud's sexuality often centres on whether she may have had lesbian wishes, as evidenced by her later long friendship with Dorothy Burlingham. Samuels' concept of erotic playback can help to move debate on from this irresolvable question to an evaluation of the nature of the erotic playback between her and her father. Certainly, in terms of her creativity, there were remarkable successes but these were possibly purchased at the price of never letting her loose. Women who retain close emotional bonds to their fathers and seek to emulate them are represented by Athena the goddess of wisdom, who was born fully grown from her father's head and who never managed much of a sexual relationship (other than being the victim of attempted rape) with anyone. From the point of view, therefore, of the theory of erotic playback, it may be that such a woman, born from her father's head, needs a mother to father her and offer her a sufficient degree of (homo)erotic playback to prevent her from becoming always like father.

Perhaps the most extended and forceful and therapeutically relevant treatment of sexuality and sexual imagery is found in Jung's work *The Psychology of the Transference* (1946). This volume juxtaposes woodcuts from an alchemical text the *Rosarium* with a discussion of the relationship between the therapist and the patient. The woodcuts show the sexual union of king and queen in various states of fusion and separation. Jung discusses their meaning at length as well as the function of erotic aspects in the transference as they bear on the individuation process. The text and Jung's work in general serve as continual reminder that sex has a purpose beyond reproduction and that its many functions and capacities are immediately manifest in the consulting room. Jung's notions of sexuality in the psychology of the transference allow for an analysis of sexual feelings in the consulting room on the part of therapist and patient which point both to the creative possibility of those feelings and to the non-sexual meanings (as well as sexual) that they may carry. Analytic – Freudian and Jungian – notions of sexuality in the consulting room are discussed further in Chapter 10:

> James in analysis one day admitted to a lifelong obsession with the image of a huge mass of writhing naked bodies piled one on top of each other writhing, suffocating, and copulating. He first linked this image with that of people in a gas chamber struggling hopelessly towards the door to get out and was particularly interested and sexually aroused by the idea that some of the people in the chamber were themselves sexually aroused. Next he thought of an orgiastic event in an opium den of the kind Sherlock Holmes would have frequented. Lastly the sweat on the bodies in his fantasy made him think that these were all foetuses in the amniotic fluid struggling to be born.

Analysts will bring a range of insights to these images, depending on other aspects of James's life and on their theoretical perspective. However, the image of people struggling, aroused, dying, being born, would certainly have for Jungians associations with the image of the '*massa confusa*', a term drawn from medieval alchemy. The '*massa confusa*' is the first substance needed in order to start the long path of chemical transformations the alchemists thought would be required to make gold. Jung thought that the alchemists were really writing psychological texts, describing the experience and process of personal growth towards integration, even though their overt concerns seemed chemical. The alchemists were keen on the idea that only a return to the basest of materials, such as shit, animality or the massa confusa, would yield the starting point for alchemical endeavours.

For a Jungian, thinking about the transference and counter-transference, the relationship between analyst and patient, the fact of James confiding these images to his therapist also suggests that he and his therapist have reached a particular stage in their relationship. They are the Jews dying together in a fatal ecstasy, the opium eaters, and the siblings awaiting birth. The images offer fractured glimpses of intense proximity. They are physical and sometimes sexual and all involve or presage unconsciousness. James's therapist didn't do much interpretively with these images but they often came to be laced into the speech between them as ways of describing things. Oddly, possibly as a result, James thought of them less desperately when he was alone.

While Jungian thought is not primarily concerned with sexual matters it is clear that it does possess a theory of sexuality whose key advantage is that it is at least potentially both permissive but also empowering. The main disadvantage of Jungian thought in this area (and possibly more generally) is that it can easily become rather otherworldly and thus seem to offer less purchase on practical therapeutic problems than other stances.

French analysts

Most of the analytic diaspora remained, unlike Jung, closer to the original ideas of Freud. In France analysts can be divided into those who owe their chief inspiration to Lacan who broke from Freud while claiming to follow him more closely and a group of others whose allegiances have remained more orthodox. Lacanian thinking with its structuralist and poststructuralist foundations and ramifications is discussed in Chapter 4 .

Two more classical analysts, Chasseguet-Smirgel and McDougall, have developed Freud's ideas on sexuality to form theories of perversion which deviate significantly from his first notion that perversion represents a failure of repression. They have instead developed notions derived from Freud's later hypothesis that more pathological defensive and repressive processes are involved in perversion, such as the splitting of the ego which occurs in fetishism. Chasseguet-Smirgel (1984a) argues that the essence of perversion is a refusal to acknowledge genital and generational differences. Thus anus and vagina become one and faeces and penis are also equated. For Chasseguet-Smirgel, as for many other writers on sexual perversion, there is a more general perversion of character and truth involved in sexual perversion. In consequence, she believes that perverse sexuality is inevitably associated with character abnormality.

Joyce McDougall has also written extensively about sexuality both conventional and otherwise. Initially she firmly stated (1985, 1986) that normal heterosexuality requires acknowledgement of difference between the sexes, of the primal scene (the image of the parents in bed), of castration, and of genital difference as the basis of sexual arousal. The phallus is a requisite and if it were absent psychotic confusion would occur. This led to a position firmly opposed to any deviation from heterosexual genitality.

McDougall's work is important because she concerns herself very directly with sex and particularly with women's sexual development. For McDougall (1985, 1995) human sexuality is inherently traumatic because we naturally desire to abolish the differences between self and other. This makes the discovery of sexual difference painful but vital. The Oedipal complex becomes a 'crisis' in which the child wants to be both sexes and possess both parents. Sexuality is shaped out of the profound importance of primal scene fantasies and crucially of psychic bisexuality. The primary homosexuality of the little girl impels her to want to possess her mother sexually, penetrate her vagina, climb right inside her and eat her up, as a way of incorporating her mother totally. At the same time she desires to be a man like her father. The boy child develops his own form of primary homosexuality in which he imagines himself as his father's love partner, incorporating his penis orally or anally and thus becoming his father. Phantasies like these coexist in the boy with the desire to take mother's place in the hope that father will give him a baby to grow inside his own imagined space:

> Harry dreamed that a metal thing like a tea strainer which was the shape of a little heart was being pushed inside his vagina by another man. The experience was one of extreme pleasure. He woke confused. His associations to the tea strainer were first to knights' armour and then to medieval torture instruments, particularly one called an iron maiden which pierced the victim with spikes while enclosing them in a person-shaped space.

Harry's dream reveals gender confusion and bisexual wishes and fears. Insides and outsides are muddled up as are pleasurable and painful experiences. Much more clinical material would be needed to reveal the details of his inner world. Clearly though, McDougall and Chasseguet-Smirgal's theoretical perspectives could serve to illuminate the material. Chasseguet-Smirgal might well point to the wish to obliterate gender differences which causes the gender confusion. McDougall would point up the bisexual elements of the dream.

Thinking about women, McDougall draws on Kestenberg's (1968) idea of inner and outer configurations of sexual organs and the girl's innate knowledge of her inner spaces as she develops her own version of Freud's developmental path for women, on the way burdening women with yet further developmental difficulties. McDougall argues that the nature of the vagina makes it more likely to be thought of as similar to mouth and anus and thus that women are more likely than men to think of their bodies as dirty. Another sexual consequence of female anatomy derives, McDougall argues, from the failure of little girls to have a genital to hold on to. This makes their inner representation of their genitals and awareness of their sexual sensations less differentiated and more condensed. Like Jones (1927), McDougall also supposes that the female version of the castration complex envisages a far more total personal obliteration than simple castration. To these many difficulties McDougall, like other feminist analysts, adds the effects of the asymmetrical pattern of early childcare with mothers doing most of the work. For McDougall this asymmetry may produce strong enduring homosexual attachments to mother which the girl may fail to give up and which may then interfere with the woman's relationship with her husband.

McDougall's radical espousal of an innate early bisexual constitution allows her to consider the individual's identifications with both sexes and also homo- and heterosexual desire. However, for the most part the outcome of these reflections is profoundly normative because McDougall insists that bisexual wishes and homosexual desires must be given up to achieve a heterosexual outcome. More recently, McDougall (1995) has retreated to some extent from this position to one more permissive of alternate sexual outcomes aided, to an extent, by her vision of all sexuality as profoundly conflicted. Psychoanalytic perspectives on homosexual orientation and on the notion of perversion are discussed further in Chapters 6 and 7.

Olivier (1989), like McDougall, concentrates on the sexual

drama of early childhood but focuses on the asymmetry of child-care arrangements and, unlike McDougall, on the sexual wishes of parents rather than those of children. Her main idea is that while mother desires her boy child sexually she does not have the same desire for a girl child. Thus little girls do not get the same incestuous erotically charged attention as little boys. They therefore mourn the loss of mother and strive to please, for example, by speaking earlier and by becoming continent earlier. For Olivier only a father can give a daughter a fully sexed position but sadly the little girl's body is not a sexually mature one so father is not sexually pleased by it. Girls strive this time to please a father who is disinterested in their body and as a result women are doomed always to seek a body other than their own. Olivier's formulations and clinical material are vivid and convincing but there are significant disadvantages in her work. She locates women in a doubly victimised and striving position and can generate no sense of female power or capabilities. She never asks why anyone would want a sexual or other relation with the striving pleaser she manages to create. She also ignores the possibility of homoerotic desire between mother and child or father and child; a desire which would, from her theoretical perspective, be liberating.

It is tempting to ascribe to some aspect of the national character to the tendency of French analysts to stress the inherent differences in sexuality between men and women, and to rely in their theorising of passion and love on something which is forever unrealised, tragic and unreachable (Budd 2001). In general, French psychoanalytic theory of sexuality gives detailed accounts of passion and conflict but repeatedly makes gender and power differences an inherent feature in the theoretical structure. By failing to question these principles French analysts risk dooming their patients to remain subject to the failings of heteropatriarchy even as they collect its blessings.

English developments

Perhaps, just like the French, English analysts also show some traces of their nationality in their work. The central question historians of psychoanalysis in England will need to answer will be to give an explanation for the rise and mesmeric rule of the

Kleinian version of the object relations account of the developing mind in English analytic thought. While the French made the object of love precarious and deficient, providing in the meanwhile an account of restless desire, the English, under Klein's influence, have problematised the capacity to love, providing accounts of envy, attack and repair enacted by the subject.

In England, as elsewhere, the male bias of Freud's theories was challenged as was the supremacy of sexual drives in motivating behaviour. Meltzer (1973) commented that British object relations theorists argued that Freud focused too much on the relief of tension rather than seeing erotic desire as linked with loving intimacy and defences against it. Fairbairn (1954) went so far as to say that libidinal attitudes do not determine object relations, rather than object relations determine libidinal attitudes. Freud's division of instinct from object was questioned, and objects not instincts became the focus of analysis. Fairbairn therefore de-emphasised sex, claiming the child's sexual attraction to a parent was not natural and by no means inevitable. It occurred when normal efforts on the part of the child to make loving contacts with a caretaker failed. The desperate child may then eroticise the relation in order to have more to offer the negligent parent. Following Fairburn's line and that of his followers, Winnicott and Guntrip, many analysts in England revised their theories of sexuality and concentrated almost entirely on intimacy and relationship issues, turning to cover sex only in its pathological manifestations (Kahn 1979, Balint 1959).

Kleinians took object relations theory in a new direction. Klein was analysed for a time by Abraham, who had taken up and developed Freud's work on oral, anal and genital stages of psychosexual development. And Klein's work, with its vivid depictions of a fantastical world of childhood imaginings, bears the marks of his preoccupations with zonal stages. She also struggled far more deeply than other British theorists with the drive model which Freud had laid out and, as a result, derived a theory halfway between drive derived models of the psyche and object relational ones (Greenberg and Mitchell 1983).

Klein believed that infants were born orientated towards the objects of their instincts – in Freud's terms already linked prior to experience. Infants connect emotionally with internal and external objects from the outset rather than requiring repeated experiences of satisfaction to forge the connection. At the centre of development is the relationship with mother and with her breast, which is experienced as both good and feeding, and bad and poisoning, by turns. Klein therefore displaced the penis as the organiser of psychic experience and replaced it with the breast:

> By regarding the infant as relating to objects from the beginning, Klein established the relationship with the breast as the primary organising experience for future development, including genital development. Sexual development was understood in terms of feeding and nurture rather than ecstasy in mutual enjoyment. (Green: 1995 877, cited in Harding 2001:4)

This has important consequences for later sexual development since attitudes towards the penis and other sexual objects contain the trace (or more than a trace) of attitudes towards the breast. As a result it became possible to desexualise sex – sex now being nothing more than a cipher for mother–baby stuff – in much the same way, if by a different route, that the theories of Fairbairn and Winnicott did. Desexualisation was not an inevitable consequence of Kleinian theory for, just as the breast can infuse the penis so, by the same token, either through deferred action (as Freud would have it), or as a result of innate knowledge (as Klein and her followers would have it), attitudes to the breast can become infused with attitudes towards the penis. In this formulation Kleinian analysts have potentially a powerful tool for analysing and unveiling layers of sexual and erotic experience:

> Franz particularly liked to reach round from behind and touch women's breasts. Sometimes he worried that he would succumb to the temptation to do this in a crowded place. Other times he felt it cramped his capacity to satisfy a partner since he insisted on making love from behind. Working with his therapist he began to feel that touching women in this way had links with the way he touched himself when he masturbated. He sometimes wished women had penises. He sometimes wished he had breasts and he could pretend he did when he touched a woman's breasts from behind. Further work with Franz revealed much earlier sexual experiences which also seemed linked: mother being kissed by father who was standing behind

her, his horror and disgust at seeing father and mother naked, a childhood fastidiousness which both parents ridiculed.

Franz's material seems apt for a Kleinian analysis, the image of the breast is linked in it chiefly to the primal scene, which seems on his account (which may be defensive) to have intruded upon him rather than being a fascinating or horrifying discovery.

Understanding Franz's material requires adding in more elements of Kleinian theory. These include the importance of pathology and the grim aspects of the Kleinian world view as they relate to the role of aggression, which is ascribed even more importance than erotic feeling. Klein thought aggression an innate part of every individual and outlined a complex and disputed ontology of its first expression in the infant. Whatever the details, for Klein and her followers there are practically never unmixed loving or hating emotions. All individuals experience aggressive and loving feelings at war with each other when they contemplate the objects in their world. In Franz's case, aggression seems absent until the fantasy of acting out sexually in public is inspected more closely. While it is not overtly presented as such, a Kleinian would probably be inclined to regard it as an aggressive wish, perhaps to take over and appropriate the breast or to intrude on the mother with her fantasied other in the primal scene.

Despite her emphasis on the breast, Klein did not abandon the Oedipus complex. She believed it to be a powerful force in mental life at a time far earlier than Freud would allow. She also believed that knowledge of the organs involved in sexual relations is innate and that the initial form of the primal scene is one in which organs penetrate each other rather than one in which people relate to each other. This distinction was incorporated into the notion of part object (organ-based) as opposed to whole-object relations. The child's recognition of the parental sexual relationship moves from an appreciation of organs towards one involving people and ideally involves relinquishing the idea of sole and permanent possession of mother. The resulting profound sense of loss may not be tolerable and may produce a sense of persecution. This experience underpins all future mental and emotional life.

Klein's repositioning of the Oedipus complex stirs up Freud's orderly developmental timetable (Young 2001). As development proceeds Klein stresses how awarenesses from each stage remain stirred together into a complex phantasy image of the parental intercourse. Hinshelwood (1991) points out that the parents are perpetually mutually feeding, incorporating each other, biting each other to pieces, messing each other inside, controlling each other as well as penetrating, cutting, caring for or protecting each other. The nature of this intercourse as phantasied by the child determines the child's thinking processes and the way things are felt to come together in its mind. To resolve the Oedipus situation the child must relinquish his claim on his parents by accepting the reality of their sexual relationship.

Kleinians can paint detailed and complex pictures of sexual experience which seem able to do justice to the fluidity of zonal preoccupations and to the transgressive, dangerous, exciting, qualities of sexual expression. They are assisted by the Kleinian interweaving of developmental stages and the use of the notion of part objects, which are parts or functions of the object seen as separate from the object. The early world of the Kleinian infant resembles the massa confusa appealed to by Jung as well as elements of the Rosarium woodcuts. Unsurprisingly, therefore, the case of James can be re-examined instructively from a Kleinian perspective:

> Shamefacedly James admitted to masturbating while fantasising about these struggling bodies. Normally he felt OK about masturbation but in the setting of these fantasies he felt shamed and dirty for masturbating.

For a Kleinian, James's fantasies are rather like dreams, they give evidence of underlying unconscious phantasies that concern James's relation with his internal and external objects. Klein thought that masturbation fantasies provided the missing relational quality to a seemingly autoerotic and unrelated act (Klein 1923, cited in Hinshelwood 1989). Thus for James masturbating while fantasising about the bodies may serve the function of gaining him phantasied admission to the primal scene which he imagines as the union of bodies in constant mutual gratifications of every sort. His aggressive and denigratory wishes can also be satisfied by the image of gassing all the participants and possibly through the image of the detective (father analyst), debased and entrapped by the opium den.

Like other analysts who followed Freud, Klein was unwilling to accept that little girls imagined they were boys until the advent of the Oedipus complex. In place of this notion she introduced the concept of the femininity phase in which children of both sexes imagine they have maternal capacities and can have babies. This is consistent with her primary focus on the body of the mother and its interior in the imaginings of the child. Father is an object conceived of as existing originally within mother and limiting access to her by his own presence. Consistent with Klein's tendency to conceive of early childhood as anxious and conflicted she also supposed that children of both sexes phantasise aggressive attacks on the interior of the mother's body, killing or robbing the babies it is thought to contain.

In the work of Klein and her followers (for example, Britton *et al.* 1989) the phantasy of a particular kind of sexual activity (parental heterosexual coitus) is taken to be absolutely central. At one and the same this particular sexual phantasy generates normal psychological structure and represents psychological truth. Just as in classical Jungian theory so in Kleinian theory the coital couple are inscribed in the matrix of the mind eternally in union. If this psychic fact is denied or attacked psychological mayhem and sexual perversion result. The consequent ineradicable heterosexism (Young 2001) of this theoretical strand is evident. But, of equal importance, this kind of Kleinian theorising amounts to claiming that a particular socially located view of the heterosexual couple is biologically foundational and psychologically forcing. In this respect therefore Kleinian theory is very close to the views of some of the most hardline sociobiologists and shares both the advantages and drawbacks of that stance.

American analysts

Otto Kernberg's ideas form a bridge between Kleinian ideas and American developments, based more on the work of Anna Freud. He has spent some time delineating a hierarchy of developmental disturbance and immaturity, and in outlining the expected consequences of a position on this hierarchy which is governed by the degree of disturbance of internal object relationships. At one end normal individuals can maintain stable boundaries between self and other while also tolerating ambivalence and allowing limited loss of boundaries. At the other end, severely disturbed individuals are unable to establish and maintain stable boundaries between self and other and oscillate between an absence of relatedness or total, confusing merger. This results from a failure to integrate good and bad object relations into a single complex relationship.

Within this grand structure Kernberg (1995) lays out a developmental pathway for sex, arguing that sexual excitement develops only after rage, elation, sadness, surprise and disgust, which he sees as more basic emotions. Once evoked, sexual excitement rapidly becomes fused with libido and both are evoked in primitive affective states of elation. It is object choice which turns sexual excitement into desire. Excitement is experienced in relation to a part object and linked to zonal stimulation. Desire, on the other hand, is linked to a whole object, and is elaborated and differentiated, amounting to excitement linked to an oedipal object.

Kernberg defines mature sexual love as desire for one person and for the formation of a joint ego ideal. Mature libido is formed from a final fusion of a range of partly integrated affective aggregates, which are themselves derived from the two great drives, and therefore are a derived series of libidinal and aggressive affects. Mature sexual love holds loving and aggressive feelings in tension. Kernberg also stresses the role of psychic bisexuality and argues that heterosexual love allows both partners the experience of the other sex which satisfies bisexual wishes. Kernberg therefore contends that mature sexual love is an amalgam of excitement, desire, tenderness, tolerance of ambivalence, identifications, and passion.

Unlike that of many other writers (except Stoller), Kernberg's system stresses the value of polymorphously perverse elements in normal heterosexual love, including a whole range of sadistic and masochistic wishes. In supporting this he cites Balint (1959), who first introduced the notion of a fusion of pre-genital and genital urges, and Wisdom (1970), who argued that oedipal and pre-oedipal urges are both involved in sexual expression, linking sexual acts with reparation and the depressive position.

At times Kernberg waxes lyrical in his praise of the healing powers of sex. He believes that a genital identification, in which heterosexual–homosexual pre-genital and genital identifications are held all at once, allows a sense of biological closeness and union with nature. Orgasm therefore integrates homosexual and heterosexual, love and hate. The partner's body becomes a 'geography of personal meanings' (Kernberg 1995:26) with polymorphous perverse, oedipal and mother–baby elements all re-enacted in a safe haven.

Kernberg's account of mature sexuality allows for a great degree of ambivalence and for a complexity of fantasy life which gives it a sense of vitality and explanatory power. By fusing object-relations theory, with its capacity to make a distinction between part object relations (sexual excitement) and whole object relations (desire), with more orthodox Freudian accounts, he maintains a capacity to chart the successive transformations of excitement and of desire which develop as different fantasies dominate or different objects present themselves. It is therefore a major disappointment to discover that Kernberg, like Freud, ultimately constrains his theorising, settling on monogamous heterosexuality as the only legitimate object-related container for these geographies and wishes. Any other preferred form of sexual union is judged pathological. This constraint creates a paradox, since nothing in Kernberg's theory so far necessitates restricting sexual expression in this way. To shore up the conclusion Kernberg tries to build in features of maturity which he judges integral to his model, and by so doing attempts to lock in the virtues of monogamy and heterosexuality. Here he is, for example, building in fidelity:

> and in sexual passion, crossing the time boundaries of the self also occurs in the commitment to the future, to the loved object as an ideal that provides personal meaning to life. (Kernberg 1995:42)

Kernberg is also particularly scathing about sex he regards as not object-related as the following condemnation of 'compulsive masturbation' reveals:

> Sexual excitement and orgasm also lose their function of boundary crossing into biology when mechanical repetitive sexual excitement and orgasm are built into self experience dissociated from the deepening of internalised love relations. (Kernberg 1995:46)

Even though it is, evidently, a long way from here to monogamous heterosexuality as the only form of legitimate non pathological sexual expression, it is a leap Kernberg is determined to make. By doing so he robs his own formulation of much of its power. If he was less determined to privilege whole object relationships over part object ones, excitement over desire and heterosexuality over homosexuality and instead able to hold these in tension with each other (rather as Bion does with his formulation of Ps and D) he would have been able to reveal a far greater range of erotic potentials and capacities. Indeed, the model of holding the tension between competing imperatives could have been developed into a far more flexible and permissive aesthetics of sexuality.

In fact, Kernberg deals with difficulties in sexuality in a fairly standard way. At neurotic levels of disturbance issues involving love and sexuality are understood, in Kernberg's system, in terms of more classical Freudian conflicts between impulses and defences. He analyses some cases of impotence, for example, as a direct consequence of oedipal anxieties. At the more disturbed end of the spectrum Kernberg suggests that sexual desire is often keyed to a particular scenario whose perverse, often violent, qualities are too disturbing to integrate into the tender, intimate side of their relationships. The passions of sexuality therefore become infused in some with meanings to do with aggression and violence. This is not inevitable, and Kernberg is keen to point out that borderline individuals may enact perverse scenarios wrapped up in seemingly normal genital sex, or may have severe sexual inhibitions:

> Gail presented with symptoms of borderline personality disorder, including repeated deliberate self-harm, an eating disorder, and persistent bored anhedonia which decompensated on occasions into excited drinking or drugs binges. Sexually she presented herself as 'entirely normal' and was accompanied by her partner who reminded the interviewer of an obedient puppy dog. Interviewed separately, he revealed dissatisfaction with their sexual life, which always had to adhere to a strict routine and which, curiously, always ended with Gail holding her partner's penis and announcing in somewhat strained tones what a nice penis it was. When she did this it always made Gail's partner scared, although he could not say why. Sexuality was

not, for a while, the focus of Gail's treatment but it later transpired that Gail had been sexually abused and that her abuser had always made her hold his penis and say how nice it was. Now Gail's 'perfectly normal' sex turned the tables on her abuser (identified with partner), controlling him both in sexual and non-sexual ways instead of being controlled by him.

Stoller, another American analyst, shares with Kernberg a lively appreciation of the variability of sexual behaviour and of the inevitability of perverse elements. Stoller argued initially that hatred was the key to sexual perversion but increasingly came to add that hostility was central to all sexual excitement. Consequently he became less interested in differentiating perversions from other forms of sexual expression. (Stoller 1993, 1996, Stoller and Levine 1993). He does not distinguish, as Kernberg does, perverse and polymorphous sexuality. Instead he puts perversion at the centre of all sexuality. The overall structure of erotic excitement is the same in everyone, differentiated only by the extent to which erotic excitement promotes or breaks down intimacy.

Stoller, like Klein, believed that the little child thinks itself female (as opposed to male). This formulation brings him to analyses of gender development which are very similar to those of feminist analysts. For example, he argues that men must dis-identify with mother so identities are both more rigid and fragile. Early anxieties about dis-identification make for dread of being gay or female and a three-way conflict: desire to regress, dread of ensuing loss of male identity and longing for revenge on mother for causing this (Stoller 1992). In later work he can be found becoming less and less sure of his founding frameworks so that by the time he writes on sadomasochism (*Pain and Passion*, 1991) he is left in his conclusion listing the mistakes Freud made in his analysis of SM rather than delineating a positive project.

However, the real strength of Stoller's developing contribution lies not in the theoretical superstructure that he develops but in the close attention to detail. As his oeuvre develops he grows increasingly disenchanted with the couch as a source of information about the phenomena he wishes to investigate and instead works outside his consulting room. Outside it he attempts to develop a 'psychoanalytic ethnography', gathering data from participants but using psychoanalytic ideas. Stoller's discussion of ethnography is, to modern eyes, one which could have benefited from some input of ideas from professionals in the field. Notwithstanding, he rapidly cottons on to the notion that the location of the ethnographer, the viewer's assumptions and the expectations and assumptions of the participants will all affect the data gathered and the interpretation placed on it.

Stoller's discussion of the aetiology of sadomasochistic sexual practices (Stoller 1991) includes biological, cultural and psychodynamic forces. He also allows for a role for perversion as subversion. In this respect he can be seen as having links to the Freudiomarxist analysts, feminist analysts and ultimately queer theorists, all surveyors of the sexual scene who seek to analyse it in ways which will prescribe the overthrow of current arrangements in favour of various alternate possibilities (see Chapter 4).

Psychoanalysis and biology: recent developments

While analytic thinking has moved, to an extent, to encompass elements of the social it is only very recently indeed that psychoanalysts, lured by developments in neurobiology and cognitive psychology, have revisited biology. Badcock (1990) has tried to marry psychoanalytic thought with evolution. More recently there has been increased interest in uniting neurobiology, neuropsychology and psychoanalysis (see, for example, Pally and Olds 1998; Bucci 2001; Solms and Lechevalier 2002, and Olagaray 1998, who writes specifically about sexuality). Westen and Gabbard, in a pair of papers (2002a, 2002b), provide a comprehensive overview of the potentialities of this new field. They try to show how neuropsychological theories of memory impact on classical analytical theories of repression. They talk for example of 'attractor states' which may be sensitised by a critical remark, and try to give an account of transference based also on the notion of 'enduring dispositions to react in particular ways under particular conditions'.

It must, of course, be a good thing that psychoanalytic theorists are re-engaging with biology. However, a flaw in current accounts lies in the nature of the relationship being forged between analytic and biological ideas. All too often biology is called in to support cherished analytic notions rather than being used to interrogate them critically. Thus the Westen and Gabbard paper generates several ideas, none of which seriously challenge psychoanalytic orthodoxy. Neurobiological insights appear on the scene suddenly as supporters rather than critics of psychoanlaytic orthodoxy, peace is restored between previously warring parties but little practical benefit has been obtained. In the case of Westen this is particularly sad since previous papers (especially Westen *et al.* 1990) freely challenged psychoanalytic orthodoxy, pointing out that on empirical evidence its developmental timetable was flawed.

A second problem which contributes to the first, and can create the notion that psychoanalytic theorists are self-serving when they pick theoretical bedfellows, is that these papers also seem to pay little attention to similar ideas produced in different traditions. The notion of attractor states, for example, bears a close relation to Jung's notion of complexes and to Bartlett's concept of schemas, taken up later by psychotherapists in the cognitive therapy tradition as schema theory (Young 1999). Psychoanalytic meditations on neuropsychology still seem threadbare and continue to reveal the years during which other disciplines were neglected.

It is not yet clear exactly whether the new relationship between psychoanalysis and neurobiology will develop fruitfully. In the area of sexuality a psychoanalytic understanding of the personal impact of cultural sexual expectations could unite beneficially with biological theories about the range of sexual strategies and social roles which may be pre-programmed into our biological sexual make-up.

A closer union between biology and sexuality has been achieved in the area of trauma (e.g. van der Kolk *et al.* 1996 and de Zuluetta 1993). These theorists have looked at the effects of trauma on the brain, and particularly in relation to its propensity to cause post-traumatic stress disorder. Their aim has been to marry up psychological with biological understandings. The dust has yet to settle in this area, particularly in view of the fact that it has positioned itself strongly on the side of developing a psychology of victims. In the case of sexuality fascinating questions remain to be answered. Some sexual traumas are more in the nature of assaults whereas others may be surrounded with ambivalence, grooming, seduction and the potential accusation of consent. Neurobiological and psychological understandings have yet to tease out the sequelae of these different kinds of event.

For the present, therefore, the impact in the consulting room of a newly re-biologised psychoanalysis is hard to evaluate. The danger is that the dialogue will be more in the nature of an infatuation, which lasts only as long as the conclusions of the reflections produced support rather than challenge psychotherapeutic orthodoxy.

Conclusion: psychoanalysis, lovemaps and the *erotic imagination*

What unifying thought can the practising therapist take from the tumult of an analytic account of sexuality? Perhaps none. At times it seems that at some time some analyst somewhere must have taken up every possible position in relation to sex. The psychoanalytic history of sexuality is after all coterminous with the history of the divisions in the analytic world. Thus Adler (1924) thought that narcissistic urges for power and superiority were more important psychologically than sex. The English object-relations theorists found sex too cold and mechanical a chore for the human psyche and substituted intimacy and its vicissitudes. Feminist analysts, as we shall see, struggled and quarrelled with the sexual submission of women, and so on. So, no single theme can be discerned to unite the many contributions other than perhaps a persistent tendency to rub or caress the palimpsest of Freud in the hope of discerning a more congenial picture beneath the surface of the canvas.

From a biopsychosocial point of view, psychoanalysis repeatedly looses its footing on one or other side of the impossibly narrow arêtes it chooses to follow between biology and psychology. Somehow analysts repeatedly arrive at a place where biology and psychology become both opposed and mutually exclusive. If analysts could have brought themselves to consider the social realm more often they might have found there room to manoeuvre between psychological and biological explanations.

Psychoanalysis has had severe and cogent critics (Gellner 1985, Crews 1995, for example) and it has certainly not been kind to people with sexual problems. Particular cruelties have been inflicted on those whose sexuality it has, in a particular manifestation, disapproved of (Socorides 1995 being a particularly virulent example). Yet the richness and drama of analytic explanations of sexuality and the extent to which its notions have penetrated the popular imagination make the discipline impossible to ignore. The sexual phantasies that analysts have dreamed up may simply be fantasies but they are gripping stuff none the less. It is difficult to find accounts of human sexuality which offer a similar degree of congruence with the emotional complexities of the experience of sexuality. Unsurprising, then, that patients frequently grasp at psychoanalytic notions as ways of interpreting their own experience. For these, if for no other reasons, psychoanalytic theories of sexuality repay study.

Psychoanalysis, however rich, cannot be left as the only psychologically based theory of sexuality. Recourse to the realm of non-psychoanalytic psychological theorising does not produce any great wealth of ideas. One important exception is Money's introduction of the concept of lovemaps (1986). Lovemaps result from the laying down at an early age of a specific script of sexual activities which channel and constrain later sexual experience. They represent an amalgam of biological, cultural and personal influences which are both idiosyncratic and stereotyped – a kind of sexual fingerprint. Money is strongly of the view that repressing children's sexual play, particularly around the ages of 5 to 8 years, is damaging to the formation of lovemaps. He argues that the chief determinant of benign sexual experience is that the participants in childhood sexuoerotic play are all roughly the same age and most importantly are at the same developmental stage sexually. When early development does not proceed correctly, for example where there is child sexual abuse, lovemaps become 'vandalised' (Money 1986) and perversions result.

Money's lovemaps are biopsychosocial constructs and consequently seem to offer therapists keen to practise in a way which respects this model a working concept. However, lovemaps seem to be seriously deficient when it comes to representing the possibility for sexually driven transformation of the self. This feature of lovemaps, that they explain how things came to be as they are but they do not give many pointers to explain how things might change, also makes it difficult for therapists to use them.

Envisaging change requires a different construct. This may be termed the 'erotic imagination'. The term imagination had enormous resonance for the romantic poets and for Warnock (1980) but has, as a concept, fallen somewhat into abeyance. By imagination the romantic poets meant something far more substantial than simple fancy. Instead they meant the capacity for creativity. Psychologically it can represent the capacity of humans to take up attitudes to their own biological, social and psychological nature and to contrive new ways of doing things, mostly within the constraints of a given state of affairs. The works of the erotic imagination are therefore aesthetic achievements. In matters of sex the erotic imagination takes the generalities prescribed by a biopsychosocial lovemap and turns them into detailed interpersonal and intrapersonal experiences which then may in turn exert transformative influences on the biopsychosocial matrix. Thus individuals are, by the exercise of the erotic imagination, released from being the sexual outcome of some complex biopsychosocial equation and instead becoming sexual agents interacting with biopsychosocial influences.

Lovemaps can be vandalised and the imagination can be wounded, most particularly by being repressed, either entirely or in part, or by being forced away from certain channels. Imagination can be delicate. Warnock (1980) chronicles the vicissitudes of the idea in the Romantic period, showing how the Lakeland poets maintained a specific view of the imagination as linked with vital, even sexual, capacities and as being capable of falling into a malaise. More serious deformations of the imagination result in a loss of the capacity for discrimination and in the capacity to build complex imaginative structures. In the worst case, a degenerate state with only two modes – the most basic biological ones – attraction or revulsion, can arise. The hallmark of disorders of the imagination is that they primarily produce aesthetic ill-effects.

The notion of the erotic imagination exercised on a biopsychosocial foundation offers a way of considering sexual matters which examines how patients make something out of their cultural, personal and genetic sexual givens. The value of the erotic imagination will be pointed up throughout the text and discussed in greater detail in the final chapter.

4

Politics

Introduction: why politics?

Political thought and activism appear, at first sight, to have no place within a biopsychosocial model of sexuality. If this were true then sexual activity would have no political consequences. However, the intensive legal regulation of sexuality in many cultures reveals at once that sexual activity has an intensely political aspect and because politics itself is a social activity it has applicability within the biopsychosocial model as a specific aspect of culture.

Therapy also seeks to change or at least take control over a state of affairs, albeit on an individual or micro social level, and there are important and complex links between politics and therapy (Samuels 2001). Therapy itself is a political activity with sexual connotations. Therapist's patients suffer or enjoy the disadvantages or benefits which accrue from social attitudes to their sexual life. Therapists may need to sort out the essentially political dilemma of deciding whether the patient's position might be most improved by changing the internal world or the external one. Patients may often share or feel that they share, with oppressed political groups, a sense of being the underdog.

The theorists and movements discussed in this chapter do generally come from the underdog position. There are, as Nietzsche pointed out, self-serving and, not entirely rational reasons why the underdogs may spend more of their time theorising their positions than the ruling elite, but even so these political visions have proved important, even revolutionary. Activist psychoanalysis, feminism (psychoanalytic and otherwise) and queer theory account between them for an important body of self-consciously political theory in sexuality. They also sequentially demonstrate an increasing dissatisfaction with orthodox ways of obtaining and evaluating knowledge. In them a naive acceptance of existing social structures, linguistic category systems and, even, the apparent 'facts' presented by the material world, has given way to an understanding of the ways in which, by dominating the discourse and presenting that domination as natural, power groups can make dissenting thought problematic. This is an important understanding and, used well, it can provide powerful and liberating ways of penetrating the assumptions of prevailing ideologies. It has also allowed commentators to develop a thoroughgoing critique of ideology and hegemony as they operate in relation to sexuality. Feminism and queer theory can offer the capacity to gain purchase on dominant ideologies and this is particularly important in our current culture in relation to sexuality. Recent sex panics and attacks of unbalanced sexual self-righteousness have demonstrated how difficult, even dangerous, it can be to question the established order, and this is the mark of a powerful tacit ideological system controlling thought. Indeed, specifically in the case of sexuality, the establishment point of view may be so well entrenched that the thought that it might be questioned never occurs:

> A man in the public eye had downloaded pornography onto his computer and had now been caught. He was pictured being hustled away by the police. A number of patients in therapy commented on this. Some were outraged at the fall of an icon, a few questioned whether the police should spend their time catching 'real paedophiles', none questioned the limits of acceptable representation or wondered why viewing pornographic representations on the internet should attract a maximum sentence of 5 years in prison, a sentence greater than the maximum 4 years given to an employee who steals £250,000 from their firm.

Radical challenges to the dominant structure of ideology can help to prevent this kind of myopia.

However, the reflexive questioning not only of categories but also of all categorisation and the accompanying refusal to accept any secure or simple grounds for knowledge, which the more radical political theories of sex propound, can be confusing. The philosophical notions involved entail abstruse epistemological twists and turns. At times theorists have become unduly preoccupied with a complex, and possibly not entirely productive, thicket of philosophical speculation about the getting and securing of certainty. Ultimately this chapter will maintain that the more extreme postmodern approaches to the nature of sex and gender impale themselves on their own logical contradictions and, as a result, do not provide a secure stance for political or therapeutic action.

Freudiomarxists

The Freudiomarxists (such as Brown 1959,. Marcuse 1970 and Reich 1961, 1962) viewed sex in a highly positive light. They took Freud's opposition between repressive civilisation and sexual wishes quite literally, but drew very different conclusions, coming down firmly on the side of sex rather than civilisation. For them sexual liberation, which they equated with the lifting of repression and the freeing of sexual impulses, including polymorphous perverse elements, would at last allow individuals to express their truest nature.

Reich's political theory derived from an eclectic appropriation of Marxism. He opposed proponents of bourgeois marriage and argued that modern society is patriarchal and its emphasis upon monogamous marriage only serves to develop authoritarian traits of character thereby supporting an exploitative social system. For Reich the fundamental mediating term between individual and repressive society was the family which created, through child rearing, the type of character structure which supported the political and economic order of society. That is, it created submissive personalities.

Reich opposed sexuality to power arguing that sexuality, appropriately expressed, is our main source of happiness and that whoever is happy is free. He developed a therapeutic method which revived Freud's early theory of actual neurosis and involved taking up bodily postures which aimed to free the body of its 'character armour' and restore sexual functioning. Reich's sexual morality and analysis of the place of the family allowed him to give particular attention to the sexual rights of children and adolescents. Even so, despite his apparent radicalism, at the heart of Reich's theory was an entirely normative vision of a natural man and a natural woman whose sexual urges were heterosexual and genital and essentially complimentary. As a result he regarded homosexuality as the product of thwarted libido and thought that it and pornography would disappear with the progressive liberation of sexuality in culture. Ironically despite the revolutionary stance of much of his thinking, the normative strand in Reich's work was used to justify highly restrictive stances (Weeks 1985). Although he spent his final years discredited and in a battle with the state over a weird contraption called the orgone box his influence can still be discerned in modern thinkers. The influential sexologist John Money (1993) holds very similar views which are based on the idea that absolutely free sexual play between children will allow appropriate 'lovemaps' to form, and perversions, which all result from distorted or vandalised lovemaps, will be eliminated or greatly reduced.

Marcuse argued that capitalist society induces sexual repression because delaying gratification is necessary for work (Battaille (1987) also held this view). Sexual repression, however, works on all the secondary or partial drives, desexualising the pre-genital zones and enforcing total and repressive genitality. Therefore the goal of human history is re-sexualisation, which means rebellion against the hegemony of procreative genital sexuality. The perversions which uphold sexuality as an end in itself should flourish. Marcuse's later work (1970) is somewhat less optimistic and utopian but highly perceptive. He talks about the liberalisation of the 1960s, not as an example of re-sexualisation but of 'repressive de-sublimation', in which a measure of highly regulated pleasure is allowed because it generates social submission. Ultimately though, Marcuse does not fully endorse the non-normative positions his theory seems to sanction. Instead, he regards perversions and homosexuality as behavioural critiques of the regime of genital sexuality. Non-repressive desublimation would be a basis for a renewed harmony with nature and under its sway all perversions would evaporate.

These thinkers are not much thought of in modern analytic theory, but modern cultural analysts of sexuality have revisited Marcuse and Reich. Weeks (1986) gives a fairly sympathetic account but he criticises Marcuse and Reich for biological essentialism, which, he argues, locks them into a moral normativity which is different from, but no less rigid than, the mainstream one. Giddens (1992) looks at these thinkers in the context of his project of charting the changes in intimacy in a society of extreme individualism whose project he sees as being self-creation. He regards them as advocates of plastic sexuality which is an element of the task of self-creation. Neither Marcuse nor Reich lives up to the definition of plastic sexuality according to Giddens. Nor, in Giddens terms, do they take account of the commodification of sex in which sex is everywhere apparent but eroticism is not in view. Giddens' judgement is too harsh. Even though Marcuse and Reich succumb to dated views about alternate sexualities, their ideas still hold revolutionary potential. Their vision of sexuality as a driver of social change envisaged something more collective than the individualism of a pure project of self-creation.

Feminism

One of the most potent criticisms that can be launched at the Freudiomarxists is that they utterly failed to appreciate the sexual oppression of women and failed to analyse heterosexuality's oppressive elements. Feminist commentators on sexuality have much to say in this area. Feminism is essentially a political movement although it has accrued a theoretical vanguard which studies the human condition from the female perspective, focusing particularly on areas where that perspective brings a distinctive approach. So, feminism is not so much a discipline located within the biopsychosocial paradigm as a politically driven approach to that paradigm, or to any paradigm, pointing up male-biased assumptions within them.

Like anthropology and sociology feminism is not a single theory. At different times feminists have adopted a wide range of opposed positions, and an awareness of the variety of sexualities attributed by women to themselves over the last four decades is a powerful antidote to any tendency to talk about 'female sexuality' or feminism as if they were a singular entity. Yet it remains fair to say that, usually, feminist perspectives on sexuality have sought to eliminate unquestioned male biases in descriptions of sexuality or in therapeutic interventions.

In the feminist polemics of the late 1960s and early 1970s, sexual autonomy and the right of women to control their own bodies was a central aspiration. Giddens (1992) argues that this surge of feminism was the result of the widespread social acceptance and use of the contraceptive pill. Writers represented sexuality, both male and female, as a biological drive, available for self-expression once sexist oppressive restraints were overcome. Women's sexuality was innate, universal and mechanical. It was a pleasure and, indeed, something of an obligation. The sexual advice manuals and magazines concentrated on the right of every woman to release previously blocked sexuality, and injunctions like 'The way to a woman's sexuality is through her clitoris' (Koedt 1970) were commonplace.

Indeed, the clitoris was to be the organ of sexual success and the clitoral orgasm was depicted as a skill to be learnt by increased self-knowledge. Women were exhorted to examine and appreciate their genitals – a task often requiring a steady hand with a mirror or considerable athletic skills. There was also a ready application of behavioural understandings developed by contemporary sexology to improve women's sex lives. Women themselves became prominent in sexology (Shere Hite 1976 being a good example). The emphasis on the clitoris and on the sexual autonomy and independence of women was not without its critics. Germaine Greer (1969, in Segal 1994) was disdainful both of 'clitoral centred' sexuality and of the growing influence of separatism and lesbianism, which she termed the 'lavender menace'. Greer regarded anything less than the straight fuck as a watered down experience, and she exhorted women to 'embrace the penis' (Greer 1970, in Segal 1994:69). Greer may have been at odds with the mainstream in the methods she advocated for liberating women's sexuality but she remained at one with it in her attempts to debunk the myth of women as the passive sex and her belief that women's and men's sexuality were equally active.

The focus of feminist theory in relation to sex changed in the 1970s, largely as a result of the increasing awareness of the extent of the violence experienced by women in their sexual experiences with men. Susan Brownmiller's influential book *Against Our Will* (1975) was a landmark in this shift. Now sexuality was seen as the primary source of men's oppression of women. Emphasis on essential differences between men's and women's sexual natures replaced concentration on their similarities. Indeed previous concentration on similarities was re-evaluated as a concentration on female sexuality only in so far as it was similar to (or aspiring to be similar to) male sexuality. Male sexuality was not active and admirable but aggressive and intrusive. Female sexuality was sensual, diffused and respectful. A particular idealised egalitarian lesbian relationship became the model for good sex and for a good relationship. Some revolutionary feminists argued that since sex is the problem, then avoiding heterosexual sex was the solution. 'Giving up fucking is taking your politics seriously' (Leeds Revolutionary Feminist Group 1981, in Segal 1987:96). Women were exhorted to limit their sexual expression to experiences of masturbation or politically motivated lesbianism. The curious paradox of this time was the combination of an essentialist perspective on the origins of women's sexuality, which was viewed as innate, with an exhortation to learn sexual orthodoxy through appropriate consciousness-raising.

At the Birmingham National Women's Liberation Conference in 1978 the motion was passed to 'make the right to define our own sexuality' the overriding demand of the women's movement (Segal 1987:96) – a war cry which had the construction of sexuality in mind. However, three years later the socialist feminist magazine 'Scarlet Woman' was still able to introduce its 1981 issue on sexuality with the essentialist affirmation 'that all women, whether lesbian or heterosexual do have the same kind of sexuality' adding 'we do think that there is a real difference between women's and men's sexuality' (Segal 1987:95). The right of women to define their own sexuality sits uneasily next to the assertion that women's sexuality is fixed by nature. This contradiction tended to be obscured within the feminist movement by the consistent notion that patriarchy had defaced an essential female sexuality which needed reclaiming.

The developing tendency in the mainstream feminist movement to collapse all discussions of heterosexuality into a case against male violence was further enforced in the early 1980s by feminists like Dworkin (1981), Morgan (1982) and MacKinnon (1987), who led a crusade against pornography. By drafting anti-pornography legislation they ensured high levels of publicity at the price of finding themselves bedfellows with the political right and fundamentalist Christians. Dworkin's attitude to pornography is uncompromising: 'the woman's sex is appropriated, her body is possessed, she is used and she is despised, the pornography does it and the pornography proves it' (Dworkin 1981:15). Sometimes she concludes that women will be free when pornography no longer exists. Sometimes she is even more pessimistic, as in her interview with Elizabeth Wilson for the Women's Press: 'women's pursuit of their own sexual pleasure is represented as itself dangerous', 'male sexuality does in fact colonize us, set our limits . . . we are in fact defined by male sexuality' (Dworkin 1982, in Segal 1994:61). Ironically, Dworkin's account of sex is remarkably like that of some sociobiologists, and although she sees pornography as a cultural phenomenon which must be eradicated it interacts, in her view, with a male biology that is immutable because 'for men the right to abuse women is elemental' (Dworkin 1981, in Segal 1987:176).

There was opposition within the feminist movement to what was seen as the troubling simplicity of the anti-pornography campaigners. This came to a head in 1982 at the Barnard Conference, which explored feminist approaches to sexuality. Feminists like Carol Vance argued that the 'hallmark of sexuality is its complexity; its multiple meanings, sensations and connections' (Vance 1984:5). The conference became the site of the first of many aggressive confrontations between pro-free speech and anti-pornography feminists. This conference also marks the beginning of the so called 'sex wars' (Vance 1984), which were to divide the feminist movement for the next decade. The intellectual 'liberal' sex radicals, as some delegates of the Barnard Conference described themselves, wanted to broaden the debate over pornography and male oppression in order 'to identify the ways in which women had been humiliated through sex without affirming that sexuality was intrinsically humiliating' (Vance 1984:xx). It was a curiously humble objective and it is hard now to understand quite why this stance should have resulted in the whole conference being surrounded by such acrimony.

Amongst the liberals the 'lesbian sex mafia' provided personal evidence of women enjoying a range of seemingly oppressive practices (for example, sadomasochism) without, as they saw it, being humiliated. Aspects of this liberalising project continued through the '90s. The sorts of practices involved were butch femme sexual role-play, consensual lesbian sado-masochism and, for adventurous heterosexuals or lesbians, sex with men! Pat Califa (1982), a sex activist, positively appropriated these practices demonstrating that when used by women they had meanings not simply reducible to power dynamics, or sexist oppression. Susie Bright, another activist, reacted against the return to passivity implied by some feminist notions of essential femininity and noted in her characteristic prose that 'women thrive on exuding as well as seeking masculine energy. It's like a Valkyrie demanding her due. The language that new women pornographers seek is not about love . . . but a roar that comes straight out of our undulating bellies' (1995:41). The strength of the lesbian sex mafia's position was that they were not taking arguments back to the 1960s when it was claimed that men and women had identical voracious sex appetites. Instead they claimed for themselves and other women the right to live out their sexual lives as they wished. They accepted and acknowledged a wide diversity of sexual wishes without the constraints of moral censorship either from patriarchy or radical feminism forcing them to conform to some mistaken view of a uniform female sexuality.

Most recently the radical feminist viewpoint has been extended by the racial or ethnic feminists, who offer a challenge to the assimilationist and universal tones of much (even radical) feminism. Anti-assimilationists argued that, insomuch as feminist thought holds to a notion of women's commonality or common oppression, sexual difference is prioritised and other differences disappear. This leaves white, middle-class, women as the norm for what constitutes woman precisely because they are not marked by these other 'distracting' distinctions. Many writers of colour have now begun to struggle with the contradictions and difficulties of identifying with more than one oppressed group. They have begun to try and tackle both white feminists for their racism and also the homophobia and sexism found in some black communities.

Post-feminism, which arose in the late 1980s and early 1990s, returned to the question of men. Camille Paglia (1993), its most vociferous exponent, argues that feminism is a victim cult in which women whine about inequality and moan about the wicked penis. She agrees with commentators like Dworkin that male aggression is a biological given, but instead of seeing it as an evil regards it as the irremovable engine of culture. Therefore women should accept rape as a risk factor for getting involved with men and compete with men on their own terms. Understandably Paglia's position is one which has aroused both considerable opposition and support. What it is not, however, is novel. Inspected more closely, Pagila's views are simply a representation of the spirit of the swinging 1960s in a new tough 1990s edition.

Feminism psychotherapy and psychoanalysis

Even though feminists have, at times, been sharply critical of therapy, seeing it as a male-driven instrument of female control, therapists, especially female ones, have been profoundly influenced by feminism. In England, Mitchell (1974) attempted to correct what she saw as an unwarranted negative stance by feminists in relation to psychoanalytic psychotherapy, arguing that it had benefits to offer women. Explicitly feminist therapies have been developed both along psychoanalytic and other lines (for example, contrast Ernst and Maguire (eds) 1987 with Dutton and Walker (eds) 1989). Patients, meanwhile, increasingly expressed their own internal anxieties over male power and female status by preferring to work with therapists of a particular gender. Another group of patients are highly politicised as feminists and this fact influences their experience of therapy and needs acceptance as an important part of their lives.

The following case vignette is designed to illustrate some of the paradoxes and perplexities which can arise for a feminist patient and her feminist therapist during the process of therapy:

Xara had been raped by an acquaintance and in the aftermath sought therapy. Her first question to her therapist was 'Are you a feminist?' Prevarication by the therapist designed to unpack the meaning of 'feminist' produced rage. Xara's rape had been brutal but also ambivalent because the rapist had been a boyfriend. Her account of her experiences at the hands of the police seemed, to the therapist, to portray them as efficient but not especially caring. Xara experienced it as a further rape by male bastards who hated and despised her. Xara's therapist felt in a bind. In desperation she changed the topic and tried to build up an alliance by discussing feminist politics a subject that they could agree on to an extent although Xara's need to have every fine detail pinned down and complete agreement meant that the therapist often ended up saying things she didn't quite agree with. The therapist wanted to try to address something of the prickly sensitivity which made Xara's experience of the world so difficult but felt she could do nothing without seeming to ally herself with rapists, police bastards and the wrong sort of feminist.

In supervision the collusion between Xara and her therapist was highlighted, as was the aggression in Xara's way of carrying on. The supervisor (a man) forcefully advised the rather uncomfortable therapist to free herself by caring less about keeping Xara in treatment and urged her to take some risks by talking about what was really going on. The therapist skipped the next supervision. When she returned she and her supervisor wondered if their respectively female and male styles might be in conflict. Another member of the supervision group commented on the difficulty of calling some styles male and others female and an argument in the group developed. It became clear that anxiety and insecurity, particularly in relation to position, status and correctness in the eyes of others, were the driving emotions behind Xara's difficulty, the therapist's difficulty, the supervisor's difficulty and all the group exchanges. As a result the therapist adopted, for the time, a policy of intervening with Xara only when she could see an anxiety was on her mind and tried just to name the anxiety and invite Xara to stay with it. This improved the emotional tone in which therapy was conducted immensely and helped Xara and her therapist establish a working alliance to replace the oscillation between distrust or collusion they had managed until then.

Amongst the different brands of therapy, psychoanalysis has received at the same time the harshest criticism from feminist therapists and the greatest contribution of theory by them. Feminist analysts from England and America have followed a range of theoretical lines. One group has adhered to a model of psychoanalytic orthodoxy which sees anatomy as destiny. Fast (1984), for example, claims that both men and women are destined by their anatomy to envy the prerogatives of the other. Gilligan (1982) and Jean Baker Miller (1978) also follow essentialist developmental theories. However, perhaps, the most influential feminist analyst has been Chodorow (1978) who uses a developmental constructivist standpoint in which gender differences are pointedly not essential but are an artefact of social structures.

Chodorow, following a line taken by Dinnerstein (1999 reprint originally published in 1977 as 'The Mermaid and the Minotaur'), founds much of her analysis on the asymmetrical distribution of the sexes in childrearing. This allows her to account for the reproduction of mothering by laying out a social rather than biological developmental line which successively reproduces patriarchy. Chodorow bases her work on Fairburn. She argues that the earliest stage of development is one of primary narcissism or oceanic feeling. From this the ego develops gradually as a result of the baby's representation of itself as separate from mother. By retaining the theory of primary narcissism Chodorow creates for her self an infant far more open to social inscription than a Kleinian infant, who is born with a pre-packaged set of anticipations of objects.

The various vicissitudes of ego and object representations which follow in Chodorow's theory are dependent on the degree of merger between mother and child and this is, in turn, affected by the sex of the child. Boys are related to as separate by mother and separation is encouraged. As a result boys repudiate mother and form an identity based on negation. Male identity is, in consequence, precarious. Ultimately boys grow up equipped for requirements of the modern labour market but not for childcare. Girls are different; they are not encouraged to separate from mother and this results in greater security of identity but at the price of a continuing sense of merger with mother. Girls ultimately grow up socialised to motherhood. All in all the final result is that girls and boys grow up to be different and in ways which reproduce that difference in the next generation. Chodorow challenges this state of affairs (unlike Winnicott 1965) and suggests changes in childcare arrangements. Her work was quickly adopted by many feminist theorists (Gilligan 1982 – *Moral Reasoning*; Ruddick 1990 – *Maternal Thinking*; Flax 1978).

Chodorow's work has largely been a theory of gender rather than sexuality but her later work (Chodorow 1994) redresses this balance. She begins with a trenchant critique of Freud, arguing that he:

presets as objective truth a final version of woman as subject that is, like the resentment of defloration, really an extension of imaginings and beliefs held by the male psyche. (Chodorow 1994:27)

Chodorow is an object-relations theorist so she does not agree with Freud that sex is the founding drive for all psychology, but she is willing to argue that sexual love presents a particular challenge to objects and their relations. In writing on the topic Chodorow's aim is to advance a more realistically complex theory, of the relationship between objects and sexual wishes, than she believes currently exists in the analytic literature. In particular she criticises the analytic literature for failing to advance more than a simplistic understanding of heterosexuality. She argues that the usual analytic account of heterosexuality, even that espoused by modern writers such as Kernberg (1995) and Person (1999), enshrines a biologically based normative account which naively links gender, identity and object-choice via the Oedipus complex. As a result female sexual experience is indissolubly linked to a view of female gender as involving passivity and masochism. Furthermore, heterosexual practice is then defined negatively by reference to the perversions, with the curious consequence of making it less exciting, less driven and less passionate than other sexual practices.

Chodorow stresses the controlling influence of culture in determining the sexual and romantic fantasies we experience. She cites as examples the 'Rebecca fantasy' which involves masochistic love for an unavailable, angry, dominating partner, whom the fantasy transforms into a gentle, loving one. This is presented as a fantasy which is gendered as feminine in our culture. A fantasy our culture genders as masculine is the 'Portnoy fantasy'. This is an obsession with a devouring hysterical mother who pushes the man towards distant women who seem unlike mother, or towards men. Chodorow also draws on the work of Espin (1984) and Moraga (1986) to chart some cultural variations. She contrasts a circum-Mediterranean pattern of male dominance, female submission and over-valuation of the penis with Latina writings which describe a Mexican cultural legacy of women portrayed as powerful temptresses.

The political punch in Chodorow's work lies in her call to the psychoanalytic establishment to review its unexamined assumptions. The political problem is caused by the fact that although her theory offers the opportunity to review current childcare arrangements in ways which might result in a less asymmetric pattern of childrearing she does not suggest how this might be achieved. Indeed, as the case of Elizabeth, Harry and Clare will illustrate, making genuine social progress on the unequal distribution of childcare would involve some very considerable social changes and probably require successful challenges to some cultural notions of 'good' childcare:

> Elizabeth brought Harry to one of her therapy sessions along with Clare, their six-month-old baby. Harry felt de-skilled because Clare always cried when he held her.
> 'She is always hungry when I have her,' he said, 'and then I have to give her back to Elizabeth to breastfeed. I want to bottle feed her.'
> Elisabeth felt frazzled because she couldn't trust Harry to do the simplest thing with Clare and added that he was always at work. She said,
> 'Harry is useless with Clare and now there is this bottle-feeding thing. You would have thought by now that Harry would know bottle-feeding is bad for children.'

Both the location of the breast and the social organisation of paid maternity and paternity leave make mothers the primary carers of their children in the very early months. This can set up an asymmetry of ease and perceived skilfulness which is impossible to shake off without considerable self-conscious effort.

Jessica Benjamin's (1992) distinctive contribution to psychoanalytic feminism is perhaps her analysis of the subjection of women in terms of Hegel's notion of the mutually dependent relationship between master and slave. She suggests that self consciousness exists only in being acknowledged by another. In our society this develops one-sidedly into master–slave dynamics. Boys emerge from their merger with mother by denying the subjectivity both of mother and women generally while asserting their own subjectivity. Girls on the other hand recognise fathers' subjectivity at expense of their own.

To analyse sexual development Benjamin focuses on the period of development described by Mahler (1968) as separation–individuation. Dealing with agency and independence is a task of this phase which happens to coincide with the psycho-sexual phase of genital development. As a result the two mix and separation–individuation issues become genitally charged. For children in this stage father represents active desire and mother desexualised regression. Because of this, the little boy's love affair with the world turns into a love affair with father, who stands for the world. The girl must represent her sense of desire by something which is not her and not feminine. Her desire is alienated because it is male sex and genitals which come to represent excitement and eroticism. Woman's heterosexuality is then formed through the over valuation and idealisation of the father accompanied by submission and compromise. Benjamin's account is important for adding the master–slave element to our understanding of sexual subjectivity but at times her argument can seem contorted. Ironically, many of these contortions result from the need to explain a link between sexuality and subjectivity which Freudian or Kleinian theory would have had in place as foundational.

An important feature of Benjamin's account is that she emphasises the role of the father more than many other feminist writers. A striking example of this is the way in which a boy can develop a heterosexuality based on an idealising love for an exciting father producing, paradoxically, a strong link between homosexual love and heterosexuality. For Benjamin such a link offers an explanation of the link between male homosocial activities and heterosexuality.

Contratto (1987, cited in Chodorow 1995), another feminist analyst, also focuses on the social role of fathers, who come and go, bringing treats and exotic stories in contrast to mothers, who are taken for granted. Fathers make their daughters feel special but these daughters also learn not to cross their father or intrude on him. They become submissive and good at working out what the other person wants. Both Benjamin and Contratto suggest that these submissive solutions undermine female sexuality. Women come to accept whatever love they can get and develop an idealising love for fathers which forms the basis for a heterosexuality based on submission and masochism.

These feminist theorists, like Freud, regard female masochistic sexuality as an outcome of psychosexual development but, unlike

Freud, they regard it as an evil and as an outcome which analytic therapists should be striving to reverse in their consulting rooms and in society. These feminists certainly brought political aims into the consulting room. Patients were to be offered therapies which disrupted their adaptation to the accepted social order rather than therapies which encouraged them to reconcile themselves more smoothly to the demands of the dominant civilisation.

Therapists working at the Women's Therapy Centre would also have had little quarrel with the positive political aims of feminist analysis. Its founders, Orbach and Eichenbaum, also span the Atlantic and possibly for this reason the theoretical work the Women's Therapy Centre has produced is somewhat less influenced by Klein than other English theoretical developments. Refreshingly, Orbach and Eichenbaum (1982) argue that women are the stronger sex, depended on by men for emotional support. Like Chodorow they are of the view that much of the psychological structuring specific to gender inequity would disappear if there were true equality between the sexes and they stress the need for fathers to share childcare equally. Mostly their work has not been concerned to characterise sexuality specifically. Instead it has largely concerned itself with gender and with specifically female pathologies, such as eating disorders.

Maguire (1995) is critical of Orbach and Eichenbaum's (1994) position on sexuality, which she regards as simplistic. She reviews much of the work of English feminist analytic writers and advances her own object–relational perspective. Like many English analytic writers, her work bears the imprint of Klein and it is possibly for this reason that she finds Orbach and Eichenbaum unsatisfactory. An advantage of her Kleinian leaning is that she is more interested in bodies and sex than are Orbach and Eichenbaum. Maguire is impressed by the idea of biologically based differences between the sexes and follows Horney (1924) in arguing that womb envy is an intense force in psychic life. She also follows Lloyd Mayer (1985) in suggesting that a girl's most fundamental anxieties are about damage to her body, not lack of a penis. This leads her to argue, somewhat improbably, that women find men closed and incapable of intimacy because they project onto men their own anxiety about losing genital openness.

Maguire also argues that female sexuality is structured both by early experiences of mothering and relationships with paternal

the biological within psychoanalysis which seem to entrench men in a position of advantage, that feminists mostly aim their fire (socio-biology is attacked for the same reason). Disliking a conclusion is certainly a reason to seek to disprove it, but dislike is not itself a sufficient disproof. Ironically, feminists often leave the field of battle having dismissed something they dislike when a devastating rebuttal was in easy grasp. In the case of biology, often feminist anxiety about its capacity to install men forever in a superior position has blinded them to simple facts such as the poor science or poor argument on which much of the sociobiological/psychoanalytical case for the institutional superiority of men is based.

Often the difficulty in aiming a final blow at sexism in psychoanalysis lies in a wish to retain valued aspects of analytic thought. Those feminist (generally non-analyst) critics who see psychoanalysis as primarily a set of moral or political claims can freely make telling moral critiques. On the other hand, those feminists who continue, even faintly, to argue that psychoanalysis is, or should be, a science, or at least a body of knowledge making truth claims, however contaminated by unwarranted and wish-fulfilling assumptions, can only seek to disinter the truths it purports to reveal, which will sometimes be palatable, sometimes not. Feminist analysts have not been able to treat psychoanalysis simply as a moral or political discourse and its sexist elements as poor morality and worse politics, because to do so would give up too much.

Another criticism of feminist theory lies in the overwhelming white–heterosexist–waged–middle-class bias that pervades feminist writing. It is a criticism which should lie heavily on feminists, whose oppressed status has been a central preoccupation. Orbach and Eichenbaum (1987), for example, discuss ethnic and cultural diversity. They announce that their patients are not diverse and therefore they are unable to consider the issue further. Other feminist writers have laid more stress on varying stereotypes of femininity, for example by showing how the sexuality of black women, thought to be primitive, powerful and free from cultural constraints, is opposed to the delicate repressed hysteria of white, middle-class women (Flax 1978). However, the analyses are generally sketchy and token and the number of case histories in the literature of patients from any non-standard background is risible. In this text also patients from different ethnic backgrounds are rare although the socioeconomic class of the patients considered varies considerably. Until a way is found of making therapy available and culturally relevant the race and class bias in the literature will continue.

Structuralism and poststructuralism

Whatever theoretical position each of the theorists discussed so far has taken in relation to the relative contributions of biology, psychology and sociology in conditioning gendered experience and sexual expression, none has doubted that such categories exist. Nor has any theorist thought to question the value of thinking in terms of femininity (or possibly femininities) and masculinity as useful categories. But some, chiefly French, psychoanalysts, some French-inspired English and American theorists and modern Queer theorists do question these easy assumptions. They do so because they rely to a great extent on a group of continental theorists who defined first structuralism and then poststructuralism. Their radical epistemological stance allows them a different take on the essentialist/constructivist debate and their radical political analysis of power structures offers them a chance to comment on forms of sexual oppression other than the gender binary.

Neither structuralism nor poststructuralism admit of easy definition. They are both complex fields contributed to by theorists all of whom possess the skill of disagreeing with each other in obscure ways. However, structuralism can be thought of as both a group of ideas and an intellectual movement. In its pure form it is concerned to privilege structure over content in the analysis of human affairs. Structuralists often consider systems which are cultural artefacts – such as food, fashion, advertising and the unconscious. Frequently structuralism suggests that language-like structures underlie each of these sorts of systems. The view of language that structuralists use is highly specific and is based on the linguistic theories of Saussure (1983) and others who argued that in any signifying system, such as language, the signifiers (in language the words) are related both to each other and to that which they signify. The relationship between signifiers is the structure and is therefore at least as important as their relationship to what is signified – the content. Structuralists therefore concentrate on describing the relationship of the interacting rules in each cultural system.

Poststructuralism, an even more elusive term, represents a radical critique of structuralism. It picks up the anti-empirical cast of structuralist thought, in particular its privileging of ideas and the relationships between ideas over material reality, as the source of our 'knowledge of the world' and extends the analysis into a thoroughgoing critique of knowledge. In a way, poststructuralism turns to attack the very idea of a fixed structure that the structuralists aimed to study. Particularly in the hands of Derrida (1976), poststructuralism repeatedly demonstrates that the binary opposition of terms such as speech/writing or presence/absence (or even penis=presence/vagina=absence), which is a feature of linguistic structures, according to Saussure, is unsupportable. This is not just because of inbuilt bias in the binary opposition to favour one of the terms, but also because of the tendency of the binary to appear to clean up but actually to conceal a host of self-contradictory ambiguities. Poststructuralist analyses attack these binary oppositions but, even as they do so lay down structure which is itself suspect. Thus a fully formed analysis resembles a game of tip and run with an infinite sequence of differences. In the light of these ideas, it is easy to see how the structure of sexual difference was always going to be a tempting topic for structuralist and poststructuralist analysis.

Psychoanalysis and poststructuralism

Lacan, an analyst and poststructuralist thinker, influenced much of French analytic thinking. He was highly influenced by Saussure and the structuralists and his work applies their notions to a wide range of subjects. In relation to sexuality Lacan's initial move, distinguishing between the penis (an organ) and the phallus (a signifier), is typically poststructuralist. For Lacan the penis – a sexual organ – is less important than the phallus, which is all that the penis stands for including the difference between men and women. Moreover, the phallus is now taken by Lacan as the prototype of all difference and consequently the prerequisite of language which can only signify on the basis of its difference, and hence requires a structure of differences to function at all. The versatile phallus also stands for the 'law of the father', which is the separation of the (male) child from its mother who is the object of his desire. This displacement from the first object of desire inaugurates a succession of dissatisfied displacements of desire from one object to another.

It is as a consequence of these views that Lacanians always see gender a problematic affair and one intimately bound up with lack and loss. Lacan stressed that adult sexual and love relations are always unsatisfying because the loved adult is always not the first love object, who was mother. Lacan also stressed the complexity, ambiguity, and restlessness of sexual relationships and of the subjects who had them. The ideal Lacanian patient struggles to speak, and attention to the subtexts of language such as pun, metaphor and allusion are central to a Lacanian analysis:

> In therapy Petra recounted how as a child in a mathematics lesson she had been introduced to the topic of mensuration (the mathematics of measuring complex shapes) by an admired mathematics teacher. Innocently she piped up that mensuration was an interesting word. A sharp and shaming rebuke from the teacher alerted Petra to the word she had failed to hear – menstruation. As an adult, Petra announced, she had always liked to get the measure of things and had particularly liked calculus.

To Lacanian ears Petra's stream of thought and association in the presence of her female analyst/maths teacher (in mathematics mensuration is an aspect of the topic referred to as calculus or analysis) represents a complex allusive discourse on the difference between the sexes and her feelings about this. When she 'pipe(s) up' and fails to hear the homophonic resemblance between mensuration and menstruation she pretends to be a boy with a measurable genital. Yet her action is unconsciously calculated to earn her firm re-entry to her own (female) side of the symbolic order where menstruation signifies repeatedly the failure of the return of the phallus in the shape of the longed for boy baby. To Lacanian ears Petra's speech represents a girl poised between the symbolic and the imaginary and poised, too, at the menarche when at last she will acquire breasts, mensurable secondary sexual characteristics.

Lacanian theory with its own relentless displacement of meaning from bodies (penises) to symbols and texts (phalluses), can feel difficult to apply to sexual difficulties in the consulting room. However, the kind of analysis in which Lacanian theory can assist, as shown by the work on Petra's slip, is one which reveals, in the fine structure of the discourse in the analytic session, a substructure of deferred meanings. These may reveal ways in which the patient strives to maintain a coherent identity at the price of doing a certain violence to the truth of their being. Certainly in sexual matters patients often veil themselves in layers of self-misrepresentation which close textual analysis can sometimes help to unwrap.

Against these advantages must be set a considerable disadvantage. Playing with words can become a detached, dazzling, entertaining and even masturbatory activity. The deliberate obscurity of many Lacanian texts, littered with terms of art and written in ways which both play with language but also obscure any sense of plain meaning, makes the texts tough, even irritating, reading (Tallis 1988). Clinically, the danger is that the analyst becomes the arbiter of the pun, the privileged interpreter of the shifting significations of the patient's text, and as a result can impose fanciful or prejudiced notions on a patient who has been robbed of any sense that the plain text of their own discourse carries weight. Even though Lacanians strive to avoid being in the place of the 'one who is supposed to know' the technical and non-dialogic nature of Lacanian analyses can risk making the analyst seem just as knowing as any other expert interlocutor but perhaps all the more frightening for denying this status.

Some feminist analysts found Lacan's theories, with their insistence on the law of the father, patriarchal and potentially destructive to the liberation of women and the celebration of femininity. Lacanian theory will certainly have no truck with essentialist feminist theories since femininity cannot be constituted by itself but only by being contrasted with masculinity within patriarchy, and this leads to problems. Sayers (1986:46) describes it this way:

Woman is dependent on man if only, paradoxically, because her existence as woman is predicated on being contrasted in opposition and antithesis to man.

Feminist Lacanians (or post-Lacanians) have struggled with this. Kristeva, for example, removes femininity from the realm of language and speech altogether, arguing that a pre-symbolic order of essential femininity can be discerned but not spoken of:

> Feminist practice can only be negative . . . In woman is something that cannot be represented above and beyond nomenclatures and ideologies. (Kristeva 1974:137, cited in Sayers 1986:92)

As Sayers points out, a problem with this line of approach is that it escapes the law of the father but at the cost of leaving feminism nothing positive to work with.

Irigary (1985), on the other hand, argues that women have a distinctive psychology given by the nature of sexual organs. Men need instruments or a hand to touch themselves but a woman's sexual organ is doubled having two labia constantly in contact. For Irigary, therefore, men interrupt the continual autoerotic pleasure of women by a brutal intrusion and they alienate women from themselves by making them become passive objects of male voyeuristic desire. So, where Lacan saw women as lacking the phallus, Irigary sees them as possessing a self-caressing, if threatened, plenitude.

Irigary criticises psychoanalysis because it reproduces as fact, a sexual theory of children which is the childish fantasy that there is only one sex – male. She argues that the only way forward for women is to assert their difference through the creation of a powerful female symbolic to represent them against the omnipresent effects of male imagery (notice that Irigary's travel is in the opposite direction to Kristeva's). Women must create new ways of speaking about, and of, their sex and may require a period of separatism. Irigary describes typical female erotic pleasures, such as caressing the breasts, touching the vulva, opening the lips gently, stroking the posterior wall of the vagina, and lightly massaging the cervix. By doing so she makes it immediately obvious that such explicit female experience is rarely, if ever, referred to in psychoanalytic literature (Irigary 1985):

> Bryony was referred to a psychotherapy service and refused her first assessment because it was with a male therapist. There was

heated debate within the unit about offering her a female therapist. One man felt that this would collude with her in her notion that 'all men are bastards'. Some female therapists agreed but others felt that if Bryony felt more able to talk to a woman then she should see a female therapist. One pointed out that men often refer to 'women's troubles' and maybe there were such things.

Bryony's request is repeated regularly throughout the public and private sector. The debates it engenders often mirror battles between essentialist feminists and more complicated views which problematise gender categories. While an essentialist feminist perspective like Irigary's promises to rescue something valuable for women – a space for contemplation unmediated by dominant culture – it has its critics. Sayers (1986) criticises Irigary for her wish to return to a pre-oedipal time, arguing that she is denying sexual difference which must be acknowledged in order to struggle against inequality. While this criticism has some force it is not entirely an accurate representation of Irigary's stated project of building a powerful female symbolic, since in Lacanian theory the symbolic requires an acknowledgement of sexual difference. A more telling criticism (and one made implicitly in Sayers account) is to take aim at Irigary's rather romantic and idealised sexualisation of the female body. Her pictures of female sex are gentle and soft focus. The female body is the locus of intrusions and rapes but never of self-originated conflicts and trials. So, even though Irigary's woman experiences pleasures of her own in a separated space, she does so at the price of being constructed as always ready to be violated:

> Charlie's life was one of perpetual insults. Everywhere she went it felt as though the world shattered her calm and threw her into an impotent rage. She lived in an all-women flatshare but then the cat they had purchased turned out to be a tom cat and her flat mates would not get rid of him. There were fights over food – how and where it should be purchased, fights over clothes, fights over make-up. These battles were matters of extreme personal pain to Charlie, who took her politics as personally as she could possibly take them. As Charlie told this to her therapist it seemed as though the rigid structure of rules

by which she lived represented the return of an authoritarian and arbitrary father and of the patriarchical world which she strove to exclude.

Charlie's troubles can be seen as resulting from her attempt to create a female space of gentle contemplation while living in a sexist world. The irony of her life is that her separatist efforts appear to depend on an authoritarian and unforgiving part of her self. Possibly this sort of contradiction requires a vision of women as more deeply divided than Irigary will allow.

Lacan's influence was not confined to France. Mitchell (1974) in England and Rubin (1989) in America both took up his work and attempted to use it to rescue Freudian insights from their wrapping of phallocentrism. Mitchell's argument was that while the Oedipus complex deeply conditioned the psychology of girls this was a structuring only of the 'imaginary' which was therefore not universal and which could be overthrown. Freudian theory, she suggested, could be useful to feminists who had abandoned it too rapidly. A weakness of her view was that she did not suggest why or how women, influenced as they were by the patriarchal imaginary, would or could rise up to overthrow capitalism and patriarchy.

Rubin in America combined her reading of Lacan with one of Lévi-Strauss to show how the structure of sexual difference also privileges heterosexuality. She looked at sexual arrangements from the perspective of kinship structures and the rules governing the exchange of women. Rubin argued that the presence or absence of the phallus carries the difference between the two sexual statuses, and this difference also includes object choice, because of the rules of the kinship structure. Thus the Oedipus complex also initiates the child into a taboo on homosexuality because, since the girl has no phallus, she cannot love women. Since the mother and all women can only properly be loved by phallus possessors the girl recognises the futility of realising active desire. In *Thinking Sex: Notes for a Radical Theory of the Politics of Sexuality* Rubin (1989) argues for a review of the traditional linkage of gender and sexuality. Her radical stance and strictly social constructivist approach, one which allows her to question the function and value of incest rules (which she sees as enforcing the normative order), makes her an important forerunner of the queer theorists.

Many other feminist writers have taken up Lacanian or post-Lacanian themes in analysing gender (for example, Brennan 1989, 1992) and sexuality. However, Mitchell and Rubin have moved away from the initial implications of their Lacanian positions. Mitchell has retrenched, wondering about the revolutionary potential of her previous stance. Rubin has moved in a queer direction, rejecting her previous Lacanian argument because of its too easy union of sexual practice and gender identity. These second thoughts, and also the difficulties already discussed with Irigary's essentialist critique of Lacan, perhaps reveal the need for a more thoroughgoing poststructuralist critique of Lacan himself, wedded as he is to binary oppositions which privilege one term over another and in general of cultural 'certainties' about the categories of language used to define gender identity and sexual preference.

This kind of critique will clearly be highly relevant to those whose object choices are non-standard and who suffer significant oppression as a result. This project has therefore been primarily the task of theorists from sexual minorities, often travelling together as 'queer theorists'. Not all the theorists discussed below would necessarily define themselves as queer however all have some stake in ensuring that current analyses of sex and gender do not obliterate or pathologise homosexual and other object choice.

Queer theory

Queer theory, like feminism, is both a political movement and a theoretical position. From a political perspective its origins can be found in the recognition amongst gays and lesbians that they were not a monolithic or homogeneous group. People of colour, transgendered people, bisexual individuals, for example, all needed a legitimate place. To an extent all were denied it in the gay and lesbian movement of the time. HIV and the issues it raised was also a major engine driving the queer movement. The theory behind the movement, however, was developed in an entirely different location, chiefly departments of English literature (Seidman 1996). As a critical practice queer theory, which tended to define itself as in opposition to anything which was unthinkingly considered normal or natural, drew heavily on postmodern ideas.

The poststructuralist critique of theory is that there can be no theoretical perspective which stands outside that theory, and poststructuralists inspect the margins of the theory for the inevitable internal contradictions which disrupt the easy certainties propounded in the theory. Queer theory is therefore an activity, or a critical exercise, whose chief aim is to show how the sexual margins are a necessary creation of heterosexuality, even as it disavows them. It also aims to show how a critique from those margins could break down the very mainstream/margin distinction itself.

Stein and Plummer (1996) helpfully point out that queer theory typically: renders sex and gender categories problematic, exposes the political power play embedded in them, uses alternative strategies for political action, and admits extreme forms of sexual expression as valuable. The alternative political strategies advocated often involve cultural comment that ridicules the established order by highlighting contradictory or cowardly positions. Therapists could usefully consider this agenda for political action as a possible agenda for therapeutic action. Certainly the use of alternative trickster strategies in therapy has been powerfully advocated in other contexts (Samuels 1986; Erickson and Rosen 1991). It is important to emphasise that tricky dealing can be used just as easily to reinforce the mainstream as it can to subvert it.

Few, if any, queer theorists have managed to write in ignorance of Foucault (for a start, Foucault 1981). His central work has been to expose in detail how mainstream social discourses regulate social practices whatever their overt agenda. Discourses, by which Foucault means both texts but also whole climates of opinion, are internalised by individuals and regulate their activity. He showed that Victorian social discourse, while overtly sexually repressive, was replete with sexuality which it categorised and medicalised for the purpose of social control. As a result, Foucault argues, sexuality became a mainstay of identity and along with it both normative heterosexuality and the notion of different sexual natures as identities. For queer theorists it was Foucault's political analysis of the body as a centre of bio power (an object of state regulation, contested social meaning and potential social change) which set the agenda for a political as opposed to a theoretical project. Queer theory has proved popular. Only a few queer theorists out of an enormous throng will be discussed.

Monique Wittig's claim (1981) that lesbians are not women derives from her theoretical position that masculinity and femininity are defined in binary opposition to each other and therefore that a woman who relates to women cannot be defined this way. She took Foucault's insight into the political nature of sexual arrangements and argued that heterosexuality is a political regime rather than a sexuality. Until then, feminism had considered patriarchy to be an ideological system based on the domination of the class of men over the class of women. For Wittig, the word 'woman' has meaning only in heterosexual systems of thought and heterosexual economic systems. Patriarchy is therefore enforced heterosexuality.

Wittig's point of view has been taken up as 'radical lesbianism' and inspires a political project which sees heterosexuality as a political regime that must be overthrown. Those inspired by Wittig's analysis argue that heterosexuality can ensure its political power only through the destruction or negation of lesbianism. There are difficulties with this position. A simple one being that lesbianism is far less policed in most cultures than male homosexuality. Another difficulty lies in a tendency for certain groups of lesbians to replace the binary male/female as a mainstay of identity with a powerful/oppressed dichotomy. If, despite their hopes of liberation, radical lesbians are defining their identity as coterminous with oppressed status then the chances of a successful overthrow of the established order are likely to be low. In therapy, for example, it is quite common to work with patients whose lesbian identity does seem dependent on a sense of being oppressed, to the extent that there appear to be resistances to change which are founded in fears of loss of identity.

In relation to gay men, calls for radical self-exposure and self-definition have not centred around opposition to heteropatriarchy, instead concentrating on opposition to the policing of male sexuality. By extension, gay men who assimilate into the straight world using what Bersani (1995) terms the strategy of being invisibly visible are also heavily criticised. Gay sex is characterised by queer theorists as explosive, revolutionary, shattering rather than friendly and assimilable into the main order. Hocquenghem (1978), for example was concerned to show the terrifying power of homosexual object-choice. He, along with Mohr (1992), is uninterested in heterosexual-like homosexuality

– monogamy, knitted jumpers and so forth. Instead, in practices like casual sex, these theorists see the nucleus of a new kind of society, neither hierarchical nor formalised. For Hocquenghem this new society is one which, because it is not reproductive, is liberated from capitalism.

Bersani focuses on the facts of gay sex and repeats the assertion that same sex desire can disrupt the dominant ideology. He focuses on the concept that some kinds of sexual experience, such as anal sex, can result in experiences of self-shattering which completely disrupt easily received identities. Sedgwick, although a feminist writer, is profoundly influenced by Bersani; indeed one of her important essays 'Is the rectum straight?' (1994) is a deliberate homage. Her concern has been to show how mainstream Western literature is replete with homosexual allusions (Sedgwick 1990). She probes the text to expose a chronic dichotomy between concealment and outing. The importance of these theorists lies in their critique of the consumerist assimilationist gay and in their revaluing of the revolutionary potential of specific sexual practices. To this Sedgwick adds an analysis of the gay subtext of seemingly straight literary texts, showing how disavowed homosexuality is shoring up the established order. It is perhaps in this area that queer theorists have their greatest therapeutic utility. If patients can recast their understandings of their sexuality as in itself political and transformative then this new attitude may serve as the source of a radical, and it is to be hoped beneficial, re-evaluation in personal life.

It could be argued that Halberstam's sweeping analysis of female masculinity (1998) carries out much the same task for women and lesbians that Bersani and Hocquenghem attempted for gay men. Her project is to analyse the nature of 'masculinity' in women. In doing so she shows how masculinity is not a property of men and reveals the transformative and revolutionary potential of gender play in challenging and subverting the sexual mainstream. Halberstam catalogues a range of female masculinities from the past 200 years. Her analysis allows another look at 'The Well of Loneliness', butch/femme, 'transgender dykes' and lesbians who pass as men. She is concerned to argue that female masculinity is its own identity and not a poor imitation of masculinity.

The intensity of the struggle that women, lesbian and heterosexual, still have with any social perception of them as masculine, and the confusion and unconscious hatred their interlocutors reveal, is frequently evident in therapy. Social denial of masculinities which are female can be an internalised as well as an external affair. Halberstam's analysis can help some patients to develop a more flexible view of their commitments which may allow greater room for social and personal manoeuvre. O'Connor (1992), for example, describes the case of a woman whose struggle for identity and sexuality involved a progressive re-examination of the consequences of lesbian and of masculine identity.

But can any identity be secure? As might be expected, queer theorists have problems with any naive notion of identity and Judith Butler (1990) is the theorist who has done most both to problematise and to re-theorise identity. Drawing on the psychoanalyst Joan Riviere's paper 'Womanliness as masquerade' (1929), she provides an analysis of gender as a performance rather than an essence. She looks first at more obvious gender performances, such as cross-dressing, and butch–femme dichotomies, but then drives the analysis forwards to argue that the heterosexuality such practices appear to ape is itself no more than a series of performative practices which imitate a 'phantasmic' ideal. The radical anti realism and anti idealism of Butler's stance has excited some criticism from those who are unable to see how any knowledge can be grounded securely in her epistemology. From a political point of view others have criticised Butler for seeming to imply that gender and object choice, being performative, can be easily changed. This is a charge Butler has strongly denied, pointing out that it rests on a misreading of her work. Butler says (1993:94):

> Sexuality cannot be summarily made or unmade, and it would be a mistake to associate constructivism with the freedom of a subject to form her/his sexuality as s/he pleases.

Despite this it is not easy to see how Butler's work, with its relentless questioning of any settled identity or identification, might transform into a political or therapeutic project. A therapy or politics that seeks always to be elsewhere may prove too elusive to provide the basis for any form of change.

Anxieties about queer theory go further than this. Possibly the most telling criticisms lie first in the political credentials of the activity itself as well as in the philosophical contradictions at its core. Queer theory is based in academe and often relies on a certain kind of text – literary and bourgeois, possibly with a gentle sprinkle of film studies or popular culture. These sources are potentially divorced from the lives of those at whom the project of liberation is launched. It stands charged therefore with bourgeois irrelevance. There are, as well, philosophical problems. One concerns the disarticulation of terms from their referents. Consider the statement by Judith Butler of the term lesbian: 'I would like to have it permanently unclear what precisely that sign signifies' (1990:14). It is an example of what Mohr (1992), a trenchant critic, calls the claim that such a thing as 'non-denoting nominalism' could exist. Mohr argues that if the terms lesbian, or homosexual, or any other term have no fixed content then the concepts simply disappear and cannot signify. Epstein (1996), linking political and philosophical objections to queer theory, points out that political theorists have on the whole used simple essentialist theories to achieve their aims rather than queer theories. Indeed it is ironic that the success of these essentialist activists in achieving equal rights for minority groups has allowed academic institutions to appoint queer theorists who can appear to deny the legitimacy of this political stance.

Sexual politics and therapeutic practice

Each of the movements discussed so far has been able to bring something positive to the politics of sexuality. Feminism, with its reshaping of the political domain embodied in the slogan 'the political is personal', can show us how therapy is also a political exercise and how political theory can offer therapy new ways to inspire personal change. Politically aware psychoanalysis has been able to show in detail exactly how social injunctions are internalised. Meanwhile the Freudiomarxists were among the first to notice the political importance of sexual liberation. Their project was taken up by gay men and lesbians and also by queer theorists and it is perhaps this insight which remains their most important contribution.

The theorists discussed in this chapter should inform therapy, but therapists practising with their contribution in mind will need to achieve the considerable feat of avoiding easy certainties while at the same time resisting adopting an 'anything goes' attitude.

Annabelle presented in her late fifties. She had been active in the feminist movement many years ago and still believed passionately in the ideals of that period. However, she had since suffered a series of serious breakdowns in her mental health and had a received a diagnosis of paranoid schizophrenia. She wanted psychotherapy to help her discontinue her medication. Such discontinuations had in the past invariably resulted in florid relapses of her illness. One of her main reasons for wanting to stop medication was that in a recent recurrence of her illness she had at last had a 'proper orgasm'. By this it turned out that she meant an orgasm which was not accompanied by a sadomasochistic sexual fantasy. Her therapist, who was radicalised during a different historical period of feminism, explored this topic with her with considerable interest. Annabelle spoke in an animated way about the importance of liberating the self from male oppression and about her conviction that sadomasochistic fantasies were a sign that this had not been achieved in her case. She clearly viewed this part of her emotional life with judgemental disgust. It was a sign that she was a contaminated Hitler woman who colluded with the enemy. She also regarded psychotropic medication itself as a sadomasochistic intrusion into her mind. 'It's mind rape and you are the rape woman,' she said leaning forward aggressively. Scared and startled, the therapist commented that 'surely people were entitled to their fantasies'. Annabelle became angry and mildly thought-disordered. She suddenly leaned forward, saying, 'You're one of them, I know you have been watching me and listening to me but you won't catch me, only my genes are safe with you Jew.' 'Them', it turned out, were both the old sex warriors of the past but also, sometimes, a more current group of oppressors, whom Annabelle was convinced were following her and persecuting her by extracting thoughts from her mind.

Annabelle's case presents her therapist with multiple dilemmas. Was her mental state such that the therapist should press further medication and even hospital admission on her? Would this be truly a rape or would it constitute proper treatment of a woman made vulnerable by terrible illness which seemed to be recurring? What of Annabelle's self-policing attitude to her sexual fantasy

5 Male and female heterosexuality

The female sexual life cycle

The nature of female sexuality

Female sexuality is generally thought to differ from male sexuality and almost every writer in the field of sexuality makes some attempt at defining the differences, for example, characterising it as receptive, gentle, enveloping, sensuous and so forth. For some writers, such as Jung, (a good collection of Jung's views in this area can be found in Jung 1983), later analysts (Irigary, 1985) and some feminists (Brownmiller, 1971, Dworkin, 1981), these characteristics are seen as essential and internal to the nature of womanhood. For others, such as Freud (1931), they are the bittersweet fruits of the conflict between the soon-to-be-crushed activity of the little girl, the demands of culture, and the facts of anatomy.

Characterisations of femininity as passive have been resisted by some and sex-positive writers have held out for an active, even aggressive, female sexuality (Califia 1982; Bright 1995). What any universal characterisation of female sexuality achieves is the obliteration of differences both between women and within a woman's lifetime. A different view might see the negotiation of these differences within a life and between women as being as important for a fulfilling female sexuality as the negotiation of differences between the sexes. Even experience of differences between the sexes will vary between women and over a life cycle. As ever, therefore, the key therapeutic task is to be aware of diversity.

Childhood and early development

The biological determinants of sexual development in early life are first the maturational processes, which occur prior to puberty, and then the onset of puberty itself. Pre-pubertal children are sexually responsive and also sexually exploratory. Thus both boys and girls 'masturbate' from a very young age, with masturbation to the point of orgasm being visible in children as young as 6 months of age. This activity is probably continuous and persistent throughout childhood, but as children get older parental disapproval of this activity in public makes its incidence less easy to study.

Puberty inaugurates a major increase in sexual interest and activity. This occurs differently for girls and boys. Most boys rapidly develop a full level of sexual responsiveness within a year of two of puberty. Girls, take longer to develop peak sexual responsiveness and the timescale is more influenced by cultural than hormonal factors (Udry *et al*. 1986). Therapists treating young girls with sexual difficulties need to take into account the likely current state of a child's biological sexual development, and the impact of likely future development. It will, for example, be at puberty that undiagnosed biological abnormalities of the reproductive system may declare themselves, particularly in girls with failure to menstruate or difficulties with first intercourse.

Expectations about, and reactions to, the developing sexuality of girls are strongly culturally determined and reflected in differing ages of consent between countries. Despite clear evidence of benign cultural variation in sexual activity, many writers have very strong beliefs about the potentially harmful effects of either too early or (often less clearly stated) too late a start to sexual experiences. For girls, cultural assumptions of purity in children and of sexual discretion in women combine with the biological invisibility of the female sexual organs to make sexual experimentation an unspoken activity. Girls are often unable to name parts of their genitalia and may not realise that what they are doing is masturbation. These findings inevitably raise the question of whether the female sexual imagination can flourish in non-verbal modes. As we have seen, French feminist Lacanian analysts, who have a keen interest in language, have tried to set out a pre- or non-verbal space for women's self-knowledge (Kristeva 1980). Welldon (1988) has also tried to talk about female sexuality as diffused over the body surface. These writers tend mostly to chart difficulties and perversions. As yet no one has seriously attempted to draw out the positive implications of a non-verbal erotic imagination.

The lack of names for female sexual experience must be set against the existence of cultural controls on female sexuality represented by the ban on masturbation and by requirements for covering up the body. This means that the question set for girls and later for women is: What are the implications for the erotic imagination of women who do not speak much of sex but whose sexuality is always emphasised by being under so much control?

Adolescence and early adulthood

Possibly adolescence and early adulthood represent the area where the most complex weave of biological, social and psychological events contribute to an experience of sexuality and sexual behaviours. The culmination of a biological process (puberty) inaugurates a period of intense, much more overt, social control and also of psychological development.

There is some evidence that puberty has been occurring earlier in our society, triggered possibly by increased nutritional status (Bancroft, 1989). There is also evidence that some of the psychological experiences which women go through at this stage are under genetic/hormonal control. Experiences of sexual desire are associated with elevations in circulating androgen levels (Morris 1997). We may therefore expect that younger girls will be facing the cultural and hormonal challenges of adolescence. The nature of these experiences is always broadly similar – sexual interest increases and sexual desire becomes a more urgent part of mental life. However, the experience of these changes is heavily conditioned by social factors and in almost all cultures first sexual experiences are the most heavily policed parts of sexuality and are frequently delayed beyond the moment when they become biologically possible (Bancroft 1989). Our personal experience of this cultural imperative can be intense and generate massive individual anxiety, and collectively a sex panic.

The prospects for adolescent sexual adventuring, in safety, improved with the advent of reliable contraception but at the same time the risk of contracting a sexually transmitted disease increased dramatically. These factors now inform the sexual imaginations of young women. Many, for example, announce intentions to remain celibate until they marry. However, their imaginations about sexual risk often have little tie to lived experience. Faced with an interpersonal situation their theoretical appreciation of risk can give way, often without much planning, to a sudden sexual experience.

First sexual experience

There is keen political interest in the age at which girls have their first sexual experience, largely related to anxieties about teenage pregnancy. However, the frequently disappointing nature of the experience of first sexual intercourse for women is less well appreciated. Rubin (1989, in Segal 1994) catalogues experiences of regret and of feeling cheated. Orgasm seems rare and many girls report a single early sexual experience which they do not repeat for a considerable time. Person (1983) is one of the few psychoanalysts who discuss this fact. She argues that the continuing social inequalities between men and women and girls and boys result in an identification by girls of themselves as the object of desire rather than as a desiring subject. This denies them access to desire and hence to experiences which could bring pleasure.

A subgroup of teenagers reports first sexual experiences which are sufficiently coercive to amount to rape or near rape. Clinical evidence suggests that rape or coercive sexual intercourse at this particular developmental stage is specially damaging to psychosexual development and self-esteem. The core pathogenic nucleus involves a mixture of ideas in which powerlessness and the removal of personal choice mix with anxieties about accusations of having 'asked for it' and images of internal damage:

> Karen's very first long solo bicycle trip aged 16 ended in disaster. She was jumped and raped by a man whom she failed (in her view) to resist sufficiently out of shock. He stole the bike and she walked a considerable distance home. She did tell her parents who were bewildered. The police took matters seriously but Karen found being examined horrid. Everyone felt it would be best if Karen put things behind her. But she did not. She became morose at school and seemed preoccupied. Ultimately

she locked herself in her room. The psychiatric team, when called, detained her in hospital under the Mental Health Act with a diagnosis of severe depression. Many months later when she was evaluated for a talking treatment she was able to say that she could not stop worrying if she had encouraged her attacker and had also convinced herself that she had enjoyed the sex.

For girls who have been raped, but also for many others, early sexual experiences are unpleasant. Patients often speak of these experiences as fulfilling social functions, such as keeping up with other girls, or retaining the affection of a boyfriend, rather than as erotically valuable. Perhaps it is because of this kind of experience that some women draw the conclusion that sexual pleasure is something that must be worked at. From the perspective of the erotic imagination this conclusion may have advantages since it makes women ready to fine tune the aesthetics of sexual experience. Sadly others conclude that sexual experiences are of no value and foreclose on their sexuality. Notwithstanding this gloomy catalogue, some adolescent girls do describe a pleasurable experience of first intercourse. In a study by Thompson (1990, cited in Segal 1994) these girls differed from the disappointed group in having a more educated erotic imagination, as evidenced by greater knowledge of sexual pleasure, masturbation and sex education and were more likely to have obtained contraception before having sex.

Separation/individuation issues

Irrespective of age, the one topic systematically omitted from sex education classes is sexual pleasure and its increase. Studies of parental sex education show a general tendency (Roberts *et al.* 1978, in Bancroft 1989) to provide mechanical or even agrarian information but to avoid discussions relating to the pleasurable aspects of sexuality. The reasons for this may lie in the challenge of separation and individuation for both the adults and the teenagers in the family unit. Our culture requires adolescents to prepare to leave home as they become adult, or at least to take on a more adult role – for example bringing in money, if they stay. There is evidence that despite this socially scripted independence adults experience rivalry with their children's growing sexuality. Parents of the same-sexed adolescent show a decline in psychological well being when their child becomes sexually active and there may be a temporary loss of interest in the spouse (Steinberg 1994). This helps us see that social taboos over discussing sexual pleasure with daughters might represent adult rivalry and vengeful control of information.

Some of the many issues which surround adolescence are evident in the following case example:

> Lisa was four months pregnant when presented to the clinic and also had a diagnosis of a genetic syndrome which was associated with mild learning difficulties. She spoke about her wish to have the baby and her anger at her parents for pressing her to have a termination and to know who the father of the child was. She left the interview announcing that there was nothing wrong with her and refused permission for her parents to be seen. A few minutes later Lisa and her parents all returned to the therapist's room. Lisa it seemed had been threatened with being thrown out of the house if she did not let her parents see the therapist. Lisa's parents painted pictures of extremely disruptive and promiscuous behaviour and, speaking over Lisa's protests, they pointed out she had no means of looking after the child and would be dependent on them. Lisa said she would go and live with her boyfriend. The parents leapt on this, claiming Lisa did not know where her boyfriend was. Argument continued futilely along these lines for some time. Repeatedly Lisa's parents appealed to the therapist to support them in treating Lisa as not competent to manage her affairs. Lisa in her turn repeatedly failed to engage with her parents' concerns in a way which would satisfy them.

The suggestion that Lisa may have a learning difficulty is adding to the normal strains which surround separation and individuation for both child and parents. In this case, the therapist's strong reaction was that there was right on both sides although he was unclear how it might ever be apportioned. Sadly, neither party could allow the therapist his own position without seeing it as in opposition to theirs. His interventions tended only to make the row more acrimonious. His decision to involve social services was forced on him because of child protection issues raised by the parents. Unfortunately this served to make a final therapeutic rupture with Lisa, who refused further treatment.

Child sexual abuse

Adolescents and adult women who have been sexually abused in childhood report particular difficulties which frequently present in therapy. There has been major controversy in the area of treating adults sexually abused as children over the notions of 'recovered memories' and of 'false memory syndrome'. Scope does not permit a discussion of this debate here and the reader is directed to the relevant literature (Mollon 1998; Brandon *et al.* 1998). Instead, this section concentrates on the vast majority of individuals who have continuous, well-formed memories of abuse:

> Clara presented with a complaint of having been sexually abused as a child. As she sat in the consulting room chair it seemed to her assessor that she presented this fact more in the way of a challenge than a complaint. Asked to tell her story, she revealed that her parents had separated when she was 4 and she had spent time shuttling between two households. When she was 6 her mother's then boyfriend had begun systematically to sexually abuse her starting with experiences in which she was encouraged to touch his penis. Later he attempted intercourse on a number of occasions. Clara did tell her father what was going on but her revelation was not made in a clearcut way. Her father then used it as a weapon in acrimonious divorce proceedings and her mother refused to credit it. She was presenting now at 28 because she had confided this fact to a friend who had reacted with horror and pressed her to seek help.

Determining an accurate rate for experiences of sexual abuse in childhood has proved almost impossible, with estimates varying wildly depending on the population researched and the definition of sexual abuse being used (Bancroft 1989). Gaining a fair view of the likely outcomes of child sexual abuse has been equally problematic. Certainly surveys of psychiatrically unwell patients have revealed an excess of cases of child sexual abuse over the base rate in the population (Buka and Kessler 2001). But, some studies have yielded equivocal results (such as Pope and Hudson 1992, looking at bulimia). The methodological difficulties which bedevil research in the area make certain results difficult to obtain (Fergusson 1997), but prospective studies overcome some of the difficulties and have demonstrated an increased incidence of psychiatric difficulties in people who were abused as children (see Fergusson *et al.* 1996 for a review). Unfortunately much of the research effort in the field seems to have been devoted to the recovered memories controversy, leading to the neglect of patients whose memories of abuse have never been in question.

Although some people abused as children display no lasting ill-effects in adulthood, many others show a range of symptoms and syndromes which include sexual and interpersonal dysfunction, post-traumatic stress disorder, depression, eating disorders, borderline personality disorder and substance abuse. Sensitivity to and empathy towards the early experiences of abuse as well as their culturally driven evaluation is clearly a major concern in therapy:

> On closer questioning it was clear that Clara had pervasive diffi-culties with her self-esteem and self-image. She was regularly self-harming and also had some traits suggestive of an eating disorder. She was currently depressed and could not remember a time when she had not felt depressed. Another difficulty was her tendency towards angry outbursts and alcohol abuse, which had on occasion led to difficulties with the police.

Clara's condition is suggestive of borderline personality disorder although a fuller history and information from people who had known Clara for a while would be needed to confirm this. In such situations treatment can proceed along standard lines (using, for example, cognitive analytic, cognitive behavioural, psychody-namic or interpersonal therapy). However, because of the history of sexual abuse very close attention must be given to the risk of regression during treatment:

> Clara's own view of her therapy needs involved the chance to go over in detail all that had occurred to her so that she could be clear about what had happened. Pretty quickly she found

weekly sessions too infrequent but when the session frequency was increased to thrice weekly this too felt inadequate. She would spend much time outside the session writing a tortured diary of all her thoughts and distress. In the sessions she sat with her jumper pulled up over her head rocking back and forth weeping. Things took an even more sinister turn when she began to make suicidal attempts and to report hallucinatory experiences. Ultimately she was admitted to a psychiatric hospital and therapy was discontinued.

Money's theory of vandalised lovemaps might go some way to explain why the experience of being sexually abused would make Clara likely to suffer from sexual symptoms, but it would not explain the wealth of other symptomatology she experienced. Some have argued that traumatic experiences in childhood produce lasting neurological damage (de Zulueta 1993) but this explanation does not ascribe any particular pathogenic power to sexual as opposed to other forms of abuse. Certainly there are cultural expectations that childhood experiences of sexual intrusion by older adults are inevitably traumatogenic and, increasingly, cultural sanctioning of a particular kind of emotional experience as offering curative properties. Clara definitely held these expectations. From a psychological perspective, analytic writers have reflected on the disruptions to the basic system for attachment to a care-giver, which all babies possess, and which normally involves an oscillation between attachment and exploration from a secure base (Holmes 1993). In Clara's case, intense attachment occurs but this is not experienced as providing either a secure base or sufficient emotional nourishment for her to venture back into the world. Fonagy (Fonagy *et al.* 2000) discussed the idea that patients find the experience of being abused so horrifying that they cannot bear to think of their abuser as minded to abuse them. To avoid this they attack their own mind and reduce what he calls their reflective self-function.

Perhaps some synthesis of these ideas can be attempted using the idea of erotic imagination. The specific trauma of sexual abuse in childhood is erotic. Children experience this trauma differently at different ages. Very young children are bewildered and sometimes physically hurt by sexual abuse. Although they are capable of erotic experiences they probably do not classify sexual abuse as erotic and take harm principally from pain, injunctions to secrecy and a shame which their abuser educates them to feel. Older children do appreciate the erotic nature of the experience and so must wonder if they too feel erotic – to the extent that they do, or are persuaded that they do, a wide range of painful imaginings become available and are often encouraged by their abuser. Some are dominated by the idea that they 'asked for it', others are filled with rage, which may also have appeared on the face of the abuser. A third group form a horrifying ambivalent bond with their abuser. These deformations of the erotic imagination are always determined by the interpersonal context of the abuse. By the same token the erotic can therefore come to fill all, or particular, later interpersonal relationships. For example, the result may be repeatedly picking abusive men for later relationships, or developing a sexually frozen or provocative style. These interpersonal failures then reactively poison the self's relationships with itself, producing the wide-ranging deficits which, for example, Clara demonstrates.

Mate selection, marriage, early adult life

Notwithstanding great changes both in the role of women and in the social expectations of sexuality, as a culture we prize and promote the female capacity to catch and keep a man. This social task, with its implied sexual activity, dominates much literature both popular and serious. Thus the single older woman is often regarded as bitter, because passed over, or irresponsible, like an adolescent. In some areas, particularly of high social privilege, the expectation of marriage has begun to break down sufficiently that reproduction with or without a male partner has begun to replace it as the new imperative. It remains to be seen to what extent this pattern of chosen late single parenthood will spread.

Certainly, despite social pressure, women are unconvinced of the advantages of marriage. Men want to be married more than women and this is true across all races and ethnic groups (Tucker and Mitchell-Kernan, 1995). Men's reasons for this desire are sound, since men benefit from improved quality of life, mental health, and professional opportunities if they marry (Dunphy 2000). Women, on the other hand, carry the greatest burden of domestic labour, even if they work full-time and earn more than their partners. Marriage therefore remains structured around the wife's dependency and flourishes best in cultures where gender inequities are greatest (Dunphy 2000). What do women look for in a mate? There is quite a lot of survey evidence to support a fairly clear set of characteristics. Women prefer men who are taller (Gillis and Avis 1980), have stable employment histories, higher educational attainment and older age (Buss 1994). Some sociobiologists have argued that women's mate selection is aimed at maximising their partner's reproductive fitness in the provider role. Other sociobiologists have suggested that entertainment value – capacity to talk, empathy, artistic skills may also be selected by females (Miller 2000). On a more cultural level, the numerous images and descriptions of attractive men to which young women are exposed will tend to channel their choices. Individual factors are also involved and psychoanalytic analyses, particularly of unfortunate mate choice (Benjamin 1988), have demonstrated the involvement of continuing parentally directed wishes.

For whatever reasons then – biological, psychological and possibly above all social- women seek out a mate. Their current strategies for achieving this aim are conceived of, by us, as age-old but in truth have not had to be deployed in quite this way for very many generations. Arranged marriages, or selections amongst a highly restricted class of suitable men, have far more often been culture's ways or pairing up its young adults, constraining their erotic ambitions to selections from a small pool of suitors. Our story of 'Mr Right' is that he waits out there amongst the teeming myriads, the romantic needle in the haystack of lonely hearts advertisements. The Mr Right of earlier fiction (for example Darcy in Jane Austen's *Pride and Prejudice*) was an exciting stranger come to disrupt the established order of spinsterhood or of preordained marital liaison.

Often therefore it is helpful for therapists who have patients struggling with this life stage, to remind them that in an era of 'plastic sexuality' (Giddens 1992) failure to find a man by the romantically prescribed route may be largely a social rather than a personal difficulty, albeit no less painful as a result. The trouble with the modern Mr Right is that since he is selected in fantasy from everybody, he has to be exactly right. The erotic image of becoming partnered is purely a matter of selection, a sort of extended shopping trip. White western culture finds the notion that erotic emotional attraction is systematically constructed by the mutual imagination of the partners after a marriage has been contracted – common among orthodox Jews, Muslims and some Hindu cultures – difficult to understand.

Female sexual pleasure in adult life

The sexual question for women in stable unions is to what extent they will be able to express a fully sexual life within that union. Clinical and survey evidence suggests that this is by no means a certainty. Explanations for female sexual discontent within marriage have been proposed by a number of commentators.

Since the mature genital relation is prized by psychoanalytic commentators, and is most usually defined by them as heterosexual union in the context of a stable marriage, there is an appreciable analytic literature on sex in married life and its failings. Kernberg (1995) is the most cogent and passionate writer in this field. For him mature sexual love involves a harmonious fusion of aggressive and libidinal urges, with admixtures of excitement, desire, tenderness and tolerance of ambivalence. Kernberg makes clear the link between this achievement and other emotional achievements, such as the depressive position. Evidently for Kernberg a romantic notion of the couple passionately in love is at the core of a general view of well-being. Not all marriages are paradigms of sexual harmony and Kernberg draws on Dicks (1967), who argues that couples form a compromise pattern out of the best fit of their psychopathologies. Thus the marriage allows both parties to bury in the unconscious of the other repressed and unacceptable material. Sometimes this mutual locking up of skeletons in each other's cupboard may have symptomatic consequences for the marriage – for example, to render it sexless. Thus for Kernberg and Dicks unresolved early conflicts are the sources of female sexual dysfunction in marriage.

These analytic explanations of sexual difficulties in marriages suffer from two main weaknesses. First, they tend to take a male-centred view of sexual expression and its desirable frequency, which blinds them both to the possibility that standards of sexual satisfaction may vary between the sexes. Their male perspective also blinds them to the possibility that the more general dissatisfactions consequent on a 'woman's lot' may be structurally entombed within the heteropatricarchal institution of marriage, rendering sex a matter of sleeping with the enemy. A second problem with the analytic perspective is that it tends to desexualise sexual distress, seeing it as inevitable evidence of deeper difficulties. This move sadly pathologises sexually 'dysfunctional' women – a group whose dysfunction is often mainly that they don't want as much sex as their partners.

From a heterosexual perspective Freud's problems with the clitoris are quite understandable. Although no discussion of female sexuality can ignore the clitoris, arguably the second most reliable organ of female sexual satisfaction after the brain, it does not seem well placed to give female pleasure during heterosexual coitus. We have seen how evolutionary psychologists have struggled to explain the function of the clitoris. Some (Gould and Lewontin 1979) have given up and suggested it is an irrelevance. Others (Taylor 1997) suggested it was never intended to be stimulated in coitus. The idea that sexual intercourse is not biologically intended to be a pleasant experience for women prevailed in Victorian times. Some doctors made considerable sums of money by anaesthetising women so that their husbands could have sexual relations with them. Interestingly, at the same time Maines (1999) demonstrates that vibrators, clearly adapted for clitoral stimulation, were openly on sale to physicians who used them to stimulate women for medicinal purposes, relieving their husbands of their task.

Dissatisfactions with coitus and distaste for penetrative sex (Dworkin 1981) has led some straight women to have discussions about the potential for female sexual pleasure which arise from the eroticisation of the whole body surface. They have, for those who have wished to continue sexual relations with men, invoked images of sexual union in which active thrusting is replaced by gentler movements (Hite 1976). Often such accounts betray considerable envy and idealisation of lesbian sexuality (Merkin 1996) although others (Greer 1969) have held out for the pleasures of penetrative sex.

The pattern of female anxiety and worry about their lack of appetite for sexual relations with their partners, combined with apparent male indifference, or simply male demand for sexual relations, is one which is clinically common. Therapeutic efforts in relation to women who are anorgasmic, or who have low sexual desire, are outlined in the chapter on sex therapy. However, the case of Abigail is given here to emphasise that for many women sexual satisfaction in relationships may not be an uncomplicated affair:

> Abigail presented alone with a complaint of anorgasmia. She had read an article in a magazine which had set her thinking. She described her partner as a nice bluff man, not given to self-reflection. They had two children aged 8 and 12. Abigail was orgasmic during masturbation but had always found it impossible to be orgasmic during sex. Further questioning revealed that Abigail never discussed sex with her partner and, in consequence, never had sexual experiences with him that were pleasurable. Encouraged by her therapist she did discuss things with her partner and, to an extent, her sexual life improved. However, at a later joint visit Abigail and her partner were still dissatisfied. Abigail recounted how her partner had asked her to look at pornographic material with him which she did not like. Abigail's partner for his part found the more extended foreplay Abigail preferred rather boring and sometimes found he lost his erection.

Abigail's experience with her partner echoes a more general problem with female discussions and anxieties over heterosexuality. Largely they have been conducted without much enthusiasm or involvement from men (although there are exceptions; see Jardine and Smith (eds) 1987). Sometimes this is because men have been excluded, but more recently a cultural story has begun to be told in which men are not expected to be able to or to want to be involved in discussions of sexual matters. In a revival often backed by biological arguments about brain structure men are constructed as the doers and women as the talkers. To be sure, this return of sexual essentialism paints male failure in female tasks more negatively than before but there is also a revival of traditional-sounding ideas which centre on the civilising and containing influence of women – an influence now viewed as a social task which women are shirking at a cost to society, in order to have careers. In the sexual sphere many (but not all) women have had little success with the task of persuading men to engage in civilising or feminising sex. They have settled either for the status quo or at best introduced mechanical variations during sex or have after sex adopted the role of a neo-maternal courtesan.

Extramarital affairs

Until recently women were more likely to be faithful in marriage than men. Reasons for this may have included needs for economic security, disproportionate social disapproval of female philandering, and the moral conservatism of women themselves. More recently women's rate of extramarital relations has risen and evened up with the male rate (Giddens 1992). The reasons behind this increase in female infidelity are probably various. Even the sociobiologists seem divided on whether female sexual wandering can be an adaptive strategy (Buss 1994) or should be very limited (Posner 1992). Culturally, standards and expectations of monogamy vary widely, but all cultures police women to an extent. Probably male needs to ensure paternity are involved. Markowitz and Ashkenazi (1999) argue that early agrarian societies which began to keep animals developed notions of correct behaviour based on the requirements of animal husbandry.

Women in stable relationships give a range of reasons for having extramarital affairs, including some which are centred on the couple. One example given is that the affair is being used to generate a crisis or to negotiate a way out of the relationship. Other reasons cited for having affairs include factors such as boredom, sexual incompatibility, and being flattered by the attentions of a worthy suitor. Psychological accounts of extramarital affairs do not in general move much beyond this list. Psychoanalytic writers have unsurprisingly tended to pathologise the wish to have affairs (e.g. Kernberg 1995). While patients may on occasion present with complaints related to a repeated tendency to start affairs which they do not feel are beneficial it is often hard to distinguish between the effects of a sexual preference which is socially disapproved of and a genuine 'condition' such as 'nymphomania', so popular in American analytic literature in the 1950s.

Whatever else an affair may be it is almost always a sign of the woman's capacity to imagine something else with a new man and of her incapacity to imagine that something else with her present partner. This needs to be taken into account when working with couples, or individual women, who have affairs and are having difficulties in handling them. Husbands are attempting to understand what has caught the erotic imagination of the woman when they ask in fury if the lover is/was better in bed than they are. This anxious question sometimes seems to miss the mark when women say that their lover is, for example, more attentive or more sensitive rather than 'better in bed'. Whilst the advantage the lover offers may not be a matter of sexual technique it is often erotic in the wider sense. Therapeutically, describing the erotic bond imagined in the affair is helpful to the woman. Sometimes the original relationship can be repaired with this new knowledge. Sometimes a new relationship or no relationship is the outcome.

Pregnancy, childbirth and lactation

From a psychoanalytic perspective, pregnancy and the birth of a son represents the normal female triumph. In her pregnancy the woman shows she has possessed the paternal penis and with the birth of a son the castrated penis will be returned to her. Sadly, any thought that the decades of feminism since Freud's announcements have improved the situation can be sharply dismissed. Contrast accounts by some women that experiences of pregnancy, childbirth and breastfeeding represent an exquisitely sexual experience (Raphael-Leff 1991), with the (often male) expert discussions of exactly how soon after childbirth women resume sexual intercourse.

Bancroft (1989) is keen to dismiss the notion that lower female desire in pregnancy has any biological basis. Instead he ascribes reduced female sexual wishes to taboos or fantasies about the safety of sexual activity. After childbirth both the demands of parenthood and perinatal genital trauma may discourage desire. Childbirth is often seen as a time when sexual dysfunction may start but Robson *et al.*'s (1981) study shows that almost all women do resume sexual intercourse by the twelfth week post-partum although quite a few have intercourse less frequently than before. Notwithstanding Hawton *et al.*'s (1986) discussion of psychosexual difficulties, he lays heavy stress on ensuring the resumption of sexual activity after childbirth, a resumption described by him as a return to normal function. Of course 'normal function' is a term open to dispute.

Only in the case of breasts, perhaps because of the visibility of them and their acknowledged potential as erogenous zones for men, is there expert acknowledgement of sexuality in childbearing. Breastfeeding is analysed as a sexual activity. Commenting that the breasts are sensual organs and that nipples are erect during both suckling and sexual arousal Bancroft (1989) argues that breast-feeding may produce either guilt or enjoyment in women and may produce vicarious sexual excitement or troubling jealousy in men. These mainly male discussions of sexuality and pregnancy seem entirely dominated by the urgent task of making women fit for further sexual activity as fast as possible. Collectively a massive failure of erotic imagination has occurred which prevents any benign consideration of erotic bonds between either parent and their child, nor is there any positive way of speaking of a different erotic relation between the parents now that a baby is present. The reason everything is couched in terms of a return to normal (i.e. previous) function may partly be a collective horror of eroticism directed towards or enacted in the presence of children.

The failure to acknowledge any erotic connection to children does little to help mothers who are revolted in a sexual way by the experience of pregnancy. Where such conditions are commented on, the analysis is generally in terms of deep failures of maternal identification (McDougall 1995) rather than in terms of failures of sexual energies. Yet crediting Welldon (1988) and Kaplan's (1974) argument for an enlargement of the scope of female sexuality, taking the whole body surface and experience of femininity into account, leads logically to describing some maternal difficulties in childbearing in sexual terms. Welldon does so but steps immediately to the extreme of perversions, citing situations where a child's body is treated as though it were an extension of the mother's body. Raphael-Leff, in her path-breaking work on childbearing (1991), goes furthest to delineate the complex web of fantasies and biological experiences involved, but sadly often not in sexual terms:

> Portia presented for help with her second child whom she hated. The baby was 4 months old and Portia had already seriously considered having her adopted. The degree of Portia's disgust was evident in her face and her whole body posture as she held the child and announced, in a theoretical sort of way, that she was sure the experience of being mothered by her was

not good for the child. Portia had had no such difficulties with her first child and had thoroughly enjoyed childcare. 'It's because he was a boy,' she said firmly. 'I ordered another boy but I didn't get one this time.' Over a number of sessions Portia came more clearly to understand her palpably sexual disgust for her second child in terms of her fantasy that this girl baby was going to suck her up, or force her to have sexual experiences she labelled lesbian. However, although her childcare seemed less forced, she never lost her distaste for her child. This fixity is consistent with the 'sexual' nature of her revulsion, as sexual tastes and distastes tend to be relatively permanent.

Later adulthood

The biological process called the menopause generally marks an important transition for women. Biological changes which result from lower oestrogen levels may make penetrative sex less easy for women and, consistent with this, statistics chart a decline in sexual interest but no decline in rates of masturbation. Notwithstanding, women retain the capacity for sexual excitement and orgasm and some women have tried to reclaim the menopause as a time for personal and sexual re-evaluation (Greer 1991). Debates about the relentless march of biology tend to neglect a number of important factors. Prime amongst these factors which condition sexual behaviour in old age are cultural stereotypes about sex in older people. Here, embedded in a general aura of disgust, double standards apply, with greater sexual licence extended to older men than to older women. The effect of this double standard has been to spawn a massive industry ministrating to the preservation of the aging female body in a state of perpetual youthfulness. The benefits of conforming to social expectations are evident in that quite large numbers of women report significant improvements in their self-image and sexual functioning following judicious cosmetic surgery (Klassen *et al.* 1996).

Conclusion

Descriptions of female experience through the life cycle draw on the accounts of successive generations of women whose experience of female sexuality has been radically different. As a result the scope of the imaginative possibilities open to them has varied. Our culture's attitude towards female sexual expression has altered and along with it the experience of successive generations of women. In this sense older women are a living history lesson and an example of the effect of culture on behaviour and experience. The rhetoric of women's natural sphere was instituted in the nineteenth century, when cities expanded and domestic and public spheres were separated. Soon women's natural domesticity was regarded as transhistorical. To overthrow this, women had to challenge the role of biology in shaping their nature and many did so by denying any role to biological factors. Recently, scientific research has restated the importance of biological factors on both psychological experience and biological form (Kimura 2000). It remains to be seen how much the pendulum will swing back towards biologically driven arguments. Sexuality has been an area where the most immoderate rubbish has often been written in relation to gender difference. This need not be the case because the great advantage of sexuality is that it is indisputably a biological process subject to natural selection. It has unquestionable psychological impacts and is impossible if psychological factors are sufficiently adverse. Lastly, it is strongly regulated and policed culturally. This should mean that sexuality as a topic is ideally placed to force a consideration of all these elements whenever the condition of women or men is discussed. When therapy or social reform are in prospect balancing these factors in an even-handed way it helps to guard against fanaticism. The transformative potential of the erotic imagination can then be employed to provide the energy for change when that is deemed necessary.

The male sexual lifecycle

'Whatever masculinity is it is very damaging to men.' (Formani 1991, cited in Giddens 1992)

As the quote beginning the section suggests, many writers in recent times take the view that male sexual psychology is profoundly troubled. Psychoanalytic commentators view these troubles as consequent on men's need to dis-identify from one parent in order to attach to another. A more psychobiological (but one Freud would certainly not have disagreed with) view might suggest that evolutionary forces have shaped elements of male sexuality for a habitat in which competition for scarce resources was paramount. Now this same sexuality must find its expression in cultural organisations in which there is relative plenty and co-operative activity is far more important. Thus a seeming over-abundance of sexuality must constantly be curbed and constrained more or less efficiently by cultural forces. The psychic experience of this constant chafing always seems uneasy and the anger and resentment it generates always feels dangerous.

Therapeutic work with men in relation to sexual issues is often much harder than therapeutic work with women. Men may often talk about sex in the locker room but it appears that they only rarely talk about it in a way which gives access to less acceptable hopes and fears – ones which require a mutually trusting relationship to reveal. Furthermore many men regard their female partner as their main confidant (O'Connor 1992), but in relation to sexual matters their partner may not be the neutral listener needed. Thus while men, unlike women, often come to therapy with quite detailed knowledge of sexual technicalities and names for body parts they often lack ways of talking about the ambivalences of sexual experience. The tendency of men to use rule-based (Kohlberg 1966) rather than relationship-oriented (Gilligan 1982) moral reasoning means that men do not soften a judgemental stance to their own or others' perceived sexual infractions even when the interpersonal context of those infractions is elucidated during therapy. For therapists this means that increased anger is a side effect of therapy with men which should not be taken lightly, especially if it is enduring. Men may also prefer physical treatments or may select from the range of talking treatments those which seem most practical or immediate.

Early development

That boys are sexual from an early age is visually evident because they experience relatively frequent erections. They also experience the power of their penis to give them pleasure and reassurance. The sight of small boys clutching their penis at times of stress in nurseries is common enough and generally treated as an endearing one. Ramsey (1943) found that later on a majority of boys, just prior to puberty, would describe the occurrence of erections in both pleasant and unpleasant, but arousing, situations. As puberty sets in, erections become more tied to sexual stimuli and adult men do not as often experience erections set off by non-sexual stimuli. Throughout childhood boys masturbate more than girls and commentators have suggested that this is a consequence of the greater visibility, even handle-ability, of the penis. Boys are also much less socially discouraged from masturbating than girls and this must also be a factor. However, not all boys who masturbate are dealt with permissively. Morris (1997) documents the ill-effects in adult life which result from the shaming and humiliation of boys punished for masturbation.

Boys display a range of other behaviours which we label masculine from an early age. These include rough and tumble play and consistently greater interest than girls in sexual matters. Studies showing that the effect of elevated male hormone levels in young girls is to produce a tendency in them to greater aggressive and tomboy behaviour and increased sexual interest (Berenbaum *et al.* 2000; Berenbaum 1999) have also been taken to indicate that much of male development may be hormonally driven. What might be the nature and difficulties of the erotic imagination for boys in our culture? In girls and women the problem was of a secret sexuality defined mostly by prohibition. In boys and men the up front nature of sexuality makes imagining easy but can also predispose to a failure of elaboration, of sensitivity, making for an energetic but crude aesthetic.

Psychoanalytic writers and other commentators have done much to show that, while biological influences are important, masculinity and male sexuality are strongly socially conditioned. Freud's psychological account of the origins of masculinity focuses on the progressive restriction of an innately varied sexual life by a stately progress through psychosexual stages to the horrific moment of the realisation of castration and the resultant submission to/identification with the father. Subsequent sexual successes and failures are the result of the degree to which the boy negotiates the giving up of mother's love and his capacity to accept the fact of castration. A consequence of this account is the idea that at the root of masculinity is a hatred of femininity born of fear (Freud 1937). Later writers (for example Horney 1967) retained the idea that men hated women but suggested the hatred was based on envy of their capacities. They argued that men hated women for what they could do (make babies) and not only for what they lacked (a penis).

There is much work by social theorists to back up the idea that masculinity is founded on hatred and repudiation. Plummer's (1999) detailed observations in the playground have demonstrated that social mechanisms for establishing hetero-patriarchy in boys are both repressive and negative. The fear of homophobia haunts boyhood and profoundly influences how boys style and present themselves to others. This fear predates knowledge of homosexual identity and instead is used to target and stigmatise 'girlie behaviour'. Thorn comments that by fourth grade, definitions of acceptable masculine pursuit have settled around team sports. Playing with girls, especially in games like skipping or gymnastics, is seen simultaneously as a sign of immaturity, of being girlish and being a fag (Thorn 1993, cited in Plummer 1999). Despite general support for encouraging boys to participate in team sports, there is evidence that they can promote aggression (Pronger 1990) and homophobia (Messner 1992).

In view of this it is not surprising that, in Thorn's words, 'boys who enter puberty earlier tend to have higher self-esteem and prestige and a more positive body image than other boys of the same age' (Thorn 1993:140). Sexual maturity, heterosexuality and socially acceptable masculinity have become united into a single identity largely negatively defined as being not something else. Stoller (1975), along with Chodorow (1978) and others, discusses underlying reasons for this. Men, he argues, (unlike women) must dis-identify with mother, which is a tricky business, and so male identities are both more rigid and more fragile than female ones. The consequent early anxieties about successful separation from femaleness make for dread of being gay or being female. Missing from Stoller's analysis is any discussion of the possibility that the need to dis-identify from mother is not pre-given but is itself a playground imperative retrospectively imposed on the developing boy. For whatever reason, though, the outcome of these factors is to ensure that the overt or covert thought not far from each erotic encounter is an anxious fear of becoming female, becoming penetrable.

Puberty and adolescence

Puberty follows a fairly predictable pattern in men. The penis and testes start to grow and pubic hair then begins to appear, about a year later the first ejaculation occurs. At some point during this time the pubertal growth spurt begins and lasts for about 18 months. Towards the end of this time the voice begins to break. Increased interest in sexual matters is sharp and quite closely linked to androgen levels (Udry *et al.* 1986) although in later life the link between circulating testosterone levels and sexual desire is not invariable. Peak sexual responsiveness is reached within two years of puberty (Bancroft 1989).

Despite this high level of biological preparedness, adolescent boys are subject to severe social anxieties in relation to their first sexual experiences. Rubin (1989) showed that as many as 90 per cent of college men were dissatisfied with their first sexual encounter. Person (1999) comments that adolescent boys experience arousal and desire at a time when they are not socially or psychologically equipped to maintain a secure sexual relationship. The psychology of the pack and continuing fears of femininity may favour portrayals of women as disdainful quarry. Sometimes these ideas can develop into both adolescent 'trying it on' and more coercive strategies for obtaining sex. Yet, as Vance (1984:386) points out, sex itself often involves activities such as taking off clothes associated with being with mother and being a baby. The erotic fantasy of the zipless fuck may be an attempt to avoid these apparently infantilising aspects of sex. Even with these strategies, for many adolescents, sex may signify both a triumph over the threat of childhood and the unlooked-for return of the threat.

Even when puberty is complete the fear of homosexuality haunts adolescents. Even choosing heterosexual activity is in itself partly related to rejecting a gay identity. Much of the function of male sexual activity is to generate sex talk with other boys after the event. Plummer points out that adolescence represents a major switch in the policing of the behaviour of boys. Enforced segregation from girls is turned into enforced and policed interaction with them. At its worst, the outcome is that girls, who were formerly avoided as companions, are now conquered sexually in order to prove that boys cannot afford to be thought homosexual (that is effeminate, or like women):

> Timothy said he was awaiting trial for rape. In truth he had been arrested on 'suspicion of rape' and the police were making further enquiries. The exaggeration was rather typical for

Timothy, who liked to hold centre stage. He had gone to a party with some friends and had taken quite a lot of cocaine. They had all gone back to his room with some girls with whom they had been flirting. More drinking and probably more drug-taking followed. Timothy said that one of the girls asked him to have sex with her and he had taken off his clothes but passed out before sex occurred. Apparently the girl's story was that she had been raped by Timothy while she was incapable of escape and had never asked him to have sex with her. In the consulting room he was worked up and fidgety. He reminded the therapist of a young child who might be clutching his penis. He was worried that his reluctance to tell the police about all aspects of his evening might have prejudiced his case. He was also concerned that his mates would avoid him. He would be seen as too dangerous if he had raped a girl. He also worried he might be teased as incompetent if he had fallen asleep before having sex with her. Certainly his friends had evaporated at the first sign of trouble and he was furious at being let down by them. Defiantly he said, 'she'd never have called rape if I had really fucked her'.

Timothy is caught between a rock and a hard place. His parents, his mates and the girls have all abandoned him to his fate, which depends now on mysterious police enquiries. Each group deserts him because he cannot be what they need him to be – neither the dutiful son to his parents, nor one of the lads, nor even the successful sexual adventurer. Denied any positive feedback for his identity as male which is not accompanied with an implied threat of humiliation and shame if he fails, he resorts to anxious posturing and relaxes into verbally attacking women – a strategy for which his companions have always rewarded him in the past.

Adult sexuality

The domain of adult male sexuality is so large that only a small part of it can be covered here. The main theme is the repeated observation that, male privilege notwithstanding, men's sexuality is ruled over by rigid but contradictory social controls. As a result the main pathologies associated with male sexuality result from the aversive consequences of social violations, some of which are unavoidable. Male sexual imagination is at once encouraged and chained and this can be seen in the policing of the male gaze, of courtship rituals and of the penis.

The male gaze

Once men are adult they are expected, to a large degree, to conform to a fairly close set of stereotypes about the nature of their sexuality. Many societies treat male sexual desire as a force requiring external regulation. In the west this requires a certain discipline of the gaze, combined with dress codes for women. In other countries the onus is on the woman to be dressed in a way which is not sexually provocative. In all countries desire, and the gaze that betrays it, is policed:

> A supervision group discussed the sexual jealousy of one of its member's patients. The patient had been hit by his wife for staring at a girl in the street. Views in the supervision group were sharply divided about what constituted legitimate and non-legitimate looking. A consensus emerged eventually that, if a man was walking down the road with his girlfriend he could look at an attractive woman but not to the extent that this involved moving his head as well as his eyes.

Studies of male sexual fantasy tend to confirm the cultural stereo-type of an unrelated impersonal desire that requires control. Person (1999) characterises male sexual fantasy as explicitly sexual and often impersonal. She adds that there may be themes of domination and it is relatively common to fantasise about forcing a woman to have sex. Person also notes that male sexual fantasy may also involve interest in multiple partners, lesbian sex or sado-masochistic sexual fantasies but she regards these as abnormal – evidence of failure to resolve the Oedipus complex. Kernberg (1995) on the other hand allows a much wider scope for the entry of polymorphously perverse elements into male sexual fantasy. Fantasy, the inner gaze, cannot be overtly socially policed but many men provide their own internalised policing and are as a result distressed by their fantasy life.

Therapeutically the most obvious difficulties encountered in the male gaze are problems related to its social regulation – those who look or wish to look at things they should not. To an extent society provides men with regulated opportunities to look and to fantasise but never without a repressive charge. Many men experience the policing of the male gaze as restrictive and demeaning. Something of this feeling may lie behind the strongly negative reactions to the political correctness that requires the removal of sexually explicit posters in the workplace. Men experience this as an attack on their erotic freedom, as curbing their erotic imaginations. This is because pornography is the erotic imagination made concrete and despite the honourable but growing exceptions of genres directed at gay men, lesbians and straight women, is to an overwhelming degree the production of erotic images directed at the male gaze.

The use of pornography may constitute a boy's first experience of pubertal sexual longing. Often its first use is a matter of bravado, the pleasure in illicit transgression being far more important than sexual arousal. Hardy (1998) documents how, when adolescents progress to the self-consciously sexual use of magazines, the context in which they are acquired changes. The gang of boys egging one of their number on to go into a sex shop gives way to a single purchaser acting secretly and with a sense of shame. Once a man is involved in relationships then a number of accommodations with the use of pornography may occur. Some men successfully introduce pornography into their sex lives although women may be reluctant or relatively uninterested. Others continue to use pornography in secret and tend to talk about its function as providing something different from the relationship. They may talk of it as offering variety or release from sexual pressures:

> Derek consulted because of anxiety over his use of pornography. He came from an orthodox Jewish background. When young he had discovered a pornographic magazine used by his father and stolen it. Later buying pornography was part of dare games with other children and partly a sexual activity. He married the girl who had been intended to be his bride within the community for a long time and had a 'satisfactory' sex life. However he still used pornography 'for a lark'.

Although men often cite sexual variety as a reason for using pornography this variety is achieved within a strictly limited series of storylines. Although not often raped the woman is mostly depicted as powerless in the face of male desire. Hardy produces possibly the most amusing example of this genre (Hardy 1998:84) when he cites the story of the vegetarian Alison who ultimately agrees to fellate a masterful and overpowering man with the despairing cry, 'But you know I don't eat meat.' Other common themes include stories of women who, because they are sexually frustrated, have voracious sexual appetites and virgins who, although initially reluctant, are ultimately overwhelmed by sexual desire as a result of sexual initiation. These themes are analysable in terms of Person's theory (1999) that men create a fantasy of the sexually omni-available women to compensate for their experiences of frustration at the hands of the mother.

Some social commentators argue that one of the harms of pornography is that it traps men in a debased form of sexuality. Thus for Segal (1994) eternal pornographic penile readiness traps men into a superhuman standard of sexual performance. Others (Morris 1997) suggest that it develops a preference for the picture perfect women portrayed in the magazines and frustration that these women are in short supply. Therapeutically the most common complaint men present with is one of using pornography compulsively. This complaint has perhaps become more common with the availability of pictures on the internet:

> Derek's use of pornography had not really troubled him over the years although he felt bad about keeping it from his wife, whom he regarded as too prudish ever to take an interest in that sort of thing. However it was repeated risky use of the internet at work which had lead to a consultation. At times he had been logged on for 6 hours. He was disappointed if he had an orgasm because he then might have to stop. Occasionally he had skin conditions of the penis consequent on irritation.

Searching for a helpful literature on the possible causes of Derek's compulsion reveals a range of answers. Pornography has been seen as compensating for the limitations of the penis (Moye 1985), resulting from a desperate attempt to allay fears of impotence, compensating for the declining social power of men, or compensating for absent female desire due to repression of female sexuality (Hardy 1998). More psychodynamically inclined writers have suggested that some aspects of pornography symbolise mother–infant interaction (Day 1988, cited in Hardy 1998) or that it compensates men for experiences of frustration and humiliation at the hands of mother. Psychoanalytic commentators are rarely pro-pornography (see, for example, Kernberg 1992; Kaplan 1979). Their commonest move is to compare compulsive use of pornography (recreational or occasional use is never discussed) to perversion. Ultimately the case against it is that psychically its use represents a hostile act of aggression and disaffiliation against an object. The aggression is thought to result from early damage to the structure of trusting relations. Interestingly, Stoller (1991), who did much to develop the theory that the core of perverse sexuality is hatred, became increasingly convinced that hatred lies at the core of all sexual excitement and in consequence took a progressively more liberal view of all kinds of non-standard sex, particularly pornography (Stoller 1991, 1993).

Moral opposition to pornography centres on two notions. First, that pornography incites men to violence against women and second, more contentious, that pornography is itself a form of violence against women. Both ideas have been hotly contested. Many studies have tried to test a link between using pornography and male violence. It seems that using pornography probably does cause predisposed men to be more violent (Malmouth *et al.* 2000) but in relation to the generality of men the findings are unclear. Pornography is probably preferentially used (particularly hard core pornography) by men who have lower socioeconomic class, have more repressive attitudes to women and are more likely to condone rape, all making it difficult to be sure that an association with violence is causal.

The more general idea that pornography is oppressive in itself to women is particularly associated with aspects of the feminist movement who struck out against male violence and the exploitation of women. A highly vocal and extreme exponent of this view was Andrea Dworkin (1981) whose views became ultimately so extreme that she argued that all penetration, depicted or actual, demeans and degrades. Against this strong condemnation of pornography sex-positive defenders, including defenders from the feminist movement, have tried to argue that pornography represents the exercise of legitimate free speech. They claim that its use enhances sexuality and individual well-being. The issues are well reviewed in Hardy (1998), who himself goes so far as to claim that pornography is a new form of female sexuality which men turn to for the rich imagery it provides. He argues that pornography tries to correct deficits in the capacity to talk about female eroticism. He centres his discussion on the lack of names for female body parts implying that pornographic representation helps to remedy this lack. The generally male production of pornography for a male readership makes Hardy's argument difficult to credit. However, his remarks are applicable to a growing genre of erotica by women and aimed at women.

Clinically and socially none of the more extreme positions adopted over pornography seem warranted. Its use is widespread through a massive range of societies and it seems to be enjoyed by men and by some women. Certainly pornographic images which are humiliating and degrading to women are associated with individuals who, and cultures that, support highly segregated gender roles, and the notion of separate spheres and the subjection of women. In such cultures rape is more common than in more egalitarian cultures (Hatfield 1996) and the same is true even of variations between states in America (Dutton 1988). However, it is difficult to see why pornography should be the cause of all these ills. It is more likely to be their consequence.

Therapeutically, social attitudes to pornography strongly condition the experience of men who complain of using it compulsively. Some feel they have a disorder which needs cure (a notion reinforced by the creation of a category for compulsive sexual behaviours including pornography; Kafka and Hennen 1999). Others feel both humiliated and shamed judging themselves by repressive social standards. A final group may or may not be overtly compliant with treatment but are secretly rebellious knowing they are right and society wrong. This group are the most likely to be reluctant attenders at clinics, often coerced into presentation by society's legal or social sanction against their preferred use of pornography, which might include internet access to illegal websites:

> Derek's experience of himself in this area was structured both around the notion that he had 'an illness' and around the alternative humiliating and shamed category of 'culpable pervert'. The immediate effect of the assessment was striking. His

pornography use escalated considerably. Telling his story in a medical setting acted, it seemed, as a kind of absolution partly allowing him to abdicate responsibility for his use of pornography on the grounds that he was doing all he could, and the matter 'was in medical hands'. Although Derek felt like a pervert in his own mind, in his assessor's mind he did not seem perverse. Her experience of him was of a warm sensitive quite sexy man who looked at one and the same time a bit grey and a bit little boy lost.

Therapy might have gone in a wide range of directions which were discussed by him and his therapist. Cognitive behavioural strategies aimed at helping Derek to control his wayward impulses could have been instituted although he balked at one strategy involving forced masturbation to satiety, claiming that such a moment would never come. A more psychodynamic approach, involving inspection of his childhood, was reluctantly passed up by him as he felt he would end up reliving *Portnoy's Complaint*. Ultimately, interestingly, he took up the offer of a treatment approach directed at his marriage. This line of thought proceeded from his increased willingness to question his initial firm statement that he would never consider talking about this aspect of his sex life with his wife. Therapy therefore focused on channelling Derek's erotic imagination into his relationship with his wife with whom, after a few sessions, he was able to discuss his use of pornography. His wife was accepting. Although she had no interest in pornography herself she readily agreed that their sex life was in disrepair and the couple agreed to make improving this one of their goals. Interviewed later Derek reported that his sex life had improved considerably and that his use of pornography was reduced. He felt he had become a more discerning consumer.

Hardy (1998) points out that pornography releases constraints on the male gaze because it authorises men to look and suggests that this authorisation can be seen by the way the model always looks back at the camera and out of the picture in invitation. Derek's use of pornography seemed to have two functions in relation to his erotic imagination. His compulsive use seemed to be a somewhat driven solution to the status of grey, little boy lost. Imaginatively, it failed to build up any complex aesthetic structures or develop any interpersonal connections, being simply a parade of images. His later use is more discerning. Images are selected, others rejected, and while still a solitary affair, his use of pornography is now based more on aesthetic criteria and probably for this reason is less compulsive. Derek was probably right to refuse the treatment option of producing satiation and habituation by forced masturbation as this might have violated his erotic imagination.

The male game – courtship and marriage

Society prescribes the acquisition of an occupation and a stable partner as the outcome of young male adulthood (Morris 1997). Although current social trends are to delay marriage, with an extended preliminary period of playing the field, the expectation is that this will end. Some men, however, find difficulty in making an ultimate choice. There is evidence that elements of mate choice are controlled genetically, having been selected for over evolutionary time. Male standards of female beauty – facial symmetry, hip–waist ratio, and male preferences for younger women are, it is argued, strategies learned in the distant past for ensuring a maximally fertile partner (Buss 1994). It is further argued that, within any available group of women, a male will select the most reproductively attractive one he is capable of retaining given his own group status.

Although it is likely that evolutionary factors still operate in mate selection there are more recent trends which will not yield to sociobiological analysis. Despite the known advantages of marriage for men (Morris 1997), the number of never-married and unhappy men is growing. In an unconscious parody of our consumer age Morris, for example, talks of 'single men in therapy [who] complain of not being able to find a quality woman with whom to establish a satisfying relationship'. Explanations for this state of affairs draw on both social and personal factors. One notion is that there are a number of new features of the courtship game which might prevent men attaining a satisfactory relationship. Giddens, (1992) for example, suggests that modern social arrangements require partners to achieve far more in their marital choices than just the formation of an acceptably amicable, economically stable, breeding pair. Instead sexual arrangements

are an act of identity formation. Possibly these changed requirements disadvantage men, who, Samuels (1999) argues, may have
given up emotional sensitivity in a bargain he terms the male deal,
in which they swapped empathy and relationship skills for temporal power. This cannot be the whole reason for men failing to
attain satisfactory relationships because temporal power has
advantages. Miller (2000) points out that modern consumer
society makes courtship skills and goods a commodity that can be
purchased by males (meals, necklaces, theatre tickets), who potentially therefore can trade lack in some fitness indicators (hunky
body) for plenty in others (wealth and status). Even so, the large
quantities of time that couples are expected to spend in each
other's company in our society make emotional deficits hard to
trade against and a storyline which depicts a woman choosing
between wealth and character in a man is well worn. To these
somewhat weighty considerations might be added the more
simple suggestion that difficulties in male courtship may also be
due now to the increasing reluctance of young women to enter an
estate which they do not perceive as especially beneficial to themselves.

For those men who do not attract a mate there are mixed
outcomes. Our culture does accord some status to single never-
married men: the happy bachelor can be an acceptable male role.
More often, though, permanently single men give every indica-
tion of living out socially and emotionally underdeveloped lives
compared to their married counterparts. For example, despite the
randy bachelor stereotype there is plenty of evidence to show that
marriage is the best way for a man to get access to regular sexual
intercourse (Schwartz and Rutter 1998).

Psychoanalytic commentators have tended to concentrate on
men's difficulties in settling down with a mate once she is found.
Braunschweig and Fain (1971), following Freud (1905b), suggest
that mothers are experienced as first stimulating and then frustrat-
ing by their boy children. This produces conflicts which make it
hard to integrate genital and tender needs and leads to ambivalence towards women who are either viewed as mothers (and so
forbidden because they belong to father) or whores (and so
unsuitable marriage material). Kernberg (1995) and Chasseguet-
Smirgal (1984a) suggest a different set of difficulties. If mother is
experienced as too seductive or gratifying then, they argue, the

boy may come to imagine his small penis could be as good as his father's penis. Such a boy does not fear castration and so does not identify with his father. As an adult he will either form dependent relationships with mother figures or become a sexually promiscuous seducer as a result of a failure of super ego formation.

Marriage, if and when it does occur, does not end the game. Infidelity has, for the most of western social history, been largely a male affair although women are now catching up. To evolutionary theorists marriage is an evanescently recent event. Miller (2000) points out that historically humans did not begin to put up with lifelong marriage until they no longer lived hand to mouth off the land. It was only once humans settled down behind a stockade that property, inheritance and exogamy became keys to tribal and family survival. Couples then had an economic incentive to continue co-operating after reproducing. Of all the potential social organisations for the mating game monogamy has never been the only, nor even the favoured, cultural structure. Indeed it is arguable that monogamy in the west was only ever a fictional affair since sexual double standards permitted men, until recently, a form of legitimised polygamy. Studies of male sexuality do point to a consistent predilection for variety and novelty and suggest this is evolutionarily programmed (Buss 1994).

With this in mind, psychoanalytic condemnation of men who 'play away' as in some way psychologically damaged may be rather historically short-sighted. Kernberg, while conceding that promiscuity in men may have many causes, gives the impression that all infidelity is pathological and results from 'incomplete identification with the paternal function'. He ignores the fact that from a cultural perspective, promiscuity in men within a stable couple relationship has always been both encouraged and proscribed. At present, in a movement counter to trends for sexual liberality in other contexts, it is increasingly condemned and curtailed. This is probably partly because more equal relationships between men and women make for multiple economic and personal problems when relationships break up and reform. In the past, unfaithful men risked far less. Women's financial dependency, socially and legislatively enforced, meant their behaviour was unlikely to destabilise the stability of their marital relationship. But altered social trends do not render extramarital sex pathological, just socially problematic.

Difficulties in negotiating the complexities of reconstituted families may have a sexual charge. Some of the anger which feeds the attacks men may make on former partners and occasionally children can be fuelled by rage over the sexual constraints imposed by the changed relationship. One common example occurs when the female partner adopts the moral high ground over a new girlfriend and, for example, refuses access to the children because of her existence. Men who have left, frequently also react very negatively when asked to behave like a guest in the original family home. They still feel like family and may feel free to take what their now ex-partners regard as liberties. In extreme situations some men attempt, or if things are very bad force, a continuing sexual relationship with their ex-partners. The common factor is that rightly or wrongly in such situations many men experience their personal sexual freedom as being crushed and demeaned by a partner turned vengeful mother/nanny.

In counterpoint to this bleak picture it is important to record that many men have a marriage and family life which represents a profoundly satisfying experience within which they grow and develop sexually and personally. While the extent to which that married life is also stimulating and enriching for the wife may be less easy to ascertain with certainty, many women describe large tracts of their marriages with evident pleasure.

The penis

A part of the thrust of the previous sections has been to represent male sexuality as, to an extent, a roving adventurous affair. The penis has become in our culture the emblem of this aspect of male sexuality. The penis becomes the emblem of the male erotic imagination successively invested with shifting identifications within and between groups of men. There are, for example, class differences in the way men use their penises. Men with lower socioeconomic status tend to prefer sexual intercourse over other forms of sexual expression such as masturbation. Men from higher socioeconomic groups masturbate more and are less promiscuous in their relationships. As well as these differences in sexual practice there are differences in the kind of reasons which men from different classes give to justify or set in context their sexual activities. Men from higher socioeconomic classes tend to appeal to sexual morality whereas those from lower socioeconomic classes tend to appeal to the idea of the naturalness of behaviour (Kinsey 1948, cited in Irvine 1990). These differences in behaviour and reasoning produce differences in the scope of different men's capacity for imagining erotic roles for themselves and their penises.

Thus the penis can be invested with a range of different qualities. One kind is rampant, autonomous, huge, animal and only satisfied by female flesh. It is owned by the male constructed as close to the earth. This desirable but dangerous prick lay behind the image of the black male rapist in America which resulted in many racist murders (Mitford 1977). The rampant primitive penis can turn into a wayward but loveable character that features in cartoons, sometimes as a messy accident-prone boy coyly requesting indulgence for its latest transgression. Set against this is the refined prick of the sensitive man. Discerning, suave and able to please, it features to an extent in female pornographic writing (Bright 1995) but not much in the mainstream of pornography directed at men. This prick, ever willing to stand up or down to order, brings roses and remembers to ask if the other person came. It can be contrasted with the pampered penis featured in reports by Segal (1990) of interviews with male clients of prostitutes. They announce that 'I go there because I can just lie down and leave it to the girls'. This penis is coaxed into performance and need pay no attention to the requirement to be object-related.

So, when Sayers (1986) comments that male adult identity is closely wrapped up in sexual performance, it turns out that there are many performances and consequently identities available to men. However, despite brief fads for conditions like sexual compulsivity syndrome (in which men try to curb their too-active sex lives), inspection of our cultural images, for example through the internet, reveals far more interest in reviving the flagging penis than in curbing the over-enthusiastic one. This is because the aspect of male identity, that is probably always present in every sexual performance is the threat of humiliation. It is as though the limp penis comes to represent all the humiliations and failures of infancy, of childhood in the playground and of adult life – humiliation grown even more corrosive because it is one which men are taught is unbearable.

Fred consulted after having been thrown out by his partner. He was furious when he came home one day to find his partner and her mother standing united in the kitchen with his possessions piled in front of them. It became suddenly clear to him that his partner had been complaining about aspects of their sex life to her mother and that the two of them had decided to humiliate him. He maintained this view even though he admitted that sex had not been discussed that day and that his wife's main complaint was that he was cruel to her and often stayed out with friends, drinking. In Fred's history was a sequence of failed relationships, all of which had ended in some form of humiliating rejection. He believed that women liked to humiliate men and particularly that he was an object of humiliation because he had an unusually small penis. As his life story was recounted it became clear that Fred, either literally or metaphorically, always had one hand covering his penis and the other balled into a fist. With women his strategy was to talk big, get them pissed, and make love with the lights out. The talking big continued during an ongoing relationship and was combined with a touchy vigilance for moments in which his partner might secretly be laughing at him. Fred tended to lord it over his partners because he thought that was the man's role. He came to a consultation but told his assessor that he could not return to further meetings. The waiting room was too humiliating. He tried to persuade his (male) assessor to agree that all men used prostitutes and ended up assuming that the assessor did too. He became jovial saying 'we'll show the tarts what's good for them', but left remarking darkly that if a prostitute commented on his penis he would make her regret it. Afterwards, the assessor felt curiously upset and cried.

Afterwards

Even after sex the debate will not end. The real challenge is explaining male post coital behaviour, going to sleep, watching football, anything but the woman's longed for heart to heart chat. It is as though, once the penis has stood down, the mind and imagination are withdrawn also. Doubtless evolutionary psychologists will, in due time, find a reason. Kernberg (1995) offers the suggestion that when men roll over they are demonstrating a normal narcissistic response to mother's own withdrawal and that by separating men are asserting their autonomy. He is keen this behaviour should not be devalued as evidence of incapacity in men. Doubtless men will find his thoughts reassuring!

Late adulthood

Even though they die younger in general, late adulthood comes later for men than it does for women. Their reproductive potential continues much longer and declines gradually and variably rather than suddenly. The trajectories of men's later lives are changing as our society moves away from the lifelong pair bonded relationship. Many men in later life have second families, and it is relatively common for the age gap between male and female partners to be large.

Biologically, as ageing proceeds there is decreased efficiency in erectile responses and tactile stimulation of the penis is needed to produce erection rather than purely psychical stimuli. Sexual thoughts also decline in frequency. Even so, sexual satisfaction in men generally remains at roughly the levels it was in middle age. Health issues may usher in a raft of sexual problems for men related to vascular disease or to diabetes (see Chapter 1 for an account). While society has less difficulty in acknowledging the sexually active older man than the sexually active older woman there may still be difficulties in persuading care-givers to acknowledge sexual needs in thinking about health care.

Conclusion

The section began with a vision of masculinity as problematic to itself. Analysts argue that this is a consequence of the task of moving from the world of mother to that of father. Sociobiologists contend that it results from an evolutionary process adapted to hominid rather than human experiences. Work on the playground experiences of boys highlights homosexuality and femininity as structuring anxieties for men. To these factors must be added another. In adult life, demanding expectations of male sexuality and masculinity are made but then subjected to repression in various forms, such as the control of gaze, and mating patterns increasingly structured at variance with other cultural messages promoting sexual licence. It is this double construction of masculine sexuality as natural but as requiring maintenance, and as unconfined but requiring regulation that does the damage. Therapists need an awareness of these contradictions in order to work in a balanced way with men. Feminist and analytic opprobrium merely threaten more shame and humiliation. Sociobiologically driven licence further alienates men from culture. Instead men need therapists who can honour masculinity without needing to idealise it. To do this involves finding a way to respect men's erotic imagination and to acknowledge that aggression and relatively unrelated sex are nonpathological parts of that imagination without falling into a collusive relationship which covertly or overtly demeans women.

6

Lesbians and gay men

Sexuality and identity

Gay men and lesbians claim an identity defined by their choice of sexual activities. It is an identity which seems to announce, first, what their minds turn to erotically. Straight men and women who are anxious about homosexuals are quick to pick this up and mirror it with the anxiety that a gay man or lesbian is thinking about them sexually. At first sight straight men and women are equally defined by their choice of sexual partner. However, most straight people asked to choose a single identity select something non-sexual, like skin colour, religion, occupation, place of abode. They take their sexual orientation for granted. It is not an identity because it is not sufficiently distinctive. Gay men and lesbians can pick out their sexual preference as giving an identity because it is less usual than heterosexual preference, but they also choose to pick out their sexual preference as their identity because it is an oppressed identity. The oppression of gay men and lesbians for their sexual choices forces them to concentrate on this aspect of their identity consciously. As a result, the erotic imagination of gay men and lesbians is often well developed although it is, also, always an erotic imagination formed in conditions of oppression. Concentrating on a sexual aspect of experience to define identity has advantages and disadvantages.

One problem with gay and lesbian identity is that it threatens to sexualise all parts of gay and lesbian life. Most of what gay men and lesbians do, cooking, working, watching TV and so forth, has little to do with sexual activity but can easily become sexualised, as the concept of the 'gay pound' (used to describe the purchasing preferences of gay men and the consequent marketing opportunities) reveals. It is true that there are ways of seeing things, attitudes to task distribution, and experiences at work which are unique to gay and lesbian experience. The distinctive nature of this experience is often, if traced back, attributable to changes in gender role expectations consequent on refusing to adopt the usual heterosexual pattern of living.

The normative nature of heterosexuality makes a sexual perspective one of a range which can be applied to experiences (and often not the first). But homosexual experience is often only viewed through a sexual perspective and this represents another problem with gay and lesbian identity – that it may be confining. Escaping from the problem of undue sexualisation and of reduced perspectives in discussions of gay and lesbian identity involves attempting the peculiar task of defining non-, or less, sexual aspects of a sexual identity. An example of such a balancing act can be found in the elaboration of the concept of camp best expounded by Sontag (1982) in her 'Notes on Camp', which represents a container fashioned by the erotic imagination in which sex is nowhere and everywhere present.

Confusion is taken to new heights in the phrase, sometimes used by therapists, 'issues of sexuality', which mainly refers to gay or lesbian orientation and all attendant matters. In this chapter some compromise has had to be made between including material which relates only to overtly sexual aspects of life and behaviour, such as is found in the chapter on heterosexuality, and including some parts of the huge amount of material about aspects of the lives of gay men and lesbians that are not directly sexual. In general a bias has been exerted towards discussing strictly sexual aspects of gay and lesbian experience.

Why are some people homosexual?

At various times homosexual object choice has been ascribed to genetic alterations, prenatal hormonal exposure, varieties of early upbringing, seduction by predators in adolescence, cultural forces which aim to mitigate overpopulation and opportunistic sexual rapacity. Even writings by gay men and lesbians on sex are often preoccupied with the debate about the 'cause' of homosexual orientation. This preoccupation is often charged with a covert or overt moral agenda. It may be argued that some causes make homosexual orientation blameless while others make it blameworthy. Findings suggestive of a biological foundation for sexual object choice have been taken by some to provide arguments for ending discrimination against, and moral opprobrium towards, gay men and lesbians. Generally causes which characterise sexual object choice as involuntary and by implication unalterable, are the ones which, it is argued, let gay men and lesbians off the moral hook. Causes which suggest choice or plasticity – often psychological causes – impose an obligation to reform and go straight. This idea is a mistake.

The cause of an activity can only be relevant to arguments about its moral standing if there is some reason to regard the moral standing of that activity as dubious or questionable from the start. For example, if someone commits a killing then the possible causes of that act – war, hatred, desire to end suffering, accident – may contribute to arguments about its moral standing because we begin to examine the matter from the perspective that killing other people is an evil that requires justification. Since neither homosexual orientation nor homosexual sex is evil their causal origin is irrelevant to their moral standing.

Biological theories about sexual object choice either focus on genetic or anatomical differences between gay men or lesbians and straight people. In general these studies have been subjected to severe scrutiny by other scientists and by theorists who probably wish generally to resist the notion of genetic or anatomical correlates for sexual behaviour. A number of genetic studies have been conducted which do tend to show a greater than chance degree of heritability for sexual orientation (Morris 1997). These findings are still very far from demonstrating either that homosexual object choice is entirely, or mostly, genetically driven in any individual, or that it is a factor in all individuals. Anatomical differences have been found in the brains of some gay men (Le Vay 1993) but again the findings are incomplete and possibly affected by the confounding variable of HIV status. Studies showing a preponderance of left-handedness have been linked to a putative early neuro-developmental cause (Lalumiere *et al.* 2000), and other work which measures the relative length of fingers may be relevant to lesbian orientation. Scientific work correlating homosexual orientation to anatomic genetic or neuro-developmental states of affairs is made difficult by problems with the definition of homosexual orientation and its discrimination from heterosexual orientation. Critics of the whole project of relating biological states of affairs to psychological or social ones have made much of these difficulties (Weeks 1985). That said, even though there are problems it is probably now possible to say that in some people, to some extent, biological factors are involved in determining object choice. In other people biological factors, strong or weak, may be overridden in either direction by cultural or psychological factors.

If homosexual orientation is genetically driven to any great extent then it must be subject to selection pressures and consequently to the process of evolution. Sociobiological theorists have had difficulty explaining homosexual orientation because it is presumed to reduce reproductive fitness and anything which does this should, over time, be selected out of the gene pool. Wilson (1975) suggests that homosexual orientation conferred advantages on the group (helping it bond, providing an extra pair of helping hands) and would therefore improve inclusive fitness and be preserved for that reason. Miller (2000) updates this argument and suggests a complex group mechanism involving selection for variability amongst offspring to reduce competition for scarce niches. However others have been sceptical. Bancroft (1989) considers that no sociobiological theory of any merit has yet been advanced to explain the persistence of homosexuality in the population. Dickemann (1995), reviewing Wilson's arguments, suggests that they are unlikely to be correct because the assumptions they make about reduced homosexual reproductive fitness and the social organisation of homosexual object choice are wrong. Even in our culture only certain people with homosexual object choice choose not to reproduce. In the past homosexual men and women may well have often had children. It seems probable therefore that, unlike biological theories of causation, the current state of sociobiological work on the origins of sexual orientation is little better than speculation.

Sociobiology provides an example of the way that universalising assumptions about homosexuality has led scientists astray in their theorising. Some cultural and social theorists have gone the other way and argued that homosexuality as an identity and a consolidated sexual preference is an invention of relatively recent times.

They have suggested that, prior to the definition and introduction (chiefly by psychiatrists) of the term homosexual in the nineteenth century, there was no consistent homosexual identity, only homosexual acts more or less proscribed, committed by individuals. This is a highly influential and widespread view (expositions can be found in Weeks 1985; Katz 1976 and McIntosh 1968). It is generally accompanied by epistemological and ontological beliefs which stress the distinction between words and the entities they describe, and question the idea of an objective world of distinct nameable objects.

There are severe philosophical difficulties with these views (see Mohr 1992 for a careful and complete refutation). Practical difficulties with this position can be revealed by inspecting one of the arguments advanced in its favour. This is the idea that homosexuality is a recent phenomenon, a suggestion supported by the contention that prior to the nineteenth century there was no term to describe homosexual identity. Mohr (1992) correctly dismisses this argument by pointing out that examples of homosexual identity can be discovered prior to the nineteenth century. He shows for example that records of the widespread practice of homosexual activity in Attic Greece describe the existence of some individuals whose homosexual practice was exclusive rather than (as for most Attic males) combined with heterosexual activity. The same is true, he points out, of compelled ritual fellation among the Sambian in Papua New Guinea. There a small group of males continue the practice while most become heterosexual. Despite the difficulties of reading between cultures, Mohr argues that a discernible entity, now called homosexual preference, can be traced through many cultures. This makes culturally specific causes of homosexual object-choice less likely.

The fierce debate over the existence of homosexual orientation in other cultures and times has had a negative effect on the field because it has detracted from careful studies of the way homosexual orientation expresses itself in different cultures. When studies of this sort are done (for example Serena Nanda's study of the Hijras of India, in Blackwood 1986) the variations between cultural organisations of homosexual orientation can be seen as variations on a theme. There are very few cultures in which homosexual orientation is freely permitted but many in which its existence is ritualised or formalised. Thus the homoerotic imagination

finds its expression in a range of circumscribed but often ingenious cultural forms.

When psychological theories of the origins of homosexual
orientation are considered, the familiar division between psychoanalytic theories and all others is again evident. In the past,
psychological theories of homosexual orientation have focused on
aspects of learning theory. Some variants of these are reviewed by
Ruse (1988). There is disagreement over the role of adverse experiences of heterosexuality, positive ones of homosexuality. Other
psychologists have proposed that sexual orientation is learned as
part of a sex-typed identity. None of these lines of thought have
proved fruitful, largely because they lack both specificity and
sensitivity. Many people who have had the supposedly causal
experiences do not become homosexual, many who do become
homosexual lack the hypothesised cause. Many theorists have
abandoned causal speculation in favour of delineating the experiences and difficulties of gay and lesbian people and researching
the cause, operation, and effects of homophobia.

Reading the wealth of psychoanalytic theorising about the cause
and nature of homosexual orientation is both painful and dispiriting. With only a few exceptions, and those more recently, psychoanalysts have chosen to view homosexuality in the most pejorative
terms and to seek out, as causal factors, early developmental cata-
strophes causing mental pain and moral failing. Fortunately Lewes
(1989) and O'Connor and Ryan (1993) have systematically read
this literature and criticised it. Since the publication of their work
a more liberal climate has to an extent prevailed, at least in some
circles. However, the higher reaches of the analytic community
continue to harbour overt homophobia. Kernberg (1992), for
example, who was until recently president of the international
association of psychoanalysts suggests multiple aetiologies for
male homosexuality, of greater and lesser degrees of pathology,
but ultimately sees all homosexual individuals as pathological.
Other analysts seem to occupy a middle position.

A paper by a leading liberal independent analyst will serve as an
example. Bolas's (1992) paper on 'cruising in the homosexual
arena' begins with a suggestion that in thinking about cruising, to
an extent heterosexuals might as well be being discussed as gay
men. Yet as the paper progresses Bolas's disapproval both of
casual sex and of 'the homosexual', a figure who appears repeat-

edly towards the end of the paper and replaces an initially cautious designation of 'some homosexuals', becomes evident. The otherwise exemplary work of Raphael-Leff (1997) bears the marks of a similar distortion.

Some commentators have tried to search the analytic literature for helpful theoretical input which may be used to treat patients (for example Burch 1989). However, much of this revisionary theory is achieved either by distorting or revising the central tenets of psychoanalysis (see Denman 2003 for this argument set out in detail in relation to Kleinian analysis and Jungian hybrids of it). This manoeuvre is acceptable to the extent that the alteration of basic theory required is explicitly acknowledged. Where overstrenuous attempts are made to preserve it (such as Carvhallo 2003 in debate with me) then the hatred and prejudice which infuses the orthodox analytic literature creeps back in and nothing can be recovered from the wreckage.

Fortunately, speckled amongst the field are a few analytic writers who abandon prejudice and propose positive analytic descriptions of gay and lesbian life. There is increasing evidence that psychoanalytic circles, particularly in America where gay men are at last beginning to figure in the analytic establishment, are revising their theories of sexuality.

What conclusions can be drawn from this review of causal speculation about homosexual object-choice? Probably the answer is that few firm conclusions emerge. The field has too often been driven in one way or another by disapproval of homosexual object-choice, so that the sort of balanced investigation into all kinds of sexual preference which might yield genuine insight still remains to be undertaken. Nevertheless, it is probably true to say that a state of being involving largely consistent preference for same-sex partners does exist in some people. The causes of this state of being, while they vary between individuals, will certainly include some biological, some psychological and some social components. While this may not seem like much in the way of a definite statement all parts of it have at times been denied by one group or another.

In the therapy context, it tends to be patients who are in the early stages of defining themselves as gay, lesbian, or bisexual who need to talk quite a lot about cause. Frequently the therapeutic task consists of providing factual information about the current state of ignorance over causes. The therapist can also reveal the concealed anxiety about the morality of a homosexual object choice which lies behind concerns about cause for, as Isay points out (1996), most gay men enter adolescence hoping they are heterosexual:

> Gerald was 17 and presented confused and distressed after a not very determined suicide attempt. After a long time he was able to reveal that he thought he might be attracted to men and had been hanging out in public toilets to try and have sex. He was tormented with repetitive anxious and compulsive speculations about the reason that he felt the way he did and returned repeatedly to a putatively causal encounter he had with another boy when he was ten. Ironically, Gerald's preoccupation with cause drove him to the internet and was the motor for an increasingly wide-ranging search for information about gay life. As time passed, his general knowledge increased and his preoccupation reduced. The therapist's task was mostly to act as a witness to the process and also to make sure that information about safe sex was clearly presented.

The early formation of the erotic imagination of gay men often involves experiences of intense anxiety and loneliness. Awareness of sexual orientation intersects with issues of separation and individuation and forces this process forward. A restless concern with cause may partly be due to an imaginatively driven wish to stitch life back together into some continuous form. In Gerald's case this process seemed to go relatively well.

General principles of therapy with gay men and lesbians

Psychotherapy with gay men and lesbians cannot, for the present, escape its own history. The gay community is well aware of the homophobic prejudice which many therapists and psychiatrists have displayed towards them. Prejudiced treatment continues and patients are, not unrealistically, wary of therapists. Therapies conducted with gay men and lesbians therefore need to overcome obstacles to the therapy relationship not found in treating heterosexual patients. Rochlin (1982) cites research that shows that gay and lesbian clients usually report dissatisfaction with therapy experiences based on one or more of three things: the therapist's lack of practical knowledge about homosexuality, the therapist's lack of positive attitude toward the client's homosexual feelings, and/or the lack of being mutually disclosing with the client.

Clark (1987), writing in a humanistic tradition, produced a set of ground rules for therapists aiming to help gay men and lesbians. Not all would necessarily command universal assent from all therapeutic orientations. Many, however, are helpful, including injunctions to eliminate homophobia within the therapist, to remember that oppression is part of the texture of all gay and lesbian lives, to encourage clients in developing a gay or lesbian support system and to encourage psycho-education (consciousness raising). A therapist taking care to follow these injunctions, and wary of the operation of covert prejudice, would go far to eliminate the first two difficulties that Rochlin cites.

Rochlin's third area of reported difficulty is more problematic. Requests by gay and lesbian patients to know the sexual orientation of their therapist is an issue which has preoccupied a number of writers. For gay and lesbian patients the wish to know their therapist's orientation can feel very pressing. In one study 70.5 per cent of lesbians said they would prefer a lesbian therapist, and less than 1 per cent preferred to be treated by a man. Analytically oriented therapists, whose training predisposes them to non-disclosure, find these requests difficult and are inclined to resist them or pathologise the patient who makes them, for doing so. They may fail to accept that a kind of 'disclosure' is often effected by assumptions of heterosexuality by the wearing of wedding rings. Quite apart from the strictures of a therapeutic modality, therapists may or may not be comfortable with self-disclosure about a range of issues for many reasons. The request may be made within the setting of complex currents within the therapeutic relationship which can make disclosure a far from simple event. Patients may 'know' that non-disclosure is a 'rule' of therapy and request information partly to test the rule. An often neglected element is that therapists have differing levels of need for privacy and a separate personal space:

In supervision Siri, a lesbian therapist, revealed her distress at being pressed to disclose her sexual orientation by a patient.

'She keeps asking me and I feel bad, as though she would take liberties with me if I told her.' They discussed from a range of perspectives why an overtly straight patient might be pressing Siri and it was clear that the patient had probably picked up some sign of Siri's sexual identity from a range of cues. Siri's reluctance to disclose personal material seemed partly related to her need for privacy and partly a response to some sexual and aggressive tensions in therapy. In supervision it was decided that Siri would again attempt to gain an understanding of the wish that lay behind the question but then, failing that, tackle the matter directly with her patient first saying that she simply did not wish to reveal her sexual orientation because she felt uncomfortable doing so. The patient was unimpressed and said quickly and contemptuously 'that means you must be lesbian and a coward also'. Siri blushed and then faltered and stammered her way through the rest of the session. In supervision the force and violence of the attack on Siri was acknowledged, as was the profoundly negative turn the therapy had taken. Even so, the supervisor stressed that Siri needed to work in a way that she felt able to maintain rather than be pressed into an action she did not want to take for personal reasons.

Siri's patient was not overtly lesbian and this means that the kinds of anxiety and fantasy which drove her insistent questioning and attack were somewhat different than would have been the case with a lesbian patient. Lesbians are often asking, amongst other things, to be reassured that they will be understood and not harmed. Some straight women are asking for permission to explore (or reassurance they can avoid) lesbian erotic imaginings or are testing to see if they are at risk of a sexual encounter with their therapist which they may perceive as exciting, threatening or a host of other emotionally laden things.

Gay men

Growing up gay

Morris (1997) consummately sums up the complexity of influences which attend the childhood of a gay man. The fact that early homophobia in the playground is not related to sexual orientation but to difference and to a hatred of un-masculine, sissy behaviour spawns a paradox for gay boys. Since a persistent sense of difference is common to the childhoods of many gay men they often become the object of homophobic bullying. Thus many gay men report an experience of being labelled as gay by other children before they accept it themselves. The effect of apparent foresight which feels uncanny to some gay men is partly a result of selection effects, in that many more children are labelled gay than become gay adults. However, it is also partly because some boys, who grow up to be gay, do objectively behave differently as children from boys who grow up to be straight (Green 1987). As boys grow older they are repeatedly exposed to homophobia, for example in team sports (Messner 1992, in Plummer 1999), which present boys who sense themselves to be different a number of ambiguous social situations which are exceedingly risky. Locker-room homophobia is set in the context of a homosocial activity in which, for example, comparing the size of penises, or joking about sex, is 'safe' only because no boy involved is identified as gay. The shaky structure of homosociality on which such experiences are built can easily turn nasty for a boy in the group who becomes identified as gay. Furthermore, frankly homosexual experiences between boys are relatively common. The quality of these encounters is often hypocritical (Plummer 1999), with homophobic group leaders indulging in gay sex from within a safe zone reserved for the powerful. The meaning and risks of these encounters for gay boys is incandescent with difficulty.

While a sense of difference sets in early, most gay boys do not define themselves as sexually different before the age of 12 (Troiden 1993) or 14 (Coyle 1994, in Davies and Neal 1996), when puberty is underway. Awareness of sex and the tribulations of adolescence inaugurate a time of severe difficulty for many gay boys. There is intense pressure to conform to a heterosexual norm and find a girlfriend and Eliason (1995) presents evidence that choosing a girlfriend is partly connected to rejecting a gay identity. Gay men report doing a good deal of heterosexual dating in adolescent years in order to avoid seeing themselves as gay (Eliason 1995).

The sexual imaginations of young gay men have therefore in our culture been subjected to the most intense pressures. Vigilant awareness of self and others, heightened awareness of the slight-est sexual cues in a situation, and self-aware social manipulation is one strategy young gay men can adopt. An alternate strategy is to suppress awareness of, or acceptance of, homosexual wishes and repackage the self as conforming. It is this second group who may try girlfriends or marriage.

For those gay boys who reject attempts at heterosexual confor-mity the difficulties of gay adolescence mean that many delay announcing their sexuality and coming out until they are 21 (Coyle 1994, in Davies and Neal 1996). Coyle's study also docu-ments fear, isolation, a sense of not fitting effeminate gay stereo-types and anxieties about the social impact of their preference. This state of affairs is dangerous in two ways. It is associated with a risk of depression and suicide (Rivers 1994; Trenchard and Warren 1984, both cited in Davies and Neal 1996) and also ignorance about sexual matters, and isolation is also paralleled by lack of knowledge about the risks of HIV (Davies and Neal 1996).

There are only a limited range of opportunities open to a young gay person for finding a partner except in urban centres. Isay (1996) suggests that opportunistic difficulties in finding a partner are a major cause of adolescent gay boys' use of anonymous or random sexual encounters. As adolescence proceeds the failure of a gay boy to conform to social stereotypes of mate selection becomes more socially apparent and, sooner or later, in some way, the question of disclosure of sexual identity (coming out) must be addressed. There is a large literature on this topic (see in Davies and Neal 1996). The main problem is the reaction, or anticipated reaction, of others. The need to come out, or the fact of having done so, can cause gay men or their relatives to present to psychotherapists in confusion and distress. Bernstein (1990, in Davies and Neal 1996) identifies five major themes in parents – social stigma, self/partner blame, anxieties over the loss of grand-children, fears and concerns for the gay child, fears of alienating their child. Not all parents are accepting, 11 per cent of gay chil-dren are ejected from the family home (Trenchard and Warren 1984) and may end up faring as best they may in care.

Acknowledgement of the many, sometimes appalling, ways in which families treat gay men on learning of their sexual choices has possibly overshadowed the often more subtle losses in relation to peers. Gay men do not come out once, but are repeatedly faced with the choice either to disclose their sexuality, or to keep silent. If things go badly chronic loneliness may result. The social unacceptability of homosexual orientation can easily make for a lonely, sexually confused adolescence and there is plenty of evidence that increased risk of suicide amongst gay adolescents (Bagley and Tremblay 1997) are linked to a lack of satisfying friendships (Heeringen and Vinke 1997).

Gay sex

Gay men take more time over sex and emphasise the exchange of pleasure between partners to a far greater degree than their heterosexual counterparts. They communicate more openly with each other and display more sensitivity to their partner's needs (Bancroft 1989). Surveys of gay men have been conducted from time to time to determine their favoured sexual activities but tastes and fashions vary. Gay sex may include mutual masturbation, oral sex of various kinds, anal sex, and use of sex toys. There are also substantial parts of the gay community who are interested in sexual activities associated with extreme experience such as fisting, or sadomasochistic sex. Listing sexual acts ignores the dimension of erotic imagination which contrives sexual activities and which provides a meaningful context at once aesthetic and relational in which they occur.

There are few distinctive features to specifically gay psychosexual difficulties. Patients may present with failures of desire or arousal and with premature or delayed ejaculation. As with straight men, organic factors always need to be considered when there is a new onset of difficulties with erection or with ejaculation. The treatment of gay men with psychosexual problems does involve specific issues. The most important of these is internalised homophobia, which may contribute to the psychological causation of disorders of desire or arousal and may be linked to any number of aspects of gay life:

> George and Alec presented for therapy because George found Alec sexually demanding and had begun to find himself turned off when Alec approached him. They were in a longstanding exclusive relationship and throughout Alec had wanted sex

more often that George. Sometimes sex was complicated because George had genital herpes with a painful inflamed penis, but Alec and George had had anal sex at those times. In separate interviews, Alec revealed his impatience with George who always seemed to submit to sex never to enjoy it. George speculated that Alec might leave him and revealed a deep homophobically driven worry about his masculinity because of his lower sex drive. Treatment involved a modification of the Masters and Johnson approach. Sex therapy exercises, primarily non-genital, sensate focusing, were instituted, and combined with couple therapy which focused on the differing expectations George and Alec had of each other.

Gay relationships

Stereotypes of gay men have not until recently pictured them in stable relationships like that of George and Alec. However, this perception may be due more to the repression of gay sexuality so that those in stable relationships either concealed their way of life or at the least kept it as quiet as may be. Where men form stable relationships they tend to be equal partners and some degree of openness to other sexual relationships is often accepted (McWhirter and Mattison 1984) although the advent of HIV has probably altered this to an extent. Recent calls for legal reform have highlighted the plight of couples in very longstanding relationships who do not acquire any of the legal rights, for example in relation to pensions associated with marriage. Indeed, much of the remaining discrimination against gay men and lesbians is directed specifically at their relationships. It still seems acceptable for many to argue, for whatever reason, that these relationships should never be allowed the status of marriage.

Casual or anonymous sex

Whatever acceptance can be found for homosexual object-choice in men evaporates rapidly in the face of promiscuous, casual or anonymous sex. Even gay authors find they need to explain this aspect of gay life in terms of damage or pathology (Isay 1996). At its most extreme, anonymous sex may involve glory holes, where a man passes his penis through a hole to have oral or manual sex anonymously with someone on the other side. Gay bathhouses, where multiple sexual encounters could occur, were also a common part of gay life, now curtailed as a result of the impact of HIV. Many studies have demonstrated that gay men have had large numbers of sexual partners during their sexual careers and sociobiologists have seen this aspect of gay life as representing the pure culture of masculinity.

Mohr (1992) presents an important and compelling defence of these aspects of gay sexual life. He argues that the pattern of casual sexual encounters, which some gay men choose, is not the alienated expression of loss or hatred that some suggest (Bollas 1992). Instead he points out a range of forgotten features of promiscuous gay male sexual expression: casual encounters often blossom into friendship, intimate accounts of life stories often follow after sex, and sexual encounters bring people from different classes together and cross-class friendship follows. He concludes that autonomous respect and mutually equal friendship are embodied in these meetings. Mohr's defence is beautifully written and convincing. The opprobrium that the straight world pours on casual gay sex is conducted from a heterosexual position which has too often sacrificed respect, autonomy and friendship for enforced sexual fidelity and relationships structured on power and dependency. Those who care to criticise casual sex should contrast the response of the gay community to HIV (a response Mohr would argue embodied the same values as casual sex) with the straight community's achingly slow response to domestic violence and rape.

Anal sex

Disapproval of anal sex is another reason people dislike gay men's sex lives. Many cultures regard the experience of being penetrated as an inferior one and to an extent this was the case in ancient Greece (Mohr 1992). In such cultures any people who allow themselves to be penetrated, women and gay men alike, are inferior. Schwartz (1995) has argued that the experience of a man being penetrated anally by a man is neither a feminine nor a passive one. While this is certainly true and important, it does not deal with the fundamental terror which many societies have of the state of being penetrated, or acknowledge the capacity of gay men to negotiate this terror and develop its erotic, imaginative possibilities. Bersani (1988) and Hocquengham (1978), writing from a poststructuralist position, which both draws from and is critical of psychoanalysis, have gone further and discussed the sexually revolutionary potential of anal sex, suggesting that it offers experiences of self-shattering which are relatively unavailable in, what Hillman (1975) would term, our Apollonian culture.

Anal sex and casual sex offer a heterosexually structured world a radically different vision of the erotic imagination. Although they are oppressed activities, stigmatised for being unrelated, they have given the gay community a strength and solidarity capable of mounting towards the AIDS crisis a social response far stronger than the straight community could have generated. In different ways they each act back on non-sexual aspects of existence. Casual sex offers new models of the relationship between friendship, loyalty and sex while anal sex offers the prospect of penetration not instantly associated with being made or making abject (Kristeva 1980).

Gay and bisexual men in marriages

A proportion of married men have homosexual relationships. Some regard themselves as gay men in heterosexual relationships, others consider themselves bisexual. A third group would deny any homosexual identity and minimise or dismiss their homosexual affairs. Married or bisexual men having gay relationships often attract ill-feeling from both gay and straight communities. It is suggested that they hide from oppression in marriages tasting the delights of the gay world but cheating both. Certainly some men regard marriage as offering a stable relationship base while their gay sexual encounters offer variety and excitement (Whitney 1991).

Isay (1996) acknowledges the theoretical existence of bisexual men but regards true bisexuality as exceptionally rare. He discusses homosexual men who marry in order to deny their homosexuality or to avoid its socially stigmatising consequences. He includes in this group men for whom psychotherapy has been conducted in such a way as to pressure a gay man into marriage. Isay's experience is that for most of these men their homosexuality ultimately becomes a major source of conflict in the marriage.

Often sexual activity in the marriage declines and sooner or later homosexual encounters begin. Once homosexuality becomes an issue within the marriage, depression and loneliness may result as conflicts over relationship break-up are combined with difficulties in making a new gay life. Isay's work is deeply felt, personal, bleak and realistic but he may overstate the generalisability of his findings, as the following vignettes demonstrate:

Vic had thought of himself as largely gay and so he was surprised to fall in love with a woman. They married, had a child and lived happily until she became unwell and after quite a long period of disability and mental decline died. During her last months Vic had a number of gay affairs. He presented with problems related to his bereavement but also with identity issues in relation to choosing a future. 'Now she is gone I could choose to be anything. I am right back where I was before I married.'

Adrian was in his early sixties. He had a number of physical and mental health problems and was married with three adult children. As a young man he had once allowed himself to go cottaging, had enjoyed the experience but recoiled from it instantly because of his fear of being caught. Now in later life he regretted the lack of sexual choice available to him in his past even though he had no thought of leaving the marriage. While in therapy he did allow himself to be clearer with his wife that he felt he was homosexual. This revelation did not surprise her and as a result of it their sex life improved because he was able to ask her to do things sexually which he had avoided before because in his mind they were gay things to do.

Gay men from ethnic minorities

Gay men who come from minority cultures struggle with double disadvantage from racial and homophobic prejudice in our culture and as well may face a homophobic home culture. Nor should it be assumed that all racists are heterosexual. Many black men talk bitterly of their exploitation at the hands of white gay men. The work of Maplethorpe, whose photography both celebrates and objectifies his black subjects, is a case in point and has been criticised on racial grounds (Mohr 1992) for 'burning in' his black subjects. Burning is a photographic technique designed to heighten contrast. Therapeutically, knowledge of the way homosexuality is expressed in different cultures is crucial when treating someone from one of those cultures. Rattigan (1995) discusses the case of a gay mixed Afro-Caribbean/white man whose preexisting problems with self-image are multiplied to a considerable extent by his unconscious acceptance of a culturally negative stereotype of homosexuality. Rattigan's patient often referred to himself as a 'fucking batty man' – an Afro-Caribbean denigratory term for homosexual men. Only a detailed knowledge of the cultural and social context of a sexual behaviour can allow the therapist to be alert to the fine structure of the interaction between personal and social structures.

Older gay men

Older gay men experience a range of problems some of which are related to having had past lives marred by homophobia. Men who have spent lives in secluded closets may look out, now, onto a world of increased liberality with a mixture of envy and bewilderment. Other problems relate to the experience of aging itself. The homosexual community prizes appearance in men and old age can be seen as unattractive in parts of the gay community. However, the gay community is also more tolerant than the straight community of age-discrepant relationships and this makes the prospects of finding relationships in later life less bleak.

Gay psychology

Psychoanalytic prejudice against gay men is only lifting slowly. There are however, now, important papers which chart the infractions of analytic neutrality in relation to gay men and attempt to restore a less pejorative stance (Mitchell 1978). Even so, there has been, as yet, little room for positive theorising in this area. Two important exceptions are Isay (1996) whose work has already been extensively cited, and who develops an approach to gay men based on the idea that homosexual orientation is a given in gay men and boys, which then has developmental effects in consequence. Isay suggests that gay men often have difficult relationships with their fathers because of fears of homoeroticism within the family. As a result they may later on have problems in relation to men and intimacy. Early experiences of homophobia, Isay argues, are also structuring and may result in increased self-reliance and autonomy.

Morgenthaler's (1988) theory of psychosexual development is important but begins from a different premise. He suggested that all psychological development involves a trade-off between security in questions of identity and security in autonomy. Homosexual men experience a need to preserve their freedom of action (autonomy) but are able to allow some identity diffusion. For gay men, relationships with other men may result in identity diffusion but offer a way of relating in which autonomy is maximised. In straight relationships, because of the difference of the other, identity is confirmed and secured but autonomy is lost because of power differentials in the relationship. This theory allows Morgenthaler both to value and to describe the way in which gay relationships may involve changing roles and considerable flexibility in relation to identity. An increasing number of theorists are now developing gay affirmative analytically oriented psychological formulations. Cornett (1995) and Domenici and Lesser (1995) are both good examples.

Characteristically non analytic psychological work in relation to homosexual orientation has eschewed grand theory and the gay character, in favour of more immediately relevant topics related to discrimination and homophobia, identity formation, and coming out (Davies and Neal 1996). In each case the psychologies involved trace, with considerable care, the experiences of gay men in modern western society. Therapists may read these with profit in order to gain an understanding of the likely varieties of experience which may present.

What remains absent from psychological theorising about gay men is a well developed theory of the ways in which the homoerotic imagination opens up possibilities for gay men which are not open to heterosexual ones. Some Jungians (such as Jackson 1993) have begun to explore this area although their theories can suffer from strange adherences to stereotyped gender patterns which lead to a curious stretching sensation.

Lesbians

Childhood and adolescence

Lesbian women are not as homogeneous as gay men in their descriptions of their first awareness of object-choice. Commonly, one of two stories is told. The first involves lifelong awareness of difference and an early awareness of interest in women. The second describes an initial heterosexual adjustment followed by a change in later life to lesbian relationships. The childhoods of many lesbians are therefore not distinguishable from those of their heterosexual counterparts. However, some lesbians report being 'tomboys' at school. Interestingly this is associated with an increase in status (Dunne 1997). Dunne suggests that tomboy behaviour at school results in closeness to boys, a greater sense of gender equality and reduced sexual attraction to them, with consequent lesbian sexuality. Against this argument (which in any case depends on the unproven assertion that difference is a requirement for sexual attraction), must be set the hardships endured by tomboys when boys and girls frequently form separate tribes at school around the age of 8. As adolescence approaches, tomboy behaviour becomes stigmatised and sexual inferences start to be drawn from it. The confining conformity to a stereo-typed femininity required by adolescent culture is well documented (Lees 1986; Connell 1995; McRobbie 1978, all cited in Dunne 1997:14) and is even evident in the tomboy character so cruelly excluded by the Jets in *West Side Story*. So, tomboy childhood notwithstanding, a significant number of lesbians, especially from educationally less advantaged backgrounds, assume future marriage and conform their behaviour in relation to dating boys to that expectation (Dunne, 1997).

Adult lesbian life

Choosing to be lesbian

The development of a lesbian identity can pass through discernible stages as the individual comes to terms slowly with an identity which marks them out as atypical in society. Cass (1979), for example, identifies the following general stages: confusion, comparison with others, tolerance, pride, and finally synthesis.

The tasks are different depending on the stage of life when coming out occurs. Burch (1989) suggests that when lesbian identity emerges later in life there may be complicated matters to resolve relating to social obligations and attachments. By contrast, a lifelong sense of difference may assist in differentiating the developing girl from her mother which may help with the process of coming out and also confer beneficial psychological consequences generally.

Burch's (1997) theory of lesbian identity involves recasting the Oedipus complex with a lesbian slant. She argues that the young lesbian tries to develop a romantic affair with her mother and that at this point the mother's reaction is crucial. Over harsh rejection may produce defensive heterosexuality (a point on which Chodorow (1978) agrees) or redoubled efforts at acceptance and, later, lesbian identity but with oversensitivity in relation to attachment. Burch suggests that the two types of trajectory towards lesbian identity (early and late) also represent two different accommodations to the Oedipus complex. Ingenious as her theory is, it suffers from a problem endemic to psychoanalytic theorising – a lack of attention to cultural variability. Dunne shows that as late as the 1960s most women still did not possess the economic independence to contemplate a single life and thus almost all married. Such marriages obscured lesbian preference. We do not know how women with lesbian desires negotiated these from within the confines of married life. Indeed, there have been passionate arguments about the extent to which friendships between married women in the past were lesbian in nature (Faderman 1981). In other cultures where female sexuality is highly policed, lesbianism is also only an option after a marriage has been contracted and perhaps broken down for some reason (Blackwood 1986). There is, therefore, every reason to suppose that the life stories of lesbian women are highly culturally determined.

While the gay male erotic imagination has been constrained and legislated against it has been acknowledged. Lesbian erotic imagination and lifestyle possibilities have never been illegal but have always been oppressed as part of the general subjection of women and the tendency to treat them as property rather than as agents. It is perhaps many women's blessing and curse often to find it possible to imagine many options within grasp and at the same time to chain the imagination to the expediency of circumstance. Until the emancipation of women is a completed project we will not know the many ways that the lesbian erotic imagination could develop.

Lesbian relationships

Lesbian psychology has focused to a very great extent on examining a tendency of lesbians in relationships to merge. This term is rarely operationalised but it most often refers to tendencies to have similar interests and hobbies, to do most things together, to indulge in intimate conversation and to express doubts over identity boundaries. Object-relational theories of female psychosexual development can provide some explanation for this phenomenon. Chodorow (1978) argues that girls will experience more boundary confusion and difficulty with differentiation during development than boys because of their sameness with mother. In adult life this means that for women the self-other boundary may remain more permeable than for men. If this is a problem for women then, the argument goes, it is multiplied by two for lesbians.

It is often suggested (Falco 1991) that merger in lesbian relationships is problematic, and specifically that it may result in sexless relationships and frequent rows, resulting in relationship break-up. There is some data to suggest that lesbian relationships don't last as long as heterosexual ones (Tanney and Birk 1978, in Falco 1991) but other research does not bear out the gloomy analysis suggested by theorists of merger. Studies show that lesbians as a group are as happy with their relationships as heterosexuals and show higher degrees of intimacy and equality than them (Peplau *et al.*, 1982 Tanney and Birk 1978; Kurdek and Schmitt 1986; Murphy 1989, all cited in Falco 1991). Lesbians are also more satisfied than heterosexual woman are with sex (Blumstein and Schwartz 1983, in Falco 1991). While merger may not be problematic, there are aspects of lesbian lifestyles which are suggestive of merger. There is, for example, often some blurring of friendly and lover relationships which may result from shifts in the structure of dyadic relationships brought about by lesbian object choice (Denman 2001). Peplau (1981) suggests that friendship is a better model for evaluating lesbian relationships than are heterosexual sexual ones. So the phenomenon called merger occurs but is not problematic. Perhaps anxieties about and pathologising of lesbian merger results from a failure to delineate the new relationship and erotic possibilities that become imaginable when women relate sexually to each other and not to men.

Lesbian parents

For many older lesbians the inconceivability of single parenthood and conception without copulation meant that they equated their sexual choice with childlessness. Others had children from heterosexual relationships but lost custody because they were lesbians. They have watched with a mixture of envy and joy a new generation of lesbians who have chosen to conceive and parent children in non-standard families or who have retained parental responsibility for children despite leaving marriages for lesbian relationships. Sufficient numbers of children have been brought up this way for studies (Davies and Neal 1996) to show that male and female children brought up this way become normal, happy and adjusted to the extent that their childhoods have been secure, stable and loving. There is no evidence that being brought up in the absence of a father damages these children and no evidence (although the numbers are small) that gay couples raising children in the absence of a mother are damaging their children. What the evidence shows does harm children is being made complicit in secrecy, painful custody battles or other traumatic factors not related to sexual orientation. Even so, there are quite a lot of complicated issues to be negotiated. These are well covered in Davies and Neal (1996) and Falco (1991).

Older lesbians

Older lesbians, like all older people, suffer from social sexual erasure based on age (Neild and Pearson, 1992). However, their problems can be much more acute for a number of reasons. They often come from a generation which found lesbian sexual orientation profoundly distasteful and have had lifelong difficulty with their orientation. Much of the 'gay scene' is aimed at younger people and there are few meeting places and venues directed at older gay women. For those lesbian women who have been in long relationships the death of a partner may represent a considerable loss, but one that is not acknowledged by society, which lacks structures for mourning and for the sorting out of financial affairs.

Since older lesbians may not have children they may also lack the family structures of support and filiation which are important in the rebuilding of relationship structures after a loss.

Lesbian sex

Much has been made of the Blumstein and Schwartz study (1983) which demonstrated a low frequency of sex in lesbian relations. Commentators have suggested that merger, loss of difference, and sensual rather than sexual tendencies accumulate in lesbian relationships to produce the 'lesbian bed death' syndrome. The idea that a certain amount of 'differentness' is required for hot sex is one espoused by many writers, lesbian and straight, on the topic of lesbians and sex (for example, Falco 1991). The reasons given for this pronouncement are always vague. For example, sex in conditions of merger is said to lack tension or to resemble incest. That lesbian writers have themselves failed to notice the inherent heterosexism in the notion of a required quantity of difference for sex is testimony to the hegemony of heterosexual ideology in culture. Noting that this idea is never applied as a reason for the lack of hot sex in male homosexual couples should suffice to explode it as a reasonable notion.

Several other potential explanations exist for low levels of sexual activity in lesbian relationships. Sociobiologists argue it provides evidence of an inborn strategy in women designed to offset the costs of pregnancy. Women maximise investment in a small number of offspring whereas men have low parental costs and low parental investment and maximise their chances by high levels of sexual activity. Falco (1991) provides a more psychological perspective, arguing that lesbians, as women, are socialised to be passive sexual partners. This combines with internalised homophobia to generate guilt over sexual experimentation and unexamined beliefs in the superiority of sex with a penis which may produce internal doubts and anxieties. They also add, helpfully, that considerable stress is also caused by socially imposed restrictions on public expression of physical affection.

However, it turns out that the large volume of speculation on this subject may fall victim to cultural shifts. Until recently, data suggested that lesbians had sex less than any other couples (Blumstein and Schwartz 1983). More recent evidence contradicts this. Creith's (1996) research not only finds no difference between sexual frequencies reported by lesbian and heterosexual women but also highlights that the population generally is having less sex than is commonly imagined. Furthermore even the picture of sexual deficit taken from the original Blumstein and Schwartz study is less monolithic than it might appear. The lesbians who were questioned were happy with their sex lives and, when they did have sex, were more successful in achieving orgasm consistently than straight women. Thus therapists who are asked to treat lesbians with low sexual desire need to be alive to the range of perspectives which exist on this problem:

> Carla and Ruth came to the clinic with a complaint that Carla was always bothering Ruth for sex and they had frequent rows over it. Ruth complained that if ever she was interested in sex Carla would leap at the chance and Ruth felt overwhelmed. Carla was worried that Ruth wasn't interested in her any more. Carla was the birth mother to Sandy, their 6-month-old baby, and said during the session 'I thought I was the one who was supposed to go off sex after having a baby!' Certainly things had gone down hill sexually since Sandy was born and the therapist was able to point out that because Carla was working Ruth was doing most of the caring, including nights, and that tiredness may be a factor. Additionally, both Carla and Ruth simultaneously had managed to label their own state of sexual desire as pathological with Carla casting herself as mannishly over-sexed and Ruth casting herself as deficient. Pointing this out made both of them laugh. Therapy concentrated on trying to improve the times when both of them did want sex.

With the image of merger and the undersexed lesbian comes a picture of the lesbian erotic imagination as languid or worse, anxiously deficient (Scruton 1986). Such images clearly help to defuse wounded male pride but they also serve rapidly to suppress any attempt to define an active sexuality for women. When lesbians did try to expand this area of the erotic imagination they met with opposition from some unexpected quarters. The common theme underlying this opposition was always a failure to imagine any kind of active eroticism that was not masculine.

Internal and external pressures on lesbian sexual practices

Throughout the 1970s and 1980s political war reigned over the nature and appropriateness of lesbian sexual expression. When the radical feminist movement appropriated the term lesbian (Wilton 1996) it defined all woman–woman relationships as 'lesbian' (Rich 1993) and it also exerted strong disapproval and condemnation of certain forms of sex which it felt reproduced the structures of hetero-patriarchy. These included assertive, active sex, penetrative sex and any form of unequal role play in sex. This constrained expressions of sexual desire within a vision of femininity which at times constructed it as too refined and sensitive for the coarseness of sexual desire (Morgan 1984, in Wilton 1996). This view of women repeats many of the romantic male notions of womanhood which were so successfully employed to confine them in the domestic sphere in the nineteenth century (Giddens 1992). Two groups led a backlash: sex radicals (e.g. SAMOIS 1982) and older, largely working-class lesbians who had often experienced severe oppression for their specifically sexual choices and did not care to have them defined as male-identified. Many lesbians who took part in those debates are politicised to an extent and if they want to use sex toys (dildoes), butch–femme roles, or SM, they may need to negotiate the still-smoking debris of previous political battles.

The most depressing aspect of these debates within the lesbian community about what constituted acceptable sexuality was that they were largely conditioned by external and pejorative views of lesbian sex. The Lacanian distinction between the phallus and the penis (Lacan 1958 translated by Rose 1982) can provide a helpful way of thinking about these debates. The finer points of the distinction between the penis and the phallus are subtle and disputed but for practical purposes the term penis refers to the male organ and the term phallus to the complex of ideas, social privileges and roles associated with it. The straight view of lesbians, as both mannish and deficient, and unable to have real sex, is based on intolerance in the straight world of anything which either denies the power of the phallus/penis or separates power (the phallus) from possession of a penis. Lesbians, also, fail to credit the possibility of a genuine separation of phallus and penis and so worry about being mannish or question the reality of their active sexual desire. One strategy is to renounce the phallus and all its works. Lesbians who have done this feel that the penis (or its substitute) should also be renounced. They forbid activities involving penetration, arguing that being penetrated amounted to acquiescence in the straight world.

In this political atmosphere and, possibly, also because of their allure for Lacanian feminists, for whom the distinction between phallus and penis meant much (Adams 1989, 1990; Wittig 1982), dildoes were, for a while, possibly more theorised than used. For their opponents dildoes appeared to reaffirm the idea that lesbians were deficient men who needed fake penises. A dildo-wielding lesbian was, from a Freudian perspective, one who had failed to renounce phallic sexuality and the reality of castration for the compensations of femininity. Some radical feminists, even if they hated Freud, would have agreed at least that using a dildo was an unfeminine and unsisterly act. Other lesbians (such as Wilton 1996) responded by claiming that lesbians who used dildoes were radically reclaiming phallic power by destroying the link between the phallus and masculinity.

Similar political considerations applied to the question of butch–femme role play. Were lesbians who adopted erotic roles, which imitated aspects of masculinity and femininity aping hetero-sexuality or were they radically redefining gender and sexuality in a revolutionary way? Again the heterosexual perspective of main-stream culture interacted with internal political agonising in unac-knowledged ways. Academic psychiatric textbooks which refer to lesbianism have always made much of the butch–femme distinc-tion. Often the pejorative suggestion is that the use of role play to create a pale reproduction of heterosexuality is all that is left to those sad creatures who choose lesbianism. Some lesbians have rejected butch–femme role play, seeing in it, as do the medical text books, an aping of heterosexuality. Others have looked more closely at these roles, showing them to be more complex and less stereotypical than their critics supposed. For example, Creith (1996) shows how a butch's attentive and nurturing style is rather feminine. The heated debates have largely cooled off now. A Pride study showed that while almost all lesbians can identity themselves as to an extent butch (masculine) or femme (feminine), these roles have little personal meaning for all but 5 per cent.

Yvonne came into her therapy assessment in full biker's leathers with dyke in studded capitals on the back. As she stripped off her leathers in the consulting room she gave the curious impression of getting smaller and smaller so that by the time she sat down she looked petite, androgynous and very sexy. She took a while to find a way to say that her sexual relationships were with women but her sexual fantasy life increasingly involved fantasies about having sex with men. She had become frightened to masturbate and, increasingly in her sex with other people, which often had an SM flavour, she avoided orgasm and made sure she had the top role. The therapist's counter-transference thought in the first session was that it would be a terrible shame if she was really straight. During an analytic therapy with Yvonne a host of issues were explored. Yvonne wondered whether she was 'really straight' (she checked this out by trying sex with some men which she judged 'sort of OK I suppose'). Her therapist suggested that her need to be part of an accepting group and the difficulty she had had in coming out might make accepting a bisexual or heterosexual orientation costly for her. She responded that, for her, having built up a studiedly butch persona, it would be more costly and risky to come out as femme. This allowed her to try out the idea that she was femme and that her butch role covered up longings to be conventionally pretty and wear dresses which, because of aspects of her childhood, seemed particularly forbidden. Eventually she settled, at least for the present, on the notion that she was a 'butch bottom', which for her meant that she liked her biker clothes and masculine role but sexually wanted to be penetrated and dominated.

Although political debate in the gay and lesbian community about the nature of sex has definitely been influenced by the attitudes of the heterosexual world enclosing it, some solidity and tolerance is becoming possible. Interestingly, the wider culture shows signs of an increasing engagement with gay and lesbian sexualities and sensibilities. Creith (1996) cites a newspaper article referring to kd lang: 'She stopped acting like a masculine woman and became a feminine man. It looked much better.' Such a comment betrays more tolerance of gender nonconformity while revealing a resid-ual underlying misogyny. It also reveals, perhaps, that the drive behind this engagement is a need to renegotiate the nature of masculine and feminine sexuality and gender role. It remains to be seen whether this movement gathers pace or whether, particularly if war or economic hardship becomes prevalent, it falters and retreats.

Conclusion

Perhaps there are four great streams of the sexual imagination: straight male, straight female, gay male and lesbian. If so, lesbian sexuality is very much the youngest daughter in the family. It is less commodified, less discussed and less imaged than the other kinds of sexuality. As a result the factionalised infighting within the community has been pretty brutal at times but the complexity and subtlety of some of the argumentation has been correspondingly exciting. It remains to be seen if the mainstream culture will allow the lesbian erotic imagination any greater space to exert powers for radical transformation other than short haircuts and snappy suits.

7 Transgressive and coercive sex

Western society regulates sexuality by making some sexual behaviour illegal and by sanctioning other sexual behaviours with social disapproval. Some prohibitions seem rational – for example, rape. Other prohibitions seem inexplicable – for example, sexual, sado-masochistic acts involving cutting or harming other people's penises, which are illegal both for the person who does the cutting and, intriguingly, for the person who consents to it (Thompson 1994). Satz (1990) points out that the state's interference in sexual behaviour is far greater than is warranted by its interest in avoiding personal harm or promoting social benefit. Quasi-legal control has been exercised by medicalising some sexual activity under the term 'perversion' or a more modern synonym. This chapter deals with both legally and medically proscribed sex. It introduces two terms to describe sexual activity: transgressive sex and coercive sex. Transgressive sex is sexual activity which attracts social disapproval or legal sanction. Coercive sex involves activities in which one party has not consented. It is argued that this categorisation divides sex more rationally than either medical or legal categorisations.

While the distinction between coercive sex and transgressive sex can be made on quasi-logical grounds, there are individuals for whom the two kinds of sex are bound up. These are people for whom the transgressive nature of sex is the source of excitement and who lapse into coercive sex because of the thrill involved in this ultimate transgression. The Marquis de Sade (1948) would be a prime example of such an individual who revels in murderous and licentious acts precisely because they take him beyond and above the compass of the common man. When such individuals are encountered in practice they may claim that the transgressive and radical nature of their sexuality renders them beyond legal sanction. It seems self-evident that while coercive sex may be indulged in because it is experienced as transgressive from the perspective of social policy it should be primarily thought of and treated as coercive.

Transgressive sex and perversion

Defining perversion preoccupies all theorists who approach the topic. Many writers dislike the term and replace it with synonyms, suc as sexual deviation or paraphilia. Even so, a range of difficulties still troubles the whole field. Perversions were initially defined as departures from heterosexual activity, but changes in social norms mean that this definition threatens to rule unacceptable many pleasurable and common activities. Theoretical efforts are therefore made to find a new classification system, liberated to an extent from the heterosexual norm. Theorists also attempt to distance themselves from suggestions that moral judgements are being exercised in their writings, replacing culpability with pathology. Often these efforts fail and moral judgements are freely expressed in the text without being acknowledged as such. While psychoanalytic theorists have been prominent in this regard, therapists of all persuasions have adopted pathologising and covertly moralising stances towards transgressive sex.

The term 'transgressive sex' avoids many of the these difficulties because it emphasises the way in which the category 'perverse' is always defined in relation to a cultural standard of normality. This standard varies through history and between cultures. Transgressive sex is sex that breaks current cultural rules for sexual behaviour. At different times and in different places it has ranged from failure to wear a burka, through sexual intercourse with someone of a different skin colour to enjoying masturbation and group sex. These are sexual activities that different cultures would view very differently. Using the term transgressive sex makes it plain that indulging in and sanctioning these acts are moral stances, but it also highlights the potential value of transgressive sexual acts. Imaginative development can often involve transgression. The idea of broken boundaries in the service of advance in art is an important expression of one way in which imagination works. If the erotic imagination is to mean anything positive then transgression must be one of its modes of expression.

Transgressive sex is a newly coined term if not a new idea (for an older version see Battaille, 1987). Therefore when another author's work is being discussed the term used by that author will be used.

Causes of transgressive sex: psychoanalytic views

Kernberg (1995) summarises three main stages in the psychoanalytic development of a theory of perversions. The first stage derives from Freud's later formulation of perversion, which views it as a defence against an underlying neurotic conflict – castration anxiety. He takes the second stage from British-object relations theorists, who stress pre-oedipal mechanisms involving aggressively charged representations of parents' early sexual relations infusing adult sexual activity. There are links between this formulation and that of Stoller (1991), who argues that the fundamental core of perverse sexuality is hatred and the overcoming of it by triumphal re-enactment of a humiliating early scenario. Kernberg's final stage develops from the French approach represented by McDougal (1970) and Chasseguet Smirgel (1984a), for whom perversions are linked to anality involving regression to a pseudo-genital faecal phallus which permits denial of generational and sexual difference. Each of these three approaches characteristically discusses a favoured perversion. For Freud the fundamental perversion was fetishism, the English object relations theorists mostly choose to discuss sadomasochism. French analysts for whom anality is at the core of perverse sexuality focus on any anal sexual activity as the defining paradigm for perversion.

All the psychoanalytic accounts of perversion suffer from severe difficulties which relate to their attempt to disavow a prior prejudice against certain kinds of sex and to develop the theory of perversion from scientific or objective foundations. For example, Kernberg himself relates perverse sexual activities to failures to relinquish the desire to be both genders. He attempts to analyse the specific dynamics of perversion while at the same time permitting, within a stable heterosexual union, as non-perverse, even essential, many affects and acts which in other contexts he wishes to argue are perverse. Doing so forces Kernberg to make some pretty tight and not entirely convincing distinctions between perverse and permitted practices. He relies to a great extent on a highly romantic vision of heterosexual sex, using this vision as a protective covering for all kinds of sexual activity.

McDougall struggles more successfully with the moral over-tones in perversion by separating out homosexual and neo-sexual categories from the group and trying to reserve perversion as a term to cover coercive sex. Her formulation is strikingly reminis-cent of Money's (1986) account, which emphasises the impor-tance of free, age-congruent, sexuoerotic play. She says that maternal distress over sexual bodily functions results in damage to children's representations of their sexual bodies. To combat the resulting sense of inner libidinal deadness, patients short-circuit the Oedipal stage and in so doing also circumvent the elaboration of the depressive position. McDougall's concept of deadness allows her to draw an analogy between perversion and addiction. Both addictive substances and perverse sex she argues dissipate the forces of infantile rage, maintain the illusion of omnipotent control (shattered only by maternal anxieties), and anaesthetize psychic pain.

For Kleinian theorists the term perversion spreads beyond sexual activity and is used to describe an attitude of hostile antipa-thy towards truth and beauty caused by the need to hold psychotic anxieties at bay. The Kleinian literature is thus replete with descriptions of perverse transferences or relationships but paradoxically contains little by way of formal discussions of perversion. Ruth Riesenberg Malcolm (1970 in Spillius (1988)) discusses the case of a woman who, according to Malcolm, encap-sulates her psychotic parts in a perverse syndrome. The case report is an example of the standard Kleinian theory on perversion and also displays both the strengths and the weaknesses of many Kleinian accounts. Its chief strength is in developing an analysis that refers to forces commensurate with the power of sexual desire. A serious weakness is the persistent inflation of the magni-tude of any pathology involved. Malcolm's patient's sexual fantasy life and a brief incestuous sexual relationship with her sister become evidence of severe perversion. The patient's masturbation fantasy and its relation to the patient's life are analysed by

Malcolm in Kleinian terms as serving the function of supporting a fragile psyche troubled by the need to defend against envy of the breast and of parental intercourse, and the impression is given that the phantasy staves off psychosis.

Meltzer and Williams (1988) introduce an extension of Kleinian theory in this area with their notion of aesthetic conflict. They suggest that, for a range of reasons, the normally developing infant holds a negative view of the interior of mother's body while defensively idealising its exterior. When aspects of this development go wrong and the balance of aesthetic conflict is not maintained, envy of beauty and perverse wishes to spoil the beautiful are entrained and these are the cause of perverse sexual activities which embody a wish to spoil the beautiful. Meltzer and Williams' theory comes the closest of many to acknowledging the power of the erotic imagination and the aesthetic dimension to sexual life. Sadly they insist on hobbling their conceptions with an outdated and, worse, unacknowledged moral order, the imposition of which vitiates much of the potential of their work.

Causes of transgressive sex: non-analytic perspectives

Non-analytic writers on transgressive sex have adopted a range of views, often taking in elements of psychoanalytic theory. One of the most innovative and controversial is Money. Money (1993), like the psychoanalysts, can do no better than to define the perversions by reference to their deviation from what he terms 'peno-vaginal pairing'. He talks about displacements – where a non peno-vaginal aim replaces peno-vaginal sex – and inclusions – where an obligatory addition is made of a component 'not ordinarily integral to an erotosexual pairing' (Money 1993:205). He next introduces the idea of a lovemap, which is a blueprint of information about an ideal sexual partner and preferred set of sexual activities. Lovemaps are personal, like fingerprints, and may be either normophillic (presumably peno-vaginal) or paraphillic. Paraphillic lovemaps result from thwarting or warping of sexual development during the period between 5 and 8 or 9 years of age, when normal juvenile sexual play forms the lovemap on a biological substratum. Money regards paraphilic love maps as 'vandalised', either through deprivation or neglect of healthy sexual development, or by excessive prohibition and punishment, or by coercive or conspiratorial deceit with respect to learning or doing things sexual. When a lovemap is vandalised affectionate love and erotic lust become segregated instead of remaining united. Lust becomes excommunicated from the pure and spiritual realm of the lovemap and each paraphillic lovemap maps out a stratagem, no matter how weird, for avoiding the complete annihilation of lust. Money (1970) claims in support of his theories that paraphillias are not present in the aborigines of Arnhem Land, where sex play is freely endorsed.

In one of the most interesting and useful parts of his theory Money (1993) calls on opponent process theory (Solomon 1980) to explain paradoxical enjoyment of pain in paraphilia. Opponent processes are called forth by any strong stimulus and result in its extinction or diminution over time. They are, for example, responsible for the common experience of becoming able to tolerate a very hot bath after a few minutes. Opponent processes become stronger with repeated trials and also they tend to carry on working for a while after the provoking stimulus has been removed. The effect of this is that, after repeated trials, a strong aversive stimulus can call forth an opponent process which at first moderates the aversive stimulus and then produces a euphoric rush when the aversive experience ceases but the opponent process carries on. Examples include sky diving, exercising, and possibly smoking. Money's theory probably does explain why some sadomasochistic practices are tolerable and it is an important advantage of his theorising that he integrates social and biological factors into a psychological picture. However, accounts by practitioners of transgressive sex do not always fit the picture described by Money and he remains locked in as much of a peno-vaginal mindset as mesmerised the analysts.

Freund and co-workers (1986, 1993 and 1998) have elaborated an evolution based theory for some paraphilias. They suggest that voyeurism exhibitionism, compulsive touching and compulsive rubbing of sexual parts against another person (frotteurism) represent forms of 'courtship disorders'. They are respectively distortions of the four stages of courtship behaviour: finding and appraising a potential mate, pre-tactile interaction, tactile interaction, and finally genital sex. There are apparently no courtship stages after genital sex. Other sexual behaviours including paedophilia and fetishistic preferences result from what they call 'erotic target location errors'. In both cases the failure of inbuilt adaptive and evolutionary programmed sets of social and sexual behaviours are hypothesised. It must surely be the case that there are inborn mechanisms subject to natural selection which deal with successful reproduction. However, for evolutionary psychology to advance our knowledge in this area theory must do more than re-describe the already known with an evolutionary wrapping. Rape is a coercive rather than transgressive sexual behaviour but Thornhill's account (Thornhill 2000) of its evolution is a better example of evolutionary argument in this area. Thornhill suggests that rape results from the activation of an adaptive strategy used by men when females are in short supply. He has gathered considerable amounts of evidence to show that men whose reproductive options have been constrained commit rape and that their typical victims (newspaper accounts notwithstanding) are women of reproductive age.

Transgressive sexual acts and psychiatric disorders

Linking perversions with other psychiatric disorders is important to psychoanalytic theorists because it helps to establish that transgressive sex is pathological. This idea is central to analytic notions of ordered genital sexuality between stably coupled adults as a mark of general psychological maturity having been attained (Freud 1950) or as the founding image of the psyche (Jung 1946; Klein 1945). Kernberg (1992) has gone furthest to systematise this linkage by correlating perversions with psycho-structural developmental categories. At the severe end of the spectrum, borderline patients suffer from excessive hatred towards parental figures, which results in distorted perceptions of parental sexual relationships. From this a range of ill effects flow, including exaggerated prohibitions against sexual relationships, masochism or almost any kind of positive perverse sexual practice. Kernberg approves of Meltzer's (1973) idea of defensive confusion of sexual zones in perversion, arguing that this applies well to borderline personality disorders. Even more unwell are patients with malignant narcissism, whose object representations are, according to Kernberg, almost exclusively of sadistic enemies. Genital penetration is equivalent to destroying the genitals or filling the body with shit, and the penis is seen as a source of poison.

While analytic writers find no shortage of seriously unwell patients with more or less unusual sexual preferences to discuss, single case reports can never constitute good evidence for a reliable association between transgressive sex and psychopathology. Reliable evidence of the co-presence of sustained transgressive sexuality with psychological health would severely challenge central elements of psychoanalytic theory. A problem with much of the data collected is that sexual offenders, often imprisoned for coercive rather than transgressive acts, are the most commonly studied population. The survey literature search does reveal some evidence of increased psychiatric illness amongst sexual offenders (see, for example, Raymond *et al.* 1999). However, this group might be expected, for various reasons, including imprisonment and harassment by inmates for being sex offenders, to be most severely unwell and the conditions reported – depression, anxiety, and substance misuse – are as likely to be consequent upon, as opposed to causally related to, the sexual behaviour in question. Some workers have suggested links between obsessive compulsive disorder and paraphillias (Bradford 1999). But here the suggestion is that the paraphilias are a form of obsessive compulsive disorder. This is difficult to sustain since obsessions and compulsions are experienced as ego alien whereas paraphilias may be unwelcome but are not ego alien. So, all in all, it appears that, as yet, the evidence to support a linkage between most transgressive sex and other psychopathology is absent.

Women and transgressive sex

At root, medical, psychoanalytic and psychological discussions of perversion all share in common a failure to contemplate the possibility of satisfying non-reproductive sex. Despite their varying attitudes to the phenomenon of transgressive sex, they steadfastly refuse to consider social and cultural contributions to sexual experience. Possibly these two omissions are linked. If so, the relative absence of classical perversions in women might have caught their eye and assisted them in developing a more wide-ranging perspective. Sadly, thinkers in the field elected to follow a different course. Instead of re-examining the concept of perversions they decided to extend the definition to encompass pathologies previously seen as non-perverse but more frequently seen in women.

Welldon (1988) has done much to develop the concept of female perversion, arguing that since in women the whole body is eroticised (as opposed to the emphasis on the penis in men) perverse activities will have a different form than occurs in men. However, Welldon says that classical perversions also do occur in women, suggesting that prostitution is a female perversion because it affords the opportunity to practise perverse activities while disowning the desire to do so (Welldon 1988). Kaplan (1979) takes a very similar tack, giving as examples of female perversions conditions such as anorexia bulimia, self-mutilation, and kleptomania. Maguire (1995) points out that analysts like Meltzer and other Kleinians define perverse character structures that have nothing to do with sexual acts So they have little difficulty with extensions of the definition of perversion to include women. Welldon and Kaplan's extension of the concept of perversion, based on a sexualisation of the female body and the inclusion of many acts not seen traditionally as sexual, has been criticised by McDougall (1995) because it threatens the integrity of concept of perversion. McDougall points out the existence of perverse masturbation in her women patients. By this she means both auto-erotic activity involving inserting harmful objects into the vagina or anus and the use of urine or faeces in order to achieve orgasm.

The notion of perverse motherhood is an important one well developed by Welldon (1988). Controversially, she sees verbal bullying of children and giving them sexual misinformation as being as harmful as incest and would regard a mother who does these things as perverse. For Welldon female castration anxiety is an important force, and women enact the resulting rage and insecurity it causes on their own bodies or against objects (babies) which they see as their own creations. Welldon's descriptions of problems in mothering are convincing but it is unclear to what extent women see their baby-making bodies as inherently sexual (and thus capable of being used perversely), nor is it clear to what extent children may be viewed in the same light. For misinforming a child, or bullying one to be perverse, the activity would need to give the mother sexual or at least sensual pleasure. There is no evidence that this is the case, and clinically the affect which accompanies most of the acts of maternal harm towards children, which are not directly and actively aggressive, is intense anxiety. Welldon's perversions of motherhood are probably best categorised as disorders of self-esteem (narcissistic difficulties), with the child being seen as an extension of mother's social self. Through its behaviour the child subjects its mother by proxy to a range of threats of humiliation.

Specific forms of transgressive sex

Subcultures devoted to certain sexual practices exist and much of the lack of social and cultural grounding in the discussion of transgressive sex can rapidly be dispelled by investigating the social structures of individuals who prefer these kinds of sex. Such subcultures can be thought of as communities of individuals whose interest at that time is to explore the potentials of a certain manifestation of the erotic imagination. Unlike the descriptions in the medicalised discourse, very few of those involved exclusively practise one kind of sex and there is much mobility between cultures.

Sadomasochism

Both the practice of and opposition to sadomasochistic transgressive sex arouses heated passions and creates strange bedfellows. It is, for example, a topic on which the Christian right, the psychoanalytic mainstream and the lesbian left all unite to condemn. Sadomasochism is a sexual subculture in which 'devotees' indulge in a range of practices, including verbal humiliation and submission, bondage, various forms of hitting, cutting, or hurting aimed at erotic effect, and a range of other sexual practices, such as fisting (the insertion of a hand into the anus or vagina), which involve mental or physical pain and physical achievements. A vital distinction needs to be maintained between sexually sadistic criminals and sadomasochistic (SM) devotees. Dietz (1990) distinguishes criminal sexual sadists from SM devotees by reference to a number of criteria. Criminal sexual sadists secure unwilling partners, force sexual acts on victims, have an unemotional detached demeanour, use torture, and have no tendency to switch and take the role of victim. SM devotees display none of these characteristics.

Thompson (1994) points out that, in contrast to criminal sexual sadists, SM devotees go to great lengths to ensure the physical safety of their partners. They have their own techniques, rules, beliefs and language to reduce the possibility of harm. The psychological features which characterise this form of sex are dominance and submission, role playing, consensual behaviour, sexual context and mutual exploration. SM forms a community, more or less closely united by internet sites, specialist shops, clubs and magazines but it is not an exclusive or obligatory form of sexual activity. Thomson (1994) reports that the participants have straight sex far more often than they have SM sex and that they mix these two forms of sexual expression freely. SM practitioners are often demonised as dehumanised or unrelated to each other. This characterisation is both far from the truth and reveals a failure of understanding of SM practice. The complex nature of an SM scene and the importance of trust between the participants means that close relationships are vital to a successful scene. Weinberg *et al.* (1984, cited in Thompson, 1995), for example, in their study stressed the need for a discussion and a bargaining process in the construction of the scene.

A participant's perspective on sadomasochistic practice, chiefly describing the sadistic or dominant position, is given by Dietz (1990). He is keen to emphasise that devotees are not abnormal psychologically and this is reinforced by Gosselin and Wilson's 1980 study. Dietz reports that members of the SM community favour causal explanations based on an early ingrained preference, and also suggests that altered states of consciousness may also be involved. His description of the socio-cultural world of SM makes its diversity plain. He describes a community which has members who are gay and straight, dominant and submissive, and male and female. Various considerations bind these participants together, even as the diversity of sexual preferences and practices separates them. Chief among these unifying factors are rules concerning safety. The emphasis on safety in the SM world is partly sexually tinged, serving to emphasise the possible danger involved. But the concern and care is also genuine and runs strongly counter to the public prejudice against SM practitioners, who are seen as danger-ous and illogical addicts indulging in increasingly excessive, dangerous and licentious acts.

The delights of SM practice have proved remarkably resistant to explanation. The biological function of pain is to stimulate a rapid withdrawal from the stimulus which causes it and seems absolutely at variance with the aims of sexual pleasure. There have been a number of attempts to explain exactly how masochism works. Some theorists have suggested that pain responses diminish during erotic excitement so that the pain is not really painful or that the arousing effect of the pain overwhelms the noxious element. Money (1993) uses opponent process theory to produce a similar explanation. Bancroft (1972), taking a more evolutionary line, discusses whether male dominance is required for male sexuality and suggests that irrespective of whether this is the case men who are dominant can use sex as a method of control. His arguments sit uneasily with the preponderance of male masochists in the SM sex scene (Gosselin and Wilson 1980), whose existence is hard to explain on this account. Bancroft tries to suggest that masochistic fantasies are fuelled by the pleasures of giving up responsibility, which may assuage sexual guilt. Since sexual guilt is on the whole more commonly felt in women this is a less than convincing explanation for male masochism.

Freud's thought is similar to Bancroft. For Freud, sexual sadism is a natural exaggeration of masculine aggression (Freud 1950), and as a result he had difficulties explaining masochism. First he suggested that masochists had turned their sadism on themselves but later changed his mind and ascribed primary erotogenic masochism to the influence of the death instinct in a complex theoretical formulation which links sexual masochism, feminine masochism and moral masochism. This formulation attracted considerable later criticism because it seems to suggest, amongst other things, that masochism is an inherent part of the female psyche. Psychoanalytic theorists also found Freud's formulation of the death instinct difficult to accept.

In England some analysts preferred to discuss the fate of innate aggressive urges rather than the death instinct and Glasser (1979) propounded the influential theory of the core complex. He argued that in perversions aggressive affects towards care-givers arise from conflicts between the need to be separate and also to be fused. These conflicting needs and the aggressive affects they arouse threaten the stability of the early infant and its relationships. Consequently the aggressive affects are neutralised by being sexualised and turned them into sadistic impulses, which paradoxically hurt but also preserve the loved object. Klein and her followers were happy to describe the vicissitudes of the death instinct, and sadomasochistic tendencies have become theoretically very important to Kleinian analysts. Chief amongst these is Betty Joseph (1989), many of whose papers are extended discussions of the operation of what she feels are the subtle but deadly effects of secret sadistic or masochistic impulses in the everyday lives and analyses of her patients.

There are two main problems with English analytic perspectives on sadomasochism. First, the term is used to describe behaviours and experiences which have no overt relation to sex and at times seems to be used purely as a term to describe any interaction disapproved of by the analyst. Second, it is often the case that, when sex is in question, the tone of discussion by the analysts is so relentlessly hostile, contemptuous and denigratory that all the patient's sexual and other life is at once pre-judged as hopelessly pathological and contaminated. This stance amounts often to a hatred of the patient which has evident ill-effects on therapy. The drawbacks of Betty Joseph's work in this respect are well discussed by Ryle (1993).

Two American analysts have been able to open up a somewhat more benign space. Benjamin (1988) uses Hegel's analysis of the dialectic between master and slave to suggest that a masochist does not seek pleasure in pain but rather an opportunity to surrender will in safe conditions. She describes 'ideal love' as a special version of masochism involving yearning for a heroic sadist. She argues that a woman in the grip of the fantasy of ideal love is searching for an experience of excitement and containment not found in childhood. This ideal relationship offers the chance to escape from an internal mother who is at once weak, engulfing and long-suffering. While her analysis accurately and helpfully describes one predicament of women in our culture – their entrapment in a 'masterful, sadistic, hero versus submissive, victim woman' scenario – it does not do much to analyse the nature of sexual sadism.

Stoller (1991), of all the analysts discussing this area, manages the most nuanced account of sadomasochism. He starts off well by discussing the great diversity of potential psychologies involved. His typology of 'bottoms' (people who at least overtly take a submissive role) is a good example and includes 'pushy bottoms', 'bottomless bottoms', and 'tops in bottom drag'! He is also able to acknowledge that the gender of the participants involved may not be as relevant in SM practice as other aspects of their sexual preference. Califia (1984), a lesbian, backs this up. She discusses fisting, which is the practice of inserting a hand into the vagina or anus, and describes an emotionally important sexual scene with a gay man. She describes her feeling that the intimacy created by the nature of the act was more important than the gender or declared sexual orientation of anyone involved. Stoller is also critical of psychoanalytic tendencies to emphasise the notion that SM practitioners dehumanise their partner and instead he recognises that mutual trust is a major feature of SM scenes. That said, Stoller does feel that early trauma is involved in causing SM preferences. He suggests that exposure to severe early pain may predispose people to develop a preference for eroticising pain and also argues that SM scenes allow the symbolic recreation of early humiliating experiences which are now re-enacted in circumstances that allow symbolic success rather than shameful failure. Some SM practitioners have suggested very similar theories but extend them further to claim that SM practice offers healing opportunities in relation to experiences of early abuse.

The idea that SM practice is therapeutic represents a particular strand of the erotic imagination which is important to some SM devotees. While there is no excess of co-morbid psychopathology amongst SM devotees there is no shortage of it either and SM practitioners with psychological difficulties do present. In such clinical situations it can sometimes be difficult to make distinctions between intense SM experiences and some self-abusive practices which are felt to be necessary to deal with tortured states of mind:

> Sandra presented with a ten-year history of chaos. Her work life, personal relationships and involvements with mental health services were all complex, tortured and largely unrewarding. Sandra's account of her early life included accounts of being severely and repeatedly beaten and sexually abused by both her parents and a number of relatives and family friends. By the age of 13 she had become uncontrollable at school, was truanting, suspected of prostitution and using drugs. She had a long history of involvement in psychiatric services but no 'formal

diagnosis'. Currently she lived with a female partner. Both she and her partner self-harmed when in distress but also used knives and cutting during sex. Sandra felt that she was able to distinguish the sexual cutting which she and her partner did from self-wounding. It had a ritual ordered quality which distinguished it from her episodes of self-harm, which were frenzied and desperate. Yet Sandra also worried that sometimes the sex 'goes bad' and at such times she asks her partner to cut more and more deeply in order to feel OK. Her partner responds to these bad times with disgust and mostly refuses to comply.

Sandra's different experiences of cutting threaten to meld into each other but from within the culture she has chosen there is a capacity, exercised by her partner, to distinguish deliberate self-harm from sexual ritual.

Ritual aspects of sadomasochism are well covered by Cowan (1982), whose extended work on masochism analyses this phenomenon from a Jungian perspective and sets it in a religious context. She points out that modern psychology is dominated by the archetype of the hero and by heroic consciousness. Masochism, by contrast, concentrates mind and body into a single focus, burning up the pretensions and prevarications of the ego. Cowan highlights the use of masochism within religious orders as a means of achieving ecstatic religious experience, citing the examples of Teresa of Avila and of the medieval flagellants.

Cowan's consideration of the history of masochism and its religious aspects treats SM as a cultural activity. Perhaps biological explanations for SM fail to cope with the phenomenon because it is a cultural activity appearing in organised form only in literate societies. SM resembles a theatrical production rather more than an act of sexual violence and fantasy elements involve considerable elaboration. Layered on top of the basic dominant–submissive roles is what SM devotees call 'a scene', often involving scripts and extensive paraphernalia. These scenes and fantasies are often drawn from culturally generated scenarios involving stereotyped figures. Possibly SM devotees experience the theatrical elements of SM practice as the main point of the activity. Certainly one investigator (Kamel 1983) found that most interviewees were not interested in physical pain at all but in psychological role play involving shame.

For therapists the lesson of these competing explanations must surely be to counsel caution in making causal judgements. Certainly there is no evidence to support the widespread idea that sadomasochistic sexual activity is associated with any psychopathology. Patients who present with specific sado-masochistic sexual practices that worry them need assessment on a practical basis. The first priority should be to assess and manage any risks to self or others. Next the meaning of the SM act which troubles the patient needs discussing in the patients terms so that the nature of the therapeutic request is clear. Often simple permission is needed and this can usefully be combined with advice about safe sex. Others request a more deep-rooted investigation of their sexual preference. If this is undertaken it should be non-judgemental and should pay as much attention to sociocultural as to intrapsychic factors.

Fetishism

Fetishism is a sexual preference for the presence of not normally culturally sanctioned objects during the sexual act. Technically the presence of this object needs to be an obligatory feature in the sexual act in order for it to qualify as a fetish. Innumerable and at times amusing fetishes have been described. Many are harmless (for example, a sexual preference for balloons). Some, including preferences for autoerotic asphyxia, may be life-threatening for the individual involved. Those 'fetishes' which result in danger to others (for example, paraphilic rape) tend to be separately classified. As with SM, studies of people with fetishes (Gosselin and Wilson 1980) who have not presented themselves to psychiatric services show no evidence of increased psychopathology.

Bancroft (1989) sees fetishism as an extension of people's general tendency to be aroused by body parts and visual signals although he points out that a simple conditioning model for the acquisition of a fetish cannot explain its specificity and exclusivity. Some commentators have argued that orgasm experienced in connection with a fetish serves to reinforce the fetish object, but if this were the case generally then all individuals would suffer from rigidly circumscribed sex lives.

Many people find it difficult to empathise with fetishism. Williamson (1975), a cultural analyst, however, has demonstrated, the way in which fetishism is used in more ordinary lives. The core of fetishisation is the infusion of an ordinary object with special and erotic symbolic power. Williamson argues that objects are marketed by a strategy which involves fetishising them. In advertising the infusion of extra magical, symbolic and sexual status into an object is a central strategy. Fetishisation has been particularly forced on cigarette advertisements because they are sharply restricted in the content they can use. An advertisement for Silk Cut (a brand of cigarettes), which featured a piece of purple silk slashed into a gaping vagina-like slit by a pair of sharp scissors, is a prime example of fetishisation. The absent cigarette becomes far more than itself. Possessing it gains the owner entry into a cool world of sophisticated erotic possibilities symbolised by the pliant available silk and the precise dissecting scissors.

Psychoanalytic theories of fetishism begin with Freud, for whom fetishism was the paradigm of all perversion. He argued that when the little boy sees mother naked and appreciates that she has no penis he may react to the shock of the implied threat of castration by denying what he has seen. A thing comes to stand for the missing maternal penis. Often it is an item that had been on view shortly before the shock of castration occurred, such as a pair of pants. Characteristically, later writers have increased the degree of psychopathology said to accompany fetishism. Lussier (1982), for example, suggests that male fetishists fear complete helplessness and need to exert sadistic control over a woman. The fetish is used to reassure the man that he has control. Using the fetish protects them from anxiety, tension, and fear of homosexuality. Stoller (1975) focuses on the idea that fetishisation is an act of dehumanisation. For Stoller the fetish stands for the whole human, not just for the missing penis. He argues that the fetish serves as a means of revenge used by the fetishist against someone who has humiliated him, and the fetish becomes endowed with the humanness of a now dehumanised other. Stoller's theory is interesting because it comes closest to an anthropological view of fetishism, in which the fetishised object itself is artistically created and invested with magical significance:

> Bill presented with a fetish for masturbating whilst inhaling car exhaust fumes which he felt was growing increasingly danger-ous. Bill thought a stressful experience in his current life was

associated with an increased urge to masturbate. He had been made redundant from work which had increased his social isolation and his mother had recently died. Investigation of his childhood revealed an anxious memory of being taken out by his mother one day in the car. They left in haste and during the journey the necessity for absolute secrecy was impressed upon him repeatedly. On arrival he was told to sit in the car and keep quiet. His mother got out and got into the car in front, where she began kissing a man Bill had not seen before. The engine of the car in front was still running and Bill seems to have entered a slightly dissociated and less anxious frame of mind as he watched the fumes coming out of its exhaust pipe. Later, upset, he would masturbate while thinking of his mother in the car.

The origins of Bill's fetish probably do lie partly in the early events he witnessed and his case illustrates many features common in clinical work with fetishists. There is often a strong connection between the sexual fetish and the need to sooth anxiety, which many psychoanalytic formulations, and certainly Stoller's theory, would predict. However, because this need is often present in other sexual activity, it cannot therefore be thought highly pathological. Patients consult chiefly because, as with Bill, the activity has become risky and has scared them or because of the personal guilt they have incurred through social disapproval of the non-conformist nature of their sexual preference. Some fetishists need reassurance and permission. For those whose sexual activity is dangerous, or who are determined to alter their preference, therapeutic options are narrow. Since it is hard to alter fundamental sexual preferences, treatment is generally most usefully directed at exacerbating factors. Social isolation and decreased sexual opportunity both often contribute to an increase in fetishistic activity and can usefully be tackled in therapy. Obviously in cases where the sexual preference involves danger to self or others, careful and repeated assessment of risk is required along with specialist treatment.

Celibacy

Celibacy is a term that can confusingly refer either to voluntary or involuntary abstinence from sex. In almost all cultures the expectation is that members of the culture will in more or less regulated ways have sex. Our own culture, for example, places extremely strong pressures on its members to be sexual. This is achieved through peer pressure, intergenerational pressure (generally to reproduce), and currently in the West by the commodification of sex and its exploitation in advertising. For this reason, in our culture, and many others, lives of declared or actual celibacy are lives lived in transgression of cultural norms. Notwithstanding, this transgression is often given a ritualised place, being almost always marked out as having a particular, recognised status within cultures. Sobo and Bell (2001) discuss how this status varies between and within cultures.

For women, choosing celibacy and becoming part of some distinctive social structure offers a way to avoid marriage in many cultures. It may offer increased personal and social agency although even in celibacy double standards may exist between women and men, with females subject to male authority. Other cultures use enforced celibacy for particular social situations, imprisonment, war and certain ritual groups. Here motives may involve the need for social control, for example by segregating the sexes. Often the underlying motive is the notion that sex saps energies needed elsewhere.

The most well-known group of individuals who initially choose celibate status but then have it enforced are Catholic priests, friars, monks and nuns. There is much debate over the restrictions on loving relationships which celibacy enforces on the religious. Some groups feel that the restriction should be lifted and point out that the early church did not enforce celibacy. In the press, breaches of priestly celibacy are loudly reported. They fascinate because they represent transgressions from within a transgressive group. The religious involved in transgressions report experiences which range through denial, guilt, remorse, repentance, a wish to remain in the church, or a decision to leave the church. Therapists may find themselves treating the emotional aftermath of such an event. They may also be treating the religious who are considering breaking their vows, or ex-religious who have already left the church. Guilt and doubt are common emotions especially for those who after they leave the church for a relationship find it has not worked out. Therapists need to discover as much as they can about the religious context their patients come from and not assume they already possess a firm knowledge base.

It is always helpful to keep in mind that the choice of religious celibacy which was made and may be broken is a sexual choice. Many religious are aware of this and discuss the way in which erotic energies are released for spiritual purposes by celibacy (Merton 2002). Possibly the most celebrated example is that of St Teresa of Avila, whose mystical experiences included being repeatedly pierced in the heart by an angel holding a spear. She described the transports of pleasure and pain that this experience produced, in terms whose sexual connotations are unmissable. Religious celibacy represents, therefore, a form of the erotic imagination and imposes a discipline which, like all confinements of the erotic, may be experienced by its adherents as constricting or enhancing.

Recently non-religious celibacy has gained a place as an erotic choice in current culture. Some people with celebrity status have loudly declared celibacy, which has acquired as a result the quality of something of a fashion accessory. The credibility of a celebrity's renunciation is assisted by the public perception of their celibate status as chosen rather than enforced – celebrities are assumed to have no difficulty in finding partners. Obviously some people with less access to sexual partners may 'choose' celibacy because they find themselves unable currently to choose otherwise. However, there are many who choose celibacy in order to opt out of the relentless pressures that the modern commodification of sex places on the quantity of erotic encounters and their mechanical properties in favour of a period of time in which the erotic imagination can flourish unhindered by the need to have sex.

Coercive sex

Coercive sex is sex in which one party does not or cannot consent. Fortunately coercive sex is usually considered transgressive in our society although it is worth recalling that it is not all that long since coercive sex in marriage was not considered transgressive, and there are still many societies where coercive sex is acceptable.

While there are cases of female-initiated sexual abuse and harassment these are, as yet, rare in our culture. Broadly therefore the study of coercive sex is one of male sexual activity. Unconsensual sex can occur between adults where threat, force, trickery or the abuse of a dependent relationship is required or it may involve children under the age of 16 who are presumed by society to be incapable of consent. This blanket decision about children can cause difficulties, for example when coercive sex involves children younger than this age as perpetrators.

Sexual harassment and rape

Defining the point at which sexual harassment or rape occurs is problematic and varies between genders and societies. Men tend to set the point at which sexual advances or interest turn from being welcome and flattering or neutral and mildly annoying to being upsetting, aggressive and unpleasant at a much higher level of intrusion than women. This remains true whether sexual harassment or rape is under consideration. Furthermore, both at a cultural level and at a personal one there is ample evidence to show a relationship between beliefs about the appropriateness of male dominance and cultural rates of sexual offending (Sanday 1981 and Gray 1984, in Bancroft 1983: Dutton 1988, Hatfield and Rapson 1996, in Schwartz and Rutter 1998) or personal propensities to judge sexual coercion permissible (Muehlenhard 1988, in Schwartz and Rutter 1998).

The causal factors which predispose an individual to rape or to sexually harass someone are not clearly understood. Other than a tendency by harassers to subscribe to conservative patriarchal perspectives on sexual behaviour no good distinguishing factors have been found between harassing and non-harassing men (Gutek 1985, quoted in Morris 1997). More work has been done on rape and biological, psychological, and social theories have been outlined.

Thornhill and Palmer's (2000) sociobiological theory of rape suggests that it results from a specific adaptive strategy some men can deploy when deprived of other sexual opportunities. A sexually coercive male may succeed in male–male competition for females even though he has lost in competition for female mate choice. One interesting consequence of this view is that rape is a sexual crime rather than a violent one. They argue that the general lack of gratuitous violence in most rape supports this idea. Thornhill and Palmer also argue that rape in marriage may result from an evolutionary strategy designed to compete with a potential sexual cuckolder. They suggest that perceived female sexual unresponsiveness in a relationship might signal a recent sexual encounter with a rival. Coerced sex may then serve to displace rival sperm with all possible speed. Some evidence for Thornhill and Palmer's hypothesis may be found in the fact that rape is predominantly a young male crime with a strong association with low socioeconomic class. Such individuals might be thought to have a harder time competing for a mate than older wealthier men. However there is other evidence not explained by their theory. For example, most convicted rapists reported experiencing erectile difficulties, premature ejaculation or ejaculatory incompleteness during the sexual assault (Morris 1997). If rape were an evolutionary strategy for effective reproductive sex it should not be associated with these kinds of sexual difficulty.

Cultural and social factors

The main cultural risk factor for rape is holding male-dominant views. However Russell (1984) and also Segal (1994) and Smith (1992) take this analysis further, demonstrating how cultural tendencies to define masculinity in terms of aggression and sexual vitality are combined with tendencies to downplay the role of affection in the expression of sexual needs. The cultural stereotype of unfeeling aggression which men are expected to live up to (something Samuels (1999) has termed the 'male deal') may make rape a more socially acceptable option. Although it has close links to a feminist analysis (see, for example, Brownmiller 1975), this cultural perspective tries not to demonise men but instead sees them as being as trapped by the cultural stereotype as women are. Feminists and other workers in this tradition have tended to see rape as a crime of violence (Holmstrom and Burgess 1980) and to regard sociobiological perspectives as positively dangerous in that they appear to sanction male violence and the crudest stereotypes of male and female behaviour.

Personal factors

Most men do not rape. However a fair proportion of men admit to sexual arousal during rape fantasies (Schwartz and Rutter 1998). Furthermore, about 30 per cent of men say that they would use sexual coercion to obtain intercourse if they were certain they would not be discovered (Briere and Malamuth 1983, in Schwartz and Rutter 1998) and an even larger percentage say that a woman's resistance is simply a put-up token which can be overridden. This means that we should not expect all rapists to be sharply distinguishable from the normal population. Formal studies of rapists support this notion to some extent in that no clear picture of the rape personality emerges (Bancroft 1983). However, there are important associations between rape and other criminal behaviour, between rape and sexual disadvantage, between rape and high levels of sexual activity, and between rape and sexual abuse during childhood (Groth 1979). Evidently, therefore, men rape for a range of reasons and in a range of settings and no single explanatory hypothesis is ever likely to emerge to explain all incidents of rape.

Treating sexual aggression

Most of the formal research literature on the treatment of sexual aggression focuses on working with very serious sexual offenders, such as rapists. The best evidence for treatment effects has been gathered with cognitive therapies but even here there are few grounds for optimism (Marx *et al.* 1999; Clelland *et al.* 1998). Patients who present for treatment prior to serious difficulties with the law may be doing so because of an awareness that their behaviour is growing risky or they may have had a close shave of some sort. In all cases the first and most important task is an assessment of risk, which should involve detailed enquiry about previous acts, future plans, and the extent to which the patient has already broken social taboos in pursuit of coercive sex. Risk varies with time and will therefore need to be a continuing consideration throughout the remainder of any treatment. The normal boundaries of the therapeutic situation may need to be breached if the therapist becomes seriously concerned about the risk of harm to others. Treating serious sexual offenders is a specialist task and rapid referral to a specialist unit is essential if risk to others is present.

The actual course of treatment depends on the nature of the patient's motivation for treatment and the reasons behind the urge to offend. For many, a focus on the feelings and emotional responses of the victim is appropriate and helps compensate for a lack of empathy. For those whose sexual adaptation is poor and whose coercive behaviour is driven by lack of opportunity, training in social and sexual skills may be helpful. There are no systematic trials of psychoanalytic methods in treating sexual aggression and coercion, indeed results are anecdotally disappointing. Notwithstanding it is clear that purely skills-based or cognitive behavioural approaches are struggling to make a substantial impact on a problem where individual fantasy and developmental history are clearly relevant. Psychodynamic understandings may assist a practical approach.

Child sexual abuse

The vast preponderance of those who are currently discovered to abuse children are men who are often between the ages of 20 and 40 (Bancroft 1989). Their victims may either be members of their own family or acquaintances or strangers. As a group they are heterogeneous with a proportion who have learning difficulty, psychotic illness or an alcohol problem. The kinds of sexual contact involved ranges from intercourse to indecent exposure.

Possibly the term paedophile is best reserved for a group of offenders who have a pretty exclusive sexual interest in young children generally of one or other sex and who devote considerable time and attention to this interest. While a paedophile may abuse a relative they are also likely to abuse non-related children and to abuse more than one child. Little else unites paedophiles as a group. Some are sexually inexperienced men who lack other opportunities for sexual expression, while others appear to have a fixed transgressive sexual preference for children in a particular age range.

A range of theories have been proposed to explain the origins of paedophilia. Socoredes (1988), an analyst, suggests that the paedophile is attempting to repair a damaged relationship with his mother. Social learning models have been proposed, suggesting that paedophile tendencies represent an example of the intergenerational transmission of maltreatment. Others argue that pornography serves as the vehicle which provides the learning context in which paedophiles' sexual preferences are formed. It has also been suggested that males are more likely to sexually abuse children because they are not well socialised to distinguish between sexual and non-sexual forms of affection. Instead males are socialised to be attracted to sexual partners who, like children, are smaller, younger and less powerful than themselves. Recent reports suggest a role for sexual abuse in the childhood of paedophiles as an aetiological factor (Murray 2000). None of these theories is entirely convincing and perhaps the most important causal observation is that sexual arousal in relation to children is not uncommon with 21 per cent of college males reporting some degree of sexual arousal in relation to young children (Schwartz and Rutter 1998).

The treatment of paedophilia is not likely to be successful in abolishing the nature of the sexual preference involved and, unlike other criminals, paedophiles show constant recidivism rates even many years after conviction. Treatment is therefore often based on Finkelhor's four step model (1987) which defines the successive stages by which a paedophile might give way to his sexual wish. Not all the issues that need managing during treatment involve harming children, as the following case illustrates:

> Brian presented to the clinic after he had been caught taking photographs, which he called views, of young children bathing. His flat was searched and many photographs of children were found as well as some internet pornography on the computer. He was a sad and isolated character who had never married. He freely admitted that his occupation as a school janitor had been chosen for the contact it gave him with young children and firmly denied that he would ever approach or touch a child. Being discovered resulted in the loss of his job and a conviction. He now lived in terror of being discovered by his neighbours. During therapy, which (using Finkelhor's model) concentrated on helping him to accept responsibility for his behaviour and to identify when he began to give way to temptation and set up situations in which he could photograph children, he made three serious suicide attempts and succeeded on his fourth.

Paedophiles like Brian often become depressed and are quite a serious risk to themselves once they are in trouble with the law.

Generally, paedophile wishes do not abate in therapy, which has therefore to focus on controlling wishes and taking responsibility for actions. Social opprobrium weighs heavily on paedophiles; therapy encourages them to give up something they found pleasurable. Suicide is a real risk.

Adults who engage in incestuous sexual activity with children are as heterogeneous as paedophiles and there will be some whose sexual activity with their own children or stepchildren is part of a more general paedophiliac tendency. More commonly this form of abuse is carried out by males on girls of varying ages but most often near or after puberty. The finding that stepfathers are more likely to abuse than natural fathers (Finkelhor 1993; Emmert and Kohler 1998) highlights potential evolutionary explanations, possibly involving a failure of a genetically driven incest taboo or a lessening of the curbs on sexual expression imposed by parental responsibility. Abusers may fall into a range of patterns. Some are authoritarian patriarchs whose attitude to the family is one of ownership and command. Others are supposedly 'inadequate' or responding to difficulties in their marital relationship. Yet a third group of abusers come from a family pattern in which a cycle of economic disadvantage is combined with lax intergenerational boundaries and chaotic patterns of interpersonal relatedness. In such families more than one generation may be abusing and being abused. The most common attitude that incestuous abusers adopt is one of blanket denial and this is consistent with a common announcement to their victim that they will deny anything occurred if confronted. As a result, treatment generally is not sought in voluntary settings.

Coercive sex is rightly socially sanctioned. It involves a violation of key social principles of relatedness but it is also a manifestation, albeit ugly, of the erotic imagination. Probably the destructive abusive use of an object can never be capable of producing lasting artistic or creative merit but it still represents a facet of human expression within the orbit of normal understanding. However disagreeable the idea is to contemplate, most people can identify within themselves erotic trends with coercive characteristics. The line between perpetrators and their therapists is only one of degree.

Perversion, transgression and normality

When transgressive sex is separated out from coercive sex the moral opprobrium which attaches to it is revealed as less rational. Even when coercive sex is considered, social disapproval is not evenly distributed, with paedophiles subjected at times to the rule of the mob while rape may even be condoned. It is interesting to consider the reason why some consenting sexual practices are disapproved of so violently. Taylor (1997) argues that standards of heterosexual conformity became part of culture when early man moved from an agrarian life to one which involved animal husbandry. The needs of animal breeding, particularly in relation to keeping records of animal blood lines and controlling them to improve breeding stock, encouraged early man to conceive of women and their reproductive capacity as a resource to be 'managed'.

Rubin's (1989) work supports this view to an extent. She sets out clearly the hierarchy of opprobrium to which the term transgressive sex applies, pointing out that sex where the number of people involved is not two, where toys are used, where money is involved, using pain or bondage, where age barriers are transgressed, is classified as transgressive. She shows how in each case it is degree of difference from a heterosexual ideal that unites the different forms of disapproved of sex and stratifies them by degrees of unacceptability. Rubin, unlike Taylor, points to tribal rather than agrarian concerns as the drivers of conformity, essentially arguing that patrilinial exogamous tribes need to exert tight control on women because they are seen as a negotiable resource.

So, heretofore in our culture, many sexual practices now considered transgressive may be thought of that way as a result of institutionalised practices driven by a need to control women. Now the situation is changing and transgressive sexual practices have come to stand in something of the same position that homosexual sex stood in one hundred years ago. They remain relatively forbidden but they are becoming contested ground.

Giddens (1992) addresses the reason for this social shift as a product of the general tendency to increase individual rights over and against state control. For Giddens this shift towards individualism is part of a general focus on self-creation as the task of the citizen. However Giddens is also concerned to argue that modernity involves 'the socialisation of the modern world'. He therefore combines the increasing individualisation of society with the widening sphere of activities which are socially negotiable rather than predetermined by biology, psychology or religion.

As sexuality becomes socially negotiable, part of social relations, then heterosexuality whose fixity was largely a biological, psychological or religious concern ceases to be the standard by which all else is judged.

One thing is shamefully clear. By and large medicine, sex therapy, and other therapies have lagged behind social shifts and have tended to fall back into the easy stance of pathologising any deviance from a rusting patrilineal exogamous social structure. Despite pockets of old-fashioned practice, some therapies have modernised to some degree and are practised in less discriminatory ways. Often to the extent that therapies are psychoanalytically inspired this liberalisation has come late if at all. Indeed, by and large in the case of psychoanalysis, a commitment to maintaining the sexual status quo remains. Analysts frequently restate in various ways that despite its painful compromises the sexual arrangements of patrilineal exogamy are normal and that all else is deviant to a greater or lesser degree. The best advice to patients whose sex lives involve transgressive practices is that they should at the very least be aware of this state of affairs when consulting a psychoanalytical therapist who practises in an orthodox way.

Those therapies which are able to view transgressive sex as non-pathological might benefit from taking a further leap and considering its beneficial potential. Essentially transgressive sexuality is, like all manifestations of the erotic imagination, an aesthetic activity. Carrying the aesthetic analogy forward, heterosexual monogamy might for the sake of argument be compared with, say, the neoclassical style in architecture. It is but one of many potential and fruitful formalisms which serve either to contain or to chain the creative imagination, depending on the artist. Debates within art about the extent to which new styles risk becoming trite or merely sensationalist are counterpoised with artistic manifestoes proclaiming the right of artists to explore all avenues of expression. These aesthetic debates are direct counterparts of debates in the sexual sphere about the value or otherwise of forms of erotic expression. Transgressive sex, like art, is a work of the imagination. Like art, it can go too far, becoming trite,

 Transgendered people: the plasticity of gender

Introduction

Even the earliest written records (that is from roughly about 5000 years ago) contain evidence of variations in gender identity, including evidence of the existence of individuals we might now call intersexed or transgendered (Markowitz *et al.* 1999). In modern times the legal and medical treatment of both intersexed and transgendered people has sparked debate which has extended well beyond the bounds of the therapeutic and into the political realm. Transgendered and intersexed people can present therapists with a range of predicaments and dilemmas particularly if they are supposed to control access to certain treatments. In this chapter the spectrum of intersex and transgendered conditions is outlined. Then causal theories are reviewed followed by a preliminary discussion of direct treatment options. Political debates are aired next and this paves the way for a more differentiated discussion of the role and value of psychotherapeutic treatment.

Definitions

Intersex

In intersex conditions a child is born with genitalia which are ambiguous between male and female morphology or discordant with chromosomal sex. These conditions may result from anomalies in development or from inborn errors of metabolism which expose the developing foetus or infant to abnormal levels of hormones. They manifest at all ranges of severity from the barely

noticeable to severe abnormalities with life-threatening consequences. Androgen insensitivity syndrome (AIS) is one of the
commonest causes. It results from insensitivity to testosterone,
which causes genetically male individuals to be born to a greater
or lesser extent feminised in their external appearance. Because
the development of the internal genitalia initially proceeds independently of testosterone people with androgen insensitivity
syndrome who appear to be female have two rudimentary testes
found in the abdomen, groin or labia. These structures, ironically,
produce some oestrogen and this produces the feminisation.
Many children with this condition are assigned a female sex at
birth and are raised as girls. Often the first sign of anything wrong
is failure to menstruate and go through a normal puberty. Almost
all have a secure female gender identity (their chromosomal sex
notwithstanding) and their main psychological problems arise
over issues of fertility and of secrecy:

> Frances presented in distress, at the age of 22 after a consulta-
> tion with an English physician. She had consulted him because
> she still had no menstrual periods. The physician had examined
> her and diagnosed androgen insensitivity syndrome. His expla-
> nation of the syndrome was abrupt and unsympathetic, possibly
> because he found it hard to believe she did not know the nature
> of her condition. She became distressed and was referred for
> assessment. Frances was born in Germany and raised by loving
> parents who had frequently taken her to the doctor for check-
> ups of a condition which they never quite named. Her failure
> to menstruate had been dealt with by explanations that some
> women didn't menstruate for a while and assurances that every-
> thing would be 'fine in the end'. Frances needed help to cope
> with a range of issues, such as the sudden loss of her expecta-
> tions over fertility, her sense of betrayal by her family. She also
> needed to have an operation to remove her residual testes
> which, her doctor told her, might become malignant. She
> firmly identified herself as a woman and found the revelation of
> her male chromosomal sex irrelevant to her gender identity.
> She wanted therapy to cope with her infertility and found the
> removal of her testes difficult because she felt emotionally that
> her only hope of fertility was being removed.

Francis presented as a typical case of androgen insensitivity syndrome which seems to have been dealt with in a somewhat old fashioned manner. From a psychodynamic perspective her regret over loosing potentially cancerous testes could possibly be ascribed to sadness over loosing a residual sense of maleness. However, overtly she experienced no sense of conflict in this area, being concerned mainly with a shocking loss of fertility.

Not all cases of androgen insensitivity syndrome result in complete feminisation. When partial feminisation occurs the genitalia may be far more ambiguous. Children in this situation have been reared as girls or as boys depending on the appearance of the genitalia. Virilisation as well as feminisation can occur. In congenital adrenal hyperplasia (CAH), excessive androgen production either before or after birth partially virilises a female foetus or baby girl and a more or less masculine appearance may result. In such cases children have been raised either as girls or as boys (although most often as boys). As well as AIS and CAH there are a huge range of other syndromes mostly, fortunately, rare, which cause every kind of intermediate anatomical arrangement. The study of these conditions has been exploited by scientists interested in furthering debates over the relative contributions of nature and nurture in determining human gender identity (see Money 1993; Diamond 1982, 1999, 2000). A disadvantage of these struggles has been that, on occasion, the needs and wishes of the patients have come a poor second to academic debate (Colapinto 2000). Furthermore some intersex patients have begun to protest against being subjected as children to surgery designed to 'normalise' their genitalia, surgery which has sometimes assigned a sex which the adult intersexed person finds uncongenial and which often reduces genital function, sensation and sexual pleasure.

Transgender

Unlike intersexed people, transgendered individuals are born with no discernible structural deviation from their chromosomal sex. However, at some point they come to feel dissatisfied with their biological sex and wish for a change. In the classical definition of the condition a strong desire to change biological sex and a hatred of the sex at birth, particularly combined with an aversion to their own genitals, is required. Both men and women can wish for a change in gender. Incidence estimates vary but a UK figure for people seeking gender reassignment is 1 in 33,000 for male to female transgendered people and 1 in 108,000 for female to male transgendered people (Bancroft 1989):

> Amy, a male to female transsexual consulted in order to be referred to a gender reassignment clinic for surgery. She had been living exclusively in the female role for the past year having changed her name on all her papers. She talked knowledgably about the different effects of various hormone combinations and gave her interviewer a thick and helpful wadge of information on transgender issues. She had presented to the clinic because friends of hers had given it good reports and she had a clear agenda of items to discuss. Amy found having a penis disgusting. She said, 'I feel like a woman. When I look down I am shocked. It feels all wrong.' However, she was also clear that her penis was a source of sexual pleasure and this made her confused whenever she did have sex with her partner, who was a woman. Her agenda at presentation was first to secure referral to a gender reassignment programme that would ultimately offer her surgery. Once she was assured that this would be forthcoming she began to talk about other issues she found confusing. One which preoccupied her was whether she was heterosexual or homosexual.

Amy is typical of many transgendered patients who want gender reassignment. She has found out a great deal about her condition. She is already part of a lively community of transgendered individuals who swap information and give support both in meetings and on the internet. Discussing Amy's case raises issues of terminology, which is often a problem in case accounts of transgendered people. Patients are often referred to by pronouns which oscillate between gender assigned at birth and current gender role. The oscillation probably signals difficulties in dealing with patients who challenge classical notions about gender binaries. Transgendered people mostly prefer to be referred by the sex they would like to be or have already been reassigned to. In this account therefore a genetic male who wants to live in the female role will be referred to as a male to female transgendered person, or woman.

Amy's anxieties over her sexual orientation are shared by experts, who find that the sexual orientation of transgendered people gives them trouble partly because they cannot decide whether to classify it in relation to chromosomal sex or by reference to preferred gender. Until recently transgendered patients whose pre- or post-operative partner or sexual preference was not standard had difficulty in obtaining treatment. Sullivan, a gay female to male transgendered person, was rejected for reassignment because of his interest in men sexually. Many years later following reassignment elsewhere he died of AIDS and remarked:

> I took a certain pleasure in informing the gender clinic that even though their program told me I could not live as a gay man, it looks as if I am going to die like one. (Califia 1997:187)

The early studies which show both homosexual and heterosexual adjustment before reassignment and a majority with heterosexual adjustments after surgery do not reflect a growing range of sexual choices made pre- and post-operatively so that many different pre- and post-operative sexual object choices are now being made, including choosing to live with another transgendered person (Califia 1997).

Transvestism

Transvestites are people who, for a whole range of reasons, wish to dress in clothing of the opposite sex. Those who do so, for reasons of sexual pleasure or as a result of wishes to experience the female gender, are almost overwhelmingly male in current culture. However, strong traditions exist of women dressing as men for a variety of reasons and Caplan (1987) argues that there are true female transvestites. At first glance, transvestites seem rather different from transgendered individuals and they used to be separated sharply, in relation to diagnosis, from transgendered men. In fact there is considerable overlap between the two groups and Bancroft defines a continuum ranging from fetishistic transvestite at one end through to the 'full-time' transsexual:

> Simon, a large and imposing man, worked as a lorry driver all over Europe. He presented at the clinic because of anxieties

surrounding his increasing desire to dress in female clothing. Initially he had been interested in isolated items of female clothing (often underwear) and had used these as an aid to masturbation. However as time passed he began wearing women's clothes and experienced himself as more comfortable when doing this. He began to think of himself as having a female personality who alternated with his male personality. When dressed he was Joan, when he was working he was Simon. Recently during a long journey he had dared to present himself at a place where lorry drivers meet dressed as Joan. He was amazed at the high level of acceptance he received and at the aggressive defence of him by some of the truck drivers when another group began to make disparaging comments. At present he was not seeking gender reassignment and acknowledged that this would be difficult for him for medical reasons. He was however concerned about his future if his gender dysphoria became stronger.

Simon is a fairly typical transvestite who may be moving slowly from a transvestite identity towards a more transgendered one. Bancroft points out that many transvestites are married and, typically, transvestite behaviour first shows itself in adolescence but recedes in the early years of marriage, returning later on when problems develop in the marriage. In such circumstances he argues that the transvestite behaviour is a substitute for heterosexual behaviour. Other transvestites like Simon are characterised by Bancroft as having a tendency to become more transsexual as time goes on. This transvestite transsexual shift may, according to Bancroft, either be due to underlying transsexualism or to conditioning in enjoying the female role as a result of repeated orgasms while cross-dressed. Bancroft likens the progress from transvestite to transsexual status and the breakdown of the marital relationship which often results as 'a psychological malignancy because of its unstoppable destructive effect' (1989:355). This rather pejorative judgement overshadows the important fact that in cases such as Simon's the transition between transvestite and transgendered status often gathers speed and force with age. This must be taken into consideration in managing such patients. The continuum between transvestism and transgendered status, and also the range of strengths of transgendered wishes, make it sensible to see all these conditions as points along a continuum of dissatisfaction with gender. As a result it is often better to use the term gender dysphoria to describe them.

Causes of gender dysphoria: biological and sociocultural issues

Theories about the cause of gender dysphoria are difficult to formulate largely because no reliable theory of gender identity has yet been formulated. Patients with intersex conditions have often become debating grounds for considering these issues, but even here controversy reigns. There is, for instance, the now infamous case of John/Joan a genetic male whose penis was mutilated in a botched surgical operation. He was then reared as a girl on the advice of John Money, an expert in the field. John/Joan rebelled against this as a teenager and now lives as a man. This case has been taken as evidence that gender identity depends on sex of rearing and, more recently, as evidence for the primacy of biology (Colapinto 2000). The influence of prenatal androgens does seem to be important but not decisive (Bancroft 1989). Bancroft also suggests that in transgendered men in particular there may be elevated testosterone levels. Pillard and Weinrich (1987, in Devor 1999) have developed a more complicated hormonal theory to try to classify different kinds of gender identity in relation to perinatal hormonal influences but even this theory leaves much unexplained. Notwithstanding the current lack of firm evidence, most transgendered people and the great majority of people who work with them are fairly convinced of the view that a biological cause for the condition will be uncovered sooner or later.

Sociocultural studies of gender identity reveal that gender dysphoria is quite common although it is socialised differently in a range of cultural settings. Aversion to biological sex is expressed by a proportion of girls and boys, with a peak of expression in adolescence. There are large variations between cultures in this proportion, which parallels the proportion of individuals seeking gender reassignment. Thus more people seek gender reassignment in the USA than in Sweden and, there is more gender dysphoria expressed at adolescence in the USA than in Sweden (Bancroft 1989)

Some other cultures have made institutional roles to accommodate gender dysphoria. Indian mythology is hospitable to nonstandard gender roles containing numerous examples of androgyny. In the worship of Krishna, male devotees may imagine themselves to be female, and even dress in female clothing. Another example is the Hijra, who represent an institutionalised third-gender role in India that is neither male nor female. They are believed to be intersexed, or impotent men, who undergo emasculation, adopt female dress and earn their living by collecting alms. Rituals exist within the community of the Hijra for creating family relations, such as taking a daughter. The daughters of one mother consider themselves sisters. Although their role requires Hijras to dress like women, few make any real attempt to imitate or to pass as a woman and it is not rare for them to have beards. Hijras have sexual relationships with men. They may work as prostitutes or take a husband but Hijras do not characterise their male sexual partners as homosexuals and they quite explicitly distinguish themselves from homosexuals. Many Hijras see themselves as women trapped in male bodies.

Other groups with transgendered elements include the Berdache, who are Native American Indian men living as women and honoured as shamans, and the Xanith in Oman, who retain a male name but act as the receptive partner in gay sex. The Xanith dress in clothes which are intermediate between male and female and can move freely among women in purdah, or join women singers at a wedding, but like men they have the right to go about unaccompanied. Money, discussing roles such as these, talks of 'gynemimetics', men who want to look like women but not be them. Money says that gynemimetics may take oestrogens but do not desire surgery (Money 1997). Money's distinction may be valid for the transgendered performers of Latin America, although some of these do opt for surgery, but for cultures where surgery is or was not an option his categorisation seems at best a piece of casuistry. It points up the dangers of carrying across western concepts about gender identity and role, which are embodied in the notion of transsexualism, to different cultures where gender roles are differently structured. Indeed, scholarly wars have reigned over the exact classificatory status of the practices of different cultures (a good summary can be found in Califia 1997). This debate feels far less academic if transgendered people in our own culture are viewed as less of a biological curiosity and more as a culture in the making.

While sociological and anthropological theorists have broadened our understanding of the range of transgendered experiences they have not helped to develop an understanding of its causes. What they have done instead is to underline the complexity of this search. Psychological theories of this area are all either psychoanalytic or heavily influenced by psychoanalysis. Within this class, though, there are a fairly wide range of psychoanalytic views about the origins of transgendered experiences which tend to reflect the broader theoretical background of the theorist.

Causes of male to female transsexualism

For American theorists, the work of Margaret Mahler (1968), who charted the slow and conflicted progress through many hard to remember stages of the child from fusion with the mother to a separate existence, has been a decisive theoretical influence. Person and Ovesey (1974a) argue, in common with Stoller (1968) and Segal (1965), that the origins of transsexualism, transvestism and effeminate homosexuality are pre-oedipal and stem from unresolved separation anxiety from mother. In male transsexualism the child is said to resort to a fantasy of symbiotic fusion with the mother thereby allaying separation anxiety but at the cost of ambiguous gender identity. This ambiguity of gender identity then impedes sexual development and leads to relative asexuality. This theory sets transsexuals at the most primitive end of a spectrum of developmental deficits of gender identity and sexuality. Stoller (1968), less influenced by Mahler, argues differently, suggesting that the typical male to female transsexual is a beautiful boy and the son of a depressed mother who, herself, felt unwanted in early life. She keeps the boy close and he leads a blissful life with his mother who excludes the father and makes the child into her longed for phallus. As a result he does not want to separate from her and so tries to be her.

In England, Limentani is an important theorist. He begins by discussing castration anxiety, which is seemingly absent in transsexuals who actively seek castration. This represents a major theoretical conundrum for any classical Freudian analysis of a transgendered patient. However, although castration fears are generally directed at father Limentani ultimately identifies mother as the prime source of difficulties. He argues that transsexuals seek to assuage profound early anxieties by seeking to obtain a female body which allows fusion with mother and blots out a sense of unbearable separateness. Limentani (1979) characterises the thinking of transsexuals as psychotic, by which he means that they deny the reality of their gender. Kleinians believe that acknowledging the truths of the value of the breast, the difference between the sexes, and the parental relationship involves an emotional achievement and is a requirement for psychological health. Transsexuals are denying the reality of their bodies and this signals, from a Kleinian perspective, a fundamental disturbance of consciousness and of emotional and moral capacity. Limentani's accounts of analytic treatments of transsexual patients, and other accounts in this analytic tradition, concentrate on uncovering other signs of this disturbance.

Richard Green's view of the aetiology of male to female transsexuals is conditioned by his long-running study on 'sissy boys' (1987). These are boys who display feminine behaviours and wish to cross-dress in childhood. Green and Stoller both think effeminate behaviour in childhood may be a precursor of transgendered behaviour in adult life. Green thinks that a range of factors turns childhood gender non-conformity into adult transgendered behaviour. The factors he lists are: parental unconcern over gender nonconformity, encouragement of feminine behaviour, permitting repeated cross-dressing, maternal over protection, inhibition of boyish play, excessive maternal attention and physical contact, absent father, physical beauty of the boy, and lack of male playmates (Bancroft 1989:352). Green's list is problematic because he appears to subscribe to and universalise a very parochial and now rather dated vision of healthy boyhood. Furthermore it is not at all clear that childhood effeminate behaviour does predispose to later transgendered behaviour. Ovsey and Person disagree both with Green and Stoller in this and, on the basis of a study of ten patients, argue that male to female transgendered patients do not have effeminate childhoods. Indeed, when Green followed these children up over a long period of time he found an elevated rate of homosexual orientation among them but no evidence of an elevated rate of transgendered development. While, in support of Green, there is some evidence of a lack of male role models in some transgendered people (Rekers *et al.* 1983), other retrospective surveys of cases show that in as many as half there is no evidence of early parental conditioning of the kind he elaborates. The evidence to support upbringing as a factor in the development of transgendered feelings seems weak and, at best, equivocal:

> Amy's childhood had been a happy one as far as she could remember until she went to school. In school however she had been picked on and teased for being insufficiently masculine. Certainly she would choose girls over boys for companions. She said that at this time she began to feel different from other boys and was confused by this. By about eight she was sure that she should be a girl but unclear what to do about this problem. Amy's mother was rather preoccupied with her other children and her father was 'not the sort of person you could talk to about that kind of thing'. In retrospect Amy wondered if she and her father had grown apart because her father had disliked his effeminate son. As a late adolescent Amy had become very involved in bodybuilding in order to overcome her 'odd ideas'. In this she was successful and accepted.

Elements of Amy's story accord with psychoanalytic case descriptions. Others do not. Perhaps her preoccupied mother didn't help her manage separation issues when these became more intense with schooling, as Person and Ovesey suggest. On the other hand there is no evidence of parental conditioning of the sort Green thinks important, nor does Amy's mother seem to have been over-intrusive. Rather, Amy's story is closest to the trajectory proposed by Isay (1996) for gay men, in which the psychodynamics of childhood are those of a child trying to puzzle out a sense of pre-existing difference unmediated by adults or helpful social structures.

Causes of female to male transsexualism

In general, female to male transsexuals have received less interest than male to female ones. Bancroft argues that a wish to avoid homosexuality is a strong determinant, suggesting that some lesbians who become aware of sexual attraction to females first reject these feelings and try to make relationships with boys. When this fails, they choose lesbian relationships with innocent girls who have no sexual experience and, instead of regarding themselves as lesbian, decide to regard themselves as a male in order to maintain a heterosexual identity. This theory seems far-fetched since, from the point of view of social opprobrium, choosing to be transgendered is hardly a great alternative to choosing to be lesbian. It is also not supported by the common trajectory of female to male transsexuals' lives, which often include long periods living as a lesbian before concluding that gender reassignment is the only option.

Green's view (Devor 1999) is identical to that produced for boys. He stresses early gender nonconformity and says:

> Give a female child a male derivative name, provide a stable warm father, and make mother an unpleasant or emotionally unavailable woman and reinforce rough and tumble play.

While a substantial minority of adult transsexuals displayed tomboy behaviour in childhood it is not clear what can be argued from this since while virilising hormones predispose to tomboy behaviour (Bancroft 1989) girls who are exposed to them mostly grow up into heterosexual women. Bancroft does, however, think it relevant to tell us that (1989:350) 'They may continue to show some typically male characteristics, putting careers before marriage or preferring male-type clothes.' It should by now be clear that both Green's and Bancroft's work is diminished by unexamined and dated assumptions about gender roles.

Stoller believes that female to male transsexualism is different from male to female transsexualism because females, unlike males, always become transsexual as a result of psychological trauma. Stoller argues that the process begins with grandparents who instil in the mothers of female to male transsexuals a sense that to be female is of little value. As children, these mothers dream of being boys and as adults they dream of having boys. The daughters of these mothers later became transsexual because, being girls, they did not get enough attention from their mothers. The daughters naturally turn to their fathers for comfort. They learn that their mothers are sources of frustration, take up a lot of emotional space in the family but provide little succour. Furthermore, fathers may present femaleness as less than desirable. The daughters learn that their fathers expect them to take on masculine roles and look after their weak mothers. Stoller says that most will find they are becoming romantically attracted to girls in early adolescence. Lesbianism or transgendered status follows. Stoller's work is important largely because it is contained in a lengthy and sympathetic study of a female to male transsexual seen by him over a long period of time. Although many of the views expressed are somewhat dated, Stoller does seem to have been interested in listening to his patient's experience in a non-judgemental way.

As usual there is disagreement. Person and Ovesey (1974a) do support Stoller's line of reasoning but go further, claiming that female transsexuals are all at first homosexuals with a masculine gender role identity. Limentani (1979) disagrees with Stoller and suggests that female to male transsexuals have an even more profound disturbance than to male to female ones. He says they fail to feel they can ever have a body of their own because an intrusive, over-engulfing mother has taken up all the available space. They adopt a male body in a desperate flight into the only remaining gender.

Causes of cross-dressing

Cross-dressing is a far more common presenting problem than transgendered status. Bancroft suggests that a major mechanism is sexual learning, in which the pubertal boy discovers the erotic effect of a woman's clothing, found it exciting because of its association with female genitals and used as a masturbatory aid just like a pornographic picture. He then suggests that cross-dressing may come to be used to create a fantasy woman or doppelganger partner (Bancroft 1972). Against this theoretical suggestion must be set the fact that not all fetishistic transvestites begin with erotic transvestism, some begin with non-erotic cross-dressing which only later becomes eroticised.

From a classical psychoanalytic perspective cross-dressing is a fetishistic activity. The little boy is supposed to discover the fact that his mother does not have a penis by seeing his mother with no clothes on, and in a flash, knowing that she has been castrated. This thought is unbearable to the boy, who takes the last item seen before the sight of mother's genitals as a substitute for the mother's absent/present penis. Later analysts have been less impressed by the traumatic effect of castration. Stoller prefers to suggest that the adult transvestite was actually humiliated by an older powerful woman who forced him, as a child, to dress up in female clothes. Adult cross-dressing repeats this trauma, masters it, feeds revenge fantasies against women (in ways Stoller fails to elucidate) and identifies the man with the masterful phallic woman. Kaplan suggests that the mortification of being excluded from the parental bed is a key factor. Characteristically, Person and Ovesey (1978) suggest that pre-oedipal mechanisms are involved and argue that in transvestism the mother's clothes represent mother as a transitional object and are used as a fetishistic defence against Oedipal anxieties.

The various mechanisms to which psychoanalytic theorists tend to appeal are of a sort which ought to produce character pathology as well as cross-dressing, and this character pathology is frequently described in the analytic literature. However, there is survey evidence (Brown *et al.* 1996) to show that transvestite men are not more likely to suffer from psychosocial difficulties than are normal people. Perhaps a tendency to pathologise transvestism as a perversion fundamentally involving hatred, has blinded analytic theorists to a gentler view of the origins of this condition. As Person and Ovesey point out, many children have blankets or other comfort items to hold and these are also often parts of their mother's clothing. These may be prized because they are soft and remind the child of mother's body. They are comforting and protective. The same terms are also used by transvestites to describe their experiences of being dressed. It is also common for children to masturbate both for pleasure and for comfort when anxious. Thereafter, as Bancroft points out, associative mechanisms may link the holding of, or rubbing with, an item of female clothing, with sexual arousal and particularly with sex for comfort. The link that this sexual activity retains with childhood self-reassurance in times of stress explains why it is increased in adult life when stresses multiply. Person and Ovesey's appeal to pre-oedipal anxieties and Bancroft's doppelganger theory seem to add no helpful extra-explanatory element.

Treatment options

Therapists' attitudes to transgendered patients

Patients who are being offered treatment deserve to be looked after by therapists who are able to regard them as valuable and can treat them with respect. By now it should be clear that denigration, either intentional or otherwise, is a major problem in psychologically based causal accounts of transgendered people. Person and Ovesey (1974a), for example, don't think much of their patients, characterising them as un-psychologically minded and impoverished in fantasy:

> In sum, then, primary transsexuals are schizoid-obsessive, socially withdrawn, asexual, unassertive and out of touch with anger . . . they have a typical borderline syndrome characterized by separation anxiety, empty depression, a sense of void, oral dependency, defective self-identity and impaired object relations, with absence of trust and fear of intimacy . . . they most closely resemble a subgroup of the borderline syndrome that Grinker calls 'the adaptive, affectless, defended, "as if" persons'.
> (Person and Ovesey 1974a:126)

Quotes in this vein can be discovered in good quantities from all sections of the analytic and much of the medical literature. Carefully conducted survey evidence contradicts these views. Haraldsen and Dahlis (2000) compared 86 transgendered patients awaiting surgery with similar numbers of personality disordered patients and normal controls. The transgendered patients scored in the same range as the normal controls whereas the personality disordered patients scored as having severe pathology. A chart review of more than 400 transgendered people revealed similar findings (Cole *et al.* 1997). In the light of this sort of evidence continued pathologising of transgendered people is unwarranted, prejudicial to their treatment and represents unethical and unacceptable practice. Therapists who are unable to accept transgendered people, or who might wish to deny them access to the full range of treatment options available, should not practise in this area.

Medical and surgical interventions

Transgendered patients seek a range of interventions, from hormone treatments to feminise or masculinise them through to a range of surgical options. For many patients hormonal treatment and subsequent surgical intervention produces a satisfying outcome with high levels of interpersonal satisfaction and adequate sexual adjustment. Other patients, particularly female to male transgendered people, may chose to adopt solutions which only involve taking hormonal treatment, with limited or no surgery. Here, too, outcomes are good. However, a proportion of transgendered people regret having had reassignment surgery. Because of this, gender dysphoria clinics in England operate stringent criteria (albeit without much evidence that these criteria improve ultimate satisfaction rates) before consenting to irrevocable interventions. Often regret post-operatively is based on a poor surgical outcome or on unrealistic expectations for surgery.

Surgical and hormonal interventions carry risks which increase with age and with poor health status. Some patients who are judged a poor surgical risk may be refused intervention. Some patients have found their doctors make unilateral decisions about risks and benefits in this area rather than adopting a co-operative approach. Both surgical and medical options need to be accompanied by psychological support and education, before and after intervention. This is often difficult because gender clinics tend to be few and far between so that patients travel a considerable distance to them for relatively infrequent appointments:

Some years after I had referred her to a gender dysphoria clinic Amy returned in considerable distress. She had been judged a poor candidate for both surgical and hormonal intervention and had left the programme in disgust. Since that time she had lived in the female role but had found it increasingly difficult to have any kind of sexual relationship. Amy and I spent a number of sessions discussing the difficulties involved in both surgery and hormonal intervention which resulted in part from her age – 52 – and from other medical factors which made both surgery and hormone therapy very risky in her case. It emerged that she had not fully appreciated the risks involved in hormonal therapy and surgery when they were explained to her, possibly because of the strength of her desire to begin reassignment, and possibly also because the explanation had been rather rapid.

More recently dissatisfaction about surgery has been more openly expressed in the transgendered community. Califia (1997) discusses post-operative sexuality. She points out that surgical results are disappointing, especially for female to male transsexuals, but that no attempt is made to provide sex therapy or sex education post-operatively. She suggests that some transsexuals might retain their existing genitalia if a compromise way of having sex, which did not cause increases in gender dysphoric feelings, could be found. Informal user-led surveys of outcome show that the results of reassignment surgery are not very impressive in relation to functional outcome, particularly in relation to sexual sensation. Califia is particularly scathing about the evaluation of the sexual results of male to female surgery solely in terms of vaginal size. She suggests that surgeons' puzzlement about transsexuals' sexual satisfaction when the neo-vagina is small may result from a total incapacity on their part to imagine non-vaginal sex:

> Joan was a male to female transgendered patient whose surgery had been halted after she developed a severe post-operative infection. Her neo-vagina was extremely short. Joan had been referred to the psychiatric clinic after creating an angry disturbance in the surgical outpatients, shouting 'I haven't even got a vagina, what are you going to do?'. At assessment she was livid at having been dumped by the surgeons and keen for me to arrange further surgery. We agreed to have further psychotherapy sessions while at the same time seeking a further operation. Eventually Joan was seen by a surgeon who took time to explain that further surgery could be undertaken but that there was a risk it would not work and could make her much worse. Being offered the choice to go ahead allowed Joan to choose to leave matters. In therapy Joan and I talked a lot about female sexuality and what she called 'the penetration thing'. It was something of a surprise for Joan to discover that not all women liked 'the penetration thing' and that there were other ways of expressing herself sexually. She said, 'It wasn't the sort of thing they taught me when I was a man!'

Joan also suffered initially, therefore, from incapacity to imagine non-vaginal sex. Like the surgeon's, her view of female sexuality was profoundly phallocentric. Male to female transgendered people often have not had much education of their erotic imagination in relation to female sexuality. Despite their longing to be women they, in common with men, often have highly stereotyped views of female sexual experience. Califia is right to call for sex education programmes. In some male to female transsexuals, developing erotic awareness as a woman comes as a considerable surprise once surgery is complete. Such individuals embody the radical capacity for development that the erotic imagination can display.

Psychological treatment

Psychoanalytic theorists have voiced an almost universal opposition to gender reassignment surgery, some authors comparing it to psychosurgery (Kavanaugh and Volkan 1978). Limentani's position is fairly characteristic:

> Finally I must state that as I regard the transsexual syndrome as a personality and characterological disaster, it cannot be corrected by mutilating operations which are often carried out in response to suicide threats amounting to blackmail. (Limentani 1979:150)

Making an argument against surgical treatment can be important for some patients because surgery does not always achieve all that might be hoped from it. Psychoanalysts have argued this point, but with such ferocity and in terms which seem to indicate a deep dislike of their patients that their stance is radically weakened. It would also be easier to support if there was any evidence that psychological treatments can affect the basic gender dysphoria which transgendered people experience. Accounts of analytic treatments do not give cause for optimism. Limentani and others describe analyses which are always conducted in the light of a refusal to refer for sex reassignment. Frustrated or partial (often broken-off) treatments are described. Although a few patients are reported to give up their wish for gender reassignment it is difficult to be sure whether, in the face of such implacable opposition, the patient hasn't simply suppressed the information. Given the increasing analytic tolerance for homosexuality one might have hoped for a less immoderate position in relation to transgendered people. Sadly, this does not seem to be emerging. Chiland (2000) bemoans the difficulty of analysing 'these patients because they are fixated on the body and continually press for gender reassignment'. She characterises them as having an unpsychological attitude and a narcissistic disorder.

A better therapeutic approach is to offer supportive and psychodynamically oriented therapy aimed at empowering the patient to make their own decisions about treatment and to adjust to its effects. An increasingly important area of treatment concerns the relationships of transgendered patients. Beyond documenting the likelihood that marriages will break up (even requiring it before surgery), none of the clinics give much thought to managing the pre-existing relationships of transgendered patients or to preserving them:

> Lynda and Ben presented for therapy because of difficulties in their relationship. They had been partners before Ben had gender reassignment surgery and had wanted to stay together. Lynda, however, complained that she did not see herself as a heterosexual woman but as a lesbian. She found that she now resented Ben expecting her to dress up nicely or wanting to initiate sex even though this had been their pattern of relating before gender reassignment. Ben however was struggling with difficulties about his gender reassignment. He had not opted for phalloplasty because of the poor outcome of this kind of surgery. Because his genitals were 'not properly male' he felt the need to prove himself. The atmosphere was tense and hostile. Therapeutic intervention was based on a systemic approach. The therapist theorised that Lynda and Ben had developed a well-functioning system prior to reassignment surgery but the change of roles was confusing both parties. Paradoxically, Ben was asked by the therapist to exaggerate his masculine behaviour while Lynda was asked to behave like 'a woman out of Dallas'. Next session both parties spoke freely about the experiment, some bits they had liked others seemed ludicrous beyond belief. Their tensions had reduced to an extent and it felt as though the system could reorganise more freely.

Treatments for cross-dressers

There are no well validated treatments for cross-dressing, although sporadic accounts in the literature report success in single cases. Probably, like any well established sexual wish, the urge to cross-dress is unlikely to respond to treatment although if necessary the behaviour itself could be suppressed. Behavioural interventions are particularly likely to be useful if the patient gets into risky situations which might have unpleasant consequences if he was discovered. Obviously in the rare situations where the patient behaves in ways which are a risk to others then therapy needs to deal with that as a matter of urgency and a wider team of professionals should be involved.

Supportive treatment for transvestites should often focus on their relationships. Many are married and these marriages can be placed under considerable strain when cross-dressing is discovered. Sometimes couple therapy can resolve matters, on other occasions the relationship may end. Often transvestites without relationships can be lonely and depressed. Psycho-education about support groups for cross-dressers is helpful, as is medical or therapeutic intervention aimed at low mood.

Treatments for patients with intersexed conditions

Physical treatments for patients with intersex conditions are highly controversial. Many medical experts believe that early surgery on the small baby to make the genitals clearly one or other gender is vital. By contrast, some gender activists are dissatisfied with what they regard as mutilating surgery and the consequent reduction in sexual functioning it produces. They oppose early surgery. Studies of the adult life of intersex patients show general satisfaction with life but often dissatisfaction with body image and sex life. Even so, only two in a sample of 30 said they trusted doctors and of those who had had surgical interventions on their genitalia none were satisfied with the outcome (Schober 1999). Cheryl Chase, a gender activist, is a case in point. She was assigned male gender at birth but her parents, ashamed of her small penis, reassigned her to a female gender at which point her small penis was reclassified as an over large clitoris and a clitoridectomy was performed. Cheryl points out that as a result all sexual function was removed. She founded 'Hermaphrodites with Attitude' and has picketed the American Academy of Paediatrics, pressing for a change in policy over surgery and arguing that delaying surgery until the child is old enough to express an opinion is a more respectful way of treating intersexed patients. In adult life, intersex patients need support for a wide range of potential emotional problems. Advice guiding them towards self-help organizations is useful. Therapists should also avoid the urge to fit their patients into a particular gender and be particularly careful to allow the patient freedom to move between identifications as they need.

Political considerations

Califia (1997) presents an extended analysis of the political issues involved in the management of transgendered patients. Repeatedly she demonstrates how the wishes and needs of transgendered people are subordinated to the gender prejudices and paternalism of their doctors. Even those doctors who have been willing to allow gender reassignments to occur appear to regard themselves as doing their patients a furtive favour. Many doctors still advise transgendered people to actively conceal their previous lives. Doctors dealing with patients seeking gender reassignment also find non-standard post-operative sexual choices more than they can handle. Green (1969, cited in Califia 1977:66) describes a man who wished to live as a lesbian post-operatively, as wanting to live the social life of a woman but not the sexual one – a comment which implies that lesbians do not have the sexual lives of women. While Green attacks his male to female transgendered patients for not wanting to be fully female, as he sees it, Money and Primrose (1969) cannot bear the thought that they might be fully female as mothers. They say that male transsexuals lack maternal wishes and when they are faced with a group who wish to adopt older children they suggest that wish is like wanting to own a fashionable pet:

> A woman may do an excellent job of caring for a fashionable pet. So also a post-operative transsexual, married as a female, may do an excellent job of mothering an adopted or foster child. (Money and Primrose 1969, cited in Califia 1977:75)

Doctors have not been the only people with worries about transgendered patients. There has also been a feminist backlash against them. Raymond is the most vocal (1996). Her work has been enthusiastically supported with blurbs on the cover by Dworkin and Rich (Califia, 1997:86). These feminists deny female status to transsexuals in the most virulent terms, seeking to exclude them from female colleges or organisations and suggesting, like psychoanalysts and the International Olympic Committee, that only chromosomes determine gender. This is an argument which sits uneasily with feminist rejection of essentialist theories of gender or psychoanalytic acceptance of constitutional bisexuality.

Analysts, feminists, medical and non-medical gender dysphoria specialists all seem to have at times found it acceptable to adopt views which are plainly unprofessional or unreasonable. Samuels' (1985b) theory of gender certainty may provide a helpful way of understanding why this might occur. Samuels argues that gender certainty and gender confusion are in reciprocal relation to each other. Political opponents of transgendered choices, doctors and parents who deal with intersexed children are threatened with an increase in gender confusion. They attempt to preserve the balance by manoeuvres designed to increase gender certainty. The construction of a medical category for people who wish to change sex role serves our culture's need to preserve order as much as in other cultures do the construction of roles like Xanith and Hijra. It preserves gender certainty by creating a little '*cordon sanitaire*' in which to place anything threatening. The strategy is not entirely successful. Assessors often comment on the capacity of an applicant for reassignment to pass as, or carry off, the role of a woman. The use of a term like 'passing' to denote successful entry to the new role is filled with connotations of secrecy, infiltration and betrayal while the phrase 'carry off' implies acting and dissimulation. Even if the possibility of a change of sex is granted the idea of a fluid sexuality, of remaining married to a previous partner, or of opting only for a partial gender reassignment becomes too threatening to gender certainty and doctors, analysts and feminists alike rebel.

Psychotherapy of transgendered transvestite and intersex conditions

Neither neutrality nor ignorance are helpful adjuncts to the treatment of these conditions. Successful therapy with transgendered, transvestite or intersexed patients needs to be conducted from a position that is well informed about the condition and benignly disposed towards the patient. 'Curative' efforts are pointless and also start from the position that patients who present these difficulties are ill – something which they may well deny. The best therapeutic input may either be supportive or exploratory but should always be aimed at exposing and coming to terms with the reality of the current situation rather than bending it to fit the will of the therapist:

> Charlotte presented in clinic in the female role. She was a tall young woman dressed casually and impressed the interviewer as an extremely beautiful woman. She was seeking referral for gender reassignment. Charlotte wanted to live in the female role until masculinising hormones had started to work and a bilateral mastectomy had been performed. She said, 'I don't want to be a half man I want to be a real man.' The therapist found herself struggling after the session with sexual fantasies about the patient and regret over the proposed reassignment.

Supervision concentrated on the therapist's countertransference reaction to the patient. A particularly trusting atmosphere pervaded the supervision so that the therapist's sense of regret over gender reassignment could be explored in terms of the therapist's lesbian sexual orientation, with supervisor and therapist both sharing openly thoughts about sexual attraction to women and also to more androgynous people. Once personal issues had been discussed, the possibility that the therapist's countertransference was driven by the patient's own ambivalence about gender reassignment could also be tackled:

> During the second session the therapist suggested to Charlotte that she might be ambivalent about changing orientation. Charlotte reacted angrily saying that this clinic was like everywhere else and imposed its own views on how gender reassign-

ment should be managed on patients to make them 'neat and tidy'. At this point she suddenly looked, for a second, sad. The therapist repeated the words 'neat and tidy' and suddenly Charlotte produced a stream of associative ideas centring around both the pain of being a tomboy as a child (never being neat and tidy), and also about her rage at not having a neat and tidy life but instead having to go through surgery to be 'put right'.

Subsequent therapy then developed in two stages. There was an extended period of mourning over childhood experiences and current difficulties which went on while Charlotte went through the early stages of seeking gender reassignment. Then Charlotte changed her name to Charles and described frequent struggles with the 'gender reassignment establishment', as he called it. These struggles had a practical focus but psychologically in therapy they also became a goad to the development of less rigid and bipolar notions of gender. Charles's appearance and way of living at the end of therapy were unquestionably masculine but he was not the 'absolute hunk' Charlotte had once imagined she might become.

9

Sexology and sex therapy

Introduction

A group of therapies are specifically devoted to sex as their prime therapeutic object. While they all draw on other therapeutic disciplines for their conceptualisation of change techniques they develop their own distinctive perspectives on human sexuality. For all of them a central knowledge base is the scientific study of sexual functioning and in that sense whatever their other allegiances they can all be thought of as practical applications of that study. This chapter critically reviews both scientific sexology and the therapies it spawned.

Sexology: a historical review

There is no shortage of theories of human sexual functioning. An account, itself highly theorised, can be found in Foucault's *History of Sexuality* (1981). The origins of present-day views stretch back as far as the historian can relate. Indeed, there are records of sexual practices dating from the earliest recorded script (Markowitz and Ashkenazi 1999). The nineteenth century, however, initiated a new trend by producing a raft of sexual theorists all united by adherence to a 'scientific' standpoint and by a Darwinian perspective on human behaviour, viewed as part of the natural world rather than separate from it. For example, Havelock Ellis (1934) concerned himself with the ways in which modern social developments might be causing women to reject their natural female role and maternal function. His view of female sexuality was closely derived from a supposedly animal model in

251

which a female is hunted by a male who arouses the reluctant woman to the point of surrender. Although Ellis thought of himself as a defender of women's sexuality his attitudes now seem dated and unpleasant. Later, during the interwar years, a number of marriage manuals were produced. Chiefly aimed at a male readership they drew on the new 'scientific' ideas about sex. Van de Veld (1928) used Ellis's ideas to portray women as desiring savage penetration. For van de Veld, women were sexual instruments. An appropriately informed man could, with correct handling, awake them to sexual feeling. Marie Stopes (1918) stood out in this male field as an isolated woman. However she was not particularly feminist or committed to female autonomy and her concern with birth control, relatively new amongst sexologists, was probably a consequence of her gender. Stopes still, like Ellis, portrays women as reluctant, and as needing to be chased. She was quite clear that marital relations were the only permitted ones, condemning lesbians and masturbation alike.

As the twentieth century progressed, the quest for female sexual response and the problem of frigidity which had preoccupied van de Veld and Stopes remained paramount, but the burden of responsibility for overcoming these problems and ensuring marital sexual satisfaction switched from men to women. Authors now start to inveigh against certain women, particularly those with cold natures, or those who were feminists, who actively resist responding sexually (Segal 1994). The role of the clitoris in female sexual response slowly gained prominence and began to be regarded as a training ground which might be useful to bring round a recalcitrant vaginal response. There were problems with this notion of the trainable vagina, which did not altogether fit with the idea of sexuality as an instinctive and natural response.

Kinsey's work, first published in 1948, is a logical extension of the work of Havelock Ellis and other earlier sexologists. He, too, purported to view sex as a biological function but he extended the range of permissible sexual activities by regarding more kinds of sex as acceptable. However, there is plenty of evidence of preconceived bias in his work. He emphasised the similarities between men and women, even as his research showed up considerable differences. He also produced an elaborately scientific staged model of the human's sexual response cycle that is not particularly true to life. At first sight his work was revolutionary in relation to female sexuality. Although previous writers had acknowledged the role of the clitoris they had all seen it as a staging post. By contrast Kinsey, as a result of his experiments, emphasised the role of masturbation as the surest route to female orgasmic response and was disparaging about the utility of the penis in this respect. He argued that referred sensation from the vagina or incidental clitoral stimulation were responsible for female orgasmic response during coitus. He also depicted women as multiply orgasmic and having orgasmic responses of longer duration than men. Thus, in the orgasm department, women were, at least potentially, better endowed than men. Notwithstanding, Kinsey manages to back coitus as the glue for a successful marital relationship and by extension for the stereotypic home life of the American way, 1950s style.

Kinsey, like many sexologists who followed him, has been accused of a male focus in what might be called their 'orgasmo-centrism'. Certainly he, in common with most other sexologists, ignored other aspects of female sexuality, such as pregnancy and breastfeeding. Irvine (1990) also points out that despite the seem-ingly value-neutral stance a white male value-system permeated Kinsey's efforts. His employment practices provide the strongest example. He would only hire happily married staff and this precluded hiring women since, he argued, the work involved trav-elling away from home a good deal and a happily married woman could not do this. People with odd-sounding names or ethnic names were also excluded from employment on Kinsey's team, as was anyone not born and raised in the States.

It could be argued that Masters and Johnson set out to put into practice as a therapy the scientific sexology which Kinsey had expounded. With the publication of *Human Sexual Response* (1966), scientific sexology moved from dispassionate enquiry to therapeutic endeavour. Like Kinsey, Masters and Johnson were keen to define a unified cross-gender sexual response cycle. To do this they effaced differences between the sexes even to the point of creating some very stretched parallels, such as analogising penile erection with vaginal lubrication. Much of their scientific work was not original, being either speculative or drawing on previous findings. Initially it seemed vindicated by the strikingly positive results they claimed for their sex therapy clinic. Later findings have not supported their strongest claims (Bancroft

1989), although their techniques still form the basis of modern sex therapy.

Masters and Johnson took an even more traditionalist stance than Kinsey. They maintained an exclusive focus on marital harmony and on marriage maintenance achieved through good sexual adjustment. Thus when presented with a married couple in which one partner says they are homosexual rather than heterosexual, Masters and Johnson would regard treatment to eliminate homosexual feelings as the correct course of action. For them, satisfying heterosexual coitus is a mainstay of marital harmony and, the onus for achieving this should fall very largely, on women. Their task is to initiate sexual activities which kindle their sexual capacities – capacities seen now as greater than those of men. Specific sex therapy exercises teach the couple to focus first on female pleasures, at least initially delaying penetrative sex in favour of less genital pleasures.

Some feminist commentators view Masters and Johnson's depiction of female sexuality as active and initiating rather than passive and responsive, as benign (Segal 1994). They argue that it has served to strengthen some women, giving them permission to make more demands on men in heterosexual encounters or relationships. This benign depiction downplays the fact that their focus on non genital relationships is a tactic (often making a virtue of necessity) deployed within an overall strategy designed to restore a genital relationship. They never resolve the contradiction between their acknowledgement of masturbation as the assured route to orgasm while denying its place in marital sexuality other than as a staging post.

Meanwhile the social context of sexual activity had been steadily changing from one of overt rectitude and covert social disobedience to a more self-conscious and sexually promiscuous attitude. Generally this social transformation is ascribed to the contraceptive pill, but there are a number of reasons for doubting this. First, effective birth control predates the pill by a long period. Marie Stopes after all was able to talk about birth control issues 50 years earlier. In fact the contraceptive pill had been in existence for quite a period of time before its widespread acceptance and use. This suggests that social changes were needed before the contraceptive pill could be introduced. The pattern reversed in the 1970s and 1980s and enthusiasm for sexual freedoms declined. The decline was driven at first by the feminist realisation that the new sexual freedoms seemed largely to do with freeing men to be sexually exploitative of women. Later, sexual retrenchment was fuelled by the exigencies of the AIDS epidemic and, more recently, by social anxieties (highly reminiscent of those concerning the mob which troubled Dickens) over the rise of an urban underclass which threatens to outbreed the more restrained bourgeoisie and drain state resources.

Shere Hite's work spans twenty years but she first began publishing in the 1970s. She has concentrated on accounts gathered by survey from large numbers of women and many sexologists have criticised her for presenting the views of a potentially unrepresentative sample of subjects. Her work is feminist and somewhat angry in tone. Hite, like most sexologists, has her own axe to grind. She dethrones penetrative sex as a source of orgasmic pleasure in women, systematically discounting high numbers of women in her survey who report pleasure in this form of sex (Hite 1976). Her most bitter critics were the many sexologists who were profoundly committed to preserving heterosexual marriage through better sexual adjustment. However, not all feminist commentators viewed her benignly. Some women report pleasure in penetrative sex because they enjoy its relationship functions even in the absence of orgasm. Segal (1994) criticises Hite for regarding such women as sexual slaves. Segal suggests that by focusing on the presence or absence of orgasmic response Hite dehumanises sexuality and discounts the value of a particular man in the eyes of a woman during sex. Thus Hite, who set out to humanise and personalise scientific sexology, is seen by some as being as reductionist and biologistic as her penetration-obsessed predecessors in her opposite insistence that women are not 'made for' penetrative sex.

Since Hite, sexological theory has fractured into a myriad of theories and nostrums. Perhaps of all branches of psychological knowledge and therapy it has succeeded best in the popular market, with a cornucopia of books and magazine articles. Crazes of various sorts sweep the popular imagination, such as the G spot (Ladas 1983) or a more recent craze for diagnosing sexual addiction syndrome. While contemporary sex manuals (for example, Comfort 1972 and Beck 1993) usually no longer adopt an openly sexist rhetoric they retain a strong focus on coitus as the chief aim of sex. Indeed, one value of the female G spot was its accessibility to penile penetration and stimulation within the vagina. Heterosexual sex manuals tend still to refer to all forms of sexual activity other than coitus as foreplay. The sexologists of the past have had their effect. Whereas once female pleasure in coitus was not often depicted as a male concern now male anxieties about adequacy can centre round the female orgasm. Vance (1984) points out that *The Joy of Sex* (Comfort 1972, cited in Altman 1989) instructs the female reader in detail on the technique of faking orgasm, since it is supposed that the sensitive modern woman will not refuse her partner just because she does not feel like it. Doubtless women have faked orgasms through the ages, but only recently have they felt they had to do it so often. That the faked orgasm is one enduring legacy of a scientific sexology, which emphasised humanity as part of nature, is one of the more delightful ironies in the field.

Sex therapy

Sex therapists armed themselves with the findings of sexological research and set out to devise treatments for sexual difficulties. They are spread out along a spectrum in which more or less attention is paid to the emotional and non-sexual aspects involved in causing sexual difficulty. From a biopsychosocial perspective the spectrum is the usual balancing act between biological and psychological explanations and remedies, while only the slightest nod is made in the direction of social influences or remedies.

Biologically based sex therapy

Biologically based sex therapy has concentrated on conditions where good evidence for organic difficulties have been found. A large number of different medical causes for male erectile and ejaculatory failure have been elucidated and female sexual dysfunction has also been investigated, chiefly in relation to reports of pain during intercourse. Remedies, particularly for erectile failure, have been vigorously pursued and over the past twenty years a succession of biological treatments ranging from penile implants through injections of papaverine into the root of the penis to oral Sildenafil citrate (Viagra) have been tried. At the time of writing there are likely to be a number of new drugs, in the same and related classes to Viagra, due for release. The popularity of biologically based remedies for erectile failure has fuelled a vigorous marketplace for remedies the existence of which can be traced back to the earliest written records. Their current popularity can be assessed by even the most cursory inspection of the numerous internet sites which offer both Viagra and a host of other more or less dubious remedies for sale by 'discreet' delivery after an internet consultation with a medical advisor. While none of the remedies currently available (even Viagra) are without difficulties and side effects it does seem that the balance between efficacy and inconvenience or pain has moved decisively in a beneficial direction.

The presumed balance between psychological factors and medical ones in the causation of a range of sexual difficulties has been assigned in a range of ways over the last fifty years. Probably the majority of sexual dysfunctions in fit younger individuals with no other evidence of physical disease are psychogenic in origin. However in older people, or those in an 'at risk' group (like diabetics), sexual dysfunction may raise the suspicion of an organic problem even though there is almost always a psychological component as well. Some of the conditions which cause sexual dysfunction may be seriously threatening to health. No therapist dealing with sexual dysfunction should neglect organic causes as a major consideration. Referral for a full medical history and physical examination is usually appropriate.

Biological/psychological hybrid therapies

Most modern sex therapists tend to practise in ways which represent different integrations of behavioural, cognitive/psychodynamic and relationship-oriented elements. Many have medical or scientific backgrounds and incorporate the medical elements of an assessment into their work. This predisposes them to use medical diagnostic categories and to categorise even psychologically driven sexual difficulty into a series of dysfunctions.

The core of cognitive/behavioural approaches to sex therapy is a series of behavioural exercises initially introduced by Masters and Johnson and designed to re-establish sexual communication and sexual pleasure. Couples are treated rather than individuals and the therapy involves an admixture of educative elements with systematic desensitisation in which fearful or avoided elements are introduced slowly in conditions where relaxation and anxiety reduction is encouraged. For different conditions the treatment offered will vary but a core procedure can be defined which is almost always used, at least in part.

Couples are first asked extensively about their sexual and relationship histories with the aim of eliciting information about their hopes, fears and expectations. Some sex therapists stress communication skills training at this point. The couple's understanding of sexual physiology and anatomy is also assessed and improved if necessary. Next they are asked to initiate 'non genital sensate focusing'. In this exercise both parties take it in turns to stroke or caress the other with the aim of taking pleasure in touching the other. The exercise is then extended first to incorporate giving the other pleasure in being touched and then, when both parties are comfortable, genital sensate focusing is introduced. During this time there is a ban on full sexual intercourse and, in the early stages, on sexual arousal to orgasm. This paradoxical injunction functions to allow both parties to re-establish physical intimacy and communication which may have decayed during an anxious period marked by unsatisfactory sexual encounters. As the behavioural exercises progress, intercourse may be introduced in a variety of ways.

Bancroft's detailed account of his practice (1989) gives considerable weight to relationship issues in couples who are experiencing sexual dysfunction. He characterises his treatment as paying rather more attention to the underlying relationship between the couple than had been the case in the approach of Masters and Johnson. Bancroft sees the setting of behavioural tasks in therapy as serving to expose psychological issues which need thought and attention before any focus on the mechanics of sexual activity can resume. Bancroft characterises both Masters and Johnson (1976) and the work of their followers Arentewicz and Schmidt (1983) as being both behavioural and prescriptive, with a strong implication that his work is more relational. The work of Hawton (1985) and others represents another synthesis in which new developments in cognitive therapy are incorporated rather more explicitly than in Bancroft's work.

Crowe and Ridley (1990) develop yet another hybrid. They use something they call a behavioural-systems approach to sexual problems. Their work is interesting because it draws on systemic family therapy to provide a conceptualisation of the psychological nature of the relationship in which sexual difficulties are experienced. This approach allows them to discuss, much more openly, the issues of power and gender which may underlie marital and sexual difficulty. They are also keener to use interventions drawn from the family therapy canon which serve to enhance or disrupt people's experiences of the system in which they are operating. They may use paradoxical interventions (for example, instructing the couple to have an argument) to try to enhance awareness and to alter the system. Like all sex therapists, they set behavioural sex therapy tasks within this framework. While their approach is promising there are moments in their work where something altogether less benign suddenly peeps through, revealing an unexamined and casual sexism, which thought and emotional relatedness could easily have eliminated.

Psychodynamically oriented sex therapists also practise a hybridised therapy but instead of using cognitive elements or elements derived from family therapy they tend to use psychoanalytic concepts to provide the psychological half of the hybrid. Generally their background leads them to be less interested in the biological basis of sex and to stress psychological elements. It is consistent with this that Kaplan (1979, in Bancroft 1989:71) should have been the first therapist to introduce a classification of sexual dysfunctions which involve dysfunctions in one or more of three phases characterised as desire, excitement and orgasm. Kaplan's combination of behavioural and psychodynamic techniques was highly structured. Her policy was at first to regard the cause of problems as residing in the immediate or near past and to prescribe drugs and to emphasise the biological processes involved in sex. She moved on to more psychological and specifically psychodynamic conceptualisations only if this initial approach failed. Bancroft criticises Kaplan's hierarchical approach because he feels relationship issues should be given first priority. Probably any rigid ordering of areas to focus on is incorrect. Instead, equal attention to both areas should continue until a case formulation can be constructed which is individual to the patient.

The work of Scharff and Scharff (1991) would probably be

more to Bancroft's taste. Their approach is psychodynamic, like Kaplan's, and, also like hers, a hybrid sex and psychodynamic therapy. Their emphasis is strongly on relationship and psychological aspects first. They see unconscious communication between the couples as fundamental to determining the quality of their long-term intimacy. Sex at once symbolises the longing to hold onto the image of the loving parent, the struggle to overcome the withholding parent and the attempt to synthesise the two into an internal loving couple. It is therefore a symbolic attempt at reparation. Within this object-relations framework a full range of sex therapy interventions is delivered and they make full use of transference and countertransference feelings in the therapy room. Specifically Scharff and Scharff associate each sex therapy exercise with a specific psychodynamic task so that trust and regression, for example, are required for exercises involving mutual non-genital stimulation (non-genital sensate focusing). The clinical account they give of their work is a powerfully evoked fusion of fantasy and dream interpretation with sex therapy, which can be useful with some clients. Kaplan and Scharff and Scharff are able to conceive of sex as an imaginative activity. The erotic imagination of their clients is active during sex. This is an important advantage which they share over the more behaviourally oriented sex therapists whose reflections concern the cognitions, emotions and behaviours of their patients but who do not discuss the work of the creative imagination. Regretably, in common with most object-relations theorists, Scharff and Scharff's conceptualisation of the imaginative work of their patients is one which turns both patients away from sex and back to a childhood dominated by attachment and feeding issues. It seems likely that a theoretical prediliction for breast milk over semen may not be the best stance from which to enliven the erotic imagination.

Scharff and Scharff's work is also flawed in other ways. Their assumptions about sexual normality seem ferociously dated in the current age. They are severely anti-gay and their discussion of perversion moves so rapidly to a consideration of paedophilia as to create the impression that all transgressive sex is equivalent to a desire to abuse children. Even in the area of straight sex their work assumes normative stereotypes of male and female sexual and emotional activity which could even have seemed dated in the 1950s. They privilege a male-driven view of success in coitus, without any sign of reflection over the place of women in society and the experience of sexual subjection.

Sex therapy in practice

The following case example illustrates a fairly standard case of sexual dysfunction:

> Diana presented with a complaint of low sexual desire. She reported a five-year history of disinterest in sex and had presented currently because she was worried that her husband might be having an affair. The couple had had only the most infrequent and unsatisfying sex life in recent years. Before then she said their sex life had been 'fine' but did not elaborate on the details and seemed troubled by the request to do so. After considerable discussion the following story emerged. Five years ago she had been admitted to hospital for an operation on piles. After surgery she had felt sore and sexual intercourse with her husband had been sufficiently painful that she came to dread it. Instead of getting better the pain got worse with time and she described a burning sensation on intercourse. She rapidly lost interest in sex. Her husband approached her quite often with 'a look in his eyes'. She would freeze and avoid him. Now they rarely touched each other for any reason. The therapist supposed that Diana's story could be put together as follows. Her post-operative pain had meant that sexual intercourse was unpleasant and so she had come to anticipate that sex would be a painful affair. For this reason the thought of sex and sexual foreplay were not arousing but appalling and she did not become stimulated or lubricate her vagina. Once penetration was attempted Diana's lack of arousal made penetration painful and accounted for the burning sensation. Now a negative feed-back loop of fearful anticipation and avoidance had been set up and the baleful effects on Diana's relationship with her husband were slowly increasing. However the therapist was at a loss to understand why Diana had not been able to explain to her husband in the days after surgery that sex was still too painful to be pleasant. The therapist probed back into the 'fine' sex life and then Diana admitted, with every evidence of the deepest shame, that she had let her husband have anal intercourse with

her quite a lot. She was convinced this had caused the piles which she had needed to have excised. Diana was ambivalent about anal intercourse and the therapist was unclear if this was something Diana liked but felt ashamed about or whether it was something she allowed her husband, who did seem, on her account, to be sexually forceful. However, it was clear that Diana had let her husband have vaginal sex with her after surgery as a compromise so he would not try anal sex.

How might the different sex therapists discussed so far treat Diana and her partners problem? All the sex therapists discussed so far would ultimately tend to come round to the sensate focusing exercises with Diana and her partner. However, there would be major differences in emphasis in the way that they tackled the case. Probably Masters and Johnson would move towards behavioural interventions and sensate focusing relatively early, acknowledging the problems in the relationship but possibly feeling that these would become more tractable once they were having satisfying sex. Bancroft would certainly not do this. For him the lack of communication between the couple would be the most serious problem and particularly Diana's difficulty in saying that she did not like some kinds of sex. His first move might well be to do with communication. Naturally all the therapists would be interested in the worry about an affair but Crowe and Ridley would regard an affair, or the anxiety of one, as a vital factor in the system. Probably it would be here that they would concentrate. Both Kaplan and Scharff and Scharff would look at relationship and fantasy issues even if Kaplan tried organic and conditioning manoeuvres first. Here they would find much to concern them, as psychoanalytic views of anal sex are ambivalent and Diana certainly has some fantasies about it as a damaging activity. They would want to deal with this material analytically even if they wove in some sex therapy exercises.

Would any of the therapists treating Diana improve the situation? Despite the medical model in which most sex therapy interventions are delivered the work on the outcome of treatment leaves much to be desired. Bancroft reviews the literature and chiefly reports on its inadequacy. Many couples fail to complete treatment and this failure is associated with lower socioeconomic class and poor motivation on the part of the male partner. For those who do complete conditions show a range of success rates with good results for vaginismus and generally poor ones for low sexual desire (Bancroft 1989). A five-year history of low sexual desire means that a good outcome for Diana cannot be confidently predicted.

Techniques to treat specific sexual disorders

The classification of psychogenic disorders of sexual function has been taken up by Hawton (1985), who produces the following table:

	Women	*Men*
Interest	low interest	low interest
Arousal	low arousal	erectile dysfunction/ impotence
Orgasm	orgasmic dysfunction	premature, delayed or painful ejaculation
Other types	vaginismus dyspareunia sexual phobias	dyspareunia sexual phobias

This rough and ready categorisation allows for some comparison of male and female sexual problems and also allows for differential prognoses on the basis of such outcome research as exists.

Vaginismus

Vaginismus is a condition in which there is spasm of the vaginal muscles which makes penetration either painful and difficult or impossible. Its cause is not well understood although there have been no shortage of often unflattering characterisations of women who suffer from it with implied aetiologies (Bancroft 1989). Treatment involves a combination of psycho-education, assisted self-exploration and ultimately systematic desensitisation by the insertion of either fingers or dilators of progressively increasing size into the vagina. Treatment is often very successful.

Low sexual desire in women

Low sexual desire in the female member of a heterosexual couple is one of the most common problems presenting to sex clinics (Bancroft and Coles 1976). Causes include a host of psychological factors and also physical ones, including the action of some drugs and physical debility. Social factors include religious upbringing which can lead to an aversion to specific sexual behaviours including oral–genital contact or masturbation (LoPiccolo 1980, cited in Rossi 1994). Amongst the important individual predisposing factors is sexual abuse in childhood. In one study 23 per cent of women molested as children reported sexual dysfunction. (Fritz *et al.* 1981). Degree of sexual desire also tends to be related to a conducive setting. Bancroft (1989) points out that for many families the privacy, warmth and time which a 'middle-class sex therapist' may take for granted can be difficult to gather together. Certainly children may prove barriers to privacy and to time. Since sleep deprivation tends to mostly affect the mother this may be contributing to reduced female interest in sex. In relation to children, Schwartz and Rutter (1998) comment that social sanctions against women who are not emotionally engrossed with their child may be severe so that there may be subtle social prohibitions against women with young children making time for sex.

Crowe and Ridley's (1990) systemic approach allows them to see that low female sexual desire is in effect a property of a relationship and they discuss the situation 'where the male partner is enthusiastic and demanding and the female partner is reluctant for sex' (1990:243). They call this situation equivalent to 'frigidity'. The problem is whether to consider mismatches in sexual desire in a couple as the core problem or whether the (generally female) partner with lower desire is labelled problematic and 'frigid', or more politically correctly as suffering from low sexual desire. Thus Jehu (1979), who recommends dealing with the problem by individual treatment of the woman to overcome fears of sex, is clearly subscribing to a female dysfunction model. Bancroft uses a couple approach involving sensate focus and communication skills training and adheres, at least in part, to a relationship model.

Bancroft starts the treatment of low female sexual desire with a focus on basic communication and may include some practice in the giving of clear statements about wishes both positive and negative. This establishes the foundation for the feedback partners are expected to give each other during more explicitly sexual exercises. Sensate focus is then introduced and, for most of the time, there is also a ban on intercourse which may often expose anxieties about male self-control or the right to refuse sex. The exercises are meant to become an exploration of sexual likes and dislikes. To an extent Bancroft is permissive in relation to women who do not want to fulfil certain sexual wishes expressed by their partners. He, for example, allows patients freedom not to want to do some things (e.g. touch a man's penis). However, he also wants the therapist to point out 'inconsistencies' in the aims of the individuals. For example, the therapist should highlight the 'inconsistency' between a woman's wish to please her partner sexually and her wish not to touch his penis. Thus it is clear that Bancroft's strong expectation is that a set of sexual activities represent 'legitimate' requests to which a less than willing (usually female) partner needs to be brought round to assent. Bancroft's anti-female focus also emerges in his discussion on resistance to performing the sex exercises in which he discusses what he terms female passive aggressive resistance in denying sex until other work within the relationship (like the washing up) is done.

While Bancroft is able to acknowledge the importance of hostility between the partners he does not carry this analysis much further than the notion of the disaffected wife on sex strike. Other commentators acknowledge the importance of relationship difficulties including anger and resentment (Kaplan 1979) in low sexual desire. One useful analysis views women in couples as being the emotional demanders and men the emotional withdrawers. The more powerful member of the couple is the one with the privilege of being emotionally withdrawn. This is often a male privilege so women may need to use their power to be the withdrawers in the sexual side of the relationship to even up the power balance. Crowe and Ridley (1990) also argue that sexual reluctance compensates for a male-dominated relationship. He argues for the use of a negotiated timetable for sex to clear the air and remove doubts and argues that the process of negotiating the timetable helps to bring out a range of resentments and issues.

not typically present and touching is more likely to be perfected. Schwartz and Rutter (1998) point out that men are poorly educated in how to touch women and that women may see asking for specific sexual stimulation as improper or unsavoury. Even so, the lack of discussion in sex therapy texts of ways (particularly non-mechanical) in which a couple may promote female orgasm during coitus, or before or after it, is striking. Perhaps sex therapists are tacitly subscribing to the attitude exemplified by the following quote from Crowe and Ridley (1990:344):

> it has been claimed that 95 per cent of women can achieve an orgasm with the help of a vibrator, whereas a much lower proportion do so regularly in sexual intercourse. It is this last finding which settles that a couple may often have to settle for a less than ideal relationship in which the woman achieves her climax separately from the act of intercourse.

Possibly, the situation in which female orgasm is conditioned by evolutionary forces to occur is not coitus. If, as discussed in Chapter 1, female sperm selection between different mates is accomplished by exploiting post-coital masturbation (Baker and Bellis 1993) then an orgasm during coitus may be disadvantageous to a female who wishes to select which partner's sperm results in a pregnancy. If so Crowe's 'less than ideal' relationship may be exactly what nature intended.

Male erectile or ejaculatory failure

The initial treatment of male erectile or ejaculatory failure needs to be biologically based and the introduction of Viagra has also expanded the role of biological treatments into the psychological domain. Many men find psychologically oriented discussion of their sexuality either shaming or pointless. For them the introduction of a tablet which enhances sexual function has represented a major advance in therapy.

However, Viagra does not work for all cases of psychogenic erectile or ejaculatory failure and there is a place for psychological interventions even when possible organic causes exist. A key psychological concept is that of performance anxiety. This concept tries to sum up the range of pressures which are exerted on men who are in a sexual situation. The visibility of an erection attests instantly to a man's level of arousal and this exposure is compounded by a sociocultural expectation that male sexuality should be unproblematic and that effortless sexual performance is an index of fitness and power. Anxiety reduces sexual functioning. Beck and Barlow (1984) described a negative feedback loop in which poor sexual performance sets up performance anxieties which in turn fuel both themselves and further poor sexual performance. Performance anxiety may develop in the context of personality vulnerabilities. From a cognitive perspective, underlying maladaptive assumptions predisposing to performance anxiety may include ideas like 'All proper men can always get an erection' or 'Anyone who can't get an erection is a wimp and rejectable'. Psychodynamic theorists dealing with impotence have tended to appeal to ideas based on phobic reactions. Thus men with oedipal anxieties may fear castration or may see penetration of the female body as a symbolic castration which they are unsure they will survive. Some analysts argue that such men imagine the existence of a vagina dentata ready to bite off their penis. Such ideas might seem far-fetched but perhaps the globally widespread reporting of a case in which a woman bit off her partner's penis might indicate that such fantasies hold some sway in the mind.

The contribution of multiple causes is an important feature of erectile failure and a simple separation into biological and psychological factors is not desirable. Rossi (1994) points out that in a large series of men with erectile failure 25 per cent had only an organic problem, and 40 per cent had a psychogenic difficulty. Thus a substantial number had mixed causation:

> Aleck had diabetes and presented with erectile failure. He was a well built and muscled man who clearly took a great pride in his body and perhaps had coped with his diabetes by becoming as fit and as healthy as he could manage. He was also something of a playboy and was quite open about the way in which he liked having a range of 'girlfriends' on the go at any one time. He was also insightful about his need to perform sexually with these women. 'It's not like they're going to be understanding if I can't make it with them. I mean if we aren't going to see each other for a while, it all needs to work.' Mostly Aleck worried that his erectile failure, which had increased recently,

meant that his diabetes was getting worse. In this respect the fact that he was still having nocturnal emissions and sometimes woke in the morning with an erection was a good sign. The therapist pointed out to him that his penis was still able to become erect. Aleck was physically examined and special tests were done to look at the functioning of his nerves and of the blood vessels which supplied his pelvis and legs. After review of these tests he was then taught how to inject his penis with a chemical which produces an erection. (He was treated in the days before Viagra which would probably be tried first now.) He managed this technique well but was concerned that the erection did not look entirely normal. Notwithstanding he tried using the injections on a number of occasions in the next months and reported himself cautiously satisfied at his next clinic visits. Then, after about four months he reported that he had been getting erections again without the use of the injections. Thereafter he used the injections infrequently but said he liked to have them on hand.

Aleck's case shows how biological and psychological issues can intertwine in the causation and in the treatment of erectile failure. It also shows how biological treatments for erectile failure can intervene beneficially in the psychological cycle of performance anxiety.

Some men can become erect but suffer from specific ejaculatory failure during coitus. This may have biological causes but is in such cases generally a total rather than a situational failure. Where biological causes are not present it is suggested that ejaculatory failure results from a masturbatory habit which relies on over-stimulation of the penis which cannot be replicated by vaginal penetration. Treatment involves super-stimulation of the penis in increasing proximity to the vagina and with vaginal penetration introduced at the last minute and then at an increasingly early point.

Premature ejaculation

Males with ejaculatory control problems seldom brag about how fast they can come. Culturally men are expected to delay orgasm until penetration and a modicum of penile thrusting has occurred. On this definition premature ejaculation may affect as many as a third of all men. Treatment is initially relatively easy, using the stop start technique introduced by Semans (1956). The man is asked to stimulate himself or be masturbated by his partner (depending on how much arousal he can manage) almost to the point of orgasm. Then stimulation stops and is repeated again. With repetition the aim is to lengthen the period of stimulation which can be tolerated and slowly introduce vaginal penetration as well. In men who experience orgasm very rapidly indeed, a squeeze technique is added in which the penis is squeezed fairly hard just below the glands at the moment when the man feels orgasm is immanent (Masters and Johnson 1970). While premature ejaculation responds initially to treatment it tends also to relapse (Bancroft 1989). Furthermore there is some evidence that a physiological difficulty may be the cause (Metz *et al.* 1997). For these reasons physical treatments can be helpful. These rely on the application of anaesthetic gel to the glands of the penis.

Treating older patients

The sexuality of older people has only recently become an acceptable topic. Older patients are more likely to suffer from certain forms of sexual dysfunction and to present a mixed biological and psychological picture. Rossi points out that the therapist may well be younger than their patient and this may bias them towards sexually unrealistic therapeutic goals either over- or underestimating an achievable level of sexual performance. Male sexual response changes with age so that tactile stimulation becomes more important in achieving erection with age. Also specific new sexual anxieties may occur in older patients, including the 'widowers syndrome' – guilt at having sex after the death of a wife (Rossi 1994). Crowe and Ridley (1990) adopt a sex positive message in relation to sex in older couples. They emphasise sexual creativity and advocate innovation in love-making in order to break up established patterns and rituals of sexual activity which may have become tarnished with age.

Gay men and lesbians

For far too many years the chief 'sexual' therapy offered to gay men and lesbians consisted in attempts to offer sexual reorientation with heterosexuality as its object. Slowly the culture changed, at first advocating therapy only for so called 'egodystonic' homosexuality, and now, most often, acknowledging that sexual orientation is not therapeutically alterable and that the egodystonic nature of some people's experience of their sexual preference is a consequence of societal prejudice and not a pathological condition. While many therapists would regard treatments designed to promote heterosexual desire in a gay or lesbian person as necessarily homophobic some dissent. Bancroft (1989), for example, still advocates treating egodystonic homosexuality with therapies designed to change sexual orientation and devotes a number of pages to describing therapeutic methods for increasing heterosexual desire in an unhappy homosexual. He argues that only a therapist who is genuinely accepting of a homosexual lifestyle should offer such treatment to an individual who genuinely seeks it on a civil liberties basis. Of course, a genuinely accepting therapist might be a gay man or lesbian themselves – something Bancroft does not envisage and the image of a gay man behaviourally conditioning another gay man to be straight certainly gives pause for thought. Groups of religiously inspired psychotherapists of a psychoanalytic orientation in America also offer 'reparative therapy'. In England some psychoanalysts still feel that homosexual orientation is a pathological condition (Phillips *et al.* 2001):

> Luke consulted with a complaint of erectile failure which upset his long-term lover and himself. He had always known that he was gay but had found this fact difficult to accept about himself in the context of his Scottish Presbyterian family upbringing. In his early twenties he consulted a psychiatrist and was referred to an experimental behaviour therapy programme using aversion therapy. Patients were given electric shocks if they became aroused while being shown pictures of naked men. Luke found the treatment ineffective in reducing his sexual desire but he liked the professor involved and so, at the end of treatment said he had become heterosexual so as not to disappoint him. His next burst of treatment undertaken five years later was psychodynamic and explicitly focused on attempts to promote heterosexual interest. Luke briefly contemplated a marriage but ultimately did not go through with it and left therapy. In the intervening years Luke established a stable lifestyle with a long-term partner which sat alongside a continuing interest in casual sex.

Set against Luke's negative experiences are a number sex therapy programmes. Masters and Johnson (1979) have offered sexual and couple therapy for gay men and lesbians. Even here there can be issues related to homophobia. Satsz (1990) points out that while Masters and Johnson asserted that homosexuality is not a disease they still offered homosexual men who wished to become heterosexual treatment to help them do so and claimed high success rates. They also strongly advised homosexual men who were married to conceal their true sexual preference and never advised them to accept their homosexual inclination. Little (or large) corners of unexamined homophobia are important when considering the treatment of gay men and lesbians with sexual problems. McWhirter and Mattison (1980), reviewing behavioural treatments for gay men and lesbians with sexual problems, suggested that these programmes can be successful as long as the therapist is not homophobic. Probably also therapists who have some familiarity with and sympathy towards gay sex and the sexual anxieties which gay men and lesbians may experience are advantaged over therapists without such experience. Indeed, gay men and lesbians are rightly no longer content with therapists who approach them with an 'open mind' and perhaps a trace of residual smugness for being so liberal. Instead they expect to be treated by an informed professional who does not first require an education into the ins and outs of gay and lesbian life and sexuality.

Lesbian sex therapists and sexual advisors have concentrated largely on two issues. One is 'lesbian bed death', an expression which refers to the tendency of established lesbian couples to reduce or cease their sexual involvement with each other. The other issue concerns the limits of permissible lesbian sexual expression. The extent to which either of these issues represents a therapeutic problem is almost entirely a matter of cultural or subcultural setting. In the space of a small area of San Francisco might be found groups of lesbians who regard sadomasochistic sexual wishes as vile remnants of patriarchy and other lesbians who regard sadomasochistic sexual activity as both therapeutic and life-enhancing. Wilton (1996) reviews the work of a number of 'lesbian sex gurus' including Loulan (1984) and Hall (1998). They are permissive in relation to sexual troubles, sanctioning a wide range of sexual activities. Hall is particularly interesting. In order to treat lesbian bed death she offers a set of paradoxical interventions designed to break up the ordered progression of sexual activity. Breaking down expectations over the setting for sex, its initiation and stimulation produces novelty and risk, the lack of which is thought central to failure of lesbian desire. As was seen in Chapter 5, these treatments adopt the common presumption that lesbian levels of desire are problematic. Although Hall comes closest to offering a critique of the concept of lesbian bed death she and Loulan both succumb to an extent to the temptation to read off from norms of heterosexual activity equivalent lesbian norms. Thus while it has been accepted in the lesbian community that the orgasm count is a poor index of sexual activity between women (generally resulting in the finding that the amount of sex is roughly proportional to the number of penises present) the temptation to indulge in the activity still breaks through.

Another concern of lesbian sex therapists has been to delineate or expand the limits of normally permissible sexual expression. Susie Bright and Pat Califia have devoted much time to this area. Although both act as individual therapists their chief public activities are political campaigns in various communities for sexual freedom. This combination confers on them the almost unique distinction of being therapists who take social context and the attempt to alter it as being as important as personal difficulty. Wilton characterises the difference between them neatly by labelling Califia as a sex pervert and Bright as a perverse girl guide. The advantage of these two commentators to practising therapists is that they expand the range of behaviours which are permissible between consenting adults but do not minimise any difficulties or anxieties which may arise. Bright has been willing to take considerable risks for her beliefs, staging demonstrations of sexual activity. Califia is more willing than Bright to write about the difficulties and risks of sexuality. Like Bright she extends her sexual liberalism beyond the homosexual world to create communities out of other sexual desires such as fisting or bondage. Thus Califia sees active desire as in itself subversive and liberating but does not minimise the difficulties which attend it. Her acknowledgement of the subversive potential of desire places her in the tradition of De Sade (1948) and Battaille (1987). Unlike them, she retains a strong sense of human connectedness and relationship. This clear-eyed combination makes her one of the strongest and most interesting writers in the field of sexuality today. Like De Sade and Battaille she has been able to introduce in her fiction and her serious writing the full play of the erotic imagination. Unlike them, she retains a far more delicate erotic sensibility, avoiding both De Sade's repetitious descent into coercive sex and Battaille's tendency to pompous narcissism.

Disability

In the minds of most able-bodied people disabled people are asexual or at best sexually inadequate. It is supposed that if they are not married or in a relationship this is because no one wants them, that if they are childless this is perforce and not through choice. Able-bodied people who marry disabled people are assumed to have some abnormal motive. Any relationship between two disabled people is seen as having been entered into for lack of a better choice. Sadly these prejudices can also pervade the disabled community in which sometimes fierce hierarchies of ability and desirability can build up. Along with these prejudices comes active discrimination and abuse. Disabled persons are, for example, raped and abused more often than able-bodied people.

The specific sexual difficulties of disabled people depend on the nature of their disability. Some may have physical problems involving sexual response, others may have difficulties in mobility which make sexual activity onerous or mean that able-bodied assistance is needed. In this area a key controversial issue is the involvement of carers in assisting disabled people to have sex. Carers and disabled people can become involved in very complex and emotionally painful debates over what should occur. Our cultural expectation of privacy during sexual activity makes carer involvement difficult. The emotional arousal during sexual activity may well involve all parties and the physical vulnerability of a disabled person, or of two disabled people, may make sexual exploitation a major risk.

When the handicap involves learning difficulties or mental illness then a tendency to infantilise disabled people can combine with actual difficulties over competency. Here moral questions shade into legal ones. We are terrified of the thought of letting people with learning difficulties or mental illness make sexual choices, erring almost always on the side of sexually repressing them. Yet people with learning difficulties or mental illnesses are also at risk of being sexually abused by their carers and then re-traumatised when their stories are not believed or taken seriously (Hollins and Sinason 2000).

Finally it must be admitted that the position of disability in this book resembles its position in the minds and policies of most sexual therapists and policy-makers: a small ghettoised subsection chiefly devoted to a superficial discussion of difficulties and authored by an able-bodied person. Fortunately, an intelligent, extended and sensible work does exist in this area and for further advice readers are directed to Shakespeare, Gillespie-Sells and Davies (1996).

Critique

While there has been a great deal of good work done by sex therapists and while theorists of sexual activity have also done much to create and be created by an increasingly liberal and less demonised view of sexual activity, sexology and the sex therapists have serious in built drawbacks.

Three common threads unite modern sexological theory and the therapeutic practice of sex therapy. The first is the creation of an expertise in sexual matters and sexual dysfunctions which can be marketed to the general public, who may thereby be constructed as sexually ignorant and helpless. The successful creation of this expertise also allows for the creation of an ideo-logical hegemony for scientific sexuality by developing a seem-ingly value-free stance on sex which obscures the intensely political and value-laden content of the discourse (Jackson 1987). The second difficulty, which Segal (1994) points up, is the extreme sanitisation, amounting to an ultra white boil wash, which sexological theory has performed on sex. Masters and Johnson, for example, tried to write their book in impenetrable and unsexy language, and even more 'erotic' volumes, such as *The Joy of Sex* (Comfort 1971) ignore the idea of an ambivalent, trou-bling, less controllable side to sexual desire. The last problem is that the notion of sex which sexology and the sex therapists devel-oped, the discovery of the multiple orgasms not withstanding, is both unitary and entirely masculine, with a resultant crushing of difference. These criticisms – the scientific commodification of sex, its sanitisation and its masculinisation – can be examined in turn. They are each in part a consequence of the failure to allow any space for the erotic imagination.

Commodifying sexual disorders and selling remedies involved the sex therapy community in the creation and promotion of disorders, and there is evidence that this happened. For example, the sex therapy industry advances the notion that sexual disappointment augurs poorly for the overall health of a relationship. It turns out this is not true and happy relationships may have unresolved sexual difficulties (Tiefer 1995). Even so for the sex therapy industry the notion that sexual difficulty has spreading ill-effects in other areas of life remains a key claim and an important selling point. At times the commodification of sexuality, and especially of sexual difficulty, even threatens to eviscerate the considerable value that adheres to the notion of the promotion of sexual enlightenment and wellbeing. The most cursory glance at women's magazines and at the growing genre of men's wellbeing magazines reveals any number of questionnaires, articles and letters pages devoted to sex and sexual difficulty. It is now traditional to normalise any positive sexual wish 'as long as your partner wants to join in' (note the use of the singular and the implied assumption involved). Yet nothing perceived as sexual 'deficit' is ever allowed to stand as normal. Imaginatively, the effect of this commodification is to hand over the erotic imagination to experts who then resell it in packages made to conform to the sexual morals of the age. Particularly damaging is the notion that no deficit can ever be allowed since it threatens to crowd the erotic canvas with ill-thought-out agglomerations of erotic objects.

The urge to sanitise sex is ubiquitous in our culture. In sex education classes desire is almost always obliterated by love. Sex panics, such as those which attend paedophile trials, attest to a need to sanitise areas of 'sex pests'. Sanitisation can also be seen in our wish only to imagine aesthetically appealing bodies in sexual relationship to each other (thus excluding the old or the disabled). In the 1980s the lesbian sex wars (Wilton 1996) can be read as a fight between lesbians who felt that sex should be demasculinised and rendered gentle, equal and reciprocal, and lesbians who wanted to retain a host of practices which involved power or role play. Segal (1994) points out that the ill-effects of sanitisation result from excluding the ambiguity and pain that are also part of sexual experience. From an imaginative perspective the failure is aesthetic. Excluding every note of conflict, sadness or pain from the erotic imagination forces it repeatedly to shy away from aspects of experience which keep recurring. Indeed the erotic imagination is been deprived of its main potential benefit, which is to weave together disparate elements of experience into a maintainable and aesthetically satisfying whole:

Brian suffered a medical catastrophe in his early twenties which resulted in his having a permanent colostomy (a hole in the stomach wall for faeces to emerge into a bag rather than defecating in the usual way). Initially he recovered well but as time passed he found himself unable to chat up girls for fear that he would smell. On the few occasions a sexual encounter did develop he was impotent. His GP's practice counsellor seemed unhelpful and Brian got the impression that she thought he should not want to have sex. He surfed the internet for fellow sufferers and discovered that some people like to have a penis or fingers inserted into their colostomy. Brian was disgusted but the idea dominated his mind. He eventually began to finger his colostomy and then to damage it. On referral to a psychologist he described a childhood history of a preoccupation with cleanliness in the family, enforced by his mother who probably had an obsessional disorder. He had been told about sex early on but in a matter of fact way. He said 'I hadn't realised it would feel nice'. Once he started his early sexual experiences had been aggressive and degrading to his female partners.

Brian's over-sanitising of sex and faeces has rebounded on him and he now enacts towards his colostomy a complex mix of emotions involving hatred of it, and himself, wishes to be clean and dirty, and sexual wishes mixed with disgust. Probably sanitising sexuality overmuch has ill-effects socially and for the individual if only because, as in Brian's early sex education, it takes descriptions of and arguments about sexuality too far from the actual experience of sexual activity.

Given the taboos against it in our culture it was probably only with the ground prepared by a suitable sanitisation and comodification of sexuality that Masters and Johnson could have started to use sex surrogates in therapy. Their rise and fall as a technique demonstrates that the liberalisation which commodification and sanitisation permitted was more apparent than real.

Masters and Johnson used surrogates for unpartnered men but not for unpartnered women. Cole, however, used surrogate partners for both sexes (Satsz 1990). The practice was understandably highly controversial, and unflattering comparisons have been made between surrogates and prostitutes. Satsz certainly regarded this practice as little short of the legitimisation of prostitution. In making the comparison he correctly identifies the element of commodification involved. There are without doubt serious problems with using surrogates, particularly in relation to issues of exploitation and sexual risk, but it is hard to put up any absolute and principled objection. Arguments against surrogates in sex therapy tend to rest on a privileging of monogamy, fidelity and longevity in relationships so that the use of surrogates violates a certain set of currently romantically acceptable contexts for finding a partner:

> Lawrence, unkindly and secretly nicknamed Lawrence the lizard by his therapist, presented with a mixture of paranoid ideas, that people in the street were calling him a poof, and a complaint of sexual inadequacy. Lawrence keenly felt both a failure to find a female partner with whom he could have sex and also a radical uncertainty about his performance once he had found one. Doubtless, partly because of the severe unresolved countertransference, therapy with Lawrence stalled before it had even begun. Lawrence wanted treatment from a centre where he would be given the services of a sexual surrogate and could find out what sex with a woman was like before trying it out on his own on a 'real' woman. The therapist interpreted this as a fantasy and as an attempted seduction. Only after the failure of the therapy did the therapist discover that such a sex therapy institution did exist in England at that time about which Lawrence had probably read. The therapist was left wondering if she would have referred Lawrence had she known about the centre at the time.

The difficulties of using sexual surrogates and the complex relationship entanglements which can result led to the cessation of this practice by Masters and Johnson after legal difficulty. The brief exploration of this area demonstrates the instability within our culture of a sexual liberalism achievable by commodification and sanitisation. These two strategies do not bring any true expansion of the erotically imaginable in our culture.

The scientific masculinisation of sexuality has had significant ill-effects on an understanding of female sexuality. Feminist writers documented this extensively (e.g. Reed 1978). However, Satz (1990) points out that our current perspective on sexual order results in the construction of disorders read off from a masculine norm which is itself fictitious. Thus while a quick orgiastic response in the male is now regarded as a manifestation of sexual incompetence the same response in a female is regarded as a manifestation of sexual competence. Retarded ejaculation acquires its significance from the fact that the act is not expected to cease until the man ejaculates. Yet if the partners were free to end coitus without ejaculation, then retarded ejaculation might be welcomed by the woman and be no problem for the man. Satz's shows us that the procrustean effect of scientific sexological norms damages both the female and the male psyche. A one size fits all model of sexual functioning is self-evidently a consequence of a massive imaginative failure – the same imaginative failure that occurs throughout many cultures and across a wide range of historical periods. Indeed the ubiquity of this failing has been taken by some to mean that it is normal and desirable whatever ill-effects it can be shown to have. As yet our culture, like many others, has failed to quell sexual anxiety long enough to free the imagination and to permit true sexual variation.

Improving sexology and sex therapy

Many of the deficits in scientific sexology are being slowly rectified. Women have been important in this area and for all her faults Hite was a pioneer. For some straight men and women (Samuels 1993; Segal, 1994) the gay and lesbian movement have been able to offer insights about sexuality which serve as an antidote to the dominant view. But in other areas difficulties persist. The industry of websites selling Viagra to the general public, using internet-based medical 'consultations' to avoid any personal (and presumably humiliating) contact with a doctor is worrying because of potential medical problems with Viagra but also demonstrates that many people do not agree with the medicalisation and control of a substance they see as a modern aphrodisiac. Even in one-to-one consultations the medicalisation of human encounters continues. Satz would have found much to amuse him in the 'Coital alignment technique' advocated by Pierce (2000), which along with 'orgasm consistency training' is advocated for problems such as female anorgasmia and premature ejaculation, which appear to have their origins in 'ineffective intercourse techniques'.

It will only be possible to move on from situations like these if modern sexual therapists begin to attend to the multiple ambiguities of their positions as advisers and experts in something which everybody knows how to do and in which very many different ways of doing it are equally valuable. To provide any real expertise modern sexual therapy must renounce prejudice and make itself the master of the wide range of differences that exist in sexual expression and of the different ecstasies, pleasures, difficulties and anguishes each kind of expression imposes. It needs an active and subtle theory of the erotic imagination. This erotic imagination can provide an erotic psychic content to supplement the bland behavioural and cognitive reflections of the cognitive behaviour therapists. Use of the erotic imagination might end the strange divorce in the psychodynamic therapies, which conceive of adults having sex while fantasising about breastfeeding. From such a position the therapeutic enterprise might be able to widen from the therapy of the individual to the therapy of a culture, equally prone to imaginative cramp and sexual monochrome of whatever hue.

10

Sex in the consulting room

Sexual feelings towards the therapist

Breuer's difficult experiences with Anna O (1893–5) and Freud's (1905b) summary dismissal, with two weeks notice, by Dora both had at their core sexual wishes by the patient towards their analyst. They set the scene for an analysis first of sexual wishes on the part of the patient towards the therapist and later for an analysis of sexual wishes on the part of therapist towards patient. At times these wishes lead to sexual activity. Several cardinal features of the field should be noted. First, the major commentators are psychoanalytic. No other school of psychotherapy appears yet to have produced an extended theory-driven meditation on sexuality in the consulting room. Second, it is assumed by almost all writers that sexual activity between patient and analyst is dangerous and harmful. In conformity with this, sexual relations in this setting are illegal in some countries and result in professional sanctions in almost all countries and settings. A third feature, which will become apparent, is the tension created by a desire to explore erotic feelings during therapy and the sanctions over their expression.

Freud (1915) set out the classic combination of neurotic female patients who fall in love with their male analyst. He argued that these feelings of love are displaced from elsewhere and transfered onto the analyst. As elsewhere in psychoanalytic theory his views were successively modified by later writers, often to conform them to the requirements of wider theoretical considerations. Public perceptions of analysis picked up on the erotic possibilities inherent in the activity and soon generated a stereotyped version of an aloof male analyst as the object of hopeless and somewhat demeaning love of an attractive blonde. Psychoanalysts subscribed to very similar views. For example, Greenson (1967) thought all cases of eroticised transference were of women patients analysed by men, while Racker (1968) described transference 'nymphomania', with attempts to seduce by the patient.

Freud thought initially that all transference was an obstacle to analytic progress, and even after this view was revised the erotic transference remained highly suspect and continues to be so to the present day. Schafer (1977, in Person 1983) sees erotic transference as resistance. This view is echoed by analysts from the Kleinian school, such as Joseph (1993) and Doctor (1999). The degree of pathology thought to be represented by an erotic transference depends to a large extent on the general view of pathology espoused by the analyst. Thus Kleinian analysts tend to regard an eroticised transference as involving a significant degree of disturbance.

More benign views of erotic transference can be developed. Kernberg (1995), starting from Freud's formulation, sets out a fairly classic theory of transference love but usefully contrasts it with unrequited neurotic love. Ideally, he argues, transference love, which is refused direct expression by the analyst, is relinquished slowly, mourned and lessens with time, whereas neurotic love is increased by rejection. Furthermore, unlike the secret love of the oedipal scenario, transference love is (or should be) talked about and analysed. This analysis sets Kernberg amongst a group of analysts who regard erotic transference as dangerous but useful, manifest analytic material to be mined for latent content. Kernberg argues that the erotic transference can go wrong in a number of ways. An excessive or demanding quality to the transference love implies neurotic/masochistic problems in the patient while too little evidence of erotic transference implies sadomasochistic resistances or narcissistic transferences.

Schaverien (1995), who reviews the field, points out that post-Freudian theory increasingly relies on a distinction between erotic and eroticised transference, which are thought to be, respectively, neurotic and psychotic. Chiesa (1994) describes eroticised transference as the delusional manifestation of a pathological organisation. He subscribes to the idea of erotic (good) and eroticised (bad) transference, suggesting that the appearance of the analyst in a dream is a bad sign, presaging possible involvement of analyst. He also thinks that early overt expression of erotic transference in therapy, is likely to be seriously difficult and can be distinguished from benign episodes occurring later during therapy which are self-limiting (Chiesa 1999). Patients who experience this pathological reaction have, in his experience, a history of childhood seduction and a sexualised family story.

An even more permissive view sees the erotic transference as defensive but, if handled correctly, beneficent. Covington (1996, in Mann 1999) sees erotic longing by the patient as representing a desire to find nurturing parents and to internalise a new (presumably more benign) primal scene. Schaverien (1995) takes a broadly similar view and cites Blum (1973) and Rappaport (1956) who both argue that sexual urges may be covering up wishes for, but fears of, dependency on the analyst.

However, as Kernberg (1995) points out, love which was displaced once may be displaced again and if transference love is secondarily displaced onto others then the patient may 'act out':

John's behaviour in therapy was experienced by his therapist as sexually provocative and threatening. She had already made sure to see him only at times when there were other people present in the therapy centre where she worked. The strangest thing was that nothing was stated openly and the therapist was sure that if she raised the issue of his behaviour he would laugh it off with scornful contempt accusing her of imagining things, and even possibly turn the remark into evidence that the therapist had sexual feelings about him. Matters intensified over a few sessions and the therapist's paralysis and desperation increased. Then, suddenly, it went away. The sessions were no less strained or contemptuous but the sexual edge was gone. Later the therapist found out that John had started two new relationships with women he hardly knew, one of whom he insisted on seeing once a week, only at exactly the same time each week.

John's behaviour in the later part of the sessions would certainly be seen by most analysts as 'acting out' and the feelings which were building up in the therapy, to the acute discomfort of the therapist, are latterly being discharged elsewhere. The therapist's experience is well described by the term erotic horror. This was coined by Kumin (1985, in Mann 1999) to describe the impending awareness and discomfort felt by the analyst as patient develops an erotic transference. In this case the horror dissipates, but not necessarily to the patient's benefit. The aggressive quality to the erotic transference which built up is typical of a pattern described by Kernberg in which men with narcissistic disorders use aggressive sexualisation of the transference to defend against fears of dependency. Kleinian commentators would also add that the build-up of unverbalised tension in the analyst, rather than the patient, is a sign of massive projective identification of the sort which patients need to use when unbearable psychotic anxieties dominate their mental processes.

Sexual feelings of therapists towards patients

Broadly speaking, those analytic writers who concern themselves at all with erotic feelings by therapists towards patients do so under the rubric of countertransference and tend to take a more benign view of erotic feeling in analysis generally. Mann (1999), reviewing the topic, cites Searles (1959) as taking a more progressive view than was usual at the time of both transference and countertransferential erotic feeling. Some writers on the topic are preoccupied with creating a taxonomy of the types of patients who may elicit countertransference feelings. Gorkin (1985) lists four different kinds of characters who elicit erotic countertransference – the female hysteric, the female masochist and the phallic male or female. Kernberg also produces a classification system, arguing that erotic countertransference is most intense in male analysts analysing masochistic women whose erotic longings represent impossible love for an unavailable oedipal object, and in male analysts with female narcissistic patients. For women analysts, he argues, their own masochistic traits may lead to erotic feelings towards the narcissistic men they are analysing. Kernberg's categories go beyond an anatomy of patient characteristics to suggest that features of the analyst may also be important in determining the play of erotic transference and countertransference.

A second way of viewing erotic countertransference is to highlight its function within the analytic situation. Kristeva (1983, quoted in Mann, 1999), for example, propounds a complex view of countertransference in which the analyst represents the 'father of prehistory', that is, the pre-oedipal father who is/stands for the mother's desire for the father's phallus. This leads Kristeva to argue that the experience of being acknowledged as an erotic object for the analyst helps the patient become a subject-in-process. The idea of a positive function both for erotic counter-transference has been taken up strongly by a large number of modern writers, such as Mann (1999) Schaverien (1995) Covington (1996) and Samuels (1985a). The view they hold in common is that erotic feelings are in some way crucial to the very process of analysis and that inattention to them may be damaging to the endeavour and to the patient. Field (1999), who agrees with this position, also feels that the patient's experience of the therapist's self-aware desire for the patient is curative and might be lost if erotic countertransference is neglected. These writers and others permit disclosure of countertransference feelings by the analyst as a legitimate part of technique, once a range of rather anxious criteria have been met.

This view needs to be distinguished from that of a more traditional writer such as Chiesa (1994, 1999), who discusses the adverse consequences of inattention to erotic countertransference in a patient, who, as a result of this, subsequently acted out. Chiesa does not see in erotic countertransference the opportunity for the patient to experience validation as an erotic object. For Chiesa, the valuable thing that is lost as a result of failing to attend to the erotic countertransference is the capacity to make interpretations informed by the countertransference. In analytic practice Chiesa and also Kernberg are absolutely clear that no disclosure of the countertransference should occur.

Jung differed from Freud in matters of sexuality and developed his own perspective on erotic longing in the analytic relationship. Jung sees sexuality in the transference as a progressive force and as a symbol for various patterns of relatedness (Jung 1959 CW 8:74, 1956 CW 5:7–11). His most extended work on the subject – *The Psychology of the Transference* (Jung 1946 CW 16) combines an extended meditation on the symbolism of alchemical woodcuts and on the passionate involvement of patient and analyst in the mutual process of analysis. The work repays study but is often neglected for a range of reasons, not least because modern readers find Jung's theories about alchemy as a symbolic representation of psychological processes of growth difficult to swallow. A key feature of the woodcuts is the intermingling of the bodies of the King and Queen, represented sometimes side by side sometimes in coitus and sometimes as a fused hermaphrodite. Jung thought that the goal of the psychological process was 'individuation' a term which refers to the development of the psyche into a more differentiated and integrated state. Since the woodcuts are a symbolic depiction of individuation they depict the passionate intermingling which will be needed in the analytic process for change to occur:

Wendy thought that her therapist was looking down her cleavage and said so. The therapist was mortified and chiefly felt guilty, unsure whether she had been looking down her patient's cleavage or not. On a reflex she assured Wendy that she was not looking down her cleavage and the matter appeared to rest. Some sessions later Wendy repeated the accusation and the therapist, having discussed the matter in supervision, proceeded to try to explore Wendy's 'fantasy' about her. There, overtly, matters rested again except that the therapist now had no idea where to put her eyes. Should she look defiantly at Wendy's cleavage, which was, as it happened, rather attractive now she came to think of it, or should she avoid it and look away? The problem was that each session Wendy's cleavage became bigger and bigger. In her mind the therapist even called Wendy 'the cleavage'. Pleasurable if guilty sexual fantasies alternated with a sense of disgust engendered by the notion of drowning in Wendy's cleavage. Wendy took to describing her own sexual fantasies about the therapist, which grew juicer and spicier even as the therapist struggled to interpret them, often in terms of infantile material. Eventually Wendy said, 'Come off it, you're looking down my cleavage aren't you?' Cornered, the therapist had to admit that she was, but then added, 'You started it!' With tones of extreme satisfaction Wendy said: 'They're my one good feature. Sometimes I like to watch people look at them. I know I can push people around with them if I want to.' More by luck than judgement on the therapist's part Wendy's pushy cleavage became a central image of work on someone who in other areas of life had a low opinion of herself and problems with assertion.

Wendy's case underlines the experienced dangerousness of sexual material to the therapist. Sometimes one or both parties may conspire to avoid erotic material emerging, in order to remain in the comfortable area of dependency and childhood (Lester 1985). Schaverien would agree, and adds that to do so and keep things infantile is a form of abuse of power, because while the analyst denies adult elements of sexuality in the transference he or she prevents the infantile and dependent from developing into the adult and independent.

Gender and erotic transference/countertransference

Once the idea of a reciprocal interaction in relation to erotic feelings in therapy is allowed, then a range of potential pairings are evident, each of which may interact differently. On the manifest level there are at least four pairings of analyst and patient gender. These become sixteen possible combinations if the sexual orientation of either partner is added in as a variable. Unsurprisingly, given the combinatorial complexity, the literature has not yet developed far enough to encompass accounts of, for example, gay men analysed by lesbians (or vice versa). These sixteen possible pairings become a minimum of thirty-two if the possibility that either partner may unconsciously be operating as a different sex to their overt one is admitted. It is perfectly possible to contemplate a situation in which a gay male therapist is related to sexually in the role of oedipal mother by a heterosexual woman who is exploring or fantasising, consciously or unconsciously, her inverted Oedipus complex. However, such situations have also yet to make it into the therapeutic literature and most commentators confine themselves to conscious heterosexual pairings.

Freud had little to say about analysing couples other than the female patient – male analyst pairing. Other Freudians have, however, taken up the challenge. Kernberg (1995), for example, begins to extend this range, distinguishing, as well, between neurotic and narcissistic patients. He argues therefore that a neurotic man analysed by a woman will inhibit transference love and displace it because of anxieties over sexual performance with a woman seen as the oedipal mother. Narcissistic patients fear humiliation and shaming. Thus narcissistic women do not experience sexual desires for their male analyst because this would be experienced by them as humiliating. However, narcissistic men may develop very aggressive sexualised transferences towards their female analyst as a way of defending against dependency, which is experienced as humiliating.

Apart from a gesture by Kernberg, the erotic transference and countertransference experiences of female analysts with male patients are often absent from the literature. Person (1985:163) suggests that women feel the touch of the erotic transference less. She argues that women use erotic transference in analysis as a vehicle of resistance whereas men resist the experience of the erotic because feeling erotically towards the female analyst would be experienced as undermining male autonomy. Lester (1982) agrees, arguing that cultural factors, amongst others, make male erotic transferences towards women analysts unlikely. Guttman (1984, in Schaverien 1995), argues similarly that men who want to say devaluing erotic things are not keen to tell female analysts because it is more socially acceptable to tell such things to men (locker-room talk). Chasseguet-Smirgel (1984a) suggests that a male patient who idealises the female analyst will keep sex out of the transference, presumably thereby maintaining the split between idealised mother and denigrated whore. Coming from a different tradition, Meltzer (1973) produces a different reason for the lack of erotic transferences, arguing that male analysts are drawn into an infantile form of sexual excitement in perverse patients whereas women analysts tend to idealise the patient within maternal transference.

Maguire (1995) disagrees and argues that sexualised male patient to female analyst transferences do occur. She suggests that female therapists may not discuss sexual transferences because of anxieties about being seen as provocative. She cites in evidence Gornick (1986) who points out the existence of a film theme of the woman analyst who restores her male patient by having sex with him. The suggestion is that women analysts are scared of being boxed into the role of therapeutic prostitute and therefore crush signs of erotic transference. Arguing from her own clinical experience, Maguire contends that sexual transferences tinged with aggression and contempt, born of fear and envy of a woman in a superior position, do occur. Her experience is echoed by Schaverien (1995), whose extended case reports involve a range of male patients who experienced erotic transferences towards her. She usefully argues that women analysts' erotic transference and countertransference experiences with male patients are structured by the ways women are viewed by men, pointing out that erotic or loving feelings towards female analysts are often treated as maternal rather than erotic. So, female clinicians do report experiences of heterosexual transference with men, but there are differences which reflect the relationship between sex and authority and sexuality.

Schaverien is also willing to admit the possibility of erotic feelings between female–female analysing pairs, and cites O'Connor and Ryan (1993), who discuss the lack of any extended discussion of lesbian transference and countertranference feelings in the literature but who also remedy this deficiency with case history material. Schaverien acknowledges sexual feeling towards her female patients but says these were not as strong as towards male patients and attributes this to her heterosexuality. Person (1999) will not even go this far and downplays the erotic element, even of erotic transference between heterosexual women, suggesting that feelings are affectionate and tender rather than sexual. By contrast she suggests that homosexual women develop very strong erotic transferences and that this situation is redoubled when the analyst is also homosexual. Person also discusses male patients analysing with male analysts and suggests that the erotic transference is muted largely because of taboos on homosexual expression in heterosexual men.

Where non-analytic literature discusses sexual feelings on the part of the patient towards the therapist the general tendency is either to borrow some of the simpler and more evidently rationally based formulations of psychoanalytic theory or to regard expressions of sexual attraction by the patient as carrying simply their manifest meaning. Scharff and Scharff (1991) summarise sex therapy attitudes to countertransference. Masters and Johnson (1970) thought it dangerous and tried to design it out of their treatments. Dicks and Strauss (1979) acknowledge its importance as a threat to treatment. Kaplan (1974) regards it as important but gives no guidance on its use. Scharff and Sharff, being analytic in orientation, use countertransference analytically as an explicit therapeutic tool within a mixed therapy involving both behavioural and analytic elements. There are extra difficulties with this approach since the behavioural elements of treatment may be experienced as provocative within the transference, but clearly attempting to ignore transference elements, as Masters and Johnson do, is no solution.

Sexual orientation and erotic transference/ countertransference

It is clear in all these discussions that psychoanalytic theorising about sexual transference and countertransference and gender is an area where social custom and cultural forces demand accommodation. Despite the relentless focus in psychoanalytic theory on the inner world, analysts considering the manifestations of the transference and countertransference have been forced to give the outside world's social conventions pride of place in determining the nature, direction and strength of the erotic reactions which may occur in therapy. This makes accounts of the interaction of sexual orientation with erotic experiences in therapy particularly interesting as there is less (or at least a different) weight of social convention structuring gay relationships. Issues involving sexual orientation issues have until recently not been well discussed. Elise (1991), for example, has a go but her account both lacks detail and is rather denigratory. She discusses an intense lesbian transference on the part of a patient who idealised her. When the idealisation broke down threats of rape and murder followed, plus a confession that she had raped her last lover!

The complicated if flawed account given by Elise of the analysis of Dale stands in sharp contrast. Elise (1991) develops a powerful erotic countertransference over an extended period of time and speaks personally about the difficulties of managing bodily expressions of attraction like blushing or a vulnerable smile. Despite acknowledging the importance of erotic transference and the need to take it at face value rather than analyse it away as a defence, Elise maintains a rigid boundary of concealment between herself and her patient in relation to countertransference. Part of her reason may lie in her view that: 'the intensity of erotic transference and erotic countertransference can lead to the therapist feeling out of control. These feelings of vulnerability are out of character with our role. Direct discussion can even increase these feelings' (Elise 1991:64). The strain of the effort on her part to conceal her feelings is terrible. 'I was attempting to work through these issues with Dale, yet I felt terribly concerned even after months and years of treatment with an unfailing therapeutic demeanour on my part, that a fraction of a second of possibly perceived sexualised vulnerability on my part would undo my role and my power to be helpful to her' (Elise 1991:62).

Elise suggests that lesbians who know of their sexual orientation very early (and presumably Dale is one) are 'more masculine' and avoid vulnerability or dependency. She argues that because of the difficulties of growing up as a lesbian they do not have anxiety-free experiences of platonic friendships and also that they defend against dependency with erotic feelings. This analysis, while welcome because detailed, threatens to turn Dale into a man manqué and by extension to suggest that passionate or difficult lesbian feelings result only from internalised masculinity. Furthermore it provides no justification for the way in which Elise manages her countertransference feelings.

More extended accounts of gay men as analysing couples are beginning to occur in the literature (Domenici and Lesser 1995), although the dead hand of the analytic past still hangs over these attempts. Occasional accounts can be found of sexual issues developing between gay men analysing straight men, where one difficult situation is accusations of attempted seduction made by a frightened patient as a way to avoid threatening dependency or attraction. Sexual contempt is also an issue which may threaten gay analysts working with straight men. Therapists can be torn between their political and personal commitment to their orientation and the patient's overt or covert contempt for homosexual orientation. Such matters become particularly acute when the therapist feels the patient is probing to find out about the therapist's sexuality. Negotiating this unknown territory can be a frightening and bewildering experience for a therapist. The danger is generally not ignorance, but rather practice based on the knowing assumptions of a standard model. The following case vignette illustrates the value of attending sequentially to a hierarchy of possible explanatory sources for a phenomenon; first real world explanations, then personal material from the therapist, then conscious elements in the patient and only last unconscious forces or defences:

Gudrun's therapist knew he was in trouble as soon as she told him she was a lesbian. His immediate reaction was 'what a waste'. She had been brought up in Germany but her father had been an American serviceman and had been absent rather a lot as his job took him here and there. The family had also moved frequently and Gudrun's developing lesbian sexuality had combined with her mother's language difficulties on American bases to make her always feel an outcast. As the therapy progressed the therapist fought to shake of his persistent sexual feelings for Gudrun, which were evidently not reciprocated. The therapist reckoned that anyone with half an eye for beauty would think Gudrun very attractive and felt confirmed in this view by a co-worker who had spotted her in the waiting room and remarked upon her spontaneously. He also knew of his own tendency based on a first love experience on a school trip to find unavailable German women attractive. He wondered whether his own mother's frightening tendency to remark, when angry, that if they were lucky his father would have to go and fight the Germans again and leave them in peace, might be part of the equation. The therapist felt confident that consciously sex was not a feature of the therapy relationship as far as Gudrun was concerned, but unconsciously he felt that he might represent the absent father for his patient. Sadly, he never plucked up the courage to raise the issue with Gudrun because he was terrified of the resulting humiliation he might experience.

Further inspection of this case vignette reveals an array of possibilities almost as dizzying as that opened up by contemplating all the possible analysing pairs and their potential erotic experiences. The therapist's use of the phrase 'what a waste' for example has links with the war and the Germans. Angry and dismissing mothers and fathers on the therapist's side are linked in a delicate quadrille with mute or absent ones on the patient's. But through it all the vulnerable nature of sexual feelings in a setting where they seem both permitted and forbidden runs like a constant thread.

The renunciation of sex in the consulting room and in the Oedipus complex

Of course even the most sex-positive writers on erotic counter-transference are against enactment. Instead they advocate the advantages of a kind of sailing close to the wind. Wrye and Welles (1994), for example, develop the idea that the basis for eroticism is a body love print based on the way mother deals with infant's body fluids. Maternal erotic transference and countertransference recreates the sensual erotic contact that the baby once had and is an important positive and necessary transforming process in treatment. If the therapist defends herself from experiencing counter-transference feelings the therapy may stall. Instead the therapist must tolerate the feelings without fanning the flames.

Mann (1999), writing in his own edited volume, makes powerful claims for the value and power of the erotic in therapy. He argues that the purpose of the erotic bond is to deepen an individual's capacity for connection and relatedness to others. Thus the therapist's sexual feelings allow him or her to participate with the patient in an erotic manner in a way that is 'supercharged with unconscious incestuous and murderous desires'. Supposedly the therapist then brings to the encounter 'an erotic subjectivity that may be characterised as good enough, incestuous, and murderous desires' (1999:77). Mann sees both repression and license as bad but restraint as good and the motor for development. Something of the Christian horror of license also fills Schaverien (1995) as she describes the, fantasised as unsatisfying, sexual encounter of bodies alone which might have followed an enactment of her erotic countertransference towards her patient (Schaverien 1995).

It is, therefore, an odd irony that this very Christian idea should be linked by writers to a tribal taboo on incest and a Greek myth. Schaverien, for example, links the theme of renunciation with the incest taboo and the growth potential it possesses. This view is a Jungian one and is echoed by Samuels (1995b) who argues that the purpose of incestuous desire within the family setting is to foster psychological growth and that this growth is destroyed by too much or too little 'erotic playback'. Searles view (1959) is very similar, but differentiates the countertransference to a pre-oedipal patient from the countertransference to an oedipal one. He argues that, in a pre-oedipal patient, the countertransference love is parental whereas in an oedipal patient it is more erotic. He links the renunciation of sex in analysis with the successful outcome of the Oedipus complex where renunciation of incestuous wishes is said to be a result of recognition of separateness.

Transference, countertransference and the erotic imagination

The amazing thing about all these accounts is that none will credit the existence of a truly plastic and sexual realm of the unconscious or of the imagination. While Freud was able to suggest that humans are born constitutionally bisexual and polymorphously perverse, no analyst seems able to grapple fully with the notion that the unconscious structuring of desire may not run in accord with anatomy or overt sexual orientation, nor are they able to accept that desire for the analyst or their patient may be just that. This means that while writers can agree that social forces structure permissible expression, they are not able to discuss the ways in which the tensions between social and unconscious realms condition the erotic imagination or the ways in which the imagination might transcend either realm.

The development of the notion of the incest taboo as the model for renunciation in the analytic situation provides a convenient analogy by which therapists can legitimate their strictures on sexual expression in the consulting room and at the same time permit themselves the right to explore sexual feelings, while withholding or revealing their own, as their theoretical whimsy takes them.

Jung's theory of individuation and creativity could have led Jungian writers to accord the erotic imagination its own wayward spirit but this has, by and large, failed to occur. Instead, his concept of holding the tension has come to serve as the model for correct management of erotic feeling in the consulting room. While holding the tension does offer one aesthetic for the expression of the erotic imagination it should not be elevated above all other aesthetic options. If the difficulty with at least some patients is imaginative cramp born of anxiety over the unruly demands of desire, then erotic transference and countertransference can be recast as expressions of an erotic imagination which has been partly liberated in therapy. Helping the patient to develop this new potential presents the patient with a better curative offer than transference interpretations or pale corrective sexual emotional experiences provided by an analyst, always constructed as in the powerful position of being more loved than loving.

Sexual relationships between therapist and patient

It is agreed by all that sex between therapist and patient breaks the fiduciary duty which the therapist owes the patient, damages the patient, and is unethical. Most professional organisations have severe penalties for breaches of sexual abstinence during treatment and often for a longer or shorter period of time afterwards. In some states in America sexual breaches have been made illegal and in England it is illegal to have a sexual relationship with someone who is detained under the provisions of the Mental Health Act. The basic argument behind these prohibitions is that patients are, for a range of reasons, not capable of valid consent to sex and therefore that the sex involved is always coercive.

Despite this, sexual activity does occur and recent interest has been stimulated by high-profile scandals and increasing evidence that sexual acting out is rather common. Gabbard (1995) and Gabbard and Lester (1995) announce that acting out of erotic feelings between therapist and patient is more common than acknowledged. Jehu (1994), whose book length treatment of the subject is authoritative, reports on a survey of American psychologists (Pope, Keith-Spiegel and Tabachnick 1986) in which 95 per cent of men and 76 per cent of women reported having been sexually attracted to patients on at least one occasion, 46 per cent reported engaging in sexual fantasies about patients rarely and 25 per cent more frequently, lastly 9 per cent of men and 2 per cent of women had acted out these feelings in some way.

Who has sex with their patients and why do they do it?

The vast majority of therapists who become involved with their patients are older men and most of their patients are younger women, but women do abuse at a rate of about 2 per cent. There is an infamous case, reported by McNamara (1994), of exploitation of a male patient by a female psychiatrist/psychoanalyst, ending in the patient's suicide. The case involved intense sexual fantasies by the patient and sexually suggestive letters both ways resulting in a curious, eroticised regression. McNamara points out that, consistent with our tendency to view female transgression more seriously, this case produced outrage and national coverage but cases of male sexual exploitation, which were much worse, did not. There are accounts of sexual exploitation between homosexual analysing couples and sufficiently many accounts have accumulated in the literature for there to be suggestions that lesbians analysing lesbians may be at particular risk of sexual acting-out, although no reliable estimate of numbers has been produced.

Attitudes to and explanations for sexual activity during therapy depend largely on the extent to which the experience of sexual attraction is thought to need any independent explanation. Those therapists whose views about sexual expression are most normative tend to regard the desire to have sex outside of a standard relationship (however defined) as pathological and needing explanation. Those therapists whose views about sex are more permissive or less theorised see sexual attraction as, to an extent, inevitable and focus mainly on controlling sexual expression.

In the former group Thompson (1999) sees sexual acting out in the consulting room, for all its grown up appearance, as an example of regression to mother–baby dynamics. She suggests that the analytic couple have come to fantasise that all their needs will be met by sex. Lasky (1989) takes a different tack, arguing that male analysts identify with their female patient's heterosexual desire and feel homosexual or feminine. This makes them anxious and leads to sexual abuse of patient by the therapist who is trying to prove he is masculine and actively sexual. Kernberg argues that, in general, narcissistic pathology is involved in analysts who sexually act out but admits oedipal dynamics, including a wish to be found out, may be involved.

Amongst those in the more permissive group, a number of writers have tried to anatomise the risk factors which predispose a therapist to begin a sexual relationship with a patient. Jehu (1994) lists personal distress, isolation, grandiosity, dominating character and antisocial traits as vulnerability factors. Schoener and Gonsiorek (1989) identify impulsive and sociopathic character disorders in abusive therapists. The former have longstanding problems with impulse control and have poorly controlled sexual behaviour in their personal lives. Sociopathic abusers tend to be more deliberate and cunning; they may abuse serially and see the therapy situation as one in which they can procure sexual experiences. Typically they are cool and calculating and detached. POPAN (Prevention of Professional Abuse Network: www.popan.org.uk – an organisation to help people who have been abused in therapy) stresses isolation and turmoil in the therapist's personal life as risk factors. They mention the more serious serial and calculating abuser but stress that such individuals are rare. Finkelhor (1987) has written generally about sexual transgressions and deviant sexual behaviour and suggests a range of different factors, including wishes for sex and love or for the patient to assuage the therapist's distress. Against such factors may be reasons for restraint which include internal inhibitions, external constraints, and resistance by the patient. Jehu says that therapists who have sexual contact with one patient are at a high risk of re-offending and remarks that 80 per cent of offenders had had sexual contact with more than one patient.

Who is abused?

Many of the individuals exploited by therapists appear to have a pre-existing psychological vulnerability to abuse and can therefore seem, to a suitably predisposed therapist, to be asking for it. Patients reporting abusive experiences show a tendency to develop erotic transferences to therapists and to reverse roles with the therapist and start caring for them. Some patients also lack sufficient and accurate knowledge about the impropriety of sexual relationships with their therapists or may need to achieve power over the therapist by developing a sexual relationship. At the more extreme end of psychopathology some patients with borderline personality disorder, dissociative identity disorder or complex post-traumatic stress disorder may have a range of symptoms including dissociative reactions, sexualised behaviour, confusion over boundaries, or extreme dependency. These symptoms both offer an exploitative therapist excuses for breaking boundaries and initiating sex and also may reduce inhibitions on sexual activity by increasing the therapist's evaluation of the chances for successful concealment.

Jehu (1994), Gardner (1999) and POPAN (www.popan.org. uk) all remark that as many as 80 per cent of cases reported to them involve patients sexually abused in childhood. The mechanisms by which sexual abuse experiences in childhood ultimately results in sexual exploitation in therapy are probably various. Some people who are sexually abused in childhood appear not to be seriously damaged by it but a large proportion of patients with personality difficulties, depression, and major psychotic disorder are found to have had unwanted sexual experiences in childhood. Patients with these conditions are likely to be vulnerable to sexual abuse in therapy. The prevalence of childhood sexual abuse is so high in cases of sexual exploitation in therapy that a history of it can serve as a useful warning marker to guide extra caution in managing such patients. A past history of over-sexualisation is reported by 51 per cent of patients, (Jehu 1994), who say that they have had over-sexualised relationships. The reasons for this may include difficulty in distinguishing sex and affection, having a compulsive need for sex as proof of being loved, and using sexuality to serve as a self punitive function.

The process of sexual boundary violation is reported by most patients in therapy settings as involving a gradual erosion of customary boundaries. These commonly include unorthodox therapeutic arrangements, suggestive talk, physical contact, extra therapeutic relationships and excessive self-disclosure by the therapist. However a softly softly approach is not invariable and severe psychological pressure may be applied, or therapists may physically intimidate or assault their victims. Sexual experiences in therapy often continue for a while. Jehu's survey showed that therapy ended immediately after the first sexual contact in 34 per cent of cases and, of these, in over half the immediate ending of therapy also ended sexual contact. For the remainder sexual relations and therapy continued. This is important for the psychology of the patient. Someone who returns to a sexual situation which is transgressive, for whatever reason, potentially lays themselves open to internal and external accusations of complicity:

Harriet was a highly damaged woman whose early promise as a brilliant academic had given way to a life of obsessional cleaning and self-recrimination for reasons which remained stubbornly obscure even after twenty years of psychiatric treatment.

By the time she was referred to her present therapist she was on her fifth psychiatrist and seventh psychotherapist. In therapy she soon revealed that her previous therapist had sexually abused her and that she felt guilty and upset about this. The story, as gathered both from her and from others involved at the time, was that she had been referred to her previous therapist at a time when his stock was high and he was thought both a brilliant teacher and clinician. Sessions had been initially formal and restrained but had then been moved to an evening slot. As winter drew in the therapist often let the room grow dark. The patient grew increasingly dependent on the therapist and felt she had been reassured that he would stick with her whatever it took. One day when the patient was in deep distress she asked to hold the therapist's hand and he let her do so and let her put her head on his lap. This established a pattern of encounters which she found beneficial and supportive. Then, one day the therapist under the guise of helping her to stand placed his hand on her breast. She was shocked and upset but said nothing. At the next session she placed the therapist's hand on her breast. Again nothing was said. Now a new pattern had been established in every session there was some ambiguously sexual element. Some months later the therapist announced his retirement. Harriet was furious and threatened to disclose the sexual element to the sessions if he did not go on seeing her. The therapist denied the existence of any sexual element to the sessions.

This account of a sexually exploitative experience in therapy illustrates many of the complexities which often arise. The therapist's behaviour is clearly on the wrong side of the line and yet it is not the kind of outrageous barn door transgression which usually comes to mind when sexual transgression is discussed. Classic vulnerability features are present in the patient, in the therapist and in the setting, all of which promoted regressive dependency which could have been picked up by someone with sufficient expertise. In this case the local expert was the abuser. The patient, because of her pathology, does much to worsen the situation but deserves to be protected not exploited. It is not clear whether the broken promises, leading to abandonment, or the sexualisation of the relationship was the more harmful or the most unprofessional.

Opinion is divided about the probity of sexual relationships once therapy has ended. Some people and organisations feel that a fiduciary duty continues in perpetuity (Gonsiorek and Brown 1989, in Jehu 1994) while others set down a range of strictures and limitations which amount to a cooling-off period. Most commentators (see www.popan.org.uk) would agree that there remains a power differential between therapists and patients even after termination, so that coercive influence may still be exerted after the end of treatment. Broadly, those patients who were vulnerable to sexual exploitation in therapy remain vulnerable to exploitation in post-therapy sexual relationships.

The outcome of sexual relationships in therapy

Survey data (Jehu 1994) reports that predominantly adverse psychological consequences for patients follow therapy abuse. Negative effects on personality occurred in 34 per cent of the patients, including depression, loss of motivation, impaired social adjustment, significant emotional disturbance and suicidal feelings. Hospitalisation was necessary in 11 per cent of the cases. 14 per cent of patients attempted suicide and 1 per cent were successful in committing suicide. The problem with interpreting these figures lies in deciding how much of the pathology to attribute to pre-existing conditions. In contrast to these adverse affects, 16 per cent of the patients were reported to have become healthier and in 9 per cent of cases no effect was found. Therapists who were sexually intimate with patients tended to report positive effects. These were also more likely if the patient initiated the sex or if the initiation of sex was mutual. Obvious biases in reporting make the interpretation of this data difficult. It is a simple matter to spot the likely effects of self-justificatory bias in those therapists who report the value of their erotic attentions to patients. However, successful sexual outcomes may be underreported by patients who, well aware of the consequences of reported transgressions by their therapists, keep the matter secret. Some unsuccessful outcomes may never be revealed by patients who are too traumatised to complain.

Those psychological factors which predispose patients to a greater likelihood of sexual exploitation also predispose them to a more severe outcome. Labelling the psychological consequences of adverse events depends, to an extent, on diagnostic debates over the use of the term post-traumatic stress disorder (PTSD). Jehu (1994) freely uses this diagnostic category and finds it to be a frequent outcome in patients. A huge range of symptoms, including loss of sexual interest, many forms of addiction, self-damaging behaviour, and denying, minimising, playing down or rationalising the abuse, or feeling emotionally dead, numb, being unable to recall their abuse experiences in some degree, and dissociative reactions including 'spacing out' and depersonalisation, all fall under the rubric of PTSD. Reactions are grouped into blocks which involve intrusive thoughts, phobic avoidance, chronic arousal and emotional numbing. At the severe end of the spectrum PTSD shades into dissociative identity disorder. Patients can experience a PTSD diagnosis as helpful because it co-ordinates a wide range of symptoms into a coherent whole. However, a major disadvantage of the diagnosis lies in the way that it ignores the specific interpersonal complexities of the trauma of sexual exploitation by a therapist having been fashioned with reference to major catastrophe. Treatments based on the condition often fail to analyse feelings of complicity sensitively enough. Worries about complicity may occur in any trauma but have added force in interpersonal traumata.

Treating patients who have been sexually exploited

The first major problem with all accounts of treatment for patients who have had sexual relationships with therapists is that they fail to allow for the possibility that no treatment may be needed or wanted. Jehu, for example, stresses the need to facilitate disclosure and suggests that if abuse is not disclosed then the therapist may gently probe the patient. His argument is probably based on the use of exposure to the avoided stimulus in the cognitive behavioural treatment of PTSD, and for many patients facilitating disclosure will be valuable. In other situations the fact of abuse may not be the primary thing the patient needs to deal with and it may even be the case that preoccupation with it is impeding progress.

Harriet threatened to make the entirety of her new therapy an obsessional rumination on her abusive experience at the hands of her former therapist. It was only when her new therapist had the courage to say 'I think one reason you keep on thinking about what he did to you is that now after years of being let down, you've at last got something solid to pin on all of us health workers,' that Harriett began to move on in therapy.

An equal and opposite problem is that therapists may deny that abuse has occurred or disbelieve the account which they are given. This may arise from a range of reasons, but one of the most pathogenic is the application of prior beliefs to the patient in ways that obliterate the patient's own account of what is being said:

> Edward was abused by his therapist in a children's home. He repeatedly disclosed this fact to staff but always at times when he was emotionally worked up or was threatened by some punishment for a transgression. Staff would say 'This is not the time to bring it up'. To make matters worse Edward had made accusations of abuse before about another much liked member of staff and had then withdrawn them. When, as an adult, Edward saw in the newspaper that his former therapist had been successfully prosecuted for abusing children Edward's reaction was of extreme distress and anxiety. He consulted a therapist, whose first comment was, 'I wonder why you are bringing all this up now.' Edward did not return to a second session.

A second area of difficulty may be the legal consequences of the disclosure and the effects of decisions by the therapist to give an account of what has occurred to other professionals. As a general rule if patients do not consent to their details being revealed then the therapist must not breach their confidentiality, and getting round this by pushing patients towards taking formal action has been termed intrusive advocacy. However, there may be situations (for example if a patient was raped) where the public interest elements involved are so marked that a breach of confidentiality may need to be weighed against an immediate risk of danger to the public. In two situations the duty of confidentiality may quite easily be overridden: where a child may be at risk, or where the transgressor is a medical doctor.

A third area of special difficulty lies in the subsequent transference and countertransference difficulties that bedevil a new therapy. Patients who feel exploited and abused are likely either to lack trust in their subsequent carers or to idealise them as rescuers. Therapists are likely to have their own emotionally laden views about the topic under discussion. Some react with denial and try to move the patient off the topic. Others experience excited curiosity and a morbid pleasure at the possession of secret knowledge about another therapist's downfall. Perhaps therapists are the wrong people to be treating patients who have suffered at the hands of their colleagues. POPAN (www.popan.org.uk) does help patients to get into therapy if they wish it but also runs self-help groups which bring together patients who have been abused in a setting which is egalitarian and open.

Primary prevention of abuse

This may be difficult. Provocatively, Jehu (1994) reports that in a survey of psychiatrists in the USA it was found that offenders were more likely than non offenders to have completed an accredited residency and to have undergone personal psychoanalysis or psychotherapy. A survey of social workers (Jehu 1994) also showed that personal therapy was not associated with lower rates of abuse by therapists. It is not clear why more highly qualified therapists may be more likely to abuse patients but it is possible that their professional status and prestige could help them to avoid detection. Jehu also reports that education does not seem to deter people from abuse and helpfully adds that factors like personal distress, tendencies towards professional isolation, grandiosity or domination, or an antisocial personality disorder, are likely to be relatively impervious to educational influences.

Regulation of psychological treatment from professionals seems a sensible step and ensures that patients have a properly constituted organisation that can hear complaints. The absence of such an organisation represents a considerable difficulty for patients who are complaining about an unregistered practitioner. However, there are disadvantages to regulation in some areas when professionals have a range of affiliations each of which takes independent disciplinary action and where each such procedure requires evidence from the patient. The repetitive and drawn-out nature of the proceedings does not help the patient to move on.

Because re-offending rates are appreciable, wherever therapists are employed it is sensible to have checks to ensure that previous disciplinary procedures have not been initiated in this area and also clear written policies on standards of conduct. Jehu and POPAN both recommend supervision as another means of prevention. However, while supervision can be valuable, it should not be thought a sufficient guard against the professional isolation which may accompany and predispose to sexual boundary violations. Single-handed practitioners in private practice are evidently at risk but isolation amounting to single-handed practice within organisations also occurs. Both kinds of situation should be rigorously avoided:

> Laura supervised Andrew, a psychiatric nurse with a second qualification in psychotherapy. His special qualification and position in a local community team had led to his being referred a portfolio of women with borderline personality disorder with whom he had built up a reputation for working well, even charismatically. Although Laura did not like Andrew much she had little to say faulting his work, as reported to her by him, but she had no contact with the clinical team and no independent check on what he did. When a patient made a very serious and well founded allegation of sexual misconduct against Andrew Laura was 'both surprised and not surprised'. This was a general reaction throughout the service as people slowly realised that no one knew what Andrew was doing most of his working week. While the organisation was able to respond, slowly, to the allegation which had been made it was still not entirely able to acknowledge the challenge of this incident for organisational practice. It did not, for example, consider contacting any of Andrew's other patients as it would have done if Andrew had been a surgeon with an infectious condition. It also did not find time or energy to review its working practices in relation to professional isolation.

The organisation's response to the allegations of abuse bears the marks of fear which is fostering avoidance. Obviously complacency is equally worrying and can be found even in professional publications:

My patients may have eroticised fantasies about me from time to time, but they are in no way disturbing or uncomfortable for them or me, nor is there any expressed wish to act them out.
(Gordon 1999:50)

Discussing the taboo

One topic is almost never discussed in the current literature on sexual misconduct or experience in the consulting room, and that is the reason for the taboo nature of the subject. At times the way the topic is discussed amounts to a sex panic. Granted that the outcomes for patients may be poor for some but it remains unclear that the results of sexual encounters between patient and therapist are much more seriously damaging than other, less investigated, technical errors in therapy. Furthermore, it is often the taboo nature of the sex which both excites and upsets the patient, who becomes complicit in the transgression of a social taboo and is therefore to an extent damaged by sex in the consulting room more because it is taboo than for any other reason.

Analysts have, to an extent, adopted the notion of taboo in relation to this phenomenon by relating the incest taboo to the taboo on sex in the consulting room. Yet they cannot say convincingly why a taboo on sex in one area (incest) should translate other than by analogy to a taboo on sex in another area (therapy). Admittedly they can draw on parallels between the analytic relationship and parent–child relationships but the therapeutic relationship also has many dissimilarities from early relationships. For example, money changes hands. Because commentators always start by assuming that the taboo on sex in the consulting room must exist they are handicapped in any effort to understand its origins. Even seriously considering the value and nature of the prohibition is itself taboo and can provoke public censure because questioning the taboo raises the possibility that the questioner may have broken it or be about to break it.

Samuels (1999) does take up some of these issues. He notices the harmful effects of sex panic on analysis, arguing that the effect is to promote the analysis of all erotic feeling as rooted in early mother–baby dynamics and thereby to do 'safe analysis'. However, he too rapidly returns to a safe zone by arguing for an eroticism that is experienced but not enacted in therapy. He also fails to acknowledge an important undertone in his metaphor of safe analysis which alludes to the idea that conducting a dangerous analysis would lead to the spread of a deadly virus through the profession. Some of the ways in which the taboo on sexual expression in analysis is enforced, including the way some patients who have experienced it are treated with exaggerated caution, do carry the imprint of a fear of infection and contamination. This is consistent with Battaille's (1987) idea that the threat fought off by a taboo is one of contamination of the ordered world of work by a sexuality that is too sticky, confused, dangerous and related to death, to be easily contained by the world of work. Analytic dissection into oedipal versus pre-oedipal urges or reflective discussion in supervision might prove equally inadequate. Battaille's analysis of taboo provokes the sobering thought that a necessary prohibition on sexual exploitation in the consulting room may also serve to civilise psychotherapy, fitting it and helping it to fit others for the work of ordered production and drawing them away from the dark excitements of the underworld.

The taboo on sex in the consulting room is therefore not, as Samuels sees it, a necessary good which if managed right may be productive for the patient. Instead, it is probably a necessary evil which protects the patient from coercion and exploitation while chaining aspects of the erotic imaginations of both parties. The necessity for the taboo is partly driven by the need of our culture to restrain sexual forces in order to maintain social control. The other restraining force is the constitution of social space for therapy in our culture, which demands sharp demarcation from prostitution or courtesanship, both of which might have been seen as having had therapeutic functions in other cultural settings. Erotic imagination, while shaped by culture is often able to transcend it, and so it frequently threatens to escape from the confines of the permissible, even in therapy.

The therapeutic implications of seeing the restraints on sexual expression in therapy as a necessary evil rather than as a difficult good are important. It means that the the restraint on the freedom of the erotic imagination in therapy can be genuinely mourned because it is genuinely being acknowledged as a loss. This mourning does not necessarily have some ultimately therapeutic or beneficial outcome for the patient but it is preferable to the currently practised options. Feverish transference analysis in an attempt to transmute sexual desire into baby longing may well be an exercise in bad faith. The apparent acceptance of loss but with the offer of the redemptive value of renunciation is a bit better and might be helpful for some, possibly those whose erotic imaginations take a Judaeo-Christian turn, but it runs the risk of being a straitjacket in that there is no necessary advantage (for the patient) in the renunciation of sex.

11 Conclusion

Taking stock

It would seem self-evident that, in order to deal effectively with sexual issues therapists of all persuasions must be informed about sexuality, as free of prejudice as possible in relation to sex, and be comfortable hearing and talking about sex. These qualities are not common in our society, where silence about sexual matters alternates with sudden, often prejudiced or salacious outbursts. It follows that education about sexual matters must form part of training courses for therapists and that the continuing professional development of therapists also needs to help them stay abreast of developments in the field.

Of course, therapists will only be helped by the education they receive if the theory that they use is well informed, free of prejudice, sensible about sex, effective, and sophisticated. It is worth reviewing the capacities of different theoretical perspectives on sexuality to achieve this aim.

Some therapies have ignored sex or treated it only as an afterthought or even a nuisance (for example, for different reasons, some versions of group therapy and interpersonal therapy). These therapies tend neither to consider sexual difficulties nor to theorise them. The extent to which this deficiency weakens them as therapies will depend on whether it is believed that sexuality is a pervasive feature of human experience that can, in consequence, never be ignored. In practice, of course, sexuality varies in its therapeutic salience, and for sufficiently many purposes these therapies are highly effective. Where sexual matters do become relevant then the therapists in this area must either turn eclectically to other theoretical backgrounds, suppress the topic, or refer on.

Ironically, therapists of other persuasions, or integrative therapists dealing directly with sexuality, can derive much of value from these therapies. The interpersonal approach takes as its central idea that the pleasures and pains of being an agent in the social world are central to mental wellbeing. Chronic interpersonal diffi- · culty causes psychological ill health and resolving that difficulty will assist in resolving psychological ill health. In sexual matters, too, interpersonal issues are often central to the experience of satisfactory or unsatisfactory sex. Conflict, hostility, and resentment are, on the whole, poor settings for satisfying sex. Interpersonal therapy's notion of interpersonal disputes which have settled into a prolonged unstated, or understated, cold war possibly with occasional flair ups, is often highly relevant in relation to sexual difficulties between couples. Exposing and then if possible resolving these conflicts is a crucial element of successful sex therapy.

Cognitive analytic therapy, which was discussed in Chapter 2 as an example of a therapy well armed with tools to analyse social situations and social entanglements, has had, as yet, little time to turn its mind to sexual matters. I have, with a colleague (Denman and De Vries 1998) discussed its use as a therapy for a gay man in a slow but ultimately successful coming-out process. CAT's way of framing our knowledge of our social world, in the form of reciprocal roles and of framing our agency within the inner and outer world through the notion of procedural sequences, could offer a powerful theoretical framework for the analysis of sexual experience and difficulty. However, CAT as a therapeutic endeavour is not particularly given to positive projects of self improvement. For CAT therapists the danger of lengthy processes of accompanied self-development lies in the risk that the potential prejudices and predilections of the guide will come to predominate. CAT therapists prefer to be in the role of navvies, removing roadblocks and then waving the motorist/patient a cheery good-bye as they drive off to explore the newly accessible terrain. It is therefore unlikely that CAT will turn it resources towards charting the potentialities of the sexual domain, although very likely it will flesh out its account of sexual roadblocks and their rapid removal.

Therapies such as attachment-based psychotherapy and some Jungian approaches repeatedly and deliberately subordinate sexual experience to other needs, or drives. They tend thereby to see sexual difficulty as symptomatic of more fundamental difficulty in another domain. These therapeutic approaches are valuable because they remind therapists, first, that sex isn't everything and, second, that sex may stand for something else. These are important points to make. Some of Freud's successors reacted against the mechanical nature of his formulations about instinctual gratification and, in consequence, elevated the importance of the object, and of object-seeking, replacing erotic gratification at the hands of mother, with desire for an object-relation as the primary cause of the attachment between mother and baby. A similar sensibility allowed Bowlby and Harlow to show that a distinct attachment-based instinctual process exists alongside instincts with nutritive and reproductive aims. Dethroning sexuality from pride of place in the instinctual pantheon allows therapists to see that during sexual activity or erotic imagining desires which are not purely erotic may be being satisfied or may compete. For many children who are subjected to sexual experiences by abusers in which there is a period of grooming rather than violent coercion, a later consequence is the fusion or confusion of attachment needs with erotic ones, with symptomatic outcomes such as promiscuous but unsatisfying sex. Thinking back on the events of their abuse, adults may have difficulty in separating pleasure in the meeting of attachment needs by a seductive abuser from feelings about more sexual touching. This retrospective confusion confounds attempts to attribute guilt or responsibility and often perpetuates a victims own tendency for self-blame.

While Jung's aim was to replace sexuality with spirituality rather than attachment, he too wanted to argue that sexuality could very well point to somewhere other than the bluntly erotic. Therapists working within classical Jungian traditions are likely to redirect sexual material in another potentially advantageous direction, that of creativity or spirituality. Eastern religions and some new wave elements have associated sexual activity with spiritual practices. Attempts to import these into the West have often had a poor public relations profile as various spiritual leaders have been discovered, with greater or lesser justice, to have more interest in the sensual side of sexuality than its spiritual potential. It is interesting to wonder why linking spirituality and sexuality has so frequently resulted in a rather tacky failure. Possibly the fact that the high-profile failures have largely involved male exploitation of women or children, while the rather less public or prestigious female sexual spirituality movements have generally not resulted in exploitation, may be relevant. Arguably, also, women in the West have access to a longer history of sexualised spirituality from classical antiquity to draw on (Downing 1996). Apart from trying to be spiritual while having sex, Jungians may also see non-sexual issues related to creativity in sexual dreams or material in therapy. The capacity to de-literalise the erotic can be powerful and important in the therapeutic context. However, the danger in both Jungian and attachment-based therapies is that they risk denying or downplaying the intrinsic value of sex and of the erotic imagination. Patients who have sexual difficulties or undeveloped sexual potentials may find these are left to resolve themselves as a side-effect of the main field of operations.

Of those therapies which treat sex as central to their theorising, psychoanalysis has the longest history and the greatest weight of theory. Doubtless it is partly on account of volume alone that psychoanalytic theories contain plenty that is wrongheaded or, worse, harmful about sex. Volume is probably also partly responsible for the enormous range of often-contradictory thoughts that have been expressed by psychoanalysts writing on sex. This multiplicity makes it very difficult for a therapist confronted with sexual difficulties in a patient to use a psychoanalytic framework because they must first decide which, of many, psychoanalytic ideas about sex are valuable. Nor is it always clear how to use the ideas derived from psychoanalysis in practical form. Often their use in therapy seems to turn upon the extent to which they can be alloyed with practical techniques derived from cognitive behavioural therapies.

Notwithstanding, psychoanalytic theories of sex do represent an area where the erotic imagination has flowered to a very great degree, forming a baroque structure or perhaps agglomeration of repellent/fascinating/useful/useless ideas. It therefore represents an area replete with possibilities for invention and theoretical innovation in relation to the erotic imagination. Indeed, the structure of psychoanalytic theorising about sex may resemble the structure of the erotic imagination, or a part of the erotic imagination itself. This sense of the potential of psychoanalytic thought makes it especially disappointing that, for the most part, theorists have not done as well as they might have in welding biological and psychological and even social or cultural processes together. There are, of course, honourable exceptions to this criticism and among them are some of the most liberal-minded and creative analysts and psychoanalytic psychotherapists. Stoller's approach comes closest at times to a genuine biopsychosociology. Stoller's work offers the practitioner a consistent focus on the specificity of the patient's material combined, via his ethnographic explorations, with a respect for the diversity of human self- and sexual expression. Chodorow gives a detailed culturally and socially sensitive rereading of Freud's formulations on heterosexuality which shows that it is a compromise formation. By doing so she allows therapists to glimpse the powerful forces and warring desires which may underlie even an apparently tranquil sexual surface. Sadly, though, her work does not acknowledge – it even repudiates – biological influences. Samuels, an analyst from the Jungian tradition, has engaged with sexuality, and particularly with its political struggles, but, despite his interest in bodies and the bodily experience of countertransference, his work lacks much interest in formal biology. Yet therapists can use Samuels' account as a springboard for understanding the political dimension of their patient's sexual struggles and experiences. Kernberg's output attempts an integration of biological and psychological elements but his lack of cultural perspective may account for his sudden descent into prejudice against non-standard sexualities. Therapists can take from his work a development of Stoller's idea that hostility and aggressive longings are positively bound up in erotic desire and sexual expression and that this intermingling may be at times both beneficial and harmful.

Richard Isay has theorised about gay men, offering a strongly biologically and psychologically based account which has proved controversial within those elements of the gay community committed to a social constructionist account of homosexual identity. Isay's work, differentiating as it does between being homosexual and becoming gay, has particular relevance to gay men. However, it can also be read backwards (as it were) with profit. Heterosexual individuals can make a helpful distinction between being heterosexual – a biological sexual inclination, and (to reclaim a term) becoming straight – a social and sexual iden-

tity. Rattigan, Cornell and Schwartz have in their separate ways all
contributed culturally sensitive and emotionally specific work
about the experience of gay men, though some may regret that
their particular theoretical location has led to a failure to acknowledge biological influences or to weave them in creatively. Often
an important positive contribution, directly encouraged by the
poststructuralist tradition of almost perverse readings, has been to
take so-called negative features of sexual identity and recast them
in a positive form. Thus Schwartz (1995) can give an important
and vital account of the experience of being penetrated which is
not feminine, and Phillips (2001) can look at the negative over-
sexualised experiences of gay adolescents in the supposedly sex-
free atmosphere of a segregated changing room. Lesbian
psychoanalytic psychotherapists are for socio-political reasons
thinner on the ground. Those individuals who have emerged
(such as O'Connor and Ryan 1993, and Glassgold and Iasenza
1995) tend to adhere more to a postmodern, even a queer,
agenda. Their work is therefore chiefly centred in a critique of
current certainties and in a disruption of accepted categories. To
the postmodern element of this critique they are able to add
greater layers of complexity which derive from their psychoanalytic appreciation of the shifting vicissitudes of desire.
Therapeutically, therefore, they offer clients the possibility to
explore new internal and external locations. As with much
psychoanalytic thinking they generally fail to give very much space
to the literal body, though Irigary (1985) is an important exception. Even as this group of analysts mount a cogent critique of
seemingly physically derived categories such as gender they refuse
to rub up (as it were) against the material implacability of bodies.
This is not the case in the works of transgendered individuals (a
group who have yet to gain access to analytic spaces) who have
combined considerable interest in expanding the definitions of
femininity and masculinity with as literal and as unpostmodern an
interest in their bodies as it is possible to get. Their synthesis may
be helpful here (Califia 1997).

Sex therapy draws largely on techniques which were developed
first by behaviourally oriented, and later by more cognitively
inspired, therapists. These may be combined with family therapy
(Crowe and Ridley 1990) or psychoanalytic ideas (Kaplan 1974).
These therapies have a practical biological goal-oriented cast but

maintain a more or less psychological focus. They may be contrasted favourably with purely biologically based treatments for sexual conditions, in which psychological factors are either minimised or ignored entirely in favour of biologically based causal statements. The great advantage of sex therapy, even in biological guise, is that it is easy to evaluate whether it does what it says on the packet. Patients who seek relief from specific sexual difficulties are offered a solution that may well be congruent with their own terms of reference and which, if effective, may satisfy. Therapists should be familiar with the major sex therapy techniques, although putting them into practice can be quite a skilled and a creative activity and probably requires some specialist training. That said, sex therapists and their literature are at acute risk of neglecting both culture and imagination in favour of a theory of sexuality cast purely in terms of performance, as measured against a stereotype of good sex, whose cultural relativity has until recently not been properly acknowledged.

Things are changing and therapists in this area have started to develop a more socially aware vision of sexual matters. A good example would be Tiefer (1995), who has developed an approach to women's sexual health which is quite biological in orientation but which also includes psychological factors. Importantly, it contains a sharply critical feminist perspective on the medical community's tendency to define female diseases by reference to supposedly analogous male conditions. She has proposed a reclassification of female sexual disorders to include, amongst other things, a category of sexual disorders which arise from the cultural or political position of women.

Therapists treating sexual difficulty must consider if their treatment will work. Curiously, statements like this are considered controversial by many therapists but the arguments for it are important. Patients come and either directly or indirectly pay money in exchange for a service. It is this exchange which makes the space where sex therapy, as opposed to simple sex gossip or neighbourly advice, can occur. This exchange also commits both individuals to the social rules of a commercial engagement. One of the consequences is that ideas like value for money, being cheated, advertising standards, and professional conduct become relevant. The notion of value for money may contain all kinds of elements but should involve some congruence between patient and therapist's ideas of value. The presenting problem very often represents important elements of the patient's notion of value and therefore for this reason it is important to know, in terms of the presenting problem, whether a therapy is effective. While failure or success in relation to this problem does not in every case establish whether a therapy offers good value (as in: the operation was a success but the patient died) they are very often a good first thing to measure. The best scientific evidence of efficacy has been obtained for purely biological treatments. Some scientific evidence of efficacy exists in relation to cognitive behaviourally based sex therapies but very little scientific evidence of efficacy has been gathered in relation to all other treatment. The quality of evidence also varies between different conditions. Broadly speaking, the evidence base is best for simple difficulties of sexual function constructed as manifesting directly in the genitals (impotence, premature and delayed ejaculation, vaginismus, and dyspareunia) (Hawton *et al.* 1986). The state of the evidence is largely a function of the allegiance, disposition to gather evidence, and diligence of the evidence-gatherers. For many therapies evidence is absent. From the point of view of giving a sufferer advice about therapeutic interventions an adviser is therefore forced to say that the choice is between therapies which have some (not wonderful) evidence of efficacy in certain sexual conditions and others which may make more or less appealing theoretical sense of the problem but which lack direct evidence of efficacy or otherwise.

The erotic imagination

The existing therapeutic approaches to the erotic difficulty are at best modestly satisfactory. Future developments in neurobiology, neurochemistry and, though much less certainly, in social tolerance probably offer the best immediate hope to some groups of sufferers. It is hard to see immediately any likely avenues for advance in the therapy of sexual difficulties based on describing and explaining the causal origins of sexual pathologies. The difficulty which pathology-based approaches present is their concentration on what has gone wrong – a particularly problematic concept in the area of sexuality, where normality and pathology are often as much matters of social consensus as of biological malfunction.

Throughout the text the idea of the erotic imagination has been gestured at as a potential corrective to a focus on pathology which is too exclusive. Using the concept of the erotic imagination allows for a radically different approach to sexual problems and may present the best opportunity for developing therapeutic approaches to sexuality which are not exclusively based on correcting pathological deviations from a presumed state of normality.

Theories of imagination

Historically the term imagination has been associated with two major philosophical debates. The first concerns somewhat abstruse issues in the philosophy of mind. The second relates to its use in the area of aesthetics. It has also often been associated with moral judgment and to an extent these areas of discourse have informed each other. The introduction of the term itself is generally credited to Aristotle, who was concerned to develop the theory of thinking. Imagination was the faculty that presented images before the mind. As such it was associated with the capacity to want something which is based in the capacity to imagine a thing as present before the mind in its absence. It was this feature of the imagination which led early Christian philosophers to link imagination with concupiscence and to emphasise the need to discipline the imagination by the exercise of reason. Early on, therefore, imagination moved from a topic solely based in the philosophy of mind into closer connection with the moral sphere. The English empiricists – Locke and Hume prominent amongst them – used the idea of the imagination extensively, to discuss our way of gaining certain knowledge of the world and our way of manipulating ideas. Images of things formed from sense impressions could be represented in their absence (memory or desire) or combined to create new images not directly presented from sense data. In this sense we can imagine things, such as a purple lemon, that have never been seen in the world. It is this faculty of the imagination, 'to body forth the substance of things unknown' as Shakespeare would have it, that caught the eye of the Romantic philosophers and Lakeland poets. Later philosophers of mind have exposed in detail the many difficulties with the image-based approach to mental processes and it would probably be fair to say that modern philosophers of mind no longer give imagination a central role in their theoretical structures.

The Romantic re-evaluation of the imagination has roots in England and Germany and is bound up with the enormously complex set of reflections on the nature of knowledge and the limits of the knowable. Coleridge, who was not only a powerful poet but also an important literary critic, was concerned to develop a philosophical and aesthetic theory which was coherent and consistent. He was powerfully influenced by German idealist philosophers and most particularly by Kant, from whose monumental philosophical work he is now thought to have borrowed extensively. Kant thought that the imagination was crucial, indeed conditional, in all thought, providing a link between sense data and the construction placed upon that data without which they cannot be known. Kant is prepared to grant far greater activity and constructive power to the mind than the empiricists. In Kant's contribution to aesthetics the faculty of the imagination is that which produces art. He is also concerned to distinguish between individual likes and dislikes and aesthetic judgement, which he wishes to establish on the grounds of 'common sense'. By 'common sense' he means not a practical down to earth approach to things but, instead, a supposedly universal faculty for distinguishing what is beautiful and delighting in it. The Lakeland poets and others found in Kant's formulation of the actively synthetic mind a representation of human creative capacities more congenial than, for example, Locke's collection, association and accretion of sense data. Shelley characterises the imagination as the creative agent of the psyche with reason in second place, as its handmaid. In Coleridge's hands these ideas, and those of the British empiricists which preceded them, are contrasted in the notion of two kinds of imaginative activity. In 'fancy' ideas are merely combined or reordered, whereas in the operation of the 'imagination' a much more radical and active synthesis of ideas is attempted in which often contrary ideas are juxtaposed and unified. Coleridge was also concerned to characterise the imagination as itself involving a particular union of two difficult-to-juxtapose mental faculties: reason and emotion, a view he shared with Wordsworth.

Both the Kantian and the Lakeland poets' conception of the imagination involve both moral and aesthetic judgements. The active life of the imagination and the activity of the imagination can both be subjected to critical judgement, although Coleridge certainly did not find Kant's moral philosophy always congenial. The imagination remained a topic in moral, aesthetic philosophy and the philosophy of mind, being taken up by people like Sartre, who had both aesthetic and philosophical interests in it. Recently there has been another burst of interest. Moral philosophers have turned from considering the rights and wrongs of specific actions to considering lives led as a whole. This topic, known as virtue ethics, concentrates both on a longer time perspective than has been traditional in moral argument, centring on specific acts, and also on the details of particular moral contexts. For an agent to evaluate moral action in a whole life perspective, and in a context rich in detail, requires imaginative perception, union of thought and feeling and the capacity for subtly nuanced judgements. There are evident connections between such a formulation and the capacities required for an aesthetically sensitive reading of the work of art.

In recent times one of the most important philosophers to contribute to theories of the imagination has been Mary Warnock. Two comprehensive works (1980, 1994) on the subject of imagination are densely argued and defy easy summary. However, the conclusion *Imagination and Time* (Warnock 1994) sets out her views succinctly. Warnock is concerned to argue that imagination is responsible for connecting the momentary with the permanent, that it allows humans a sense of timelessness by virtue of the very fact that they are located in time. She suggests that each person is dependent on having a sense of connectedness to the past and the future and that this is achieved by imagination. Warnock therefore thinks memory and desire are both at least served by, if not being functions of, the imagination. She also argues that it is physical existence, vital for providing us with recollections, which give us continuity. Imagination and memory give us a sense of timelessness, although perhaps her apparent intent might be better conveyed by a phrase such as 'time beyond us' or even 'time around us'. Next, Warnock is concerned to argue that intrinsic to the notion of a significant act or to the idea of valuing something is an element of public generalisable declarability. She, following Kant, uses the idea of a common sense but she also ascribes important significance to the communicative value of aesthetic acts. Imagination for Warnock becomes, through these generalisable values, the faculty which allows us to experience sympathy with others.

Warnock cannot, like Kant, rely on a notion of universal or innate moral and aesthetic judgements to anchor her moral judgements. Yet she believes that the unruly behaviour of children shows that some values need to be taught and she believes that the history of ideas and development of the common view or set of values are the most important things to learn. Warnock's concern to school the imagination might simply risk a return to the early Christian attempts to constrain the wayward imagination were it not for her concern to develop in children both a sense of history and a stance on history that they can argue for with integrity. In addition, unlike the early Christians, who distrusted the senses, she is still interested to argue that there are some things intrinsically worth doing for their own sake because they bring a sense of joy. The difficulty is establishing by what criteria something might be intrinsically worth doing for its own sake. Some have argued that this is impossible without an external guarantor, like God. Warnock's position is that the imagination, combined (although this is tacit within her argument) with our (imaginative) relationship to others and to the whole human community and possibly with the basic conditions necessary for a whole human community to exist, can act as that guarantor. This argument leads Warnock into a discussion of how situations on which moral judgement is divided should be adjudicated and, interestingly, she argues strongly for a legal system based on the majority consensus, even siding with Lord Justice Devlin, who was opposed to the Wolfenden Report liberalising the law on male homosexuality on the grounds that the majority found homosexuality abhorrent.

Warnock's treatise is an attempt to use the imagination as the basis for both a moral and an aesthetic sense of value. Ultimately the communitarian aspects of her argument appear to lead her into some difficulties but these should not obscure the importance of her work in showing the creative and communicative capacities of the imagination in the moral and aesthetic spheres.

Warnock's work and the work of Kant and of the Lakeland poets offer a reading of the capacities of the erotic imagination in relation to creativity, aesthetics and morality as they apply to sexuality. The aim of the following remarks is to show how, specifically in relation to the erotic imagination, Warnock's view of imagination can be applied.

Defining the erotic imagination

By the erotic imagination is meant those imaginative capacities or activities concerned with sexuality. It has psychological expression in day dreams, sudden attractions, sexual conversation and experiences of moral or sexual horror. The erotic imagination is also specifically active during sexual activity, when it may often be at its most bodily or at least at its most directly sensory and concerned with immediate somatosensory desires and wishes. The erotic imagination also has a social dimension evident in innumerable ways: for example, the dissemination of smutty jokes across the internet, the presentation of scantily clad women draped over motorcars, or a sudden upsurge of rage over a paedophile scandal.

The erotic imagination operates on multiple levels and over a range of different time periods. It also has different levels of aesthetic attainment. Following Coleridge, it is possible to suggest a distinction between erotic fancy and erotic imagination proper. Such a distinction would be based on elements such as the duration of the enterprise, or the radical nature of the juxtapositions attempted. A flight of erotic 'fancy' might be, for example, admiring a pretty person in the street, perhaps a one night stand. A work of the erotic 'imagination' might be a sustained erotic fantasy, a long-running love affair or a well-worked-through sado-masochistic scene. Being able to give some flesh to a distinction between erotic fancy and erotic imagination is useful because it begins to show the way in which aesthetic and moral judgements of erotic acts might be made using the concept of erotic imagination. However, it is important to note that these judgements are not simply a matter of reading off the desired level of complexity and duration of erotic activities. Coleridge was too hard on 'fancy' as we know it now and it would certainly be wrong to eliminate all fancies from life as morally inferior. It is, as ever, a question of what, how much and when . . .

Another of Warnock's concerns is to emphasise the capacity of the imagination to give access to experiences which are timeless.

In relation to this she makes the powerful point that it is the capacity of the imagination to give us the power of sympathy that is the source of these experiences. From an erotic point of view Warnock's formulation would have the effect of contradicting a commonplace of conventional sexual wisdom. The conventional aesthetic notion (perhaps largely derived from male-centred views of sexuality) is that the best erotic experiences result in loss of individuality and in fusion with the other. This view is not supported by Warnock's formulation. Instead, a theory of the erotic imagination derived from Warnock would tend to see the best erotic experiences as those which offer a perspective on time by drawing in, through memory and anticipation, many other experiences. Such an experience would be one which engendered sympathy or relation to the other and required individuality rather than fusion.

Warnock's difficulties with morality derive from her wish to give universal value to certain imaginative products. She discusses the idea of the communicative value of art in ways that perhaps imply that great art must command a large audience. Many people would have difficulties with the idea that the aesthetic values of art are necessarily linked with the commercial values embodied in producing art but it is very likely that such linkages are important. One of the features of commercial art is often its capacity to be dislocated from the original space of its production. Its capacity to be reproduced in a variety of ways is also related to its value, with scarcity conditioning both economic and aesthetic value. From an aesthetic perspective erotic experiences follow the opposite rule and appear to be valued when the number of people involved is small (although in general it should be greater than 1!) and when there is no audience. Those products of the erotic imagination which are reproduced are often regarded with considerable suspicion unless they can piggyback onto the commercial domain of high art. Admitting erotic experiences into the domain of the aesthetic may involve a redefinition of art which looks back to activities which predate the mass media, such as family entertainment, storytelling, and chamber music.

Danto, in his important book *The Transformation of the Commonplace* (1988), suggests that art is exactly that imaginative activity through which whatever is commonplace can be transformed and presented anew. Although he does not discuss them, his formulation seems particularly ideal when applied to what we might call local or commonplace arts and what we might think of as commonplace transformation of the commonplace. The task of constructing an aesthetic fit for the local arts in general and the erotic imagination in particular may come to prove part of any psychotherapy in which increasing creativity is a key aim.

Such a therapy might wish to take seriously the idea that the faculty of the erotic imagination needs to be taught. This certainly involves an acknowledgement that erotic imagination might well be unruly. Warnock's argument that all imaginative faculties require education is important because she sees the function of this education as grounding the individual in a sense of history. Warnock does not want children to be taught a particular point of view but instead to be taught the history of differing points of view and a sense of the importance of holding a coherent point of view for oneself. Patients with psychosexual difficulties have rarely been taught anything of great value about sexual matters. Current sex education has abandoned any concept of the imagination at all. Instead, the current social function of sex education is the promotion of hygiene and of sexual social control. Our society has enormous difficulty in conceiving of a positive project of developing erotic sensibilities in children and regards the activity as close to perverse. Within therapy the opportunity to talk in detail about sexual matters is best developed in some psychoanalytic treatments where the detail and variety of the discourse produced is often highly developed. In the best treatments these conversations become sources of creativity but psychoanalytic strictures about sexual expression can get in the way and psychoanalytic methodologies do not sanction the active promotion of a historical sense of the development of the sexual behaviour of others, nor are the sources of such historically relevant material easy to discern.

Developing the necessary documentary history of sexual activity would also help therapists and moralists who wish to apply the notion of virtue theory to the development of a moral project for sexuality. One way of getting hold of the virtuous sexual life would be to develop a set of accounts which chart erotic lives of varying apparent virtue. These could serve as inspirations or indeed as cautionary tales. They would not be prescriptions any more than an individual painting prescribes those which succeed it. The internet with its capacity for the rapid distribution of personal accounts to any who might choose to read them may be one vehicle for such a project and such accounts already exist in certain areas. They are commonplace in the gay and lesbian community and also in the transgendered community. As yet, however, heterosexual accounts which cross racial and religious divides are infrequent and those which do exist often spend considerable time hammering home a point. The task of judging accounts of this sort from a moral and aesthetic perspective cannot be escaped if they are to serve the purpose of a historical/moral education in the virtuous erotic life. Warnock's suggestion that many convergent notions may be needed to come to a moral judgement seems sensible, even if the level of moral certainty she desires to achieve may be greater than is possible. One helpful aspect to consider is the historical development of accounts.

Gay and lesbian personal stories involving coming out and sexual experience have a long history. Reviewing them, it is possible to see how waves of dichotomised stridency (such as the lesbian sex wars or early debates on HIV) are succeeded by waves of diversity as the 'common sense' evolves. It may therefore be possible, by having a well-developed knowledge of the common sense, to pick on those accounts which manage to allow the maximum human diversity consistent with an ordered narrative and with social order. This formulation – one which contrasts diversity with order – is close to that suggested by Coleridge when he valued daring juxtaposition brought into a sense of order, but it also draws strongly on Warnock's use of the idea of history as providing the matrix of accounts on which judgement is based.

The foregoing remarks on imagination and on the erotic imagination have been designed to show how psychotherapists working with sexuality might be able to take up the concept as a valuable tool for promoting creativity in patients. The challenge of such an activity is to promote creativity as opposed to scribbling, and this means that the aesthetics and the morality involved in trying something new and creative need to be maintained as important criteria for judging the value of the activity.

Pathology and the erotic imagination

One way of viewing pathology is as a roadblock which obstructs the creative and positive potential of an individual. Armed with at least some notion of the erotic imagination it is now possible to review those conditions which have traditionally been thought of as representing pathologies of sexuality from a new position. The mechanical difficulties which can present, such as premature ejaculation or vaginismus, have been seen by some as failures not in the individual but in the social realm. Satsz suggested that premature ejaculation in particular is simply a condition which represents failure to live up to social standards about sexual activity. There is much to be said for this view as there is for its complete contrary: that these conditions will turn out to be biologically based. However, whatever the cause, premature ejaculation often results in, a failure of imagination about relation. Commonly, the men involved show little creativity about what to do next. Few, for example, consider possible further sexual activity. Vaginismus on the other hand seems to involve either an organic difficulty leading to pain and possibly thereafter to a self-reinforcing pain cycle or, when it is more purely psychogenic, it involves erotic revulsion. In such cases it can be helpful to enlarge on the erotic fantasies involving pain and disgust which underlie the difficulty.

Male and female sexual desire often fail to conform to socially accepted or self-imposed norms. Low or high, it causes interpersonal difficulty as individuals fail to match up their relationship needs to their erotic ones. One way of thinking about these issues is to see the aim of matching erotic activity with a certain kind of exclusive relationship for example as having a specific aesthetic aim, rather like that involved in trying to write a fugue or pen a sonnet. Viewing it this way allows therapists to suggest avenues for further development. The patient might chose to continue to struggle with the difficult form or might decide on a different kind of aesthetic exercise. The use of sexual stimulants is particularly interesting in this regard. While aphrodisiacs of all kinds have been freely available for thousands of years the new availability of drugs sanctioned by medical science (and possibly with greater efficacy) has caused a paroxysm of anguish, especially over the notion that an illness called low female sexual desire might exist.

From the point of view of the erotic imagination the question can be de-medicalised. The question now becomes whether it is aesthetically appealing, imaginatively helpful, for women of any level of sexual desire to take aphrodisiacs. Put this way it is clear that the answer must be that for some women it will be. Whether the state should fund this activity on the grounds it is treating an illness, or on any other ground, is simply a matter of public policy.

Wishes to look at pornographic pictures, read erotica, choose strange sexual objects, perform sex in unusual ways seem all of a part with one another. They represent manifestations of the erotic imagination, and individual reactions to them demonstrate individual differences in sexual taste. The interesting element is the strength of the negative opinions which people can hold about certain sexual acts. Aesthetic judgements about painting and poetry seem not to get as strong as those about sex, and the best analogy is given by aesthetic responses to foods. It is this strength of response which fuels the easy notion that whatever is unappealing to the individual should be universally condemned. Instead of using such criteria therapists would do better to recall the concept of the virtuous life and of its evaluation by the accretion of multiple similar accounts. Patients with unusual sexual interests often do benefit from meeting other individuals with similar tastes and the internet makes this much easier and, on the whole, safer to do.

One thing which is not easy or safe or, indeed, a virtue of the internet, is accessing pornographic pictures of children or being someone whose (even passing) sexual interest is in children. In thinking about theorising the erotic imagination a crucial question is whether some sexual acts, broadly the non-consensual ones, must necessarily involve some deformation of the erotic imagination so severe that it can be thought universally aesthetically unappealing. To do so would involve accepting that at some level the erotic imagination must involve consent. Such a notion is tempting but De Sade would not have thought it true. Probably the matter cannot be settled, but one controversial alternative possibility is to accept that the creative imagination may also be evil and deployed in ways that accord with an aesthetics of evil. Some serial killers and some popular culture seem to be exploring this aesthetic. In practice, however, most individuals who indulge in coercive sex do not have a highly developed imagination. Their activities are neither highly creative nor complex but instead often reveal sad, crumpled lives and evidence of abuse in childhood.

This brief review of some pathologies does not give an easy sense of the way in which the erotic imagination might be exploited in therapy. The following case example illustrates how the erotic imagination can develop in a therapy. It also illustrates that an almost quietist approach to therapy, without apparent technicalities but in practice involving considerable skill, can be helpful to individual development:

Bernard was a devout Roman Catholic who sat rigid in the chair, tense and immobile. His complaint was of depression and loneliness. He worked as a computer operator in a large factory and lived with his mother. He had intense contacts with his church, which involved Bible study, attending worship three or four times a week and going out to do good works. He had never had a partner. The assessor guessed he was gay but the matter was not openly discussed with Bernard.

Bernard was assigned to a male therapist of considerable experience. He began a long-term therapy. The therapist had to begin many of the sessions with questions for fear that a silence so profound that it would be irretrievable would fall. This strategy seemed effective and Bernard slowly came awake in the sessions. A few sessions followed when he would talk freely about his problems. People let him down, they promised to do things with him but then they did not turn up. His mother was preoccupied and never paid him any attention. He had no real friends. The therapist continued to help the process along by asking questions about Bernard's life and experience that seemed relevant. Bernard now revealed that he thought he was probably homosexual but that this was forbidden in his religion. The therapist made no special comment.

The following session there was no mention of the matter but after a while Bernard told his therapist that he had consulted someone at the church who had been kind but plain about Bernard's responsibilities.

Next the therapist noticed that in the middle of each session was a period of increased tension when Bernard would fall silent and then mutter, 'I don't know what to do next'. He asked Bernard what he meant by this and Bernard looked highly embarrassed and refused to say. The therapist became convinced there was an erotic relationship between Bernard and himself and while this was not voiced between them the crackling in the air and Bernard's lingering glances left no doubt. Bernard began to dream about the therapist in a frankly erotic way. He and the therapist would be having anal sex in the therapy room; someone would come in and discover them, sometimes that person would join in. Eventually Bernard told the therapist that the figure in the dream was his mother. As the dream series developed Bernard's sexual interest in his mother increased and, in a series of dreams that he found particularly horrific he had sex with her while shouting 'Fuck Mary, fuck Mary!' These dreams were told with an air that was partly sexually provocative and partly angry. The therapist had a curious and sustained attack of double vision throughout this part of the therapy. Although he was straight and felt homosexual sex rather disgusting he was strongly aware of Bernard's wishes towards him and curiously rather jealous of his mother.

At the same time as Bernard was telling the dreams he brought a series of drawings. The therapist felt that these, which were of androgynous figures often very well drawn with evident care, were brought to him in the same way that a child might bring a drawing. There were often too many, but to the therapist's relief the atmosphere in the room was much less sexual and more dependent. What was noticeable was that Bernard no longer complained endlessly about how everyone in his life let him down. In fact he had a new job and seemed to have a more active social life. He also talked about a flat of his own, but never acted on this. He also talked about entering the priesthood.

The therapist wondered about the many juxtapositions in the situation. In the dream the therapist and the church (Mary) are possible sexual partners counterpoised with each other. In Bernard's transference to the therapist, maternal and erotic love are juxtaposed

Matters proceeded until one day Bernard said bluntly that he knew that the therapist knew he was attracted to the therapist but the therapist never mentioned it. The therapist said, 'I know that you feel sexual towards me and I think this is an important part of your therapy, but I think it must be very painful for you.' As was his way, Bernard received this statement silently, the atmosphere in the room became unbearably tense and the therapist was seized with the feeling that he was about to pucker his lips. They seemed to him to be shaking uncontrollably. Bernard's eyes bored into him. Then Bernard said he thought his therapist was copping out. There followed a fairly heated exchange during which Bernard clearly wanted to extract a confession of love from his therapist.

The therapist eventually said that it was true that he had felt attracted to his patient. He said that also he had felt like looking after him as though he was a little boy. The therapist pointed out that some of what he and Bernard were feeling was real but at the same time it was also only possible because of the way in which they met in a social space set apart from each of their lives. Bernard cried bitterly and the therapist said again that the pain of loving and longing was a terrible thing for Bernard.

The following week Bernard talked at length about his choices in life. He told the therapist that he had been thinking about what to do. He had decided that his religious life was more important to him than his sexuality at present and that he was not going to act on his sexual wishes. Bernard said that he did not think the church was right when it came to this matter but he thought that obedience was an important virtue which he should not give up. The therapist did not especially like this life choice so he was heartened by the use of the phrase 'at present' in Bernard's account. He asked Bernard if he might not be copping out after the upset of last week. Bernard with a flash of humour remarked that he could hardly be said to be choosing the least painful option.

When the therapy ended Bernard remained highly religious and celibate. Indeed, towards the end of therapy he summed up his progress in therapy as having moved from being sexless but masturbating a lot, to being celibate and still masturbating a lot. He was considering ordination. He and his therapist spent a few sessions comparing the renunciation of sex in the therapy and his planned renunciation of sex in the church. The therapist, worried, said that lots of priests jumped over the wall because they found they couldn't live without sex. Bernard responded that lots of therapists jumped onto the couch for the same reason. The therapist said, 'But not me,' to which Bernard replied, 'No, not you.'

Throughout the therapy the therapist made no 'interpretations' of any sort except the sort of thing a friend might say, such as 'You must have felt rotten when she said that', or 'It sounds much like last week when you told me he ignored you that time.' His only activity was to ask questions or make comments with the aim of getting Bernard to speak more about whatever he was currently speaking about. The therapist's reasoning in proceeding this way was that the rapid engagement which Bernard made and particularly the eroticised nature of that engagement made it plain that his imaginative self had been hooked in by the therapy. The presence of another person who wants to know and who responds in a way that shows this involvement is genuine can act as an armature[1] which the patient can use to elaborate a new account of a virtuous life. In Bernard's case the virtuous life he chose worried the therapist who was not keen on religion. Despite his dislike of Bernard's choice the therapist remained clear in his own mind that Bernard's choice was made openly and not unduly defensively.

Erotic imagination and culture

The final part of this chapter considers the potentially wider value of the erotic imagination. Imagination has been presented as, amongst other things, an aesthetic and moral capacity. Erotic imagination is that part of imaginative activity which is concerned with sex. It has been suggested that it has bodily, psychological and social components. It has been argued that the imagination's capacity to embody knowledge of the past and a vision of the future, along with its relationship functions and its creative capacity, give it transformative potential. The specific transformative potential of the erotic imagination in relation to psychotherapy has been considered. Giddens (1992) thought that changed views

---

1 The notion of an armature – a sculptor's device for holding the basic form of clay or wax to be made into the model – is analagous to Ryle's notion of scaffolding. However, because it is inside and related to sculpting rather than the building industry it leaves more room for the work of the creative imagination.

of the erotic were important in shaping current culture. It is worth, therefore, considering whether the erotic imagination, if taken seriously, might have further transformative potential in culture.

It might be argued that our culture could do with a great deal less bodily, sensual and erotic engagement. Western culture is characterised by a great number of commodities sold in a profusion and variety which primarily serves to delight the senses rather than to fulfil utilitarian purposes. But it is a mistake to see that much of a genuine aesthetic in the wide range, for example, of different kettles we may purchase. These commercial activities are primarily purchases for display and therefore serve a function almost exactly similar to that of a peacock's tail. Instead of transforming the commonplace our domestic 'aesthetic' acts run the risk of displaying merely purchased novelty, which is the ideal commodity since it must always be renewed.

Our culture has tried manfully (?) to commercialise erotic activity and has to some extent succeeded. It has certainly often succeeded in eroticising the commercial. However, the happy fact that individuals all possess their own means of erotic production has always set sharp limits on the extent to which a market in Eros can be cornered. This means that there is genuinely liberating potential in a revaluing of an erotic, bodily and historical imagination. The wider importance of the erotic imagination for culture is therefore that it offers a way for individuals to create and take part in democratised aesthetic acts chiefly aimed at communication. This activity stands in sharp contrast to the activity of purchasing and passively consuming commercialised aesthetic objects chiefly aimed at ostentation.

References

Adams, P. (1989) 'Of female bondage', in T. Brennan (ed.), *Between Feminism and Psychoanalysis*. London: Routledge.

Adams, P. (1990) 'Representation and Sexuality', in P. Adams and E. Cowie (eds), *The Woman in Question*. London: Verso.

Adler, A. (1924) *The Practice and Theory of Individual Psychology*, trans. P. Radin. London: Kegan Paul, Trench, Trubner.

Altman, M. (1989) 'Everything they always wanted to know: the ideology of popular sex literature', in C. Vance (ed.) *Pleasure and Danger*. London: Pandora, pp. 115–30

Amir, M. (1971) *Patterns in Forcible Rape*. Chicago: University of Chicago Press.

Arentewicz, G. and Schmidt, G. (1983) *The Treatment of Sexual Disorders*. New York: Basic Books.

Arndt, W. B. (1991) *Gender Disorders and the Paraphilias*. Madison, CT: International Universities Press.

Badcock, C. R. (1990) *Oedipus in Evolution: A New Theory of Sex*. Oxford: Blackwell.

Bagley, C. and Tremblay, P. (1997) 'Suicidal behaviours in homosexual and bisexual males', *Crisis* **18** (1): 24–34.

Baker, R. and Bellis, M. (1993) 'Human sperm competition: ejaculate adjustment by males and the function of masturbation', *Animal Behaviour* **46**: 861–85.

Balint, G. (1959) *Thrills and Regressions*. London: Hogarth Press.

Bancroft, J. (1972) 'The relationship between gender identity and sexual behaviour: some clinical aspects', in C. Ounsted and D.C. Taylor (eds), *Gender Differences: Their Ontogeny and Significance*. Edinburgh: Churchill Livingstone.

Bancroft, J. (1989) *Human Sexuality and its Problems*. (2nd edn). Edinburgh: Churchill Livingstone.

Bancroft, J. and Coles, L. (1976) 'Three years experience in a sexual problems clinic', *British Medical Journal* **1**: 1575–7.

Battaille, G. (1987) *Eroticism*, trans. M Dalwood. London: Marion Boyars.

Baumeister, R. F. (1989) *Masochism and the Self*. Hillsdale, NJ: Lawrence Erlbaum.

Beck, A. T. (1988) *Love is Never Enough: How Couples Can Overcome Misunderstandings, Resolve Conflicts, and Solve Relationship Problems though Cognitive Therapy*. New York: Harper and Row.

Beck, J. (1993) *How to Have Multiple Orgasms*. New York: Avon.

Beck, J. G. and Barlow, D. H. (1984). 'Current conceptualizations of sexual dysfunction: A review and an alternative perspective', *Clinical Psychology Review*, **4**: 363–78.

Bell, D. (1992) 'Hysteria – a contemporary Kleinian perspective', *British Journal of Psychotherapy* **9**: 169–80.

Beneke, T. (1982). *Men on Rape*. New York: St Martin's Press.

Benjamin, J. (1988) *The Bonds of Love*. London: Virago.

Berenbaum, S. A. (1999) 'Effects of early androgens on sex-typed activities and interests in adolescents with congenital adrenal hyperplasia', *Hormones and Behavior*. **35**(1): 102–10.

Berenbaum, S. A. Duck, S. C., Bryk, K. (2000) 'Behavioral effects of prenatal versus postnatal androgen excess in children with 21-hydroxylase-deficient congenital adrenal hyperplasia', *Journal of Clinical Endocrinology and Metabolism*. **85**(2): 727–33.

Bernstein, B (1990) 'Attitudes and issues of parents of gay men and lesbians and implications for therapy', *Journal of Gay and Lesbian Psychotherapy*, **1**(3): 37–53.

Bersani, L. (1988) 'Is the Rectum a Grave?', in D. Crimp (ed.), *AIDS: Cultural Analysis, Cultural Activism*. Cambridge, MA: MIT Press.

Bersani, L. (1995) *Homos*. Cambridge MA: Harvard University Press.

Beaumont, P. J. Abraham, S. F. and Simson, K. G. (1981) 'The psychosexual histories of adolescent girls and young women with anorexia nervosa', *Psychological Medicine*. **11**(1): 131–40.

Blackwood, E. (ed.) (1986) *Anthropology and Homosexual Behaviour*. Binghamton, NY: Haworth.

Blanchard, W. H. (1959) 'The group process in gang rape', *Journal of Social Psychology*, **49**: 259–66.

Blum, H. B. (1971) 'On the conception and development of the transference neurosis', *Journal of the American Psychoanalytic Association*, **19**: 41–53.

Blum, H. B. (1973) 'The concept of the eroticized transference', *Journal of the American Psychoanalytic Association*, **21**: 61–76.

Blumstein, P. and Schwartz, P. (1983) 'American Couples', in B. Green and G. M. Herek (eds), *Lesbian and Gay Psychology: Theory and Research Implications*. Thousand Oaks, CA/London: Sage .

Bolas, C. (1992) *Being a Character*. London: Routledge.

Bradford, J. M. (1999) 'The paraphilias, obsessive compulsive spectrum disorder, and the treatment of sexually deviant behaviour', *Psychiatric Quarterly*, **70**(3): 209–19.

Brandon, S., Boakes, J., Glaser, D. and Green, R. (1998) 'Recovered memories of childhood sexual abuse. Implications for clinical practice', *British Journal of Psychiatry*, **172**: 296–307.

Braren, V., Slonim, A., Warner, J. J., O'Neill, J.A. Jr, Burr, I. M. and Rhamy, R. K. (1980) 'True hermaphroditism: a rational approach to diagnosis and treatment', *Journal of Urology*, **15**(6): 569–74.

Braunschweig, D. and Fain, M. (1971) *Eros et Anteros*. Paris: Payot.

Brennan, T. (1989) (ed.) *Between Feminism and Psychoanalysis*. London: Routledge.

Brennan, T. (1992) (ed.) *The Interpretation of the Flesh: Freud and Femininity.* London: Routledge.

Briere, J. and Malamuth, N. M. (1983) 'Self-reported likelihood of sexually aggressive behaviour: attitudinal versus sexual explanations', *Journal of Research in Personality*, 17: 315–23.

Bright, S. (1995) *Susie Bright's Sexwize.* San Francisco, CA: Cleis Press.

Brindley, G. and Gillan, P. (1982) 'Men and women who do not have orgasms', *British Journal of Psychiatry*, 140: 351–6.

Britton, R., Feldman, M. and O'Shaughnessy, E. (1989) *The Oedipus Complex Today: Clinical Implications.* London: Karnac.

Brown, G. R., Wise, T. N., Costa, P. T. Jr, Herbst, J. H., Fagan, P. J. and Schmidt, C. W. Jr (1996) 'Personality characteristics and sexual functioning of 188 cross-dressing men', *Journal of Nervous and Mental Disease*, 184(5): 265–73.

Brown, G. W. and Harris, T. (1978) *Social Origins of Depression: A Study of Psychiatric Disorder in Women.* London: Tavistock.

Brown, N. (1959) *Life against Death: The Psychoanalytic Meaning of History.* Middletown, CT: Wesleyan University Press.

Browne, A., and Finkelhor, D. (1986) 'Impact of child sexual abuse: A review of the research', *Psychological Bulletin*, 99(1): 66–77.

Brownmiller, S. (1975) *Against our Will: Men, Women, and Rape.* Harmondsworth: Penguin.

Bucci, W. (2001) Toward a 'psychodynamic science': the state of current research, *Journal of the American Psychoanalytic Association*, 49(1): 57–68.

Budd, S. (2001) '"No sex, Please, we're British": sexuality in English and French psychoanalysis', in C. Harding (ed.) *Sexuality: Psychoanalytic Perspectives.* Hove, Sussex: Brunner-Routledge.

Buka, S. L. and Kessler, R. C. (2001) 'Child sexual abuse and subsequent psychopathology: results from the National Co-morbidity Survey', *American Journal of Public Health*, 91(5): 753–60.

Burch, B. (1989) 'Unconscious Bonding in Lesbian Relationships: The Road not Taken'. Unpublished doctoral dissertation, Institute of Clinical Social Work, New York.

Burch, B, (1997) *Lesbian/Bisexual Experience and Other Women: Psychoanalytic Views of Women.* New York: Columbia University Press.

Burns, J. (1983) 'Sexuality, sexual problems, and people with learning difficulties', in J. M. Ussher and C. D. Baker (eds), *Psychological Perspectives on Sexual Problems: New Directions in Theory and Practice.* London: Routledge.

Buss, D. M. (1994) *The Evolution of Desire.* New York: Basic Books.

Butler, J. (1990) *Gender Trouble: Feminism and the Subversion of Identity.* New York and London: Routledge.

Butler J (1993) *Bodies that Matter. On the discursive Limits of 'sex'* New York: Routledge .

Califia, P. (1994) 'Gay Men, Lesbians and Sex; Doing it Together', in *Public Sex: The Culture of Radical Sex.* San Francisco, CA: Cleis Press.

Califia, P. (1997) *Sex Changes: The Politics of Transgenderism.* San Francisco, CA: Cleis Press.

Callery, P. (1998) 'Sex and children in the past and the present', in T. Harrison (ed.), *Children and Sexuality: Perspectives in Health Care.* London: Ballière Tindall.

Campbell, A. (1993) *Women, Men, and Aggression.* New York: Basic Books.

Caplan, P. (ed.) (1987) *The Cultural Construction of Sexuality.* London: Routledge.

Carvalho, R. (2003a) 'Comment on Denman', in Withers (ed.), *Controversies in Psychology.* Hove and New York: Brunner Routledge.

Carvalho, R. (2003b) 'Reply to Denman's Response', in Withers (ed.), *Controversies in Psychology.* Hove and New York: Brunner Routledge.

Cass, V. C. (1979) 'Homosexual identity formation: a theoretical model', *Journal of Homosexuality*, **10**: 105–26.

Chasseguet-Smirgel, J. (1984a) *Creativity and Perversion.* London: Free Association Books.

Chasseguet-Smirgel, J. (1984b) 'The femininity of the analyst in professional practice', *International Journal of Psychoanalysis*, **65**: 169–78.

Chasseguet-Smirgel, J. (1991) 'Sadomasochism in the perversions: some thoughts on the destruction of reality', *Journal of the American Psychoanalytic Association*, **39**: 399–415.

Chiesa, M. (1994) 'Some thoughts on erotic transference', *Psychoanalytic Psychotherapy*, **8**(1): 37–48.

Chiesa, M. (1999) 'Erotic transference in clinical practice', in D. Mann (ed.) *Erotic Transference and Countertransference: Clinical Practice in Psychotherapy.* London: Routledge.

Chiland, C. (2000) 'The psychoanalyst and the transsexual patient', *International Journal of Psychoanalysis*, **81**(1): 21–35.

Chivers, M. L. and Bailey, J. M. (2000) 'Sexual orientation of female-to-male transsexuals: a comparison of homosexual and nonhomosexual types.' *Archives of Sexual Behavior*, **29**(3): 259–78.

Chodorow, N. (1978) *The Reproduction of Mothering: Psychoanalysis and the Sociology of Gender.* Berkeley, CA: University of California Press.

Chodorow, N. (1994) *Femininities, Masculinities, Sexualities: Freud and Beyond.* Lexington, MA: University of Kentucky Press.

Clark, D. (1987) *The New Loving Someone Gay.* Berkeley, CA: Celestial Arts.

Clelland, S .R., Studer, L. H. and Reddon, J. R. (1998) 'Follow-up of rapists treated in a forensic psychiatric hospital', *Violence and Victims*, **13**(1): 79–86.

Colapinto, J. (2000) *As Nature Made Him: The Boy Who was Raised as a Girl.* London: Quartet books.

Cole, C. M., O'Boyle, M., Emory, L. E. and Meyer, W. J. (1997) 'Comorbidity of gender dysphoria and other major psychiatric diagnoses', *Archives of Sexual Behavior*, **26**(1): 13–26.

Cole, C. M and Dryden, W. (eds) (1988) *Sex Therapy in Britain.* Milton Keynes: Open University Press.

Coleman, J. C. and Hendry, L. (1990) *The Nature of Adolescence.* London: Routledge.

Coleman, W. (1985) 'Countertransference some clinical uses of Jung's alchemical metaphor', *International Review of Psycho-Analysis,* **12**: 199–212.

Comfort, A. (1972) *The Joy of Sex: A Gourmet Guide to Lovemaking,* London: Mitchell Beazley.

Contratto, S. (1987) 'Father presence in women's psychological development', in G. M. Platt, J. Rabow and M. Goldman (eds), *Advances in Psychoanalytic Sociology.* Malabar, FL: Krieger.

Cornett, C. (1995) *Reclaiming the Authentic Self: Dynamic Psychotherapy with Gay Men.* Northvale, NJ: Jason Aronson.

Covington, C. (1996) 'Purposive aspects of the erotic transference', *Journal of Analytic Psychology,* **41**: 339–52.

Cowan, L. (1982) *Masochism.* Dallas, Tex: Spring Publications.

Coyle, A. (1994) 'Coming out sane: gay identity and mental health in adolescence', in D. Davies and C. Neal (eds) (1996), *Pink Therapy: A Guide for Counsellors and Therapists Working with Lesbian and Gay and Bisexual Clients.* Buckingham: Open University Press.

Creith, E. (1996) *Undressing Lesbian Sex.* London: Cassell.

Crews, F. (1995) *Memory Wars: Freud's Legacy in Dispute.* New York: New York Review of Books.

Crisp, A. H. (1984) 'The psychopathology of anorexia nervosa: getting the "heat" out of the system', in A. J. Shinkard and E. Stellar (eds), *Eating and Its Disorders.* New York: Raven.

Crowe, M. J. and Ridley, J. (1990) *Therapy with Couples: A Behavioural-systems Approach to Marital and Sexual Problems.* Oxford: Blackwell.

Crowe, M. J., Gillan, P. and Golombok, S. (1981) 'Form and content in the conjoint treatment of sexual dysfunction: a controlled study.' *Behaviour Research and Therapy,* **19**: 47–54.

Danto, A. C, (1981) *The Transformation of the Commonplace: A Philosophy of Art.* Cambridge, MA: Harvard University Press.

Darwin. C. (1859) *On the Origin of Species by Means of Natural Selection.* London: John Murray.

Daskalos, C. T. (1998) 'Changes in the sexual orientation of six heterosexual male-to-female transsexuals.' *Archives of Sexual Behavior,* **27**(6): 605–14.

Davies, D. and Neal, C. (1996) (eds) *Pink Therapy: A Guide for Counsellors and Therapists Working with Lesbian and Gay and Bisexual Clients.* Buckingham: Open University Press.

Day, G. (1988) 'Introduction', in G. Day and C. Bloom (eds), *Perspectives on Pornography: Sexuality in Film and Literature.* London: Macmillan.

Deaux, K. and Hanna, R. (1984) 'Courtship in the personals column: the influence of gender and sexual orientation.' *Sex Roles,* **11**: 363–75.

Denman, C. and De Vries, P. (1998) 'Cognitive analytic therapy and Homosexual orientation', in C. Shelley (ed.), *Contemporary Perspectives on Psychotherapy and Homosexualities.* London: Free Association Books.

Denman, C. (2001) 'Women's friendships: theory and therapy', in S. Izzard and N. Barden (eds), *Rethinking Gender and Therapy: The Changing Identities of Women*. Buckingham: Open University Press.

Denman, C. (2003a) 'Analytical psychology and homosexual orientation', in Withers (ed.), *Controversies in Psychology*. Hove and New York: Brunner Routledge.

Denman, C. (2003b) 'Response to Carvalho', in Withers (ed.), *Controversies in Psychology*. Hove and New York: Brunner Routledge.

Derrida, J. (1976) 'Of Grammatology', trans. Gayatri Chakravorty Spivak. Baltimore, MD: Johns Hopkins University Press.

Deutsch, H. (1946) *The Psychology of Women*. London: Research books.

Devor, H. (1999) *FTM Female-to-Male Transsexuals in Society*. Bloomington, IN: Indiana University Press.

Diamond, M. (1982) 'Sexual identity: monozygotic twins reared in discordant sex roles and a BBC follow-up.' *Archives of Sexual Behavior*. 11(2): 181–6.

Diamond, M. (1999) 'Pediatric management of ambiguous and traumatized genitalia', *Journal of Urology*. 162(3/2): 1021–8.

Diamond, M. (2000) 'The field of sex research: responsibility to ourselves and to society', *Archives of Sexual Behavior*. 29(4): 389–95.

Dickemann, M. (1995) 'Wilson's Panchreston: the inclusive fitness hypothesis of sociobiology re-examined', *Journal of Homosexuality*, 28(1–2): 147–83.

Dickes, R. and Stauss, D. (1979) 'Countertransference as a factor in premature termination of apparently successful cases', *Journal of Sex and Marital Therapy*, 5: 22–27.

Dicks, H. V. (1967) *Marital Tensions*. New York: Basic Books.

Dietz, P. E. *et al.* (1990) 'The sexually sadistic criminal and his offences', *Bulletin of the American Academy of Psychiatry and the Law*, 18(2): 163–78.

Dinnerstein, D. (1999) *The Mermaid and the Minotaur*. New York: The Other Press.

Doane, I. and Hedges, D. (1992) *From Klein to Kristeva: Psychoanalysis and the 'Good Enough' Mother*. Ann Arbor, MI: University of Michigan Press.

Doctor, D. (1999) 'Understanding the erotic and eroticised transference and countertransference', in D. Mann (ed.), *Erotic Transference and Countertransference: Clinical Practice in Psychotherapy*. London and New York: Routledge.

Domenici, T. and Lesser, R. (1995) *Disorientating Sexuality*. New York: Routledge.

Downing, C (1996) *Myths and Mysteries of Same Sex Love*. Continuum International Publishing Group. New York.

Dumb, A. D., Lloyd, E. and Phelps, C. (1979) 'Sexual assertiveness in spinal cord injury', *Sexuality and Disability*, 2(4): 293–300.

Dunne, G. (1997) *Lesbian Lifestyles*. London: Macmillan.

Dunphy, R. (2000) *Sexual Politics: An Introduction*. Edinburgh: Edinburgh University Press.

Dutton, D. (1988) *Domestic Assault on Women: Psychological and Criminal Justice Perspectives.* Newton, MA: Allyn & Bacon.

Dutton, D. M. A. and Walker, E. L. (1989) (eds), *Feminist Psychotherapies: Integration of Therapeutic and Feminist Systems.* Norwood, NJ: Ablex.

Dworkin, A. (1981) *Pornography: Men Possessing Women.* London: Women's Press.

Eibesfelt, I. (1989) *Human Ethology.* New York: Aldine.

Eliason, M. J. (1995) 'Accounts of sexual identity formation in heterosexual students', *Sex Roles,* **32**(11/12): 821–34.

Elise, D. (1991) 'When sexual and romantic feelings permeate the therapeutic relationship', in C. Silverstein (ed.), *Gays, Lesbians, and their Therapists.* New York: Norton.

Ellis, H. (1934) *Man and Woman: A Study of Secondary and Tertiary Sexual Characteristics.* London: Heinemann.

Elvik, S., Markowitz, C., Nicholas, E., Lipman, L.,and Inkelis, S. (1990) 'Sexual abuse in the developmentally disabled: dilemmas of diagnosis', *Child Abuse and Neglect,* **14**: 497–502.

Emmert, C. and Kohler, U. (1998) 'Data about 154 children and adolescents reporting sexual assault', *Archives of Gynecology and Obstetrics,* **261**(2): 61–70.

Engel, G. L. (1980) 'The clinical application of the biopsychosocial model', *American Journal of Psychiatry,* **137**(5): 535–44.

Epstein, S. (1996) 'A Queer encounter: sociology and the study of sexuality', in S. Seidman (ed.), *Queer Theory/Sociology.* Oxford: Blackwell.

Erickson, M. H. and Rosen, S. (1991) *My Voice Will Go With You: The Teaching Tales of Milton H. Erickson, MD.* New York: Norton.

Ernst, S. and Maguire, M. (1987) (eds) *Living with the Sphinx: Papers from the Women's Therapy Centre.* London: Women's Press.

Espin, O. (1984) 'Cultural and historical influences on sexuality in Hispanic Latin women: implications for psychotherapy.' in C. Vance (ed.), *Pleasure and Danger: Exploring Female Sexuality.* New York: Monthly Review Press.

Faderman, L. (1981) *Surpassing the Love of Men: Romantic Friendships and Love between Women from the Renaissance to the Present.* New York: Morrow.

Fairbairn, W. R. D. (1954) *An Object-Relations Theory of the Personality.* New York: Basic Books.

Falco, K. L. (1991) *Psychotherapy with Lesbian Clients: Theory into Practice.* New York: Brunner/Mazel.

Fast, I. (1984) *Gender Identity: A Differentiation Model.* Hillsdale, NJ: Analytic Press.

Faust, B. (1991) *Sex,Feminism and Sociobiology: Apprenticeship in Liberty.* North Ryde, Australia: Angus & Robertson.

Feldman, M. P. (1973) *Criminal Behaviour: A Psychological Analysis.* Chichester: Wiley.

Ferguson, A. G. (1997) 'How good is the evidence relating to the frequency of childhood sexual abuse and the impact such abuse has on the lives of adult survivors?' *Public Health*, **111**(6): 387–91.

Fergusson, D. M., Horwood, L. J. and Lynskey, M. T. (1996) 'Childhood sexual abuse and psychiatric disorder in young adulthood: II. Psychiatric outcomes of childhood sexual abuse.' *Journal of the American Academy of Child and Adolescent Psychiatry*, **35**(10): 1365–74.

Field, N. (1999) 'O tell me the truth about love', in D. Mann (ed.), *Erotic Transference and Countertransference: Clinical Practice in Psychotherapy*. London and New York: Routledge.

Finkelhor, D. (1979) *Sexually Victimized Children*. New York: Free Press.

Finkelhor, D. (1987) *Child Sexual Abuse: New, Theory and Research*. New York: Free Press.

Finkelhor, D. (1993) 'Epidemiological factors in the clinical identification of child sexual abuse', *Child Abuse and Neglect*. **17**(1): 67–70.

Fisher, S. (1973) *The Female Orgasm*. New York: Basic Books.

Flax, J. (1978) 'The conflict between nurturance and autonomy in mother–daughter relationships and within feminism', *Feminist Studies*, **4**(2): 171–91.

Fonagy, P., Target, M. and Gergely, G. (2000) 'Attachment and border-line personality disorder. a theory and some evidence', *Psychiatric Clinics of North America*, **23**(1): 103–22.

Fordham, M. (1971) *The Self and Autism*. London: Heinemann.

Formani, H. (1991) *Men: The Darker Continent*. London: Mandarin.

Foucault, M. (1981) *The History of Sexuality, Vol. 1; An Introduction*. Harmondsworth: Pelican.

Freud, S. and Breuer, J. (1893–5) *Studies on Hysteria*, Pelican Freud Library edn, 1974. Harmondsworth: Penguin.

Freud, S. (1900) *On Dreams*, Vol. 5 of the Standard Edition of the Complete Psychological Works of Sigmund Freud, ed. James Strachey and Anna Freud. London: The Hogarth Press and the Institute of Psycho-Analysis, 1974.

Freud, S. (1905a) *Fragment of an Analysis of a Case of Hysteria*, Pelican Freud Library edn, 1977. Harmondsworth: Penguin.

Freud, S. (1905b) *Three Essays on the Theory of Sexuality*, Vol. 7 of the Standard Edition of the Complete Psychological Works of Sigmund Freud, ed. James Strachey and Anna Freud. London: Hogarth Press and the Institute of Psycho-Analysis, 1974.

Freud, S. (1914) *The Origins of Psychoanalysis. 1887–1902*, Vol. 23 of the Standard Edition of the Complete Psychological Works of Sigmund Freud, ed. James Strachey and Anna Freud. London: Hogarth Press and the Institute of Psycho-Analysis, 1974.

Freud, S. (1914) *On Narcissism: An Introduction*, Vol. 14 of the Standard Edition of the Complete Psychological Works of Sigmund Freud, ed. James Strachey and Anna Freud. London: Hogarth Press and the Institute of Psycho-Analysis, 1974.

Freud, S. (1915) *Observations on Transference-Love*, Vol. 12 of the Standard Edition of the Complete Psychological Works of Sigmund

Freud, ed. James Strachey and Anna Freud. London: Hogarth Press and the Institute of Psycho-Analysis, 1974.

Freud, S. (1931) *Female sexuality*, Vol. 21 of the Standard Edition of the Complete Psychological Works of Sigmund Freud, ed. James Strachey and Anna Freud. London: Hogarth Press and the Institute of Psycho-Analysis, 1974.

Freud, S. (1937) *Analysis Terminable and Interminable*, Vol. 23 of the Standard Edition of the Complete Psychological Works of Sigmund Freud, ed. James Strachey and Anna Freud. London: Hogarth Press and the Institute of Psycho-Analysis, 1974.

Freund, K. and Blanchard, R. (1986) 'The concept of courtship disorder', *Journal of Sex and Marital Therapy*, 12(2): 79–92.

Freund, K. and Watson, R. J. (1993) 'Gender identity, disorder and courtship disorder', *Archives of Sexual Behavior*, 22(1): 13–21.

Freund, K. and Seto, M. C. (1998) 'Preferential rape in the theory of courtship disorder', *Archives of Sexual Behavior*, 27(5): 433–43.

Friedman, L. J. (1971) *Virgin Wives: A Study of Unconsummated Marriages*. London: Tavistock.

Friedrich, W. N., Grambsch, P., Broughton, D., Kuiper, J. and Beilke, R. L. (1991) 'Normative sexual behaviour in children', *Paediatrics*, 88(3): 456–64.

Fritz, G. S., Stoll, K. and Wagner, N. (1981) 'A comparison of males and females who were sexually molested as children', *Journal of Sexual and Marital Therapy*, 7: 54–9.

Frosh, S. (1993) 'The seeds of masculine sexuality', in J. M. Ussher and C. D. Baker (eds), *Psychological Perspectives on Sexual Problems: New Directions in Theory and Practice*. London and New York: Routledge.

Gabbard, G. O. (1995) 'The early history of boundary violations', *Journal of the American Psychoanalytic Association*, 43: 1115–36.

Gabbard, G. O. (2000). 'Disguise or consent: problems and recommendations concerning the publication and presentation of clinical material', *International Journal of Psycho-Analysis*, 81(6): 1071–86.

Gabbard, G. O. (2001) 'Disguise or consent: problems and recommendations concerning the publication and presentation of clinical material', *International Journal of Psycho-Analysis*. 81: 1071–86.

Gabbard, G. O. and Lester, E. P. (1995) *Boundaries and Boundary Violations in Psychoanalysis*. New York: Basic Books.

Gardner, F. (1999) 'A sense of all conditions', in D. Mann (ed.), *Erotic Transference and Countertransference: Clinical Practice in Psychotherapy*. London and New York: Routledge.

Gellner, E. (1985) *The Psychoanalytical Movement, or The Coming of Unreason*. London: Paladin Books.

Giddens, A. (1992) *The Transformation of Intimacy: Sexuality, Love and Eroticism in Modern Societies*. Cambridge: Polity Press.

Gillan, P. and Gillan, R. (1976) *Sex Therapy Today*. London: Open Books.

Gilligan, C. (1982) *In a Different Voice*. Cambridge, MA: Harvard University Press.

Gillis, J. S. and Avis, W. E. (1980) 'The male taller norm in mate selection', *Personality and Social Psychology Bulletin*, 6: 396–401.

Glasser, M. (1979) 'Some aspects of the role of aggression in the perversions', in I. Rosen (ed.), *Sexual Deviation*, 2nd edn. Oxford: Oxford University Press.

Glassgold, J. and Iasenza, S. (1995) (eds) *Lesbians and Psychoanalysis: Revolutions in Theory and Practice*. New York: Free Press.

Goldenweiser, A. (1937) *Anthropology*. New York: Crofts.

Gonsiorek, J. C. and Brown, L. S., (1989) 'Post therapy sexual relationships with clients', in G. R. Schoener *et al.* (eds), *Psychotherapists' Sexual Involvement with Clients: Interventions and Prevention*. Minneapolis: Walk in Counselling Centre.

Gordon, S. (1999) 'Bringing up Eros: a Kohutian perspective', in D. Mann (ed.), *Erotic Transference and Countertransference: Clinical Practice in Psychotherapy*. London and New York: Routledge.

Gorkin, M. (1985) 'Varieties of sexualised countertransference', *Psychoanalytic Review*, 72(3): 421–40.

Gornick, L. (1986) 'Developing a new narrative: the woman therapist and the male patient', in J. Alpert (ed.), *Psychoanalysis and Women: Contemporary Reappraisals*. Hillsdale, NJ: Analytic Press.

Gosselin, C. and Wilson, G. (1980) *Sexual Variations; Fetishism, Transvestism and Sadomasochism*. London: Faber & Faber.

Gould, S, and Lewontin, R. (1979) 'The Spandrels of San Marco and the Panglossian paradigm: a critique of the adaptationist programme', *Proceedings of the Royal Society of London*, B205: 581–98.

Gray, J. P. (1984) 'The influence of female power in marriage on sexual behavior and attitudes: a holocultural study', *Archives of Sexual Behavior*, 13: 223–32.

Green A. (1995) 'Has sexuality anything to do with psychoanalysis?' *International Journal of Psychoanalysis*, 76(5): 345–50.

Green, A. (1986) *On Private Madness*. London: Hogarth Press.

Green, R. (1969) 'Psychiatric management of special problems in transsexualism', in R. Green, and J. Money, *Transsexualism and Sex Reassignment*. Baltimore, MD: Johns Hopkins University Press.

Green, R. (1987) *The 'Sissy Boy' Syndrome and the Development of Homosexuality*. New Haven, CT: Yale University Press.

Greenberg, J. and Mitchell, S. (1983) *Object Relations in Psychoanalytic Theory*. Cambridge, MA: Harvard University Press.

Greenson, R. (1967) *The Technique and Practice of Psychoanalysis*. London: Hogarth Press.

Greer, G. (1969) 'A groupie's vision', in L. Segal (1994), *Straight Sex*. London: Virago Press.

Greer, G. (1991) *The Change: Women, Aging and the Menopause*. London: Hamish Hamilton.

Gribbin, J. and Gribbin, M. (1988) *The One Per Cent Advantage*. Oxford: Blackwell.

Griffin, S. (1971) 'Rape: the all-American crime', *Ramparts*, 10: 26–35.

Grosskurth, P. (1987) *Melanie Klein: Her World and Her Work*. London: Karnac.

Grossman, W. I. (1991) 'Pain, aggression, fantasy, and the concept of sadomasochism', *Psychoanalytic Quarterly*, **60**: 22–52.

Grosz, E. (1992) 'Pphallic mother', in E. Wright (ed.), *Feminism and Psychoanalysis: A Critical Dictionary*. Oxford: Blackwell.

Groth, A. N. (1979) *Men who Rape: The Psychology of the Offender*. New York: Plenum.

Grunberger, B. (1989) *New Essays on Narcissism*. London: Free Association Books.

Guggenbuhl-Craig, W. (1980) *Eros on Crutches: Reflections on Psychopathology and Amorality*. Dallas, TX: Spring Publications.

Gundersen, B. H., Melas, P. S. and Skar, J. E. (1981) 'Sexual behaviour of preschool children: Teachers' observations', in L. L. Constantine and F. M. Maninson (eds), *Children and Sex*. Boston, MA: Little, Brown.

Gutek, B. (1985) *Sex and the Workplace*. San Francisco: Jossey-Bass.

Guttman, H. A. (1984) 'Sexual issues in the transference and counter-transference between female therapist and male patient.' *Journal of the American Academy of Psychoanalysis*, **12**(4): 187–97.

Halberstam, J. (1998) *Female Masculinity*. Durham, NC and London: Duke University Press.

Hall, M. (1998) *The Lesbian Love Companion: How to Survive Everything from Heartthrob to Heartbreak*. San Francisco, CA: Harper.

Haraldsen, I. R. and Dahl, A. A. (2000) Symptom profiles of gender dysphoric patients of transsexual type compared to patients with personality disorders and healthy adults', *Acta Psychiatrica Scandinavica*, **102**(4): 276–81.

Harding, C. (2001) 'Introduction', in C. Harding (ed.), *Sexuality: Psychoanalytic Perspectives*. Hove, Sussex: Brunner-Routledge.

Hardy, S. (1998) *The Reader, the Author, his Woman and her Lover. Soft-core Pornography and Heterosexual Men*. London: Cassell.

Hatfield, E. and Rapson, R. L. (1993) *Love, Sex and Intimacy: Their Psychology, Biology, and History*. New York: HarperCollins.

Hatfield, E. (1996) *Love and Sex: Cross-Cultural Perspectives*. Needham Heights, MA: Allyn & Bacon.

Hawkes, G. (1996) *The Sociology of Sex*. Buckingham: Open University Press.

Hawton, K. (1985) *Sex Therapy. A Practical Guide*. Oxford: Oxford Medical Publications, Oxford University Press.

Hawton, K., Catalan, J., Manin, P. and Fagg, J. (1986) 'Long-term outcome of sex therapy', *Behaviour Research and Therapy*, **24**, 665–75.

Heeringen C. van and J. Vincke (1997) 'Suicidal acts and ideation in homosexual and bisexual young people: a study of prevalence and risk factors', *Social Psychiatry and Psychiatric Epidemiology*, **35**(11): 494–9.

Hillman, J. (1975) *Loose Ends*. Dallas, TX: Spring Publications.

Hillman, J. (1983) *Healing Fiction*. Barrytown, NY: Station Hill Press.

Hinshelwood, R. D. (1989) *A Dictionary of Kleinian Thought*. London: Free Association Books.

Hite, S. (1976) *The Hite Report: A Nationwide Study of Female Sexuality*, New York: Dell.

Hocquenghem, G. (1978) *Homosexual Desire*, trans. D. Dangoor. London: Allison & Busby.

Hofferth, S . L. (1990) 'Trends in adolescent sexual activity, contraception, and pregnancy in the United States', in I. Bankcroft and J. M. Reinisch (eds), *Adolescence and Puberty*. New York: Oxford University Press.

Hollins, S. and Sinason, V. (2000) 'Psychotherapy, learning disabilities and trauma: new perspectives', *British Journal of Psychiatry*, **176**: 32–6.

Holmes, J. (1993) *John Bowlby and Attachment Theory*. London and New York: Routledge.

Holstrom, L. L. and Burgess, A. W. (1980) 'Sexual behaviour of assailants during reported rapes', *Archives of Sexual Behavior*, **9**: 427–46.

Horney, K. (1924) 'On the genesis of the castration complex in women', *International Journal of Psychoanalysis*, **5**: 5–65.

Horney, K. (1967) *Feminine Psychology*. New York: Norton.

International Committee of Medical Journal Editors (1995) 'Protection of patients' rights to privacy', *British Medical Journal*, **311**: 1272.

Irigaray, L. (1985) *This Sex Which Is Not One*, trans. C. Porter with C. Burke. Ithaca, NY: Cornell University Press.

Irvine, J. (1990) *Disorders of Desire: Sex and Gender in Modern American Sexology*. Philadelphia: Temple University Press.

Isay, R. (1996) *Becoming Gay: The Journey to Self Acceptance*. New York: Random House.

Jackson, G. (1993) *The Living Room Mysteries: Patterns of Male Intimacy*. Toronto: Inner City Books.

Jackson, M. (1984) 'Sex research and the commodification of sexuality: a tool for male supremacy?' *Women's Studies International Forum*, **7**: 451–72.

Jackson, M. (1987) 'Facts of life or the eroticisation of women's oppression? Sexology and the construction of heterosexuality', in P. Caplan (ed.) *The Cultural Construction of Sexuality*. London: Routledge.

Jacobson, E. (1964) *The Self and the Object World*. New York: International Universities Press.

Jankowiak, W. R., Hill, E. M., and Donovan, J. M. (1992) 'The effects of sex and sexual orientation on attractiveness judgements: An evolutionary interpretation', *Ethology and Socio-biology*, **13**: 73–85.

Jardine, A. and Smith, P. (1987) (eds) *Men in Feminism*. New York and London: Methuen.

Jeffreys, S. (1990) *Anti-Climax*. London: Women's Press.

Jehu, D. (1979) *Sexual Dysfunction. A Behavioural Approach to Causation, Assessment and Treatment*. Chichester: Wiley.

Jehu, D. (1991) 'Clinical work with adults who were sexually abused in childhood', in A. C. R. Hollis and K. Howells (eds), *Clinical Approaches to Sex Offenders and their Victims*. Chichester: Wiley.

Jehu, D. (1994) *Patients as Victims: Sexual Abuse in Psychotherapy Counselling*. Chichester: Wiley.

Jones, E. (1927) 'The Early Development of Female Sexuality', *International Journal of Psycho-analysis*, **8**: 459–72.

Joseph, B. (1989) *Psychic Equilibrium and Psychic Change: Selected Papers of Betty Joseph*, New Library of Psychoanalysis. London: Tavistock/Routledge.

Joseph, B. (1993) 'Transference: the total situation', *International Journal of Psycho-analysis*, **66**: 447–57.

Jung, C. G. (1956) *Symbols of Transformation*, Vol. 5 of Collected Works (1976 edition). Princeton, NJ: Bollingen.

Jung, C. G. (1946) *The Psychology of the Transference*, Vol. 16 of Collected Works (1976 edition). Princeton, NJ: Bollingen.

Jung, C. G. (1959) *The Transcendent Function*, Vol. 8 of Collected Works (1976 edition). Princeton, NJ: Bollingen.

Jung, C. G. (1982) *Aspects of the Feminine*. Princeton, NJ: Princeton University Press.

Kafka, M. P. and Hennen, J. (1999) 'The paraphilia-related disorders: an empirical investigation of nonparaphilic hypersexuality disorders in outpatient males', *Journal of Sex and Marital Therapy*, **25**(4): 305–19.

Kahn, M. M. R. (1979) *Alienation in Perversions*. New York: International Universities Press.

Kamel, G. W. and Weinberg, T. (1983) *S and M: Studies in Sadomasochism*. Buffalo, NY: Prometheus Books.

Kaplan, H. S. (1974) *The New Sex Therapy: Active Treatment of Sexual Dysfunctions*. New York: Brunner/Mazel.

Kaplan, H. S. (1979) *Disorders of Sexual Desire, and Other New Concepts and Techniques of Sex Therapy*. New York: Brunner/Mazel.

Katz, J. (1976) *American Gay History*. New York: Crowell.

Kavaler-Adler, S. (1992) 'Mourning and the erotic transference', *International Journal of Psycho-analysis*, **73**: 527–39.

Kavanaugh, J. G. Jr and Volkan. V. D. (1978) 'Transsexualism and a new type of psychosurgery', *International Journal of Psychoanalytic Psychotherapy*, 7: 366–72.

Kernberg, O. F. (1992) *Aggression in Personality Disorders and Perversion*. New Haven, CT: Yale University Press.

Kernberg, O. F. (1995) *Love Relations: Normality and Pathology*. New Haven, CT: Yale University Press.

Kestenberg, J. (1968) 'Outside and inside, male and female', *Journal of the American Psychoanalytic Association*, **16**: 457–520.

Kimura, D. (2000) *Sex and Cognition*. Cambridge, MA: MIT Press.

Kinsey, A. C., Pomeroy, W. B., Martin, C. E. and Gebhard, P. H. (1948) *Sexual Behaviour in the Human Male*. Philadelphia: W. B. Saunders.

Klassen, A., Jenkinson, C., Fitzpatrick, R. and Goodacre, T. (1996)

'Patients' health-related quality of life before and after aesthetic surgery', *British Journal of Plastic Surgery*, 49(7): 433–8.

Klein, M. (1923) 'Infant analysis', in *The Writings of Melanie Klein*, Vol. 1. New York: Doubleday Random.

Klein, M. (1945) 'The Oedipus complex in the light of early anxieties', *International Journal of Psycho-analysis*, 26: 11–33.

Klein, M. (1932) The psychoanalysis of children, in *The writings of Melanie Klein*, Vol. 2. New York: Doubleday Random.

Klerman, G. L. and Weisman, M. (1994) *Interpersonal Psychotherapy of Depression*.Northvale, NJ: Jason Aronson.

Knight, R. A. and Prentky, R. A. (1987) 'Motivational Components in a Taxonomy for Rapists: A Validation Analysis.' Unpublished paper, cited in J. Bancroft (1989), *Human Sexuality and its Problems*. Edinburgh: Churchill Livingstone.

Koedt, A. (1970) 'The myth of the vaginal orgasm', in L. Tanner (ed.), *Voices for Women's Liberation*. New York: Mentor.

Kolk, B., van der, McFarlane, A. and Weisaeth, L. (1996) *Traumatic Stress: The Effects of Overwhelming Experience on Mind Body and Society*. New York: Guilford Press.

Kohlberg, L. (1966) 'A cognitive-developmental analysis of children's sex role concepts and attitudes', in E. E. Maccoby (ed.), *The Development of Sex Differences*. Stanford., CA: Stanford University Press.

Kristeva, J. (1974) 'Women can never be defined', in E. Marks and I. de Courtrivon (eds) (1981), *New French Feminisms*. Brighton, Sussex: Harvester.

Kristeva, J. (1980) *Desire in Language*, trans, L. S. Roudiez. Oxford: Basil Blackwell.

Kristeva, J. (1983) *Tales of Love*. New York: Columbia University Press.

Krivacska, L. J. (1992) 'Child sexual abuse prevention programs: the prevention of childhood sexuality?' *Journal of Child Sexual Abuse*, 1(4): 83–117.

Kumin, I. (1985) 'Erotic horror: desire and resistance in the psychoanalytic setting', *International Journal of Psychoanalytic Psychotherapy*, 11: 3–20.

Kurdek, L. A. and Schmitt, P. (1986) 'Relationship quality of partners in heterosexual married, heterosexual cohabiting, and gay and lesbian relationships', *Journal of Personality and Social Psychology*, 51(4): 711–20.

Lacan, J. (1958) 'The meaning of the phallus', trans. J. Rose, in J. Mitchell and J. Rose (eds), *Feminine Sexuality: Jacques Lacan and the Ecole Freudienne*. London: Macmillan.

Ladas, A. L., Whipple, B. and Perry, J. D. (1983) *The G Spot and Other Recent Discoveries about Human Sexuality*. London: Transworld/ Corgi.

Lalumière, M. L., Blanchard, R. and Zucker, K. J.(2000) 'Sexual orientation and handedness in men and women: a meta-analysis', *Psychological Bulletin*, 126(4): 575–92.

Lasarus, A .A. (1976) *Multimodal Behavior Therapy*. New York: Springer.

Lasky, R. (1989) 'Some determinants of the male analyst's capacity to identify with female patients', *International Journal of Psycho-analysis*, **70**: 405–18.

Leonard, M. R. (1966) 'Fathers and daughters: the significance of fathering in the psychosexual development of the girl', *International Journal of Psycho-Analysis*, **47**, 325–34.

Lerner, R. M. (1992) *Final Solutions: Biology, Prejudice, and Genocide*. Pennsylvania: Pennsylvania State University Press.

Lester, E. P. (1985) 'The female analyst and the eroticized transference', *International Journal of Psycho-Analysis*, **66**: 283–93.

Lester, E. P. (1990) 'Gender and identity issues in the analytic process.' *International Journal of Psycho-Analysis*, **71**: 435–53.

LeVay, S. (1993) *The Sexual Brain*. Cambridge, MA: MIT Press.

Lewes, K. (1989) *The Psychoanalytic Theory of Male Homosexuality*. London: Quartet.

Limentani, A. (1979) 'The significance of transsexualism in relation to some basic psychoanalytic concepts', in *Between Freud and Klein*. London: Free Association Books.

LoPiccolo, L. (1980) 'Low sexual desire', in S. Leiblum and L. Pervin (eds), *Principles and Practice of Sex Therapy*. New York: Guilford Press.

Loulan, J. (1984) *Lesbian Sex*. San Francisco, CA: Sisters Ink/Aunt Lute.

Lussier, A. (1982) *Les déviations du désir: Étude sur le fétichisme*. Paris: Presses Universitaires de France.

MacKinnon, C. (1987) 'Not a moral issue', in *Feminism Unmodified: Discourses on Life and Law*. Cambridge, MA and London: Harvard University Press.

Maguire, M. (1995) *Men Women Passion and Power. Gender Issues in Psychotherapy*. London: Routledge.

Mahler, M. S. (1968) *On Human Symbiosis and the Vicissitudes of Individuation*, Vol. I: *Infantile Psychosis*. New York: International Universities Press.

Maines, R. P. (1999) *The Technology of Orgasm: Hysteria, the Vibrator, and Women's Sexual Satisfaction*. Baltimore, Md: Johns Hopkins University Press.

Malamuth, N. M., Addison, T. and Koss, M. (2000) 'Pornography and sexual aggression: are there reliable effects and can we understand them?' *Annual Review of Sex Research*, **11**: 26–91.

Malcolm, R. R. (1970) 'The mirror: a perverse sexual phantasy in a woman seen as a defence against psychotic breakdown', in E. Spillius (1988), *Melanie Klein Today: Developments in Theory and Practice*, Vol. 2. London and New York: Routledge.

Mann, D. (ed.) (1999) *Erotic Transference and Countertransference: Clinical Practice in Psychotherapy*. London and New York: Routledge.

Marcuse, H. (1968) 'On Hedonism', in *Negations: essays in critical theory*. London: Penguin Books.

Marcuse, H. (1970) *Eros and Civilisation*. London: Allen Lane.

Margolin, G. (1986) 'Ethical issues in marital therapy', in N. S. Jacobson and A. S. Gurman (eds), *Clinical Handbook of Marital Therapy*. New York: Guilford Press.

Markowitz, F. and Ashkenazi, M. (eds) (1999) *Sex, Sexuality, and the Anthropologist*. Urbana and Chicago: University of Illinois Press.

Marx, B. P., Miranda, R. and Meyerson, L. A. (1999) 'Cognitive-behavioral treatment for rapists: can we do better?' *Clinical Psychology Review*, 19(7): 875–94.

Masson, J. M. (1984) *The Assault on Truth: Freud's Suppression of the Seduction Theory*. New York: Farrar Straus & Giroux.

Masters, W. H. and Johnson, V. E. (1966) *Human Sexual Response*. London: Churchill.

Masters, W. H. and Johnson, V. E. (1970) *Human Sexual Inadequacy*. Boston, MA: Little, Brown.

Mayer, E. L. (1985) 'Everybody must be just like me: observations on female castration anxiety', *International Journal of Psycho-Analysis*, 66: 331–47.

McDougall, J. (1970) 'Homosexuality in women', in J. Chasseguet-Smirgel (ed.), *Female Sexuality: New Psychoanalytic Views*. Ann Arbor: University of Michigan Press.

McDougall, J. (1985) *Theaters of the Mind: Illusion and Truth on the Psychoanalytic Stage*. New York: Basic Books.

McDougall, J. (1986) 'Identification, neoneeds, and neosexualities', *International Journal of Psycho-Analysis*, 67: 19–33.

McDougall, J. (1995) *The Many Faces of Eros*. London: Free Association Books.

McDougall, J. C., Morin, S. and McGill, U. (1979) 'Sexual attitudes and self-reported behaviour of congenitally disabled adults.' *Canadian Journal of Behavioural Science*, 11(3): 189–224.

McIntosh, M. (1968) 'The homosexual role', *Social Problems*, 16(2).

McNamara, E. (1994) *Breakdown: Sex, Suicide and the Harvard Psychiatrist*. New York: Simon & Schuster.

McWhirter, D. P. and Mattison, A. M. (1980) 'Treatment of sexual dysfunction in homosexual male couples,.' in S. R. Leiblum and L. A. Pervin (eds), *Principles and Practice of Sex Therapy*. New York: Guilford Press.

Meltzer, D. (1973) *Sexual States of Mind*. Strath Tay, Perthshire: Clunie Press.

Meltzer, D. and Williams, M. H. (1988) *The Apprehension of Beauty*. Strath Tay, Perthshire: Clunie Press.

Merkin, D. (1996) 'A closet of one's own' in M. Daly (ed.), *Surface Tension: Love, Sex and Politics between Lesbians and Straight Women*. New York: Touchstone.

Merton T. (2002) *The Intimate Merton: his life from his journals*, ed. P. Hart and J. Montaldo. London: Lion Publishing.

Messner, M. A. (1992) *Power at Play*. Boston: Beacon Press.

Metz, M. E., Pryor, J. L., Nesvacil, L. J., Abuzzahab, F. Sr. and Koznar,

J. (1997) 'Premature ejaculation: a psychophysiological review', *Journal of Sex and Marital Therapy*, **23**(1): 3–23.

Miller, E. M. (2000) 'Homosexuality, birth order, and evolution: toward an equilibrium reproductive economics of homosexuality', *Archives of Sexual Behavior*, **29**(1): 1–34.

Miller, G. (2000) *The Mating Mind*. London: Heinmann.

Miller, J. B. (1978) *Toward a New Psychology of Women*. Harmondsworth: Penguin.

Miller, D. K. (1975) 'Sexual counselling with spinal cord-injured client,.' *Journal of Sexual and Marital Therapy*, **1**(4): 312–18.

Millet, K. (1969) *Sexual Politics*. New York: Ballantine.

Milner, M. (1987) *The Suppressed Madness of Sane Men*. London and New York: Routledge.

Mitchell, J. (1974) *Psychoanalysis and Feminism*. London: Allen Lane.

Mitchell, S. A. (1978) 'Psychodynamics, homosexuality, and the question of pathology', *Psychiatry*, **41**(3): 254–63.

Mitchell, S. A. and Black, M. J. (1995) *Freud and Beyond: A History of Modern Psychoanalytic Thought*. New York: Basic Books.

Mitford, J. (1977) *A Fine Old Conflict*. London: Michael Joseph.

Mohr, R. (1992) *Gay Ideas: Outing and Other Controversies*. Boston, MA: Beacon Press.

Moir, A. and Moir, B. (1999) *Why Men Don't Iron*. London: HarperCollins.

Mollon, P. (1998) *Remembering Trauma: A Psychotherapist's Guide to Memory and Illusion*. Chichester: Wiley.

Money, J. (1986a) *Lovemaps: Clinical Concepts of Sexual/Erotic Health and Pathology, Paraphilia, and Gender Transposition in Childhood, Adolescence and Maturity*. New York: Irvington.

Money, J. (1986b) *Vandalized Lovemaps: Paraphilic Outcome of Seven Cases in Pediatric Sexology*. Buffalo, NY: Prometheus Books.

Money, J. (1993) *The Adam Principle: Genes, Genitals, Hormones, and Gender: Selected Readings in Sexology*. Buffalo, NY: Prometheus Books.

Monty, J. and Primrose, C. (1969) 'Sexual dimorphiosm and dissociation in the psychology of male transsexuals', in R. Greg and J. Money (eds), *Transsexualism and Sex Reassignment*. Baltimore: The Johns Hopkins University Press.

Moore, M. M. (1985) 'Non-verbal courtship patterns in women: context and consequences', *Ethology and Sociobiology*, **6**: 237–47.

Moraga, C. (1986) 'From a long line of Vendidas: Chicanas and Feminism', in *Feminist Studies, Critical Studies*, Teresa de Lauretis, (ed.), pp. 173–90. Bloomington: Indiana University Press.

Morgan, R. (1982) 'Feminism is the key to our survival and transformation', in *The Anatomy of Freedom*. Oxford: Martin Robertson.

Morgan, R. (ed.) (1984) *Sisterhood is Global: The International Women's Movement Anthology*. Harmondsworth: Penguin.

Morganthaler, F. (1988) *Homosexuality, Heterosexuality, Perversion*. Hove and London: Analytic Press.

Morris, L. (1997) *The Male Heterosexual: Lust in his Loins, Sin in his Soul?* Thousand Oaks, CA and London: Sage.

Moye, A. (1985) 'Pornography', in A. Metcalf and M. Humphries (eds), *The Sexuality of Men*. London: Pluto.

Muehlenhard, C. L. (1988) '"Nice women" don't say yes and "real men" don't say no: how miscommunication and the double standard can cause sexual problems', *Women and Therapy*, 7: 95–108.

Muehlenhard, C. L., Danoff-Burg, S. and Powch, I. G. (1996) 'Is rape sex or violence? Conceptual issues and implications', in D. M. Buss and M. M. Malmuth (eds), *Sex Power and Conflict: Evolutionary and Feminist Perspectives*. New York: Oxford University Press.

Murphy, B. C. (1989) 'Lesbian couples and their parents: The effects in perceived parental attitudes on the couple', *Journal of Counselling and Development*, 68: 46–51.

Murray, J. B. (2000) 'Psychological profile of pedophiles and child molesters.' *Journal of Psychology*, 134(2): 211–24.

Nanda, S. (1986) 'The Hijras of India: cultural and individual dimensions of an institutionalized third-gender role', in E. Blackwood (ed.), *Anthropology and Homosexual Behaviour*. Binghamton, NY: Haworth.

Neild, S. and Pearson, R. (1992) *Women Like Us*. London: Women's Press.

Nelson, N. (1987) 'Selling her kiosk: Kikuyu notions of sexuality and sex for sale in Mathare Valley, Kenya', in P. Caplan (ed.), *The Cultural Construction of Sexuality*. London: Routledge.

Nicolson, P. (1993) 'Public values and private beliefs. Why do women refer themselves for sex therapy?' in J. M. Ussher and C. D. Baker (eds), *Psychological Perspectives on Sexual Problems: New Directions in Theory and Practice*. London and New York: Routledge.

O'Connor, P. (1992) *Friendships between Women: A Critical Review*. New York: Guilford Press.

O'Connor, N. and Ryan, J. (1993) *Wild Desires and Mistaken Identities: Lesbianism and Psychoanalysis*. London: Virago.

Olagaray, J. (1998) 'Biology and sexuality', *International Journal of Psycho-Analysis*, 79: 991–4.

Olivier, C. (1980) *Jocasta's Children*. London: Routledge.

Orbach, S. and Eichenbaum, L. (1987) *Bittersweet: Facing Up to Feelings of Love, Envy and Competition in Women's Friendships*. London: Century.

Orbach, S. and Eichenbaum, L. (1994) *What Do Women Want?* London: HarperCollins.

Ortner, S. B. (1981) 'Gender and sexuality in hierarchical societies: the case of Polynesia and some comparative implications', in S. Ortner and H. Whitehead (eds), *Sexual Meanings: the Cultural Construction of Gender and Sexuality*. Cambridge: Cambridge University Press.

Owen, F. (1982) 'Advertising for a partner: varieties of self-presentation', *Bulletin of the British Psychological Society*, 35: 72.

Paglia, C. (1993) *Sex, Art, and American Culture*. Harmondsworth: Penguin.

Pally, R. and Olds, D. (1998) 'Consciousness: a neuroscience perspective', *International Journal of Psycho-Analysis*, **79**: 971–89.

Palmer, C. T. (1988). 'Twelve reasons why rape is not sexually motivated: A sceptical examination.' *Journal of Sex Research* 25: 512–530.

Parsons, T. (1951) *The Social System*. London: Routledge & Kegan Paul.

Peplau, L. A., Pedesky, C., and Hamilton, M. (1982) 'Satisfaction in lesbian relationships', *Journal of Homosexuality*, **8**(2): 249–51.

Person, E. (1980) 'Sexuality as a mainstay of identity', *Signs: Jounal of Women in Culture and Society*, **5**: 605–30.

Person, E. (1983) 'The influence of values in psychoanalysis: the case of female psychology', *Psychiatry Update*, **2**: 36–50.

Person, E. (1997) *The Force of Fantasy: Its Roles, its Benefits and What it Reveals about Our Lives*. London: HarperCollins.

Person, E. (1999) *The Sexual Century*. New Haven and London: Yale University Press.

Person, E. and Ovesey, L. (1978) 'Transvestism: new perspectives', *Journal of the American Academy of Psychoanalysis*, **6**(3): 301–23.

Phillips, S. H. (2001) 'The overstimulation of everyday life: I. New aspects of male homosexuality', *Journal of the American Psychoanalytic Association*, **49**(4): 1235–67.

Phillips, P., Bartlett, A. and King, M. (2001) 'Psychotherapists' approaches to gay and lesbian patients/clients: a qualitative study', *British Journal of Medical Psychology*, **74**(1): 73–84.

Pierce A. P.(2000) 'The coital alignment technique (CAT): an overview of studies', *Journal of Sex and Marital Therapy*, **26**(3): 257–68.

Pillard, R. and Weinrich, J. (1987) 'Periodic table model of gender tranpositions: Part 1. A theory based on masculinization and defeminization of the brain', *Journal of Sex Research*, **23**: 425–54.

Pipher, M. (1994) *Reviving Ophelia: Saving the Selves of Adolescent Girls*. New York: Putnam.

Plummer, D. (1999) *One of the Boys: Masculinity, Homophobia and Modern Manhood*. New York: Harrington Park Press.

POPAN http://www.popan.org.uk

Pope, H. G. Jr. and Hudson, J. I. (1992) 'Is childhood sexual abuse a risk factor for bulimia nervosa?', *American Journal of Psychiatry*, **149**(4): 455–63.

Pope, K. S., Keith-Spiegel, K., and Tabachnick, B. G. (1986) 'Ethics of practice: the beliefs and behaviours of psychologists as therapists', *American Psychologist*, **34**: 682–9.

Porter, R. (1982) 'Mixed feelings: the Enlightenment and sexuality in eighteenth-century Britain', in P. G. Bouce (ed.) *Sexuality in Eighteenth-Century Britain*. Manchester: Manchester University Press.

Posner, R. A. (1992) *Sex and Reason*. Cambridge, MA: Harvard University Press.

Preston, J. and Swann, G. (1987) *Safe Sex: The Ultimate Erotic Guide*. New York: New American Library.

Pronger, B. (1990) 'Gay Jocks: a phenomenology of gay men in athletics', in M. A. Messner and D. F. Sabo (eds), *Sport, Men and the Gender Order*. Champaign, IL: Human Kinetics Books.

Racker, H. (1968) *Transference and Countertransference*. New York: International Universities Press.

Rahman, L., Richardson, H B. and Ripley, H. S. (1939) 'Anorexia nervosa: psychiatric observations', *Psychometric Medicine*, 1: 33, 55–65.

Ramsey, G. V. (1943) 'The sexual development of boys', *American Journal of Psychology*, 56: 217–34.

Raphael-Leff, J. (1991) *Psychological Processes of Childbearing*. London: Chapman & Hall.

Raphael-Leff, J. (1997) *Female Experience*. London and New York: Routledge.

Rappaport, E. A. (1956) 'The management of an eroticized transference', *Psycho-analytic Quarterly*, 25(5): 15–29.

Rattigan, B. (1995) 'Inner world, outer world: exploring the tension of race, sexual orientation and class and the inner world', *Psychodynamic Counselling*, 1(2): 173–86.

Raymond, J. (1996) 'The politics of transgenderism', in R. Ekins and D. King (eds), *Blending Genders: Social Aspects of Cross-Dressing and Sex Changing*. London and New York: Routledge.

Raymond, N. C., Coleman, E., Ohlerking, F., Christenson, G. A. and Miner, M. (1999) 'Psychiatric co-morbidity in pedophilic sex offenders', *American Journal of Psychiatry*, 156(5): 786–8.

Reed, E. (1978) *Sexism and Science*. New York: Pathfinder Press.

Reich, W. (1961) *The Function of the Orgasm*. New York: Farrar Straus & Giroux.

Reich, W. (1962) *The Sexual Revolution*. New York: Farrar Straus & Giroux.

Rekers, G. A., Mead, S .L, Rosen, A. C. and Brigham, S. L. (1983) 'Family correlates of male childhood gender disturbance', *Journal of Genetic Psychology*, 142: 31–42.

Rich, A. (1979) *Of Woman Born: Motherhood as Experience and Institution*. London: Virago.

Rich, A. (1993) 'Compulsory heterosexuality and lesbian existence', in H. Abelove, M. A. Barale and D. M. Halperin (eds), *The Lesbian and Gay Studies Reader*. London and New York: Routledge.

Rivers, I. (1994) 'Protecting the gay adolescent in school.' Cited in D. Davies and C. Neal (eds), (1996), *Pink Therapy: A Guide for Counsellors and Therapists Working with Lesbian and Gay and Bisexual Clients*. Buckingham: Open University Press.

Riviere, J. (1929) 'Womanliness as masquerade', *The International Journal of Psychoanalysis*, 10: 303–13.

Riviere, J. (1937) 'Hate, greed, and aggression', in M. Klein and J. Riviere (eds), *Love, Hate and Reparation*. London: Hogarth Press.

Roberts, E., Kline, D. and Gagnon, J. (1978) 'Family life and sexual learning : a study of the role of parents in the sexual learning of children' Vols 1–3. *A Report of the Project on Human Sexual Development*,

3 vols. Cambridge, MA. Cited in Bancroft, J. (1989) *Human Sexuality and its Problems*. Edinburgh: Churchill Livingstone.

Robson, K. M., Brant, H. A. and Kumar, R. (1981) 'Maternal sexuality during first pregnancy and after childbirth', *British Journal of Obstetrics and Gynaecology*, **88**: 882–9.

Rochlin, M. (1982) 'Sexual orientation of the therapist and therapeutic effectiveness with gay clients', in J. C. Gonsiorek (ed.), *Homosexuality and Psychotherapy*. Binghamton, NY: Haworth.

Rosenfeld, H. (1971) 'A clinical approach to the psychoanalytic theory of the life and death instincts: an investigation into the aggressive aspects of narcissism', *International Journal of Psychoanalysis*, **52**: 169–79.

Rosenfeld, H. (1975) 'Negative therapeutic reaction', in P. L. Giovacchini (ed.), *Tactics and Techniques in Psychoanalytic Therapy*, vol. 2: *Countertransference*. New York: Jason Aronson.

Rossi, A. S. (1994) 'Eros and Caritas: a biopsychosocial approach to human sexuality and reproduction', in A. S. Rossi (ed.), *Sexuality across the Life Course*. London: University of Chicago Press.

Rossi, A. S. (1997) 'The impact of family structure and social change', *Children and Youth Services Review*, **19**(5/6): 369–400.

Rubin, G. (1989) 'Thinking sex: notes for a radical theory of the politics of sexuality', in C. Vance (ed.), *Pleasure and Danger: Exploring Female Sexuality*. London: Pandora Press.

Ruddick, S. (1990) *Maternal Thinking*. London: The Women's Press.

Russell, D. (1984) *Sexual Exploitation: Rape, Child Sexual Abuse and Workplace Harrassment*. Thousand Oaks, CA and London: Sage.

Ruse, M. (1988) *Homosexuality: A Philosophical Inquiry*. Oxford: Blackwell.

Russell, D. E. H. (1990) *Rape in Marriage*. Bloomington: Indiana University Press.

Rutter, M., Graham, R., Chadwick, O. F. D. and Yule, W. (1976) 'Adolescent turmoil: fact or fiction?', *Journal of Child Psychology and Psychiatry*, **19**: 35–6.

Rutter, P. (1989) *Sex in the Forbidden Zone*. Los Angeles: J. P. Tarcher.

Rycroft, C. (1968) *A Critical Dictionary of Psychoanalysis*. London: Penguin.

Ryle, A. (1990) *Cognitive Analytic Therapy: Active Participation in Change*. Chichester: John Wiley.

Ryle, A. (1993) 'Addiction to the death instinct? A critical review of Joseph's paper 'Addiction to near death', *British Journal of Psychotherapy*, **10**(1): 88–92.

Ryle, A. and Kerr, I. (2002) *Introducing Cognitive Analytic Therapy: Principles and Practice*. Chichester: John Wiley.

Sade, Marquis de (1948) *Les Cent-vingt Journées de Sodome*. Paris: Oeuvres Complètes. Cited in G. Bataille (1987) *Eroticism*. London: Marion Boyars.

SAMOIS (1982) *Coming to Power*. Allyson Publications Inc, Boston Mass.

Samuels, A. (1985a) 'Symbolic dimensions of Eros in transference–countertransference: some clinical uses of Jung's alchemical metaphor', *International Review of Psychoanalysis*, **12**: 199–214.

Samuels, A. (1985b) *The Father: Contemporary Jungian Perspectives*. London: Free Associations.

Samuels, A. (1986) *Jung and the Post Jungians*. London: Routledge.

Samuels, A. (1989) *The Plural Psyche: Personality, Morality and the Father*. London and New York: Routledge.

Samuels, A. (1993) *The Political Psyche*. London: Routledge.

Samuels, A. (1999) 'From sexual misconduct to social justice', in D. Mann (ed.), *Erotic Transference and Countertransference: Clinical Practice in Psychotherapy*. London and New York: Routledge.

Samuels, A. (2001) *Politics on the Couch: Citizenship and the Internal Life*. London: Profile Books.

Sanday, P. R. (1981) 'The socio-cultural context of rape: a cross–cultural study', *Journal of Social Issues*, **37**: 5–27.

Satsz, T. (1990) *Sex by Prescription: The Startling Truth about Today's Sex Therapy*. Syracuse, NY: Syracuse University Press.

Saunders, D. (1985) *The Woman's Book of Love and Sex*. London: Sphere.

Saussure, F. (1983) *Course in General Linguistics*, trans. R. Harris. London: Duckworth.

Sayers, J. (1986) *Sexual Contradictions*. London: Tavistock.

Schafer, R. (1977) 'The interpretation of transference and the conditions of loving', *Journal of the American Psychoanalytic Association*, **22**: 459–89.

Scharff, D. E. and Scharff, J. S. (1991) *Object-relations couple therapy*. Northvale, NJ: Jason Aronson.

Schaverien, J. (1995) *Desire and the Female Therapist: engendered gazes in psychotherapy and art therapy*. London: Routledge.

Schober, J. M. (1999) 'Quality-of-life studies in patients with ambiguous genitalia', *World Journal of Urology*, **17**(4): 249–52.

Schober, J. M. (2001) 'Sexual behaviours, sexual orientation and gender identity in adult intersexuals: a pilot study', *Journal of Urology*, **165**(6 Pt 2): 2350–3.

Schoener, G. R. and Gonsiorek, J. C. (1989) 'Assessment and development of rehabilitation plans for the therapist', in G. R. Schoener *et al.* (eds), *Psychotherapists' Sexual Involvement with Clients: Intervention and Prevention*. Minneapolis: Walk in Counselling Centre.

Schwartz, D. (1995) 'Current psychoanalytic discourses on sexuality: tripping over the body', in T. Domenici and R. Lesser (eds), *Disorienting Sexuality*. New York: Routledge.

Schwartz, P. and Rutter, V. (1998) *The Gender of Sexuality*. Thousand Oaks, CA: Pine Forge Press.

Scruton, R. (1986) *Sexual Desire: A Philosophical Investigation*. London: Weidenfeld & Nicolson.

Searles, H. (1959) 'Oedipal love in the counter transference', in *Collected Papers on Schizophrenia and Related Subjects* (1986 edn). London: Maresfield.

Sedgwick, E. K. (1990) *Epistomology of the Closet*. Berkeley, CA: University of California Press.

Sedgwick, E .K. (1994) 'Is the rectum straight? Identification and identity in *The Wings of a Dove*', in *Tendencies*. London and New York: Routledge.

Segal, L. (1987) *Is The Future Female?* London: Virago.

Segal, L. (1990) *Slow Motion: Changing Masculinities, Changing Men*. London: Virago.

Segal, L. (1994) *Straight Sex*. London: Virago.

Segal, M. (1965) 'Transvestisism as an impulse and as a defense', *International Journal of Psychoanalysis*, **46**: 209–17.

Seidler, V. (1989) *Rediscovering Masculinity*. London and New York: Routledge.

Seidman, S. (1996) 'Introduction' to Seidman (ed.), *Queer Theory/Sociology*. Oxford: Blackwell.

Semans, J. H. (1956) 'Premature ejaculation, a new approach', *Southern Medical Journal*, **49**: 353–7.

Shakespeare, T., Gillespie-Sells, K. and Davies, D. (1996) *The Sexual Politics of Disability*. London: Cassell.

Sidman, J. M. (1977) 'Sexual functioning and the physically disabled adult', *American Journal of Occupational Therapy*, **31**(2): 81–5.

De Silva, P. (1983) 'Sexual problems in women with eating disorders', in J. M. Ussher and C. D. Baker (eds). *Psychological Perspectives on Sexual Problems: New Directions in Theory and Practice*. London: Routledge.

Silverstein, C. (ed.) (1991) *Gays, Lesbians, and their Therapists*. New York and London: W. W. Norton.

Sinason, V. (1986) 'Secondary mental handicap and its relationship to trauma', *Psychoanalytic Psychotherapy*, **2**(2): 131–54.

Singer, I. (1973) *The Goals of Human Sexuality*. London: Wildwood House.

Smith, J. (1992) *Misogynies: Reflections on Myths and Malice*. London: Fawcett.

Sobo, E. J. and Bell, S. (eds) (2001) *Celibacy, Culture, and Society: The Anthropology of Sexual Abstinence*. Madison: University of Wisconsin Press.

Socarides, C. (1988) *The Pre-oedipal Origin and Psychoanalytic Therapy of Sexual Perversions*. Madison: Connecticut International University Press.

Socarides, C. (1995) *Homosexuality: A Freedom Too Far. A Psychoanalyst Answers 1000 Questions about Causes and Cures and the Impact of the Gay Rights Movement on American Society*. Phoenix, Arizona: Adam Margrave Books.

Solms, M. and Lechevalier, B.(2002) 'Neurosciences and psychoanalysis', *International Journal of Psychoanalysis*, **83**(1): 233–7.

Solomon, R. (1980) 'The opponent-process theory of acquired motivation: the costs of pleasure and the benefits of pain', *American Psychologist*, **35**: 273–5.

Sontag, S. (1982) *A Susan Sontag Reader*. New York: Farrar Straus & Giroux.

Spence, S. H. (1991) *Psychosexual Therapy: A Cognitive Behavioural Approach*. London: Chapman & Hall.

Sprecher, S. and McKinney, K. (1993) *Sexuality*. Thousand Oaks, CA and London: Sage.

Stein, A. and Plummer, K. (1996) 'I can't even think straight': 'Queer' theory and the missing sexual revolution in sociology', in S. Seidman (ed.), *Queer Theory/Sociology*. Cambridge, MA: Blackwell.

Steinberg, L. (1994) *Crossing Paths: How Your Child's Adolescence Triggers Your Own Crisis*. New York: Simon & Schuster.

Stern, D. (1985) *The Interpersonal World of the Infant*. New York: Basic Books.

Stevens, A. and Price, J. (1996) *Evolutionary Psychiatry*. London and New York: Routledge.

Stoller, R. J. (1968) *Sex and Gender*. New York: Jason Aronson.

Stoller, R. J. (1975) *Perversion: The Erotic Form of Hatred*. Exeter: Wheaton.

Stoller, R. J. (1976) *Sex and Gender the Transsexual Experiment*. Northvale, NJ: Jason Aronson.

Stoller, R. J. (1991) *Pain and Passion: A Psychoanalyst Explores the World of S & M*. New York: Plenum.

Stoller, R. J. (1992) *Observing the Erotic Imagination*. New Haven, CT: Yale University Press.

Stoller, R. J. (1993) *Porn: Myths for the Twentieth Century*. New Haven, CT: Yale University Press.

Stoller, R. J. (1996) *Coming Attractions: The Making of an X-Rated Video*. New Haven, CT: Yale University Press.

Stoller, R. J. and Levine, I. S. (1993). *Coming Attractions: The Making of an X-Rated Video*. New Haven, CT: Yale University Press.

Stopes, M. C. (1918) *Married Love: A New Contribution to the Solution of Sex Difficulties*. London: A. C. Fifield.

Tallis, R. (1988) *Not Saussure: A Critique of Post-Saussurean Literary Theory*. Basingstoke: Macmillan.

Tanney, M. F. and Birk, J.M. (1978) 'Women counsellors for women clients? A review of the research', in L. W. Harmon *et al.* (eds), *Counselling Women*. Monterey: Brookes/Cole.

Taylor, T. (1997) *The Prehistory of Sex*. London: Fourth Estate.

Thompson, B. (1994) *Sadomasochism*. London: Cassell.

Thompson, J. (1999) 'Eros: the connecting principle (or the complexities of love and sexuality)', in D. Mann (ed.), *Erotic Transference and Countertransference: Clinical Practice in Psychotherapy*. London and New York: Routledge.

Thompson, S. (1990) 'Putting a big thing into a little hole: teenage girls' accounts of sexual initiation', *Journal of Sex Research*, 27(3): 253–00.

Thorn, B. (1993) *Gender Play: Boys and Girls in School*. Buckingham: Open University Press.

Thornhill, R. and Palmer, C. T. (2000) *A Natural History of Rape.* Cambridge, MA: MIT Press.

Tiefer, L. (1995) *Sex is not a Natural Act, and Other Essays.* Boulder, CO: Westview.

Trenchard, L. and Warren, W. (1984) *Something to Tell You.* Londons Gay Teenage Group.

Troiden, R. R. (1993) 'The formation of homosexual identities', in L. D. Garnets and D. C. Kimmel (eds), *Psychological Perspectives on Lesbian and Gay Male Experiences.* New York: Columbia University Press.

Tucker, M. B. and Mitchell-Kernan, C. (1995) *The Decline in Marriage among African Americans: Causes, Consequences and Policy Implications.* New York: Russell Sage.

Tuckett, D, (2000) 'Reporting clinical events in the journal: towards the construction of a special case', *International Journal of Psycho-Analysis*, **81**(6): 1065–9.

Udry, J. R., Talbert, L. M. and Morris, N. M. (1986) 'Biosocial foundations for adolescent female sexuality', *Demography*, **23**: 217–27.

Ussher, J. M. (1993) 'The construction of female sexual problems: regulating sex regulating women', in J. M. Ussher and C. D. Baker (eds), *Psychological Perspectives on Sexual Problems: New Directions in Theory and Practice.* London: Routledge.

Vance, C. (ed.) (1984) *Pleasure and Danger: Exploring Female Sexuality.* London: Routledge & Kegan Paul.

Veld, T. H. van de (1928) *Ideal Marriage: its Physiology and Technique.* London: Heineman.

Waals, H. G. van de (1965) 'Problems of narcissism', *Bulletin of the Menninger Clinic*, **29**: 293–311.

Walsh, P. (1983) 'Normal family ideologies, myths and realities', in J. C. Hansen and C. J. Falicov (eds), *Cultural Perspectives in Family Therapy.* Rockville, MD: Aspen.

Warnock, M. (1980) *Imagination.* London: Faber & Faber.

Warnock, M. (1994) *Imagination and Time.* Oxford: Blackwell.

Watson, C. and Rogers, R. S. (1980) 'Sexual education for the mildly handicapped adolescent', *Health Education Journal*, **39**: 87–95.

Weeks, J. (1985) *Sexuality and its Discontents.* London: Routledge & Kegan Paul.

Weeks, J. (1991) *Against Nature: Esseys on History Sexuality and Identity.* London: Rivers Oram Press.

Weinberg, M. S., Williams, C. J. and Moser, C. (1984) 'The social constituents of masochism', *Social Problems*, **31**(4).

Welldon, E. (1988) *Mother, Madonna, Whore.* London: Free Association Books.

Westen, D. and Gabbard, G. O. (2002a) 'Developments in cognitive neuroscience: I. Conflict, compromise, and connectionism', *Journal of the American Psychoanalytic Association*, **50**(1): 53–98.

Westen, D. and Gabbard, G. O. (2002b) 'Developments in cognitive neuroscience: II. Implications for theories of transference', *Journal of the American Psychoanalytic Association*, **50**(1): 99–134.

Westen, D., Ludolph, P., Block, M. J., Wixom, J. and Wiss, F. C. (1990) 'Developmental history and object relations in psychiatrically disturbed adolescent girls', *American Journal of Psychiatry*, 147(8): 1061–8.

Whitney, C. (1991) *Uncommon Lives: Gay Men and Straight Women*. New York: New American Library.

Williams, C. (1983) 'Sexuality and Disability', in J. M. Ussher and C. D. Baker (eds), *Psychological Perspectives on Sexual Problems: New Directions in Theory and Practice*. London: Routledge.

Williamson, J. (1975) *Decoding Advertisements*. London: Marion Boyars.

Wilson, E. (1975) *Sociobiology: The New Synthesis*. Cambridge, MA, and London: Harvard University Press.

Wilton, T. (1996) *Finger-Licking Good: The Ins and Outs of Lesbian Sex*. London: Cassell.

Winnicott, D. W. (1965) *The Family and Individual Development*. London: Tavistock.

Wisdom, J. O. (1970) 'Freud and Melanie Klein: Psychology, ontology, and Weltanschauung', in C. Hanly and M. Lazerowitz (eds), *Psychoanalysis and Philosophy*. New York: International Universities Press.

Wittig, M. (1981) 'One is not on a woman', *Feminist Issues*, Winter: 47–54.

Wittig, M. (1982) 'The category of sex', *Feminist Issues*, Fall: 62.

Wrye, H. K. and Welles, J. K. (1994) *The Narration of Desire: Erotic Transferences and Countertransferences*. Hillsdale, NJ: Analytic Press.

Wyatt, G. E. (1989) 'Re-examining factors predicting Afro-American and white American women' s age of first coitus', *Archives of Sexual Behavior*. 18: 271–98.

Wyatt, G. E. (1992) 'The sociocultural context of African American and white American women's rape', *Journal of Social Issues*, 48(1): 77–91.

Wyatt, G. E. and Newcomb, M. (1990) 'Internal and external mediators of women's sexual abuse in childhood', *Journal of Consulting and Clinical Psychology*, 58: 758–67.

Wyatt, G. E., Newcomb, M. and Notgrass, S. S (1990) 'Internal and external mediators of women's rape experiences', *Psychology of Women Quarterly*, 14: 153–76.

Wyatt, G .E., Newcomb, M. D. and Riederle, M. H. (1993) *Sexual Abuse and Consensual Sex*. Thousand Oaks, CA: Sage.

Young, J. E. (1999) *Cognitive Therapy for Personality Disorders: A Schema-focused Approach* (3rd edn). Sarasota, FL: Professional Resource Press.

Young, R. (2001) 'Locating and relocating psychoanalytic ideas of sexuality', in C. Harding (ed.), *Sexuality: Psychoanalytic Perspectives*. Hove, Sussex: Brunner Routledge.

Young-Bruehl, E. (1989) *Anna Freud: A Biography*. London: Macmillan.

Zetzel, E. R. (1968) 'The so-called good hysteric', *International Journal of Psycho-Analysis*, 49(2): 256–60.

Zinkin, L. (1969) 'Flexibility in analytic technique', in M. Fordham (ed.), *Technique in Jungian Analysis*. London: Karnac.

Zulueta, F. de (1993) *From Pain to Violence: The Traumatic Roots of Destructiveness*. London: Whurr Publishers.

Index of Names

Abraham, C. 71
Abuzzahab, F. Sr 270, 347
Adams, P. 195, 331
Adler, A. 95, 331
Anna, O. 281
Arentewicz, G. 258, 331
Aristotle 316
Ashkenazi, M. 38, 145, 251, 227, 331, 346
Avis, W. E. 141, 340

Badcock, C. R. 93, 331
Bagley, C. 181, 331
Baker, R. 34, 267, 331
Balint, G. 84, 89, 331
Bancroft, J. 16, 22, 24, 25, 133, 331, 137, 146, 147, 153, 172, 181, 209, 213, 220, 221, 230, 232, 233, 236, 238, 139, 240, 258, 260, 262, 263, 264, 266, 270, 271, 331
Barlow, D. R. 268, 331
Bartlett, F. C. 94
Bartlett, A. 271, 349
Battaille, G. 46–7, 200, 273, 306, 331
Beck, J. 255, 268, 331
Bell, D. 67, 332
Bell, S. 216, 3 53
Bellis, M. 34, 267, 331
Benjamin, J. 111, 112, 141, 210, 332
Berenbaum, S. A. 151, 332
Bernstein, B. 180, 332
Bersani, L. 125, 126, 184, 332
Birk, J. M. 190, 354
Black, M. J. 73, 347
Blackwood, E. 189, 332
Blanchard, R. 171, 344–5
Blum, H. B. 283, 332
Blumstein, P. 190, 192, 332
Boakes, J. 137, 332
Bolas, C. 174, 183, 332
Bradford, L. M. 205, 332
Brandon, S. 137, 332

Brant, H. A. 146, 351
Brennan, T. 123, 332, 333
Breuer, J. 281
Briere, J. 220, 333
Brigham, S. L. 237, 350
Bright, S. 106, 131, 165, 273, 333
Brindley, J. 22, 333
Britain, R. 88, 333
Brown, G. 55, 100, 333
Brown, G. R. 240, 333
Brown, L. S. 300, 340
Brownmiller, S. 193, 131, 219, 333
Brunschweig, D. 162, 332
Bucci, W. 93, 333
Budd, S. 83, 333
Buka, S. L. 138, 333
Burch, B. 175, 189, 333
Burgess, A. W. 219, 342
Buss, D. M. 3, 33, 35, 141, 145, 163
Butler, J. 27, 128, 333

Califia, P. 106, 131, 194, 211, 231, 234, 243, 244, 247, 248, 273, 313, 333, 334
Caplan, P. 231, 334
Carvalho, R. 175, 334
Cass, V. C. 188, 334
Catalan, J. 146, 341
Chase, C. 246
Chasseguet-Smirgel, J. 80, 82, 162, 200, 288, 334
Chiesa, M. 282, 283, 285, 334
Chiland, C. 245, 334
Chodorow, N. 109, 110, 152, 189, 190, 312, 334
Christenson, G. A. 205, 350
Clark, D. 177, 334
Clelland, S. R. 220, 334
Cole, C. M. 241, 334
Coleman, E. 205, 350
Coleman, W. 335
Coleridge, W. 317–18, 320, 323
Coles, L. 264, 331

Comfort, A.   255, 256, 275, 335
Contratto, S.   112, 335
Cornett, C.   187, 335
Costa, P. T. Jr   240, 333
Covington, C.   283, 285, 335
Cowan, L.   48, 212, 335
Coyle, A.   179, 180, 335
Creith, E.   193, 195, 196, 335
Crews, F.   66, 95, 335
Crowe, M. J.   259, 262, 264, 265,
   267, 270, 313, 335

Dahl, A. A.   241, 341
Danto, A. C.   321, 335
Darwin, C.   29–30, 31, 335
Davies, D.   180, 187, 191, 335
Davis, D.   275, 353
Day, G.   158, 335
Denman, C.   55, 190, 175, 309,
   335, 336
Derrida, J.   117, 336
Deutsch, H.   74, 336
Devlin, P. (Lord Devlin)   319
Devor, H.   238, 336
DeVries, P.   55, 309, 335, 336
Diamond, M.   229, 336
Dickemann, M.   172, 336
Dickes, R.   289, 336
Dicks, H. V.   142, 336
Dietz, P. E.   207, 208, 336
Dinnerstein, D.   109, 336
Doctor, R.   282, 336
Domenici, T.   187, 291, 336
Downing, C.   311, 336
Dunne, G.   188, 189,337
Dunphy, R.   140–1, 337
Dutton, D.   107, 159, 218, 337
Dworkin, A.   104, 105, 106, 131,
   143, 158, 248, 337

Eibesfelt, I.   35, 337
Eichenbaum, L.   113, 114, 115,
   348
Eliason, M. J.   179, 337
Elise, D.   290–1, 337
Ellis, H.   251, 252, 337
Emmert, C.   223, 337
Emory, L. E.   241, 334
Engel, G. L.   2, 337
Epstein, S.   128, 337
Erickson, M. H.   124, 337
Ernst, S.   107, 337
Espin, O.   110, 337

Faderman, L.   189, 337
Fagan, P. J.   240, 333
Fagg G.   146, 341
Fain, M.   162, 332
Fairbairn, W. R. D.   84, 85, 109,
   337
Falco, K. L.   190, 191, 192, 337
Fast, I.   108, 337
Feldman, M.   88, 333
Fergusson, D. M.   138, 338
Field, N.   285, 338
Finkelhor, D.   222, 223, 297, 338
Fitzpatrick, R.   148, 344
Flax, J.   109, 115, 338
Fonagy, P.   139, 338
Formani, H.   149, 338
Foucault, M.   49, 124, 125, 251,
   338
Freud, A.   78
Freud, S.   8, 21, 64, 66, 67, 68, 69,
   70, 71, 74, 75, 76, 100, 131,
   143, 151, 162, 204, 209, 281,
   312, 338, 339
Freund, K.   203, 339
Fritz, G. S.   264, 339

Gabbard, G. O.   7, 8, 9, 295, 298,
   339
Gabbard, G. O. 93–4, 355
Gagnon, J.   135, 350
Gardener, F.   298, 339
Gebhard, P. H.   17, 252, 343
Gelner, E.   95, 339
Gergely, G.   139, 338
Giddens, A.   49–53, 102, 103 141,
   145, 161, 194, 224, 329, 339
Gillan, P.   22, 333
Gillan, P.   330, 335
Gillespie-Sells, K.   275, 353
Gilligan, C.   108, 109, 150, 340
Gillis, S. J.   141, 340
Glasser, D.   137, 332
Glasser, M.   209, 340
Glassgold, J.   313, 340
Goldenwiesser, A.   38, 340
Golombok, S.   330, 335
Gonsiorek, J. C.   296, 300, 340, 352
Goodacre, T.   148, 344
Gordon, S.   305, 340
Gorkin, M.   284, 340
Gornik, L.   288, 340
Gosselin, C.   208, 209, 213, 340
Gould, S.   34, 143, 340

Gray, J. P.   218, 352
Green, A.   85, 340
Green, R.   137, 332
Green, R.   179, 236, 237, 238, 247, 340
Greenberg, J.   84, 340
Greenson, R.   103, 340
Greer, G.   143, 148, 340, 282, 340
Grosskurth, P.   8, 341
Groth, A. N.   220, 341
Guggenbuhl-Craig, W.   77, 341
Gutek, B.   218, 341
Guttman, H. A.   288, 341

Halberstam, J.   126–7, 341
Hall, M.   272, 273, 341
Hamilton, M.   190, 349
Haraldsen, I. R.   241, 341
Hardy, S.   156, 157, 159, 160, 341
Harris, T.   55, 333
Hatfield, E.   159, 218, 341
Hawkes, G.   50, 341
Hawton K.   146, 258, 263, 315, 341
Heeringen, C. van   181, 341
Hegel, G. W. F.   111, 210
Hennan, J.   159, 343
Herbst, J. H.   240, 333
Hillman, J.   8, 184, 342
Hinshelwood, R. D.   87, 342
Hite, S.   5, 25, 103, 143, 342.
Hocquengham, G.   125–6, 184, 342
Hollins, S.   275, 342
Holmes, J.   139, 342
Holmstrom, L. L.   219, 342
Horney, K.   74, 113, 151, 342
Horwood, L. J.   138, 338
Hudson, J. I.   138, 349

Iasenza, S.   313, 340
International Committee of Medical Editors   7, 342
Irigaray, L.   120, 121, 123, 131, 313, 342
Irvine, J.   165, 253, 342
Isay, R.   180, 182, 184–5, 186, 187, 237, 312, 342

Jackson, G.   187, 342
Jackson, M.   275, 342
Jardine, A.   144, 342
Jehu, D.   264, 295, 296, 298, 300, 301, 303, 304, 343

Jenkinson, C.   148, 344
Johnson, V. E.   16, 17, 253 258, 262, 270, 272, 275, 278, 289, 290, 346
Jones, E.   82, 343
Joseph, B.   202, 210 343
Jung, C. G.   76, 78–9, 87, 94, 131, 204, 285, 293–4, 310, 343

Kafka, M. P.   159, 343
Kant, E.   317–9
Kaplan, H. S.   16, 147, 158, 206, 240, 259, 260, 262, 265, 266, 289, 313, 343
Katz, J.   173, 343
Kavanaugh, J. G. Jr   244, 343
Keith-Spiegel, K.   295, 349
Kernberg, O. F.   88, 89, 90, 91, 92, 110, 142, 145, 155, 158, 162, 163, 166, 174, 200, 204, 282, 283, 285, 287, 288, 296, 312, 343
Kerr, I.   55, 351
Kessler, R. C.   138, 333
Kestenberg, J.   82, 343
Khan, M.   84, 343
Kimura, D.   149, 343
King, M.   271, 349
Kinsey, A. C.   17, 165, 252, 343
Klassen, A.   148, 344
Klein, M.   8, 12, 84, 85, 86, 87, 88, 204, 344
Klerman, G. L.   55, 344
Kline, D.   135, 350
Koedt, A.   103, 344
Kohlberg, I.   150, 344
Kohler, U.   223, 337
Kolk, B. van de   94, 344
Koznar, J.   270, 347
Kristeva, J.   120, 132, 184, 284, 344
Kumar, R.   46, 351
Kumin, I.   283, 344
Kurdek, L. A.   190, 344

Lacan, J.   117, 118, 122, 194, 255, 344
Ladas, A. L.   255, 344
Lalumière, M. I.   171, 344–5
Lasky, R.   296, 345
Le Vay, S.   171, 345
Lechevalier, B.   93, 353
Leeds Revolutionary Feminist Group   104

Lerner, R. M.   32, 345
Lesser, R.   187, 291, 336
Lester, E. P.   295, 339
Lester, E. P.   287, 345
Lévi-Strauss, C.   122
Levine, I. S.   92, 354
Lewes, K.   174, 345
Lewontin, R.   34, 143, 340
Limentani, A.   236, 239, 244, 345
Locke, J.   316, 317
LoPiccolo, L.   264, 345
Loulan, J.   272, 345
Lussier, A.   214, 345
Lynsky, M. T.   138, 338

MacKinnon, C.   104, 345
Maguire, M.   107, 337
Maguire, M.   113, 114, 288, 345
Mabler, M.   112, 235, 345
Maines, R. P.   143, 345
Malcolm, R. R.   201, 345
Malmuth, N. M.   220, 333
Manin, P.   146, 341
Mann, D.   283, 284, 285, 346
Maplethorpe, R.   185
Marcuse, H.   100, 101, 346
Markowitz, F.   38, 145, 251, 227, 331, 346
Martin C. E.   17, 252, 343
Marx, B. P.   220, 346
Masson, J. M.   66, 346
Masters, W. H.   16, 17, 253, 258, 262, 270, 272, 275, 278, 289, 290, 346
Mattison, A. M.   182, 272, 346
Mayer, E. L.   113, 346
McDougall, J.   80, 81, 82, 83, 147, 200, 201, 206, 346
McFarlane, A.   94, 344
McIntosh, M.   173, 346
McNamara, E.   296, 346
McKinney, K.   266, 354
McWhirter, D. P.   182, 272, 346
Mead, S. L.   237, 350
Meltzer, D.   84, 202, 204, 288, 346
Mendel, G.   29
Merkin, D.   143, 346
Merton, T.   217, 346
Messner, M. A.   152, 179, 347
Metz, M. E.   270, 347
Meyer, W. J.   241, 334
Meyerson, L. A.   220, 346
Miller, G.   31, 34, 162, 163, 172, 347

Miller, J. B.   108, 347
Milner, M.   67, 347
Miner, M.   205, 350
Miranda, R.   220, 346
Mitchell, S. A.   73, 186, 347
Mitchell, J.   107, 122, 123, 347
Mitchell, S.   84, 340
Mitchell-Kernan, C.   140, 355
Mitford, J.   165, 347
Mohr, R.   125, 128, 173, 183, 186, 347
Moir, A.   13, 33, 347
Moir, B.   13, 33, 347
Mollon, P.   137, 347
Money, J.   96, 101, 201, 139, 202, 203, 209, 229, 234, 247, 347
Moraga, C.   110, 347
Morgan, R.   104, 194, 347
Morgenthaler, F.   187, 348
Morris, L.   133, 151, 157, 161, 171, 178, 219, 348
Morris, N. M.   132, 153, 355
Moser, C.   208, 355
Moye, A.   157, 348
Muehlenhard, C. L.   218, 348
Murphy, B. C.   190, 348
Murray, J. B.   222, 348

Nanda, S.   173, 348
Neal, C.   180, 187, 191, 335
Neild, S.   191, 348
Nelson, N.   45, 348
Nesvacil, L. J.   270, 347
Nietzsche, F.   98

O'Boyle, M.   241, 334
O'Connor, N.   8, 127, 174, 289, 313, 348
O'Connor, P.   150
O'Shaugnhessy, E.   88, 333
Ohlerking, F.   205, 350
Olagary, J.   93, 348
Olds, D.   93, 349
Olivier, C.   82, 348
Orbach, S.   113, 114, 115, 348
Ortner, S. B.   39, 348
Ovsey, L.   235, 237, 239, 240, 241, 349

Paglia, C.   106, 107, 349
Pally, R.   93, 349
Palmer, C. T.   204, 218, 355
Parsons, T.   56, 349

Pearson, R.   191, 348
Pedesky, C.   190, 749
Peplau, L. A.   190, 349
Person, E. S.   110, 134, 153, 155,
   157, 235, 237, 239, 240, 241,
   288, 289, 349
Philips, P.   271, 349
Pierce, A. P.   280
Pillard, R.   233, 349
Pipher, M.   54, 349
Plummer, D.   152, 179, 349
Plummer, K.   124, 354
Pomeroy, W. B.   17, 252, 343
POPAN   297, 298, 303, 304, 349
Pope, H. G. Jr   138, 349
Pope, K. S.   295, 349
Porter, R.   50, 349
Posner, R. A.   145, 349
Preston, J.   27, 349
Price, J.   35, 354
Primrose, C.   247, 347
Pronger, B.   152, 350
Pryor, J. L.   270, 347

Racker, H.   282, 350
Ramsay, G. V.   150, 350
Raphael-Leff, J.   146, 175, 350
Rappaport, E. A.   283, 350
Rapson, R. L.   218, 341
Rattigan, B.   186, 313, 350
Raymond, J.   248, 350
Raymond, N. C.   205, 350
Reddon, J. R.   220, 334
Reed, E.   32, 279, 350
Reich, W.   100, 101, 350
Rekers, G. A.   237, 350
Rich, A.   194, 248, 350
Ridley, L.   259, 262, 264, 265, 267,
   270, 335
Rivers, I.   180, 350
Riviere, J.   127, 350
Roberts, E.   135, 350
Robson, K. M.   146, 351
Rochlin, M.   176, 351
Rosen, A. C.   237, 350
Rosen, S.   124, 337
Rossi, A. S.   2, 54, 266, 268, 270,
   351
Rubin, G.   122, 123, 134, 153, 224,
   351
Ruddick, S.   109, 351
Ruse, M.   174, 351
Russell, D. E. H.   219, 351

Rutter, V.   54, 162, 219, 222, 264,
   266, 267, 352
Ryan, J.   8, 174, 289, 313, 348
Ryle, A.   55, 56, 210, 351
Rade, Marquis de1273, 325, 3 51

Sade, Marquis de   198, 273, 325,
   351
Samuels, A.   77, 98, 124, 162, 219,
   248, 279, 285, 293, 305, 312,
   351, 352
Sanday, P. R.   218, 352
Sartre, J-P.   318
Satz, T.   198, 272, 278, 279, 352
Saussure, F.   116, 352
Sayers, J.   12, 119, 121, 165, 352
Schafer, R.   282, 352
Scharff, J. S.   259–60, 289, 352
Scharff, D. E.   259–60, 289, 352
Schaverien, J.   282, 283, 285, 287,
   288, 289, 293, 352
Schmidt, C.   240, 333
Schmidt, G.   258, 331
Schmidt, P.   190, 344
Schober, J. M.   246, 352
Schoener, G. R.   296, 352
Schwartz, D.   183, 313, 352
Schwartz, P.   54, 162, 190, 192,
   219, 222, 264, 266, 267, 332,
   352
Scruton, R.   193, 352
Searles, H.   284, 293, 352
Sedgwick, E. K.   126, 353
Segal, M.   235, 353
Segal, L.   104, 134, 135, 157, 165,
   219, 252, 254, 255, 275, 276,
   279, 353
Seidman, S.   123, 353
Semans, J. H.   217, 353
Shakespeare, T.   275, 353
Shakespeare, W.   316
Shelley, P. B.   317
Sinason, V.   275, 342
Singer, I.   17, 353
Smith, J.   219, 353
Smith, P.   144, 342
Sobo, E. J.   216, 353
Socaredes, C.   96, 221, 353
Solms, M.   93, 353
Solomon, R.   203, 353
Sontag, S.   170, 353
Sprecher, S.   266, 354
Stein, A.   124, 354

Steinberg, L.   136, 354
Stevens, A.   35, 354
Stoller, R. J.   47–8, 92, 93, 152,
    158, 200, 210, 214, 235, 238,
    312, 354
Stopes, M.   252, 354
Strauss, D.   289, 336
Studer, L. H.   220, 334
Swann, G.   27, 349

Tabachnick, B. G.   295, 349
Talbert, L. M.   132, 153, 355
Tallis, R.   119, 354
Tanney, M. F.   190, 354
Target, M.   139, 338
Taylor, T.   31, 32, 42, 143, 224, 354
Thompson, B.   198, 208, 354
Thomson, J.   296, 354
Thomson, S.   135, 354
Thorn, B.   152, 354
Thornhill, R.   204, 218, 355
Tiefer, L.   276, 314, 355
Tremblay, P.   181, 331
Trenchard, L.   180, 355
Troiden, R. R.   179, 355
Tucker, M. B.   140, 355
Tuckett, D.   7, 355

Udry, R. J.   132, 153, 355

Van de Veld, T.   252, 355
Vance, C.   105, 153, 256, 355
Vinke, J.   181, 341
Volkan, V. D.   244, 343

Walker, E. L.   107, 337
Warnock, M.   97, 318–19, 321, 322,
    323
Warren, W.   180, 355
Weeks, J.   49, 101, 172, 173, 355
Weinberg, M. S.   208, 355
Weinrich, J.   233, 349
Weisaeth, L.   94, 344
Weisman, M.   55, 344
Welldon, E.   132, 147, 206, 355
Wells, J. K.   293, 356
Western, D.   93–4, 355
Whitney, C.   184, 356
Williams, C. J.   208, 355
Williams, M. H.   202
Williamson, J.   213, 356
Wilson, E.   29, 172, 356
Wilson, G.   208, 209, 213, 340
Wilton, T.   194, 195, 272, 276,
    356
Winnicott, D. W.   85, 356
Wisdom, J. O.   89, 356
Wise, T. N.   240, 333
Wittig, M.   125, 195, 356
Wordsworth, W.   317
Wrye, H. K.   293, 356

Young Bruehl, E.   8, 356
Young, J. E.   94, 356
Young, R.   52, 86, 88, 356

Zetzel, E. R.   67, 356
Zucker, K. J.   171, 344–5
Zulueta, F, de   94, 139, 357

Index of Case Examples

Abigail   144
Adrian   185
Alec   268–9
Amy   230, 237, 242–3
Andrea and Paul   73–4
Annabel   129

Bernard   326–9
Bill   214
Brian   222
Brian   277
Bryony   120–1

Carla and Ruth   193
Charlie   121–2
Charlotte   249–50
Clara   137, 138–9
Colin   35–6

Dave and Fiona   57–60, 61–2
Derek   156, 159–160
Diana   261–2

Edward   302
Elizabeth Harry and Claire   111

Francis   228
Franz   85–6
Fred   166

Gail   91–2
George and Alec   181–2
Gerald   176
Gudrun   292

Harriet   298–9, 302
Harry   81
Helen and Paul   40

James   79, 87
Jane   20
Jill   67

Joan   243
Joan and Peter   3–6
John   283

Karen   134–5
Kiri   53–4

Laura and Andrew   304
Lawrence   278
Leonora   76
Linda and Ben   245
Lisa   136
Luke   271

Nora.   65

Paula and John   19
Pauline   48
Peter   23–4
Petra   118
Phillipa   76
Phil   65
Portia   147–8

Sandra   211–12
Sarah   11
Sheila   18
Shiv   43
Simon   231–2
Siri   177

Timothy   153–4
Tom   68

Vic   185

Wendy   287
William   72

Xara   107

Yvonne   196

Index of Terms

Adolescence in boys 153–4
Adolescence in girls 133
Aesthetic conflict 202
Aesthetics of sexuality 91
AIDS 26
Alchemy 79, 285
Altruism 30
Anal sex 183–4
Anatomy 10
Androgen insensitivity syndrome
   10–11, 228
Anorgasmia 22, 266
Anthropology 38
Armature (compared with scaffolding)
   329
Arousal 17
Art 321
Athena 78
Attachment based psychotherapy
   309
Attitudes to sex in 18th and 19th
   centuries 50–1

Being heterosexual versus becoming
   straight 312
Berdache 234
Bio power 124
Biological factors in gender
   development 114
Biopsychosocial approach 2–3
Birth control 254
Borderline personality disorder 67
Bottoms 210
Brain sex 10, 13
Butch and Fernme 195

Camp 170
Cardiovascular disease 24
Carers 274
Case reports 7–9
Castration 71, 73
Casual sex 182
Catholic priests 216
Celibacy 215–7
Child sexual abuse 67, 221

Childbirth 25
Childcare 83
Childhood (of gay men) 179–81
Childhood (of lesbians) 188
Chromosomal sex 10–11
Client v. patient 6–7
Clitoris 34, 35, 103, 143
Coercive sex 198
Cognitive, analytic, therapy 55,
   56–62, 309
Cognitive behaviour therapy for sexual
   problems 257–8
Coming out 180, 189
Commercial art 321
Commodification of sexual disorders
   276
Common sense (in Kant) 317
Condoms 26
Congenital, adrenal hyperplasia 209
Courtship disorders 203
Creative imagination (as capable of
   evil) 325
Creativity 322
Cross-dressing 239
Cross-dressing (psychoanalytic views
   of) 240
Cultral relativism 44

Development of boys and girls 109–11
Diabetes 22
Disability 274–5
Divorce 39

Ego dystonic homosexuality 271
Endometriosis 20, 22
Erectile failure 21
Erotic countertransference 284–5
Erotic fancy 320
Erotic horror 283
Erotic imagination 2, 97, 274, 277,
   294, 306, 315–30
in boys 151
damaged in child sexual abuse
   139–40
and transgressive sex 225

Erotic playback 77
Erotic revulsion 324
Erotic transference as defensive 283
Erotic transference/counter-
    transference and gender
    287–90
Evolutionary psychology 29
Exogamy 42
External genitalia 13
Extramarital affairs 145–6

Faking orgasm 256
Fathers and daughters 112
Female anatomy 82
Female circumcision 45–6
Female masculinity 126–7
Female sexual spirituality movement
    311
Female sexuality, sexological views
    252–3
Femininity as passive 131
Feminism 99, 102–16
    class bias in 115
Fertility 25
Fetishism 213–15
    psychoanalytic views of 214
Fiction 9
First sexual intercourse in women
    134
Fisting 211
Freudiomarxists 100–2

Gay analysts' countertransference
    feelings 291
Gay and lesbian identity 172–3
    as confining 170
    personal stories 323
Gay men from ethnic minorities of
    185–6
Gay pound 169
Gay psychology 186–7
Gay relationships 182
Gay sex 181–2
    as revolutionary 125–6
Gender assigned at birth 14
Gender certainty 248
Gender dysphoria
    biology of 233
    cultural variations 234
    politics of 247
Gender identity 14
Gender performances 127
Genital sex 69

Haussa 45
Hijra 173, 234, 248
Hindu 43
HIV 26, 27
Homophobia in boys 152–3
Homosexuality (and evolutionary
    theory) 35
Hunter gatherer tribes 30–1
Hybrid therapies for sexual problems
    258–9
Hysterectomy 25
Hysteria 66

Ideology 99
Imagination (as needing to be
    schooled) 319
Incest 223, 305
    taboo 293–4
Inclusive fitness 30
Individuation 77, 286, 294
Infidelity 163–5
Internal sexual organs 12
Interpersonal therapy 55–6, 309
Intersex 227–9
    treatment of 246–7
Intrusive advocacy 302

Jungian analysts 77
Jungian therapy 48, 62, 309

Kikuyu 45
Kinship structures 38, 39, 41
Kleinian analysis of sexuality 52
Kleinians 87

Lacanian theory (criticism of)
    119–20
Lakeland poets 97, 316–17, 319
Late adulthood (in men) 167
Legal regulation of sex 198
Lesbian analysts' countertransference
    feelings 291
Lesbian bed death syndrome 272
Lesbian feminism 105–6
Lesbian relationship 190–1
Lesbian sex
    frequency 192
    politicised 194
    seen as deficient 193
Libido 64
Love maps 96, 97, 101, 202, 203
Low sexual desire in women
    264–6

Male and female sexuality compared 104
Male erectile or ejaculatory failure 267–8
Male sexual fantasy 155
Marital harmony sexological focus on 254
Marriage 38, 44, 50
  ceremony 39–40
Married gay men 184–5
Masochism 212
Mass media 321
Masturbation 34
Mate selection 33, 140–1, 161

Neurobiology 94
Non denoting nominalism 128
Nyar 44–5

Object choice
  biological theories of 171–2
  evolutionary theories of 172
  psychoanalytic theories of 174–5
Object relations theory 84, 86, 89
Oedipus complex 68, 69, 73, 77, 81, 86, 293–4
Older lesbians 191–2
Opponent process theory 203
Orgasm 17, 18, 90
  clitoral 103
  female 35
Outcome of sexual relationships in therapy 300–1

Paedophilia (treatment of) 222–3
Parental intercourse 87
Participant observation 38
Passing 248
Pathology 324
Patient 6–7
Patients who are abused in therapy (features) 297–9
Pelvic inflammatory disease 22
Penis 33, 164–5
  size 34
Perverse motherhood 206
Perversion 69, 92
  psycoanalytic theories of 200–02
Phallus 117, 118, 119
Plastic sexuality 52, 102, 141
Politics and therapy 128
Pornographic pictures (of children) 325

Pornography 104, 105, 156–61, 325
Post-feminism 106
Post-structuralism 117
Post-traumatic stress disorder 301
Prejudice 66
Premature ejaculation 269–70
Prostatectomy 24
Prostitution 306
Psychiatric disorders in sex offenders 205
Psychoanalys 311, 313
  and feminism 108–16
Psychodynamic therapy for sexual problems 259–61
Puberty 132

Queer theory 99, 116
  weakness of 130

Radical lesbianism 125
Rape 60–1, 106, 135, 204, 218, 220
Reciprocal roles 56, 61
Reflexive modernity 51, 53
Runaway selection 31

Sadomasochisrn (SM) 92, 207–9
  psychoanalytic views of 209
Safe analysis 305
Safe sex 25–7
Sanitisation of sex 276
Scientific masculinisation of sexuality 279
Secondary sexual characteristics 13
Seduction theory of neurosis 67
Selection pressures 41
Self-creation 51
Sex after childbirth 146
Sex in marriage 142
Sex panic 99
Sex roles 14–15
Sex that is not object related 90
Sex therapy 313
  for gay men and lesbians 270–4
  integrated approach 314
  male bias in 265
  for older adults 270
Sex wars 205
Sexism 33
Sexual desire 16
  and alcohol 28
  low 2l

Sexual desire – *continued*
  and non-prescription drugs   28
  and psychiatric illness   27
Sexual development in children   132,
  150–2
Sexual intercourse (painful in women)
  20, 21
Sexual love   89
Sexual misconduct in the consulting
  them as a taboo   305
Sexual orientation   15
  and erotic transference/counter-
    transference   290–2
Sexual relationships between therapist
  and patient   295–301
Sexual relationships once therapy has
  ended   300
Sexual repression   101
Sexual response cycle   5–16
Sexual selection   32–3
Sexual stimulants   324
Sexually transmitted disease   25
Shamans   234
Sociobiology   29
Sperm   34
  competition   33, 34
Stages of sexual development   70
Structuralism   116

Taboo   306
  on homosexuality   122
Teenage pregnancy   54
Theories of imagination   316
Therapists who abuse patients (its
  characteristics)   303–4
Therapy
  with gay men and lesbians   176–8
  as political activity   98

Transference and countertransference
  79
Transgender   229
Transgendered patients
  denigration of   241
  surgery of   242
Transgendered people   13–14
Transgressive sex   198
  as culturally relative   224
  defined   199
  and perversion   199
Transsexualism
  childhood antecedents of   236
  female to male   238–9
  psychoanalytic theories of   235
  psychoanalytic treatment of   244
Transvestism
  see also cross-dressing   231
Trauma   94
Treating patients have been sexually
  exploited in therapy   301
Trickster strategies   124

Vaginismus   263–4
Venuses   42
Viagra (sildenafil citrate)   257, 266,
  267, 279–80
Vibrators   266
Violence and eroticism   47
Virtue ethics   318
Virtuous sexual life   322

Woman's therapy centre   113
Womb   75
Women analysts   74
Women and transgressive sex   206

Xanith   234, 248